The Incredible Sound Machine

Unleash the Sound Capabilities of Your Macintosh® Computer

Mark Andrews

Addison-Wesley Publishing Company

Reading, Massachusetts • Menlo Park, California
New York • Don Mills, Ontario • Wokingham, England
Amsterdam • Bonn • Sydney • Singapore • Tokyo • Madrid
San Juan • Paris • Seoul • Milan • Mexico City • Taipei

Library of Congress Cataloging-in-Publication Data

Andrews, Mark.
The incredible sound machine : unleash the sound capabilities of your Macintosh computer / Mark Andrews.
p. cm.
Includes index.
ISBN 0-201-60889-8
1. Computer sound processing. 2. Macintosh (Computer)
3. Computer composition. I. Title.
MT723.A54 1993
786.7'6—dc20 92-32346
CIP
MN

Sponsoring Editor: David Rogelberg
Project Editor: Joanne Clapp Fullagar
Production Coordinator: Kathy Traynor
Cover design: Trish Sinsigalli LaPointe
Text design: David Kelley Design
Set in 10-point Century Schoolbook by Williams Graphic Services, Inc.

123456789–MU–9695949392
First printing, November 1992

To Muktananda

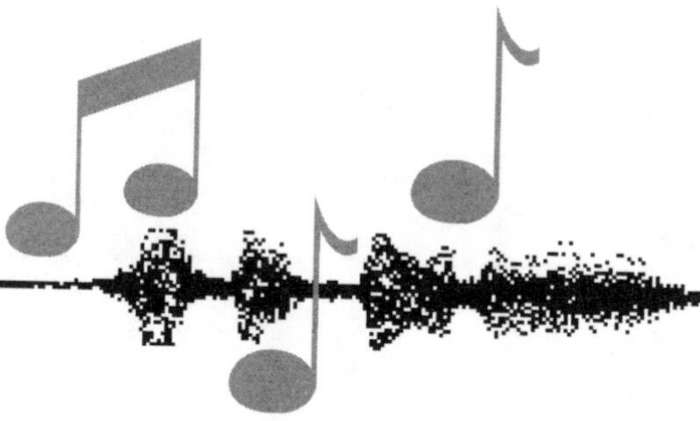

Contents

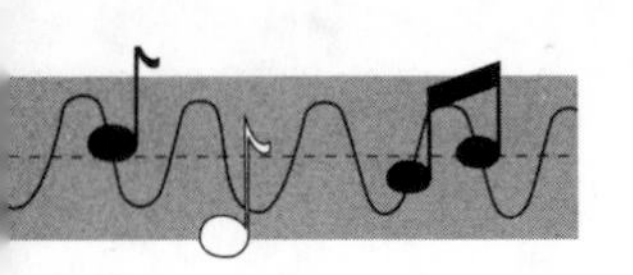

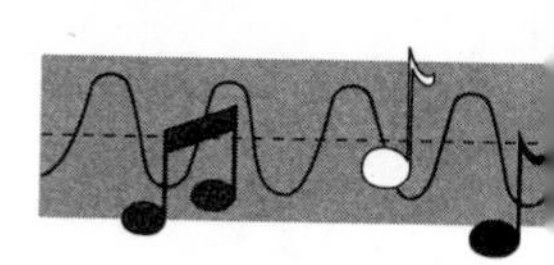

Acknowledgments

Among the people who provided tremendous help in writing this book are Dave Rogelberg, Joanne Clapp Fullagar, Amy Cheng, Tanya Kucak, Jim Reekes, Dan Wood, Frank Seide, Bruce Tomlin, Joe Fantuzzi, Greg Jalbert, Jeffrey Evans, Bill Goodman, Jeffrey Siegel, Ron Dumont, Martha Steffen, Marilyn Olson, Dan Hergert, Deborah Doyle, John Ellinger, Jerry Kovarsky, Bob Haskell, Anastasia Lanier, Jim Rosenberg, Sally Moore, David Kaplowitz, Kort Taylor, Marsha Vdovin, Renee Courington, Steve Thomas, Tom White, Cynthia Yamatata, Greg Sandell, and David How.

Introduction

Sound Trek

This looks like a computer book, but it's really an adventure book: a volume that will launch you on an amazing journey across the universe of sound and music. In each chapter, you'll visit a new and different world of sound and music. And a collection of free software and shareware, provided on a bonus disk packaged with this book, will take you on a guided tour.

Whether you own a bare-bones Macintosh Plus or a Macintosh Quadra system equipped with a $3,000 sound board, this book will show you how to make the best use of all the sound-producing ability your system offers. Best of all, the free software and shareware on your bonus disk can make your Macintosh talk, play music, and make an awesome variety of sounds.

Your bonus disk includes many powerful programs. There's the Audio Palette, a HyperCard-based sound editor that was written by Apple and was available up to now only to buyers of Macs with plug-in microphones and built-in sound circuitry. There's HyperCorder, a HyperCard application that was written especially for this book to put the Audio Palette through its paces.

Other programs on your bonus disk include HyperLab, a fun (but educational) HyperCard stack that can read typed text at variable pitches, speeds, and intonations; a demonstration version of Songworks, a new program from Ars Nova that lets you compose music on your Mac; a demo version of Listen, a music-learning and ear-training program from Imaja; and a complete, fully functioning version of Sound-Trecker, an exciting and enlightening music-playing program from Germany.

Of course, this book is much more than a collection of software. As you read this book, you'll learn how to tap the sound power of your Macintosh in ways you may never have imagined. You'll learn how to make your computer talk, imitate almost any kind of musical instrument, play amazing

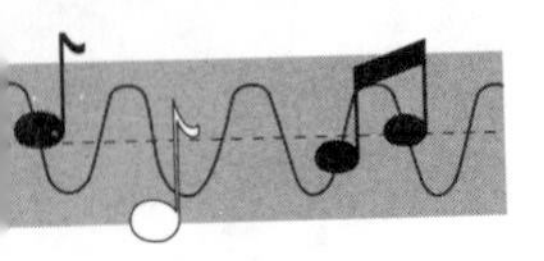

sound effects, and even sing. You'll also learn how to add music and sounds to HyperCard stacks—and, if you're a HyperCard programmer or an advanced HyperCard user, you'll get some points on adding sound to your own HyperCard stacks.

What's in This Book

Here's a chapter-by-chapter list of what this book contains.

In **Chapter 1,** you'll sit down at your computer's Sound Control Panel, where you'll start learning how the Macintosh sound system works by customizing your computer's system alert sound.

Chapter 2 introduces some of the basic principles of the science of sound. It explains some important concepts that can help you understand how electronic instruments—including the Macintosh—produce sound. To help you grasp the fundamentals of audio science, Chapter 2 documents the Sound-Trecker program: an application program on your bonus disk that's been hailed as one of the best shareware programs ever.

In **Chapter 3**—by running a program written by Apple to train software developers—you'll learn how your computer's hardware and system software work together to produce sound.

Chapter 4 introduces SoundWave, a world-class sound-editing program that is included on your bonus disk in its original version—not a crippled demo version. SoundWave is the sound-editing module that is included in Authorware Professional for the Macintosh, a multimedia application that won the 1990 Eddy award for best Macintosh multimedia program.

Chapter 5 demonstrates the sound power of HyperCard with a program called HyperCorder, which is included on the bonus disk that comes with this book. With HyperCorder—written exclusively for this volume—you can cut, copy, and paste the waveforms of sounds, using standard Macintosh cut-and-paste techniques. You can also use HyperCorder to move sounds back and forth between sound files and HyperCard stacks.

With the help of a speech synthesizer called MacinTalk, and an interactive HyperCard-based application called HyperLab, **Chapter 6** introduces the fascinating world of voice synthesizers.

In **Chapter 7,** you'll get a chance to try your hand at composing real sheet music with the help of a new notation-instruction program called Songworks from Ars Nova software.

In **Chapter 8,** you'll dive a little deeper into the field of music theory with the help of Listen, a music-instruction and ear-training program from Imaja.

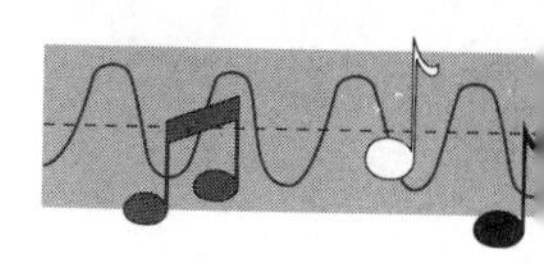

Finally, in **Chapter 9,** you'll learn how to connect your Macintosh to various kinds of MIDI devices so you can start building your dream studio, one step at a time.

Appendix A contains complete instructions—and even a schematic diagram—for building a sound recording module called the Sound Input Device, or SID. With SID—a device similar to the MacRecorder recorder manufactured by Macromedia—you can add recording capabilities to your Macintosh. Then you can use the sound-editing programs on your bonus disk to record your own sounds, as well as to edit and play prerecorded sounds.

Companies that manufacture sound-related hardware and software are listed and described in **Appendix B.** If you're interested in buying any of the commercial sound products mentioned in this book, you can find the name, address, and telephone number of the manufacturer to contact.

Appendix C describes some of the best sound-related freeware and shareware programs and tells where to find them and how to get them.

Appendix D explains how the Macintosh stores sounds in memory; **Appendix E** is a troubleshooting guide for the Sound Control Panel; and **Appendix F** provides detailed information about the architecture of sound resources and sound files. **Appendix G** describes the MIDI specification, which standardizes the interconnection of electronic musical instruments and other sound-related devices.

"It's the Law" contains licensing information about the programs on the book's bonus disk. The book concludes with a useful **Bibliography.**

What You'll Need

The way you'll use this book depends upon the kind of Macintosh system you own. Different kinds of Macintosh systems have different kinds of sound capabilities, and many varieties of sound-related software and add-on sound hardware are available.

To use this book and the software on the disk, you'll need a Macintosh Plus or better, with at least 2 megabytes of free RAM. When you load sounds into memory, they require large amounts of RAM, so if you want to create or edit sounds, the more memory you have, the better; 4MB is better than 2MB, and 8MB or more is better still. Sound files also consume enormous amounts of disk space—so a hard disk is recommended, but not required.

Even more important than RAM or disk space is the version of System Software that you're using with your Macintosh. To use the software that comes with this book, you must have System 6.0.5 or later. System 6.0.8 is better. Better still is a Macintosh running System Software Version 7. The

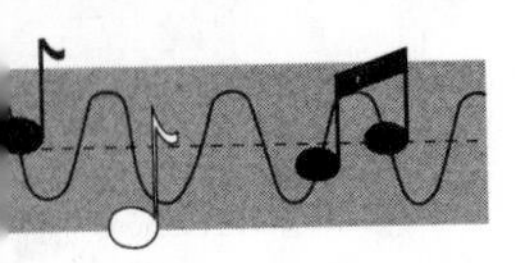

Sound-Treker program requires a 68020 chip; it will not run on a Macintosh Plus, SE, Classic, or Powerbook 100.

The sound hardware that's built into the Macintosh has improved over the years, so relatively new models produce better sound than older models do; you can get satisfactory sound from a Macintosh Plus or a Macintosh SE—but for top-grade sound, you should own a later model.

No matter what kind of Macintosh you own, you can greatly improve its sound quality by adding an external amplifier and speaker system. That automatically disables the Mac's anemic-sounding built-in speaker, which limits the sound quality of all models.

Table I–1 shows how you can use this book with different kinds of Macintosh systems. More information about Macintosh sound system configurations is presented in Chapter 1.

Table I–1 *Sound System Configurations*

If you have...	And...	Then this book...
A Macintosh computer that came equipped with a plug-in microphone	You want to learn how to record sound—and you want more sound software than you got with your system	Contains the information you need—and the software you need—to get the most out of your system
A Macintosh that *didn't* come with a plug-in microphone	You want to unleash all of the sonic power that's built into the system you own	Tells how to play, edit, and have fun with sounds, and provides the sounds and the software you need to get started
A Macintosh Plus or better and System 6.0.5 or later	A plug-in recording module (such as MacRecorder from Macromedia or Voice Impact from Articulate Systems)	Provides interesting sounds and additional software—plus valuable tips and advice about recording, editing, and playing back sound
A Macintosh Plus or better and System 6.0.5 or later	You know how to build a kit	Tells how to build a plug-in recording module for $30—provides instructions and a schematic
This book	A Macintosh with a recording module that you have bought or built	Provides you with *more* than the equivalent of a Macintosh with built-in recording capabilities!

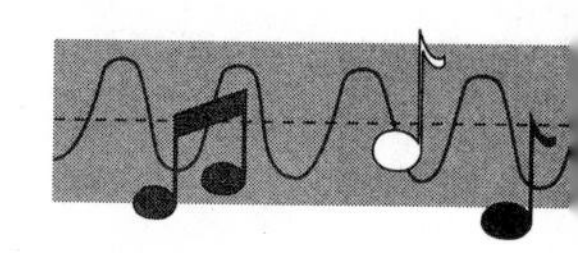

Sound Power

The sound power of the Macintosh has increased so dramatically over the past couple of years that software developers are now creating more and more applications with built-in sound capabilities. The manufacturers of Macintosh applications such as Microsoft Word, Microsoft Excel, Word Perfect, and QuickMail have all added sound capabilities to their programs.

Meanwhile, in the recording industry, musicians and audio engineers around the world are building and rebuilding sound studios around Macintosh computers. Today, more and more musicians and engineers are ripping fabulously expensive hardware components out of their studios and replacing them with inexpensive Macintosh computers running special sound software—saving vast sums of money and winding up with better studios in the bargain.

You may not be planning to build a sound studio in your living room; you may not even own a Macintosh equipped with a plug-in microphone. But no matter what kind of computer system you have—whether it's a basic Mac Plus or the newest high-end model equipped with a MIDI interface and a host of hardware—this book will help you discover and explore the amazing sound capabilities of your Macintosh. It will show you how the Macintosh sound system works, and it will teach you how to make the best use of your system's sonic power. Best of all, the diskful of sound software that comes with this volume will let you hear for yourself what your computer's sound system can do.

1 Macintosh Sound

Until the mid-1980s or so, most computers didn't know how to speak, play music, or make other fancy sounds. The best the earliest computers could do was to beep when something important was happening, or perhaps make an annoying buzzing sound when something was going wrong.

Computers didn't start learning to talk, sing, or play music very well until 1984, the year that Apple Computer, Inc., introduced the Macintosh. The first Macintosh ever built had a sound system that included three built-in sound synthesizers and a sound chip made by Sony. And those same components—slightly updated, of course, and with some supplementary components added—are still built into every Macintosh that rolls off the assembly line.

In this chapter, you'll learn about the sound hardware that's hidden inside your Macintosh, and about the system software that supports your computer's sound circuitry. You'll also find out what kinds of hardware you can add to your Macintosh system to increase its sound capabilities, and what kinds of software you can buy to record, edit, and play Macintosh sound.

This chapter also tells how to unpack the bonus disk that came with this book, and how to take advantage of the Sound Control Panel. Finally, you'll learn about a few ways to make your Macintosh an even more magnificent sound machine, how to improve Macintosh sound, and where to find even more free software.

Macintosh Sound Technology

Every Macintosh has three built-in sound generators, or *sound synthesizers*. Every Macintosh also comes with a complete set of software-based

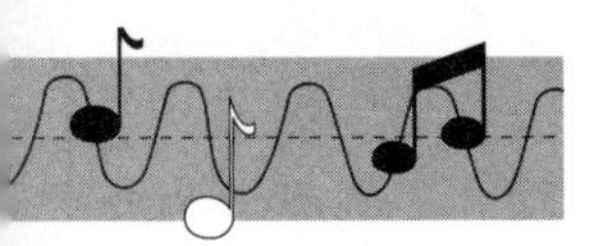

tools for producing sound. Those tools are built into the computer's *system software*—that is, the software that you get when you buy a Macintosh computer.

The sound software that comes with the Macintosh has changed more over the years than the computer's sound hardware has. Mainly because of improvements in system software, the Macintosh computers that are sold today produce better sound—with less annoying clicking and popping—than systems that were equipped with earlier versions of system software.

Advances in Sound Software

The first major advancement in Macintosh sound software took place when Apple introduced System 6. With the advent of System 6, Apple replaced an early software tool called the Sound Driver with a streamlined new Toolbox manager called the Sound Manager.

The improvements that were built into the new Sound Manager weren't immediately apparent to the Macintosh user. But they provided software developers with better sound tools and made it easier for programmers to incorporate sound into Macintosh applications.

With System 7, Apple enhanced the Sound Manager still more by adding a host of new features. The new tools included in the enhanced Sound Manager made it even easier for software developers to add sound capabilities to Macintosh applications and HyperCard stacks, and for Macintosh owners to record, edit, and play back music and interesting sounds.

Using the Latest Software

Because Macintosh system software is constantly being upgraded, you should always use the latest version of system software that can run on your computer system. That way, you can always use the latest programs that are available. Also, the programs you buy will perform better, and may even offer new features that won't work when you use older system software.

To run all of the programs that are supplied on this book's bonus disk, you need System 6.0.5 or later. If you have System 6.0.7, that's better. Better still is a Macintosh running System 7.

If you need to upgrade your system software, you can get the latest version that's available from your authorized Apple dealer.

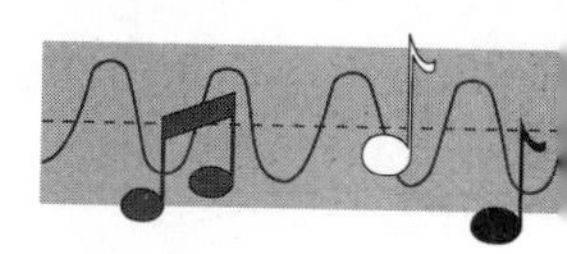

Sound Hardware

There are two kinds of hardware that the Macintosh can use to produce sound: the sound circuitry that's built into the computer, and extra hardware that you can add to a Macintosh system to increase its sound capabilities.

Factory-Supplied Hardware

Three sound generators, which Apple calls *synthesizers,* are built into every Macintosh. Except for small differences in specifications, these three synthesizers work the same way in every Macintosh, so every Macintosh has about the same capability for producing sound. However, some newer models of the Macintosh have something extra: built-in sound-recording modules, or *digitizers*.

The Three Macintosh Synthesizers

Every kind of sound that the Macintosh produces by itself—that is, without being connected to some external sound-generating device—comes from one of the computer's three built-in sound synthesizers.

These are the three sound synthesizers built into the Macintosh:

- **square-wave synthesizer**—generates the simple *system beep* that the Macintosh sounds by default when an alert dialog is displayed, or when something else happens that might require your immediate attention.
- **wave-table synthesizer**—generates sounds from a sequence of bytes that are stored in memory in a data structure called a *wave table.* The wave-table synthesizer is a versatile and memory-efficient utility, but it is not used by many Macintosh applications.
- **sampled sound synthesizer**—can reproduce sound that is recorded live, or *sampled.* Most sound-intensive Macintosh programs make use of the sampled sound synthesizer. For example, the software packages that come with sound-recording modules use the sampled sound synthesizer to record and play back sounds. The Incredible Sound programs that are supplied on this book's bonus disk also make extensive use of the sampled sound synthesizer.

These three synthesizers are described in detail in Chapter 3.

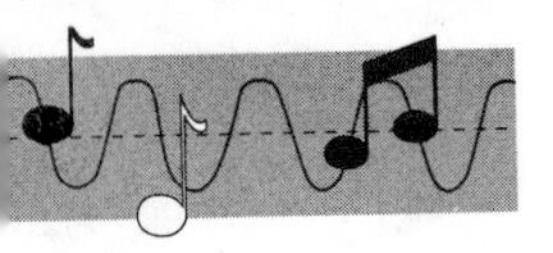

Microphones and Digitizers

Besides the three synthesizers that are built into every Macintosh, some Macs have built-in recording modules, or digitizers. Most Macs that have built-in digitizers also come with plug-in desk microphones that can be used for making recordings. Thus, if your Macintosh came with a plug-in microphone, then it also has a built-in digitizer.

Figure 1–1 shows the kind of desk microphone that comes with most recording-ready models of the Macintosh. If your Mac is equipped with a microphone like the one in the picture, then it also contains all of the hardware that it needs to record sound.

Figure 1–1. The Macintosh desk microphone

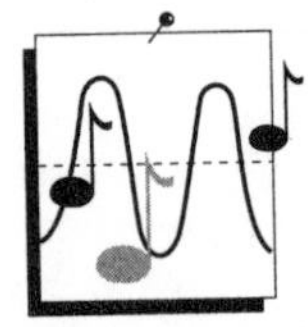

TECH TALK

Digitizers and Digitized Sounds

*Sound-recording modules are often referred to as **digitizers** because they convert natural sounds, or **analog sounds,** into streams of binary numbers that can be stored in a computer's memory and later played back in their original form. A sound that has been converted into binary numbers by a sound digitizer is sometimes called a **digitized** sound.*

*The process of recording and digitizing a sound can also be referred to as **sound sampling,** so digitized sounds are also sometimes referred to as **sampled sounds.*** ❍

The first models of the Macintosh to be equipped with microphones and sound-recording circuitry were the Macintosh IIsi and the Macintosh LC. Since then, all models have been factory-equipped for recording sound.

You can tell whether an individual Macintosh has built-in recording equipment by merely inspecting its back panel. If it has a microphone input—labeled with a picture of a microphone—then it also has built-in recording hardware.

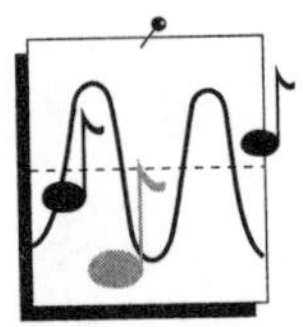

BY THE WAY

Recording Directly from Your Tape or CD Player

*If your Mac came with a mike, then it also has a jack on its back called a **line input.** Most plug-in recording modules, including MacRecorder and SID (Sound Input Device), also have line inputs.*

With a line input, you can record sound directly from an external source—such as a tape recorder, a compact disc player, or a high-quality microphone—without having to worry about background noise or the frequency limitations of a voice microphone. To connect a portable tape recorder or CD player to your recording hardware, all you need is a cable with a ⅛-inch miniplug on each end. Just plug one end of the cable into your external signal source, and plug the other end into the line input on your Macintosh or on your plug-in recording module.

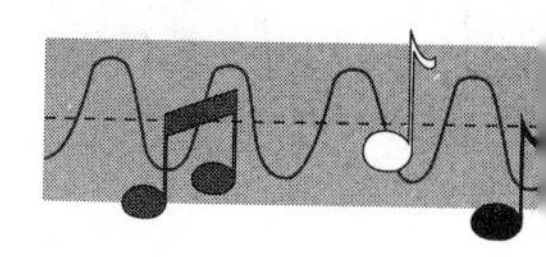

To use a component-style stereo system as a signal source, you may need a different kind of cable. If your stereo has separate right-channel and left-channel line outputs on its back panel, they are probably RCA outputs; in that case, you need a cable with a pair of RCA connectors (for your stereo system) on one end and a male monophonic miniplug (for your line input) on the other. Check the outputs on your stereo system, and if you still have questions, consult an electronics dealer. ❍

Add-on Hardware

If your computer doesn't have a microphone input on its back panel, then it doesn't have a built-in digitizer. Macs that lack recording hardware have all of the sound *playback* capabilities of models that are factory-equipped for recording. However, if your Mac doesn't have a microphone input, you'll have to buy an external plug-in digitizer if you want to *record* sound.

By the Way

There is also another way to record, edit, and play sound with a Macintosh. If you'd like to make your Macintosh the centerpiece of a professional-quality sound studio, you can buy a specially designed collection of extra hardware and software and set up a MIDI sound studio. There's more about MIDI later in this section, and Chapter 9 covers MIDI systems in greater detail. ❍

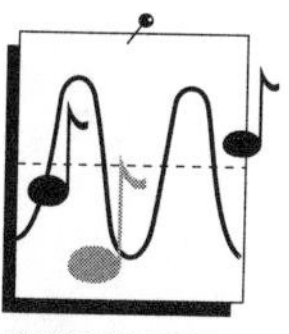
BY THE WAY

A sound digitizer is a small box that you can connect to the modem port or the printer port of any Macintosh. One popular recording module is the MacRecorder digitizer from Macromedia (formerly MacroMind Paracomp). Two other recording modules are the Voice Impact and Voice Impact Pro digitizers from Articulate Systems.

If you don't want to buy a digitizer, you can build one. Appendix A contains instructions—and even a schematic—for building a digitizer called the Sound Input Device (SID). If you've ever built a kit, or you think you'd be handy with a soldering iron, you can build SID with about $20 to $30 worth of parts that you can buy at almost any well-equipped electronics store.

MacRecorder

The granddaddy of all recording modules is the MacRecorder digitizer. The MacRecorder digitizer, originally called the MacNifty recording module, was originally created by a Macintosh user and sold in kit form by BMUG—an organization originally called the Berkeley Macintosh Users Group and now referred to only by its initials. Farallon Computing Inc. later obtained rights to manufacture the device, and it began assembling the digitizer and marketing it under the name MacRecorder. In late 1991,

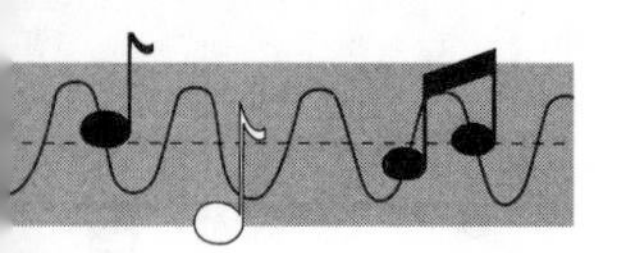

Farallon sold the rights to the MacRecorder to MacroMind Paracomp. Macromind Paracomp, now renamed Macromedia, currently markets the MacRecorder digitizer.

The MacRecorder module is a small gray or tan box that measures 4.6 inches long by 2.7 inches wide by 1.2 inches high. It has a small built-in microphone, an input for an external microphone, and a line input jack. It also has a volume control. Figure 1–2 is a picture of MacRecorder.

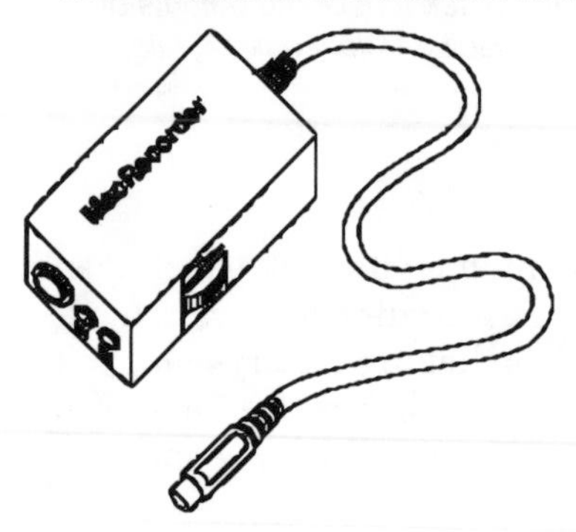

Figure 1–2. MacRecorder digitizer

You can plug MacRecorder into either the modem port or the printer port of your Macintosh. If you have two MacRecorder modules, you can record in stereo. Just plug one MacRecorder into your modem port and another into your printer port, as shown in Figure 1–3, and you can make stereo recordings.

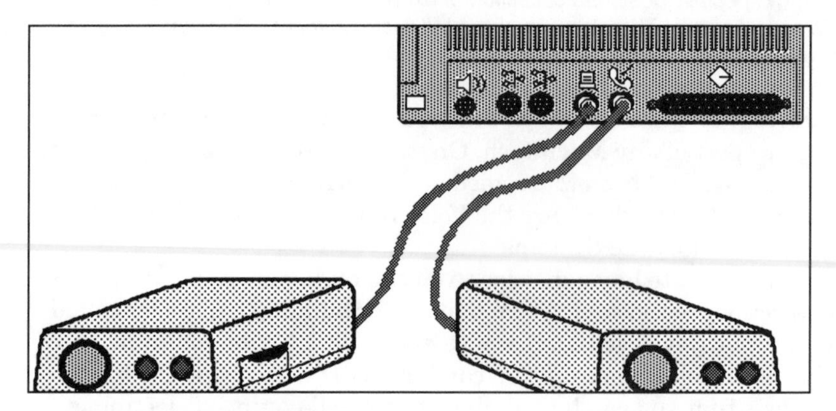

Figure 1–3. Recording in stereo

The MacRecorder system comes with a powerful recording and sound-editing application called SoundEdit Pro, as well as a set of tools for recording, playing, and editing sounds in a HyperCard environment. For more information about HyperCard sound programs, see Chapter 5.

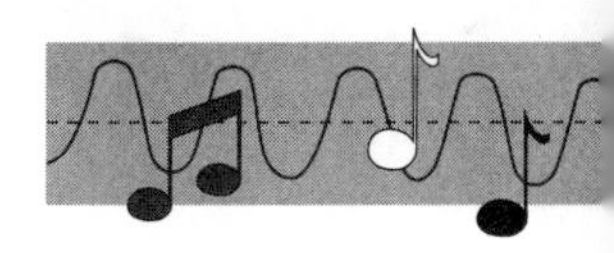

Voice Impact and Voice Impact Pro

Articulate Systems manufactures two recording modules: a basic unit called Voice Impact, and a deluxe model called Voice Impact Pro. Both devices come with a recording and editing program called Voice Record. Voice Record is provided both as an application and as a desk accessory.

Voice Impact is a tiny black box that measures just 1.3 inches wide by 1.2 inches deep by 0.5 inches high. It has a built-in automatic sound-level control and a line input. It comes with the Voice Record program, a Voice Impact sound driver, and a set of tools for recording HyperCard sound.

The deluxe recording module from Articulate Systems, Voice Impact Pro, is shown in Figure 1–4. Voice Impact Pro is almost twice the size of Macromedia's MacRecorder. It has a built-in unidirectional microphone, a line input, and a sliding gain control.

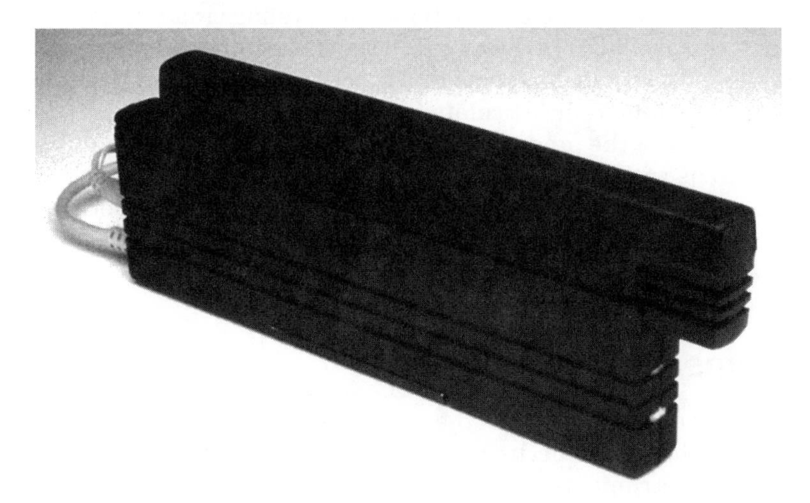

Figure 1–4. Voice Impact Pro

Unlike most Macintosh recording modules, Voice Impact Pro doesn't draw its power from the computer that it's plugged into. Instead, Voice Impact Pro has a power supply that plugs into a wall socket.

Other features of Voice Impact Pro include a built-in audio-to-digital signal processor and an on-board digital compression system that lets you save disk space by compressing sounds.

The Voice Impact Pro system comes with an impressive array of software, including the SoundWave recording and sound-editing program that's on this book's bonus disk. Other programs supplied with Voice Impact Pro include the Voice Record editing and recording program; a

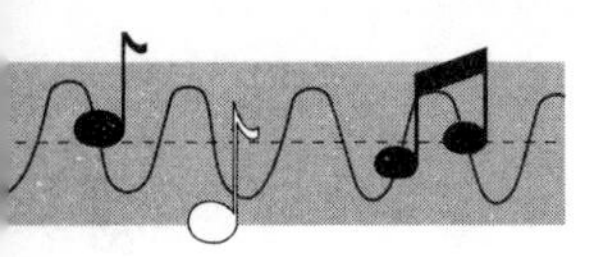

Voice Record stack for recording sound in HyperCard; and Voice Bandit, a program that enhances the capabilities of the Macintosh Sound Control Panel and other programs that access the Sound Manager.

The Sound Input Device

The Sound Input Device (SID) described in Appendix A was designed by three Macintosh fans and audio enthusiasts: Eric Gould, Jeffrey Siegel, and Dave Fleck. Siegel says that the trio put SID together, and then started giving away instructions for assembling the device simply because they wanted "to give something back to the industry."

SID, like the MacRecorder recording module from Macromedia, plugs into the Macintosh modem or printer port and draws the tiny amount of electric power it needs from the computer it's connected to. Its features include an "on the air" LED and automatic sound-leveling circuitry.

Even though you can build SID yourself, it's a state-of-the-art recording module that works much like Macromedia's MacRecorder and the Voice Impact recording module from Articulate Systems. With SID, you can record sounds for any of the programs in this book that support sound recording, as well as with most commercial sound-recording applications.

If you have experience building kit-style devices that require soldering, you'll have fun building SID; it will take only a few hours of your time, and you can buy the required parts for $20 to $30.

MIDI Systems

If you want to use your Macintosh as the centerpiece of a home recording studio, you can do that by connecting your Macintosh to various kinds of electronic musical instruments called MIDI devices.

MIDI, an acronym for Musical Instrument Digital Interface, is a language that computers and electronic musical instruments speak to each other. MIDI is also a hardware specification—and a communications protocol—that describes how synthesizers and other electronic instruments and devices can communicate with one another, and with your Macintosh. Most keyboard synthesizers and other electronic instruments manufactured today comply with the MIDI standard. That enables you to link various kinds of MIDI devices and to control them from a single spot—for example, from a Macintosh computer—in a professional or amateur sound studio.

The MIDI specification lets you connect many kinds of electronic instruments and other devices, including keyboard synthesizers, samplers, drum machines, mixers, tape recorders, VCRs, timers, and various kinds

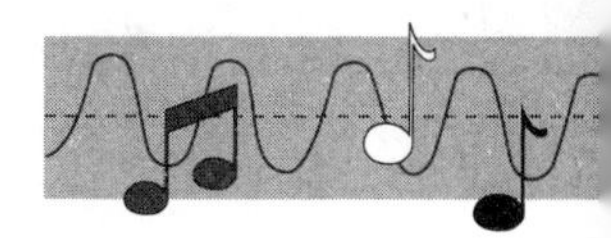

of controlling devices. Once you have set up a MIDI system, you can use it either to play live performances or to record musical sounds.

To make your Macintosh the centerpiece of a MIDI studio, you need a connection box called a MIDI interface. You can plug a MIDI interface into your computer's modem or printer port, and then you can control a virtually unlimited number of MIDI instruments and other MIDI devices from your computer.

Of course, you need software, as well as hardware, to run a computer-based MIDI system. Chapter 9 describes the MIDI standard and explains what kinds of hardware and software you need to create a MIDI system. It also contains some tips that may come in handy if you decide to go shopping for a MIDI system.

Sound Software

Sound hardware, like most other kinds of computer hardware, requires software to work properly. As mentioned earlier in this chapter, the sound hardware that's built into the Macintosh is controlled by the computer's system software.

In addition to the sound tools that are built into your computer's system software, you can use many kinds of application programs to record, create, edit, and play various kinds of sounds. The bonus disk that comes with this book contains a collection of sound-related applications. Sources for more sound-related programs are listed in Appendices B and C.

With Macs that are factory-equipped for recording, Apple supplies a limited amount of sound-recording software. The bonus disk that comes with this book contains a bigger collection of software that you can use to record, edit, and play back sound.

The programs on your bonus disk work with all models of the Macintosh: those equipped with mikes and recording hardware, those with add-on mikes and recording hardware, and those with no recording hardware at all. If your Macintosh isn't equipped with a microphone and recording circuitry, you can play and edit prerecorded sounds—which are supplied on your bonus disk—but you can't record your own sounds.

Sound Tools Provided by System Software

You can access some of the sound tools that are built into your computer's system software by opening a utility called the *Sound Control Panel* from the Apple menu or directly from the Finder. With the Sound Control

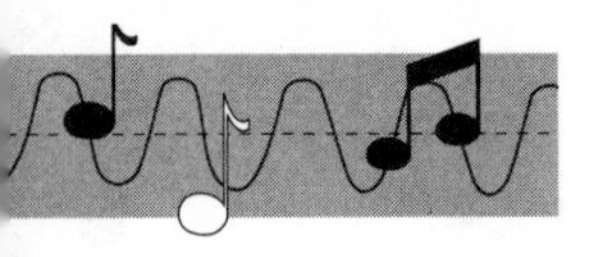

Panel, you can choose a system sound—the sound that your computer makes when it needs to capture your attention—and you can set the system sound's volume. Also, if your Macintosh has a built-in or add-on sound digitizer, you can use the Sound Control Panel to record your own system sounds. The Sound Control Panel is described in more detail in a section of its own later in this chapter.

Except for the small number of sound tools that you can access through the Sound Control Panel, most of the sound utilities that are included in your computer's system software are not designed to be accessed directly by the Macintosh user. Instead, they are accessed by sound-related programs—for example, programs that can be used to record, edit, and play back sounds. When you use a sound-related application program, the program you're using accesses your computer's basic sound tools, and what you interface with directly is the program.

This is how the process works: When you run a program that records and plays back sounds, the menus and windows you use to select recording and playback options are usually provided by the application you are running, not by the Macintosh operating system.

Suppose, for example, that you're running a typical sound-related application and you select a menu command labeled Play to play a sound. Your computer then plays the sound that you select.

The menu from which you choose the Play command is provided by the application you're running. When you make your menu selection, the application you're using accesses the system software your Macintosh is running. The system software on your computer then accesses your computer's built-in sound hardware, which plays the sound. This process is illustrated in Figure 1–5.

User
Application
System Software
Sound Hardware

Figure 1–5. Playing a Macintosh sound

Other Kinds of Sound Software

Besides the basic sound utilities that are included with your computer's system software, many other varieties of sound-related software are available. For example, you can find the following:

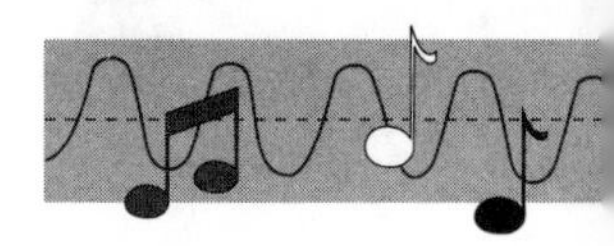

- Sound drivers
- Sound-processing programs
- HyperCard-based recording and editing programs
- Speech synthesis programs
- Musical notation programs
- Music-instruction programs
- MIDI-related programs

Examples of all of these kinds of programs are provided on the bonus disk that you got with this volume.

Sound Drivers

If your Macintosh came with a microphone and recording circuitry—or if you have bought or built a plug-in sound digitizer—you must install a *sound driver* in your System Folder before you can use your Macintosh to record sound. If your Mac doesn't have recording capabilities, or if you aren't interested in recording your own sounds, then you don't need a sound driver.

The bonus disk that comes with this book contains a popular sound driver called the MacRecorder driver. The MacRecorder driver, as you might guess from its name, was designed to access, or *drive,* the MacRecorder sound-recording module that is manufactured and marketed by Macromedia. However, the version of the MacRecorder driver provided on this book's bonus disk is specially configured to work with the SoundWave sound-editing program that's introduced in Chapter 4.

Although the MacRecorder driver on your bonus disk was designed for the MacRecorder digitizer and is modified to work with SoundWave, it also works with the following:

- The Macintosh Sound Control Panel, which you can use to record, select, and play customized system sounds
- The HyperCorder program that is provided on your bonus disk and is documented in Chapter 5
- The Sound Input Device (SID), a digitizer that you can build yourself using the instructions and schematic provided in Appendix A

Instructions for installing the MacRecorder driver in your System Folder—and using it once it is installed—are provided in the next section, "Unpacking Your Bonus Disk."

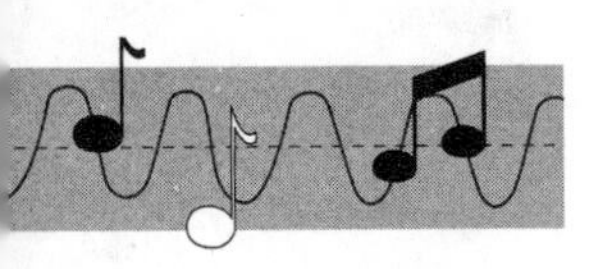

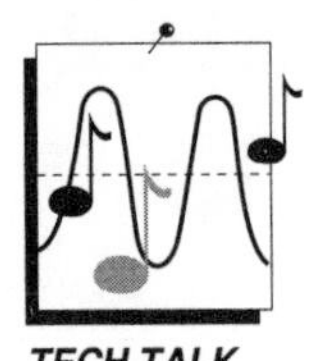

TECH TALK

How Sound Drivers Work

Although the MacRecorder driver is often referred to as a sound driver, it is technically not a driver, but a system extension that contains a device driver, or a resource of type 'DRVR'. But it's much easier to call such programs **sound drivers,** *so that's what they're usually called.*

System extensions are files that are not part of the basic Macintosh system software but do provide system-level services. Therefore, they must be loaded into memory at startup time. System extensions perform low-level tasks such as driving printers, CD-ROM drives, and voice-recording modules. Until the advent of System 7, system extensions were called INITs, or startup documents.

When the MacRecorder driver starts up, it loads a **device driver** *(a resource of type 'DRVR') into memory. From that point on, the device driver accesses the recording module plugged into your Macintosh, and it serves as a software gateway between your computer and your recording hardware.* ❍

Sound-Processing Programs

Sound-processing programs are applications that you can use to edit and play back prerecorded sounds. If your Macintosh has recording capabilities, you can also use sound-processing programs to record your own sounds. You can then use your sounds in presentations, in games, or with various kinds of applications that can play recorded sounds. Programs that can play digitized sounds include Microsoft Word, Microsoft Excel, CE Software's QuickMail, and a growing number of other commercially available applications.

One popular sound-processing program is SoundWave, which is included on the bonus disk that comes with this book. SoundWave is described in detail in Chapter 4.

Sound Programs for HyperCard

Some sound-processing programs are designed specifically for use with HyperCard. One such program is HyperCorder, which is on this book's bonus disk and is documented in Chapter 5. With HyperCorder, you can do the following:

- Cut, paste, and copy sounds
- Move sounds from one HyperCard stack to another
- Convert HyperCard sounds into sounds that can be used in non-HyperCard applications
- Convert non-HyperCard sounds into sounds that can be used in HyperCard stacks

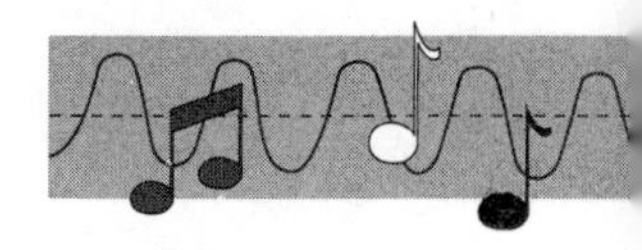

Speech Synthesis Programs

Some sound programs are designed to reproduce human speech. For example, Chapter 6 introduces HyperLab, a HyperCard-based application that can read typed text in various pitches, at various rates of speed, and with various intonations.

Musical Notation Programs

Musical notation programs are applications that musicians can use to compose musical scores. With a musical notation program, you can create and edit musical scores in much the same way that you can compose and edit documents with a word-processing program.

Musical notation programs can help you create music, transpose the keys of musical scores, and even edit musical scores using standard Macintosh cut, copy, and paste techniques. Songworks, a program included on your bonus disk (in a demonstration version) and described in Chapter 7, is an example of a musical notation program.

Music-Learning Programs

Many Macintosh programs can help you learn the principles of music. Some, like Practica Musica from Ars Nova, can serve as complete courses in music theory. Others, like the Listen program supplied on your bonus disk (in a demonstration version) and described in Chapter 8, are designed to be used primarily as ear-training programs.

MIDI-Related Programs

MIDI-related programs are applications that are designed to be used with MIDI music systems. Most musical notation programs and most music-instruction programs—including the Songworks and Listen programs provided in demonstration versions on your bonus disk—can be used with MIDI keyboard instruments. Therefore, you could say that they fall into the category of MIDI-related programs.

Other kinds of programs—for example, sequencers and editor-librarian programs—are designed specifically for use with MIDI music systems. MIDI programs, and the various kinds of MIDI devices that make use of MIDI software, are described in Chapter 9.

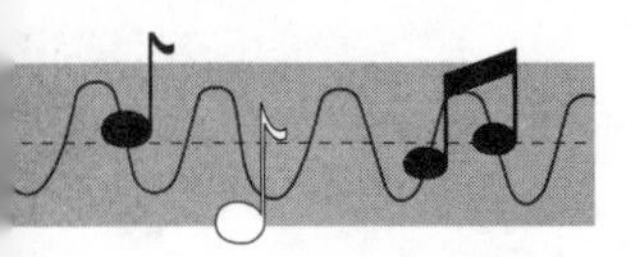

Hardware and Software Configurations

Once you've decided what sound capabilities you want, so many kinds of sound hardware and sound software for the Macintosh are available that the whole subject can get confusing. To help you sort it all out, Table 1–1 lists the kinds of sound hardware configurations that are available for the Macintosh, and tells what kinds of hardware and software each configuration requires for selected sound capabilities. For more details, see the section "What You'll Need" in the Introduction.

Table 1–1 Hardware and Software Configurations

If you have...	And...	Then...
A Macintosh that has a microphone input	You want to play, edit, and record sounds	Your computer contains all of the hardware you need; the software you need is on the bonus disk that comes with this volume.
A Macintosh that has no microphone input	You want to play and edit sounds	Your computer contains all of the hardware you need; the software you need is on the bonus disk that comes with this volume.
A Macintosh that has no microphone input	You want to record sounds	You need a plug-in recording module such as MacRecorder, Voice Impact, Voice Impact Pro, or SID (which you can build yourself using the instructions in Appendix A).
A Macintosh Plus or better	You want to play, compose, or edit music using your computer's built-in hardware	This book and its bonus disk contain some tutorials and demo programs that can get you started.
A Macintosh Plus or better	You want to play, compose, or edit music using keyboard synthesizers and other electronic instruments	This book demystifies the MIDI interface standard, tells what kinds of MIDI hardware and software are available, explains what various kinds of products do, and provides information that you'll need to shop wisely for professional-quality musical gear.

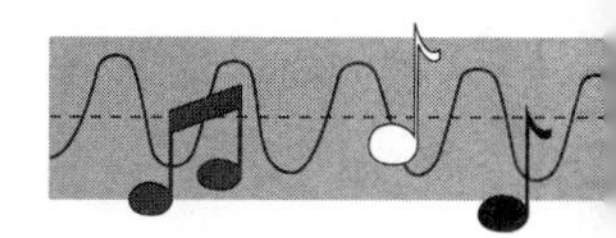

Unpacking Your Bonus Disk

Before you can use the free software and shareware that's on your bonus disk, you must unpack, or decompress, the files in which the programs are stored. The files are compressed with Compact Pro, a data compression and expansion program written by Bill Goodman and licensed for use with this volume.

It's easy to decompress the programs on your bonus disk and transfer them to another disk in their original form. You don't need a copy of Compact Pro to do that, because the compressed files are self-extracting.

If you're extracting your bonus disk archives onto a hard disk, or onto a blank 1.4Mb floppy disk, you can copy both of the archives that are on your bonus disk into the same folder. If you're copying the files onto 800K floppies, you need two blank disks. Extract the Incredible Sound 1 file onto one disk, and extract the Incredible Sound 2 file onto the other.

To expand and copy the programs on your bonus disk, just follow these steps:

1. Open your bonus disk. You'll see two icons that represent archives of compressed files. One icon is labeled Incredible Sound 1. The other is labeled Incredible Sound 2.
2. Double-click on the icon labeled Incredible Sound 1.
3. When you see a dialog window like the one shown in Figure 1–6, click on the OK button, and then do what the message says; select the volume and folder where you want your decompressed software to go, and then click on the button labeled Extract. That decompresses the files in the archive and copies them to your chosen destination. When you've finished extracting the files in Incredible Sound 1, do the same thing with Incredible Sound 2.

To decompress the files on this disk:

(1) Select the volume and folder where you want to store the extracted files.
(2) Click the button labeled "Extract."
(3) Run programs and enjoy!

Quit **OK**

Figure 1–6. Compact Pro dialog

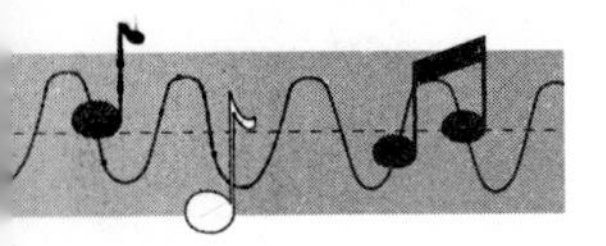

When you've finished copying the files, be sure to store your original bonus disk somewhere else for safekeeping.

When you've decompressed the Incredible Sound files on your bonus disk, you can start running the Incredible Sound programs that the disk contains. Each program on the disk is thoroughly documented in the text.

Installing the MacRecorder Driver

You can use the MacRecorder sound driver provided on your bonus disk to start exploring the sound capabilities of your Macintosh. The driver is on your bonus disk, in the folder labeled 01–Macintosh Sound.

You can install the MacRecorder driver into your System Folder by following these steps:

1. Make sure that you're running System 6.0.5 or later. You can determine the version of your system software by selecting the first item under the Apple menu (which should say About This Macintosh or About the Finder). If you discover that you're running a version earlier than System 6.0.5, you should see your Macintosh dealer about an upgrade.
2. Open the folder that holds the files from your bonus disk, and open the folder labeled 01–Macintosh Sound.
3. If you're running System 7, drag the MacRecorder driver icon into the Extensions folder that's inside your System Folder (or simply drag the icon into your System Folder; the Finder then asks you if you want to put the driver in the Extensions folder, and you can answer OK). If you're running System 6, then your System Folder doesn't contain an Extensions folder, so you can install the MacRecorder driver by dragging its icon into your System Folder.
4. Restart your computer. The MacRecorder driver is now installed.
5. Open your Sound Control Panel, using the steps described in the next section, "The Sound Control Panel."
6. Make sure that the MacRecorder driver icon is selected as the current sound-recording device. If the MacRecorder driver is selected, its icon is highlighted. If the MacRecorder icon isn't highlighted, select the driver now.

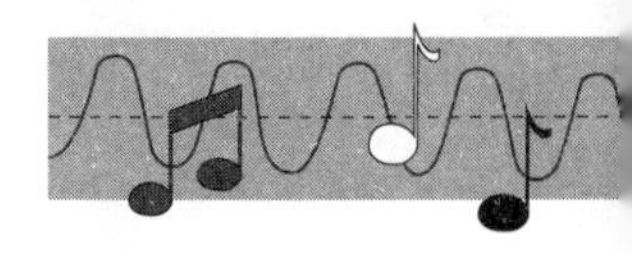

Activating the MacRecorder Driver

When your computer restarts, you may notice that a new icon appears briefly in the lower left-hand corner of your screen. That's the MacRecorder driver icon, and it's your signal that your sound driver has been loaded into memory.

Figure 1–7. MacRecorder driver icons

When the MacRecorder icon flashes on the screen, it should look like the icon on the left in Figure 1–7. If it has an **X** through it, like the icon on the right in Figure 1–7, then your driver has failed to load.

Loading Problems

If your MacRecorder sound driver doesn't load properly, the reason could be that you're running System 7 and have virtual memory turned on. If that's the case, the MacRecorder sound driver won't work because it isn't compatible with virtual memory. Also, if your computer is a Macintosh IIfx, you must install a piece of software called a serial switch, which is on your bonus disk, to make your serial ports compatible with the sound driver. Instructions for installing the IIfx serial switch and turning off virtual memory are provided later in this section.

Turning Off Virtual Memory

If you're running System 6, you don't have to worry about virtual memory being turned on, because virtual memory wasn't available until the introduction of System 7. Also, some models of the Macintosh don't support virtual memory, even if they have System 7 installed. Models that do support virtual memory are those equipped either with an MC68030 processor or with both an MC68020 processor and a 68851 memory management unit (MMU).

If you're using System 7, you can use the Memory Control Panel to find out whether your Macintosh supports virtual memory—and to turn virtual memory off if it is supported. Here's how:

1. Select the Control Panels folder from the Apple menu.
2. When the Control Panels window appears, double-click on the icon that has a picture of a computer chip on it and is labeled Memory. That opens a control panel window labeled Memory.
3. When the Memory Control Panel window opens, look for the Virtual Memory icon. The icon looks like a Macintosh blown up like a balloon, and to its right you'll see a pair of radio buttons under the label *Virtual Memory.* If your Memory Control Panel has no icon matching that description, your Macintosh doesn't support virtual memory.
4. To turn virtual memory off, click on the Off button next to the Virtual Memory icon.
5. Figure 1–8 shows a typical Memory Control Panel window. Your window may look slightly different; the contents of the panel can vary, depending on the memory architecture of the computer you're using.
6. Restart your Macintosh. Virtual memory is now disabled.

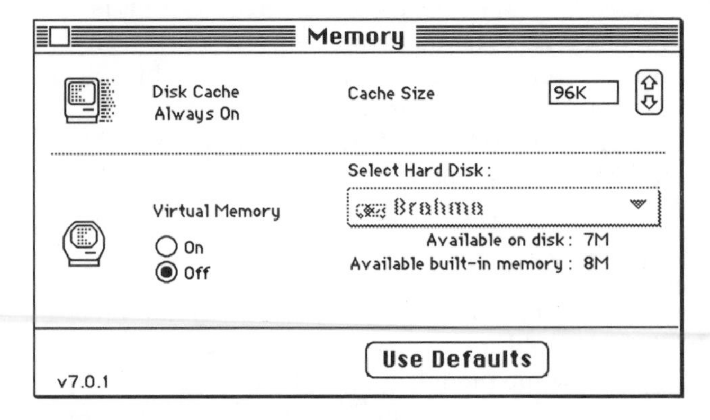

Figure 1–8. Memory Control Panel window

The IIfx Serial Switch

If you own a Macintosh IIfx, you must install a control panel device (CDEV) called the *IIfx serial switch.* You can edit and play back sounds without installing the serial switch, but you must use it to configure the serial ports on your Macintosh IIfx before you can use the MacRecorder driver.

If your computer is a Macintosh IIfx—and *only* if it is a IIfx—you should install the IIfx serial switch by following these steps:

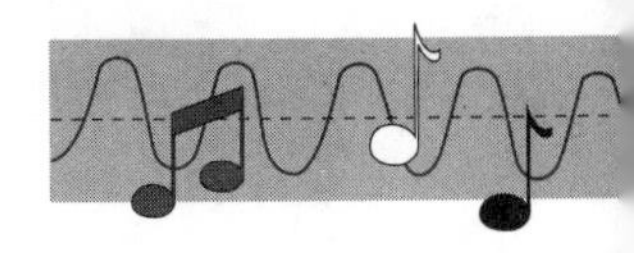

1. Open the Incredible Sound folder labeled 01–Macintosh Sound.
2. Open the folder labeled For IIfx owners.
3. Drag the icon labeled IIfx Serial Switch into your System Folder. (If you're running System 7, a dialog message will ask you if you want to store the serial switch in your Control Panels folder. Answer OK.)
4. Select the Control Panels folder from the Apple menu if you're running System 7, or select the Control Panel item from the Apple menu if you're running System 6.
5. When the System 6 Control Panel or the System 7 Control Panels window appears, select the IIfx Serial Switch icon (double-click on the icon if you're running System 7).
6. When the IIfx Serial Switch Control Panel opens, find the buttons labeled Compatible and Faster, and select Compatible.
7. Restart your Macintosh.
8. From this point on, you should set your serial switch to Compatible when you want to use your sound driver. Setting the switch to Faster makes your serial ports work slightly faster when you're using a modem or a printer.

The Sound Control Panel

When you have installed the MacRecorder driver, you can make sure that it's operating properly by examining the *Sound Control Panel:* a utility that controls many of your computer's sound-related functions. To select the MacRecorder driver as your sound driver, simply open the Sound Control Panel (as described later in this section) and select the MacRecorder driver with the mouse.

What the Sound Control Panel Is For

One important function of the Sound Control Panel is to customize the Mac's alert sound—that is, the sound that the Macintosh often makes when it displays an error message or wants to capture your attention for some other reason. The alert sound can also play when you do something illegal, such as clicking on the mouse outside a modal dialog window.

The simplest alert sound is a beep, but you can use the Sound Control Panel to change the kind of alert sound that your Macintosh makes. You can also adjust the volume of your computer's alert sound by using the

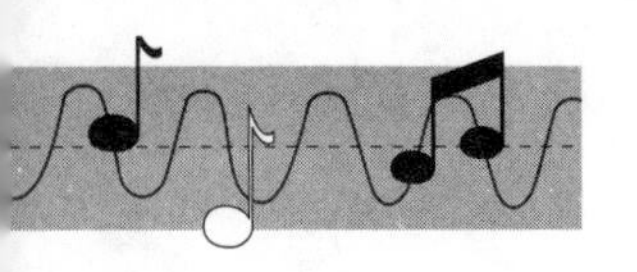

control panel. Instructions for using the Sound Control Panel to add, delete, and customize the alert sound are provided later in this section.

Differences in Sound Control Panels

A control panel, as you probably know, is a window that generally contains various kinds of controls and icons. Each control in a control panel is generally associated with a particular kind of device. By manipulating the controls on a control panel, you can access various devices—such as a keyboard, a monitor, or a CD-ROM drive—to change their behavior or their settings.

The Sound Control Panel that System 6 displays is a little different from the Sound Control Panel that you'll see if you're running System 7. The appearance of the Sound Control Panel is also affected by the kinds of sound drivers and sound-related devices that are installed.

The System 7 Sound Control Panel

If you're running System 7, you can open the Sound Control Panel by following these steps:

1. Select the Control Panels folder from the Apple menu. The Macintosh responds by displaying a Control Panels window like the one in Figure 1–9.

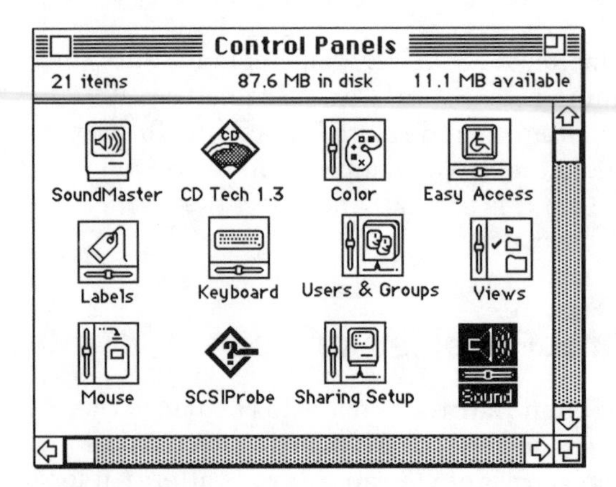

Figure 1–9. System 7 Control Panels window

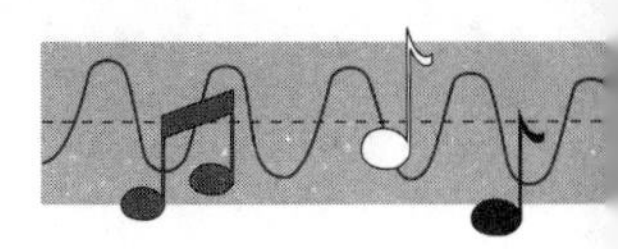

2. When you see the Control Panels window, double-click on the Sound icon. The Sound icon is a picture of a loudspeaker; it looks like the icon that's highlighted in Figure 1–9.
3. Another window now appears on your screen. That is the Sound Control Panel.

The System 6 Sound Control Panel

If you're using System 6, you can open the Sound Control Panel by following these steps:

1. Select the Control Panel item from the Apple menu. The Macintosh responds by displaying a Control Panel window like the one in Figure 1–10.

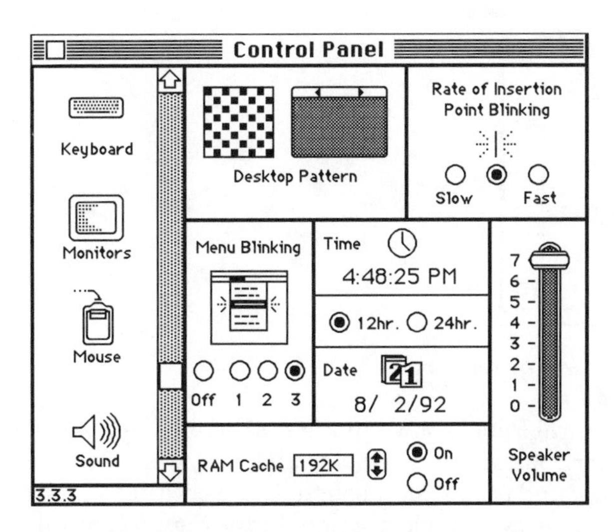

Figure 1–10. System 6 Control Panel window

2. When you see the Control Panel window, click on the Sound icon. The Sound icon is a picture of a loudspeaker; it looks like the bottom icon on the left in Figure 1–10.
3. Another window now appears on your screen. That is the Sound Control Panel.

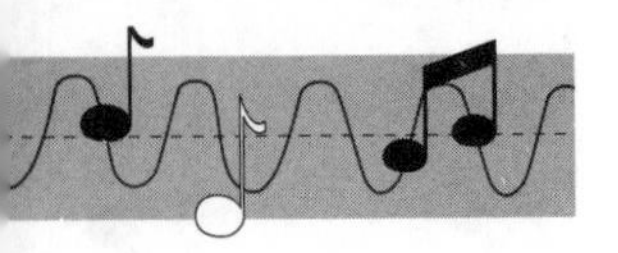

The Expanded and Collapsed Sound Control Panels

When either the System 6 or System 7 Sound Control Panel pops up on your screen, its appearance depends upon whether your system has all of the hardware and software that it needs to record sound. If a Macintosh running System 6.0.5 or later is equipped with a sound driver and compatible sound-recording hardware, it displays an expanded Sound Control Panel that offers recording capabilities. If a Macintosh running System 6.0.5 or later is not equipped to record sound, it displays a collapsed Sound Control Panel that does not support recording.

Figure 1–11 shows a collapsed, or nonrecording, Sound Control Panel. If your Sound Control Panel looks like the one shown in Figure 1–11, then your Macintosh is not equipped to record sound, or it is missing something that is needed for sound recording.

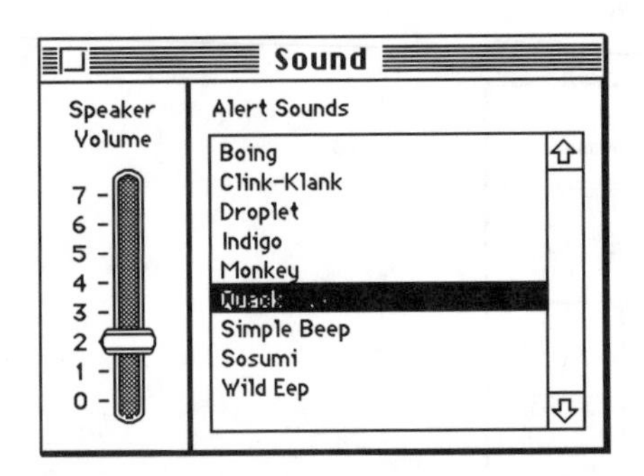

Figure 1–11. Sound Control Panel with no sound driver

The collapsed Sound Control Panel shown in Figure 1–11 has two parts: a slide for adjusting speaker volume and a list of available system alert sounds. When you select a sound on the alert sound list by clicking on its name, that sound becomes your system alert sound. In the Sound Control Panel shown in Figure 1–11, the sound of a duck quacking is selected as the system alert sound.

If your computer has recording capabilities and your system has determined that they are all working, then your Sound Control Panel resembles the expanded panel shown in Figure 1–12.

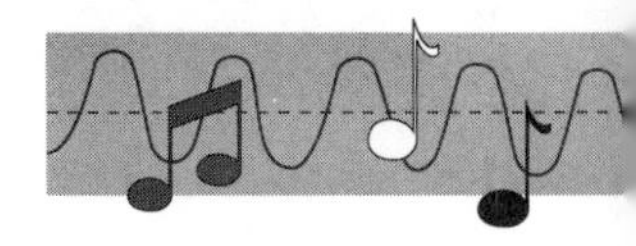

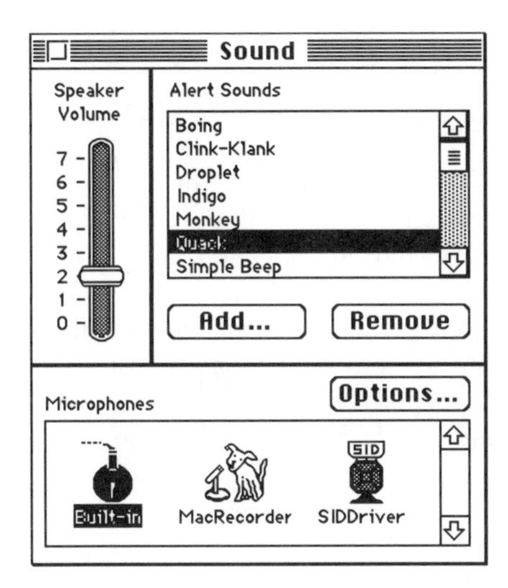

Figure 1–12. Expanded Sound Control Panel

An expanded Sound Control Panel contains three buttons: Add, Remove, and Options. These buttons work as follows:

- **Remove**—lets you remove any sound from the list of alert sounds.
- **Add**—brings up another dialog window. By clicking controls in that window, you can record a new alert sound, by either speaking into your recording system's microphone or attaching an external sound source to your system's line input and playing a prerecorded sound.
- **Options**—depends on the application you are using. Manufacturers of sound drivers and digitizers can use the Options button to list various characteristics and settings of their devices. For example, some programs let you use the Options button to find out whether your recording module is plugged into your modem port or your printer port. Some applications don't enable the Options button.

The expanded Sound Control Panel shown in Figure 1–12 has access to three different sound-recording modules: MacRecorder; Sound Input Device (SID); and Built-in, a sound driver that supports microphone-equipped models of the Macintosh. In the illustration, the icon labeled Built-in is selected. That means two things: the Macintosh being used is equipped with built-in recording hardware, and the Built-in sound driver is the one that is active.

When you display your Sound Control Panel, make sure that the sound driver you want to use is selected. If it isn't, then click on it to highlight it. When the driver you want is highlighted, that means it is selected.

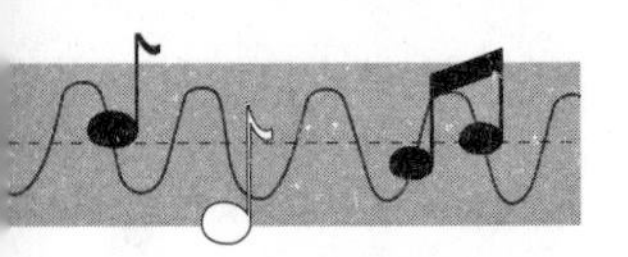

The Macintosh Alert Sound

When you open the Sound Control Panel—in either System 7 or System 6—the control panel window contains a scrolling list of available alert sounds. There's also a sliding volume control that adjusts the level of the alert sound.

If you're running System 7, you can also check to see what alert sounds are installed in your system by opening the System Folder and double-clicking on the System file. The Finder then opens a window that contains the names and icons of the fonts and sounds that are installed in the System file.

Customizing Your Alert Sound

To change your computer's system alert sound, just open your Sound Control Panel and select the name of any sound that appears in the list labeled Alert Sounds. That sound then becomes your alert sound.

Deleting an Alert Sound

By clicking on the Remove button, you can delete any sound from the list of available alert sounds. You can also delete a sound by selecting the Clear command from the Edit menu. Another technique is to remove a sound by selecting the Cut command from the Edit menu. Then, if you make a mistake, you can select the Paste menu command to retrieve the sound. The Clear menu command, like the Remove button, deletes a sound and gives you no chance to change your mind.

Recording a New Alert Sound

If your Macintosh has recording capabilities, you can use the Sound Control Panel to record customized alert sounds. Just click on the Add button, and the Sound Control Panel recording dialog window (shown in Figure 1–13) appears on the screen.

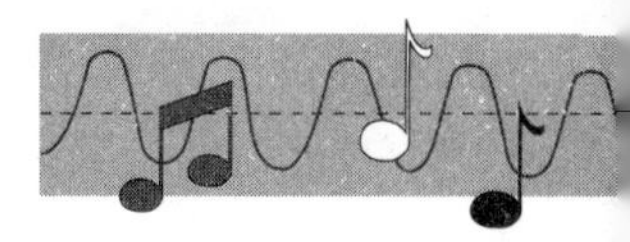

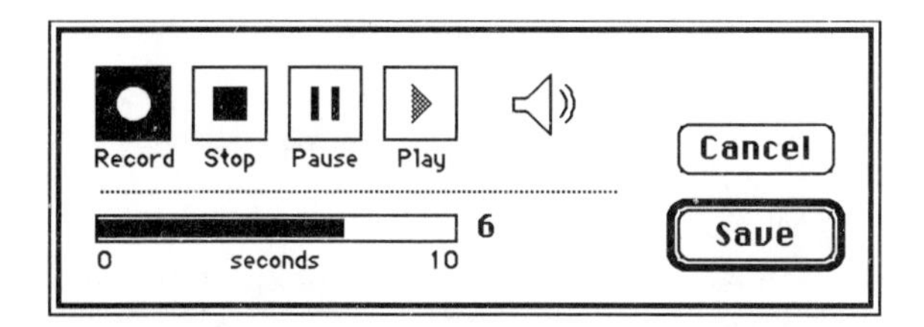

Figure 1–13. Sound Control Panel recording dialog window

The recording dialog window works like the control panel of a tape recorder. When it is on the screen, you can do the following:

- Record a sound by selecting the Record button
- Stop recording by pressing the Stop button
- Interrupt the recording or playback process by clicking on the Pause button
- Play your sound by clicking on the Play button

To record a sound, these are the steps to follow:

1. Click on the Record button in the recording dialog and speak into your recording system's microphone. As you speak, notice that sound waves appear to come from the speaker icon in the center of the dialog. The louder you speak, the more waves emanate from the speaker icon.

   If you want to record a sound directly from an external source (instead of from a microphone) and save it as a system alert sound, then connect your external signal source to your sound system's line input with a cable, and continue following these instructions.

2. Below the tape recorder pushbuttons in the window, a meter bar keeps track of elapsed recording time. Beneath the right end of the bar, a figure tells you how much total recording time you have. To the right of the bar, another number decreases as you consume available recording time.

   While observing the elapsed time meter, record your sound.

3. When you have recorded a sound and are satisfied with your sound (or have run out of time), you can close the recording dialog by selecting the Save button. Another dialog then appears, offering you an opportunity to type in a name for your sound.

4. Type in a name for your sound. The sound is then saved in the System file as a resource (resources are described in the next section, "Sound Resources and Sound Files"). Also, the sound's name is automatically added to the list of alert sounds displayed in the Sound Control Panel.

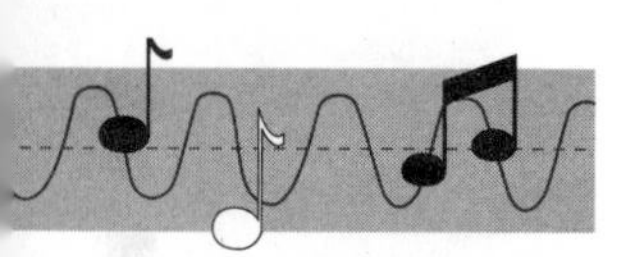

Improving Macintosh Sound

The weakest links in the Macintosh sound system are the computer's built-in amplifier and its built-in speaker (a tiny 2.25-inch cone, except on Quadra models, which have a somewhat bigger speaker). The internal speaker in your average Macintosh is too small, and too weakly amplified, to produce satisfactory sound. The Mac's internal speaker has an impedance of 32 ohms, and the amplifier that drives the speaker has an output of 250mW (milliwatts). In contrast, a typical home high-fidelity sound system usually has a pair of 4-ohm or 8-ohm speakers (speakers with lower impedance ratings require more power and can produce more forceful sounds) and an amplifier with a power rating of at least 20 watts per channel.

You can significantly improve the quality of your computer's sound by adding a more powerful amplifier and a pair of external speakers. You can use two kinds of speaker setups. You can connect your Macintosh directly to a pair of powered speakers (speakers with built-in amplifiers), or you can connect your computer to a stereo component system.

When you plug a pair of external speakers into the back panel of the Macintosh, the computer's built-in speaker is automatically disconnected.

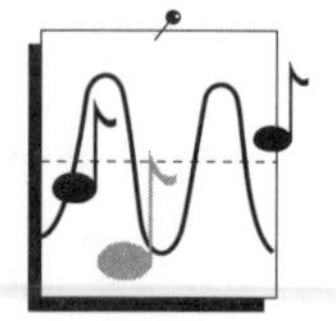

TECH TALK

Stereo and Mono Macs

The Macintosh Plus and the Macintosh SE are strictly monophonic models; they cannot reproduce stereo sound. However, the Macintosh SE/30, IIcx, IIci, IIsi, and later models can play sound in stereo.

The Macintosh SE/30 produces stereo sound in a unique way—with a method not used by any other Macintosh. The SE/30 always operates in stereo, but its internal sound circuitry mixes the two channels together when the internal speaker is used.

All other Macintosh computers that can play in stereo use a different system. In the Macintosh II and all post-Macintosh II models except the SE/30, the IIsi, and the Quadra, the internal speaker is connected only to the left channel. When a stereo amplifier is connected to the computer's output jack, both channels are activated, and a stereo signal goes to the outboard amplifier. ❍

Connecting a Macintosh to Powered Speakers

If you want to outfit your Macintosh with a pair of powered speakers, you can buy two kinds: speakers designed specifically for the Macintosh, or speakers designed to be connected to small, Walkman-style radios and tape players. Either style is fine; just make sure the speakers you select produce good sound.

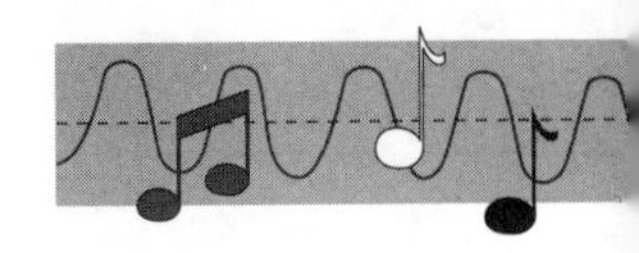

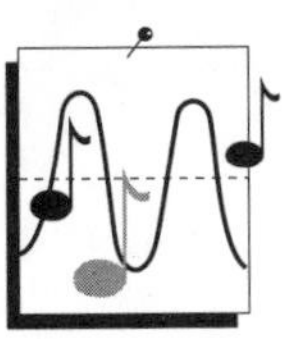

TIP

Shopping Tips for Speaker Buyers

If you buy a pair of powered speakers, be sure to choose speakers with enough power to produce good sound. Speakers that plug into a wall socket are usually more satisfactory than speakers that run exclusively on batteries. And be sure to choose speakers with some kind of volume control; the volume control in your computer's Sound Control Panel isn't sensitive enough to control the volume of an external speaker very well. ❍

Connecting a Macintosh to a Stereo System

To connect your Macintosh to a stereo amplifier, you need a cable with a male stereo miniconnector on one end and a pair of male RCA connectors on the other. You can plug the miniconnector into your Macintosh, and you can plug the RCA connectors into the auxiliary, tape, or tuner inputs on a stereo receiver or preamplifier. The audio cables that you need for this job are available at most hobbyist-oriented electronics stores.

Playing Sounds Stored on Disks

The Sound Manager can play sounds directly from a disk, as well as sounds stored in memory. However, if you want to play sounds directly from disks, here are three important points to keep in mind.

First, sounds require enormous quantities of disk space. You can save disk space by compressing sounds or by changing their sampling rates, but no matter what you do, it's a fact of life that sounds consume enormous amounts of disk space, as well as generous amounts of memory. So, if you want to play sounds stored directly from disks, you should make sure that you have enough disk space to hold the sounds that you want to play.

Second, for direct-from-disk playback, it's better to store sounds on a hard disk than on a floppy disk. When your computer has to read a sound stored on a disk, there is always some delay between the time you select a sound to be played and the time you actually hear it. Since it takes longer to access a floppy disk than it takes to access a hard disk, storing sounds on a floppy disk increases the delay.

Third, if the files on your hard disk are fragmented, that can also increase the amount of time that it takes your computer to access a sound. Disk fragmentation occurs when your Macintosh can't find enough contiguous space on your hard disk to store a file (such as a sound file) in one continuous block of memory. When that happens, your computer has to break the file down into parts, and store each part on a separate section of the disk. When you want to access the file, your computer has to retrieve

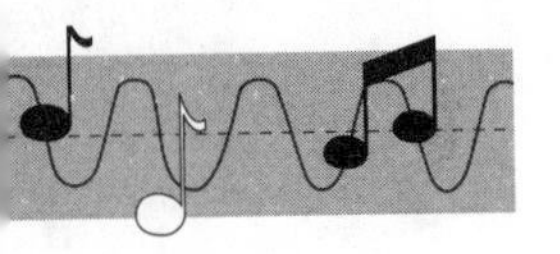

each part of the file from the section of the disk where it's stored, and then string all of the parts of the file back together again.

Hard disks often become fragmented over time, as files are saved, then erased, and then saved again. If you have a hard disk that you've used a great deal, and if you have a considerable number of files stored on it, then it's probably very fragmented. You can defragment a hard disk with programs such as SUM II or the Norton Utilities package for the Macintosh. For further details on disk defragmentation software, see your Macintosh dealer.

Playing Sound in the Background

If your Macintosh is an SE/30 or later, then the sound hardware built into your system can play a sound continuously from disk while other tasks are performed.

When an application plays sound in the background, the sound continues uninterrupted unless an application pauses or stops it.

The current version of the Macintosh Sound Manager—the enhanced Sound Manager, which was introduced with System 6.0.7—can play sounds continuously from a disk while your Macintosh SE/30 or later is performing other tasks. Furthermore, the enhanced Sound Manager can read any number of sounds from a disk, store them in buffers in RAM, and play them back simultaneously.

When multiple disk-based sounds are playing, the enhanced Sound Manager automatically mixes the sound signals it is reading as they are played back for output on the available sound hardware.

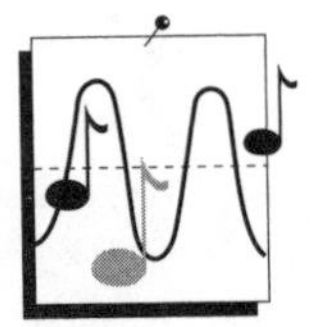

DEFINITIONS

Asynchro-what?

When a sound is being played in the background in such a way that the Macintosh CPU can perform other tasks while the sound is playing, the sound is said to be playing **asynchronously.**

When a sound claims all of the CPU's time for itself, so that no other tasks can be performed while the sound is playing, the sound is said to be playing **synchronously.**

One of the most important features of the Macintosh Sound Manager is its ability to play sounds asynchronously. When sound is played asynchronously, you can perform any task you like on your Macintosh while music or other kinds of sounds play in the background. ❍

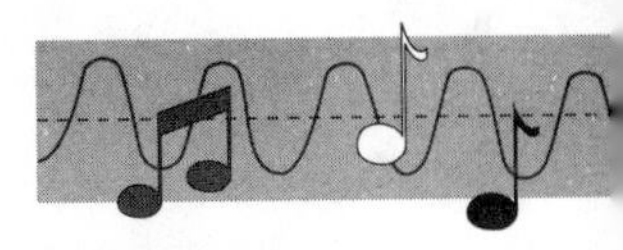

Sound Shareware

The bonus disk that comes with this book contains a great collection of sound-related software. But there wasn't nearly enough room on the disk for all of the free (and almost free) sound software that's available. Many public and commercial bulletin boards—as well as many Macintosh user groups—can provide you with many kinds of interesting sound-related applications, as well as enormous quantities of recorded sounds.

There are many sources for sound-related freeware or low-cost shareware, as well as for libraries of sampled sounds. Sources include public and private computer bulletin boards; commercial bulletin boards such as America Online and CompuServe; and computer user organizations such as BMUG in Berkeley, California.

To obtain free long-distance numbers for the commercial bulletin-board services, call the telephone company's 800 information service by dialing 800–555–1212—or buy a starter kit at a computer store.

To contact BMUG, you can connect to the BMUG bulletin board (by modem) at 510–849–2684, call 510–549–BMUG, or write to the organization (does anybody do that anymore?) at 1442A Walnut Street, #62, Berkeley, CA 94709–1496. BMUG is also accessible via America Online, AppleLink, CompuServe, Bix, GEnie, Prodigy, MCI Mail, and various other telecommunications services.

If you're more interested in the addresses of Macintosh user organizations nearer to you, consult your telephone directory or call Apple at 408–996–1010.

Some of the most popular freeware and shareware programs are listed and described in Appendix C.

Summary

This chapter covered the sound capabilities of various models of the Macintosh, and what kinds of hardware and software you'll need to record, edit, and play back sounds on the model of the Macintosh that you're using. Also, the chapter described the programs that are supplied on the bonus disk that comes with this book, and explained how to unpack and use them.

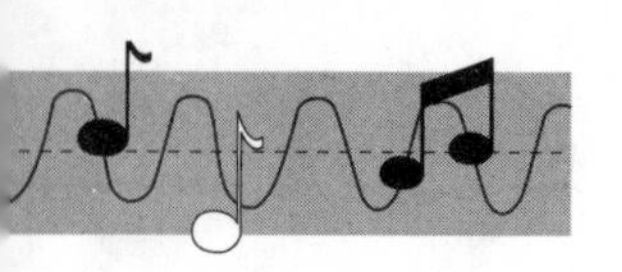

The Sound Control Panel, which you can use to select and customize the Macintosh system beep, was introduced in this chapter. The chapter explained how to install sound drivers—software utilities that are not needed for playing sounds but are required for recording sound. Some models of the Macintosh are shipped with recording capabilities installed, but others must be equipped with add-on hardware modules called digitizers, as well as sound drivers, before they can be used for recording. Along with describing digitizers and sound drivers, this chapter explained how to add recording capabilities to any Macintosh that isn't factory-equipped for recording.

Finally, you learned how you can connect your Macintosh to external speakers or to a stereo system to increase the quality of the sound produced by your computer system.

2 The Science of Sound

When you record sounds or edit prerecorded sounds, you can avoid many mistakes if you have a basic understanding of audio theory. This chapter is devoted to explaining some of the most important principles of the science of sound.

In this chapter, you'll first learn what sound is, then find out about the two kinds of sounds your Macintosh can produce—synthesized and sampled sounds. Next, you'll be introduced to and learn about waveforms, the properties (frequency, amplitude, and timbre) of sounds. Finally, I'll describe a few sampling and synthesizing techniques.

The Sound-Trecker Program

As you read about these topics, you can experiment with them by running Sound-Trecker. (Note that Sound-Trecker requires a 68020 chip; it will not run on the Macintosh Plus, SE, Classic, or Powerbook 100.) The program, written by German computer whiz Frank Seide, is one of the most acclaimed music-related shareware programs ever created. Sound-Trecker is on your bonus disk. It's introduced in this chapter because you can use it to demonstrate many fundamental principles of audio science. For example, you can use Sound-Trecker to view the waveforms of sounds; to view the sounds in a spectrum display; to adjust the range of frequencies that are being played; to listen for the phenomenon of aliasing; and to experiment with the tone, the tempo, and the volume of a sound that is being played.

What Sound-Trecker Can Do

Sound-Trecker is not just instructive; it's also entertaining. It can play four-channel stereo recordings in stereo, and can display waveforms in

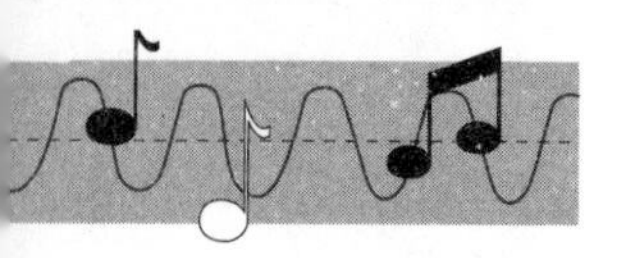

real time on two different kinds of oscilloscope screens. It can play sounds at various sampling rates; it can play a preselected series of songs; and it can do all sorts of other amazing things with music in real time.

Sound-Trecker supports full multitasking—that is, it can play background music while your computer is performing other tasks. The songs that it plays sound terrific—particularly if you have an external amplification and speaker system connected to your Macintosh—and they are stored in files that require much less disk and memory space than files of sampled sounds.

Starting Sound-Trecker

If you've unpacked the files on your bonus disk (see Chapter 1 for instructions), open the folder named 02–Sound-Trecker. Then launch Sound-Trecker by double-clicking on one or more Sound-Trecker songs in the Finder. Two songs—"Virgin" and "Canon in D"—are supplied on your bonus disk. You can obtain other Sound-Trecker songs from computer users' groups or download them from commercial and public bulletin boards.

When you have launched Sound-Trecker, the program displays a window like the one shown in Figure 2–1.

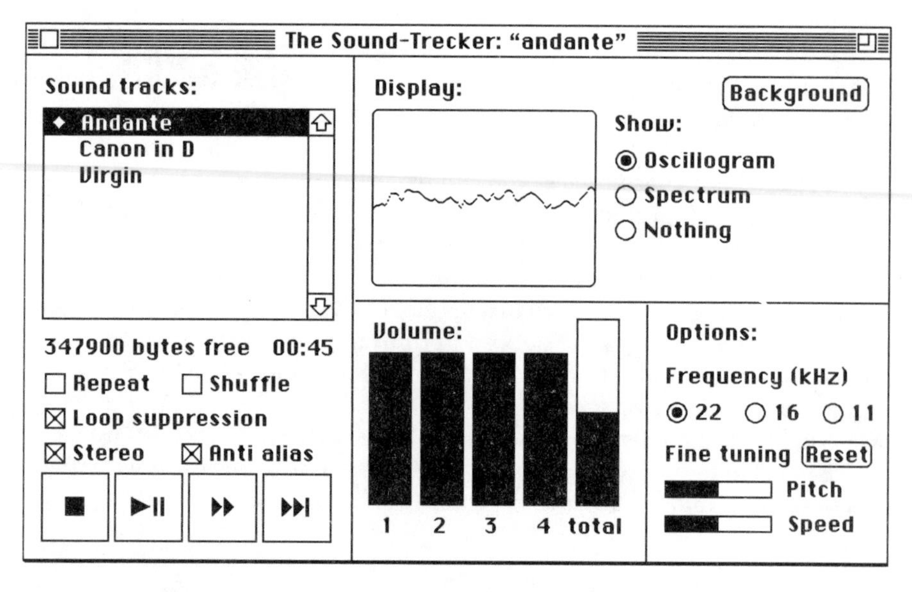

Figure 2–1. Sound-Trecker

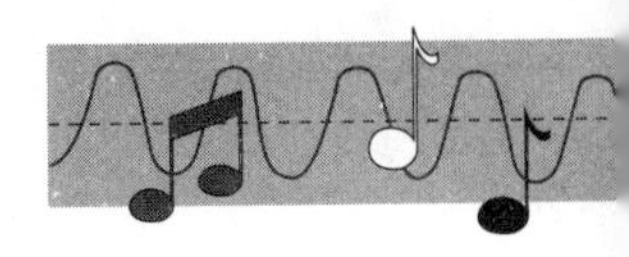

Another way to launch Sound-Trecker is to double-click on its application icon. You can then select and open a musical selection by choosing the Open command from the File menu.

The Sound-Trecker icon is a picture of a tractor—"trecker" in German—with notes coming from its exhaust pipe. The icon for a sound track file is a tractor with a note above it and a document behind. Both icons are shown in Figure 2–2.

Sound-Trecker Application

Sound-Trecker File

Figure 2–2. Sound-Trecker icons

If you're running System 7, there's a third way to launch Sound-Trecker; you can simply drag any sound track selection into the Sound-Trecker icon. That launches Sound-Trecker and starts playing the song you have selected.

When you have launched Sound-Trecker and have opened the song titled Virgin, the song starts playing automatically. You can then adjust the song's volume, frequency response, and other characteristics with the controls in the Sound-Trecker window. These controls, and what they do, are explained in detail in the section "Using Sound-Trecker" at the end of this chapter.

What Is Sound?

Sound is a change in pressure that occurs in the air around you when an object vibrates and produces sound waves. As the object moves forward, it compresses the air around it, causing the pressure of the air to increase. As the object moves backward, it rarefies the air around it, decreasing the air pressure. These changes in pressure spread out in a wavelike pattern, and they are experienced by humans and other creatures that can hear as sound.

From a psychoacoustic point of view, sound is the sensation that you experience when your auditory nerves are stimulated by vibrating air molecules. The more a vibrating object causes the air pressure around it to change, the louder is the sound that it produces. The more rapid the changes in air pressure are, the higher is the pitch of the sound.

The patterns in the air that a sound creates are called *sound waves,* and a graphical representation of a sound is called a *waveform.* A

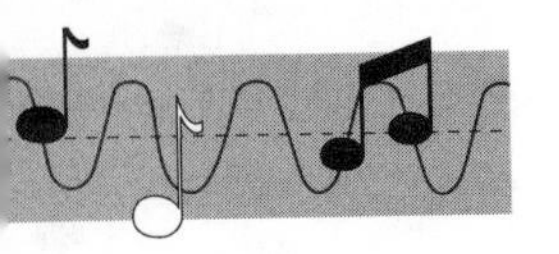

waveform provides a picture of a sound's characteristics, or *properties.* The properties of a sound include its *pitch,* or *frequency;* its *loudness,* or *amplitude;* and a combination of various other tonal qualities, which together make up a characteristic called *timbre.*

When a sound is represented as a waveform, the height of the waves that make up the waveform represent the sound's amplitude, and the width of the waves represent the sound's frequency. The simplest kind of sound wave, called a *sine wave,* is shown in Figure 2–3. A sine wave contains just one amplitude, just one frequency, and no particular timbre. A sine wave produces a steady, unwavering tone. Radio and television stations often use sounds produced by sine waves as time signals.

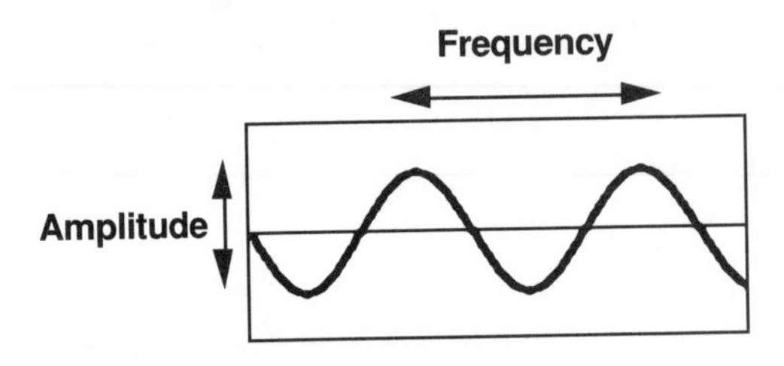

Figure 2–3. A sine wave

A *cycle* is the amount of time that it takes for the air pressure produced by a sound to rise to increase to its maximum level, fall to its minimum level, and return to its original value. A 20Hz sound is a sound that cycles through a complete wave in one twentieth of a second.

The period of time that lasts from one sound cycle to the next cycle is called a *period.* A period in a wave cycle is measured in Figure 2–4.

Most sounds don't have waveforms as simple as the waveform of a sine wave. That's because the frequency and amplitude of a sound usually vary from the time it starts to the time it ends, and because most sounds not only have frequencies and amplitudes, but also tonal colorations called timbres. The timbre of a sound is what makes it sound different from another sound, even though both sounds may have the same frequency and amplitude. For example, timbre is what makes an A note played by a trumpet sound different from an A note played by a violin.

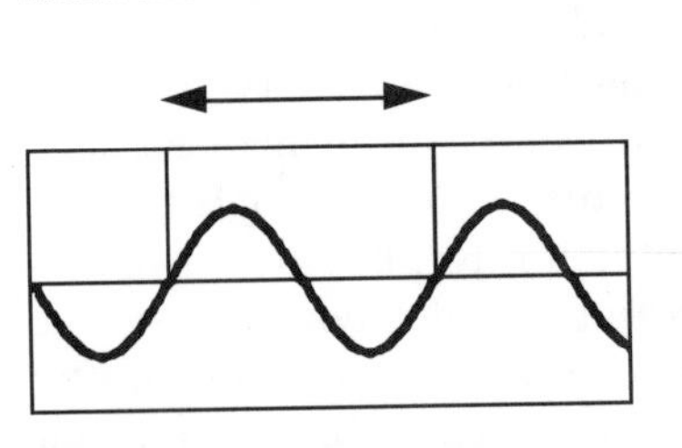

Figure 2–4. A period in a wave cycle

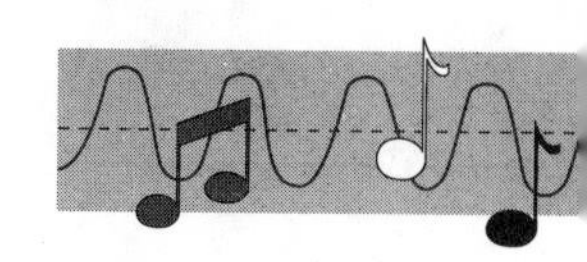

To summarize, when a sound is represented as a waveform, these rules apply:

- Fluctuations in the sound's *amplitude* are represented as variations in the height of its sound waves.
- Fluctuations in the sound's *frequency* are represented as variations in the widths of its sound waves, as measured from one cycle to the next.
- The *timbre* of the sound is represented as variations in the shapes of its sound waves.

The waveform of a complex sound is shown in Figure 2–5. In case you wonder what the sound is, it's part of the sound of a woman's voice asking, "How are you today?" You'll get to play the sound in Chapter 5.

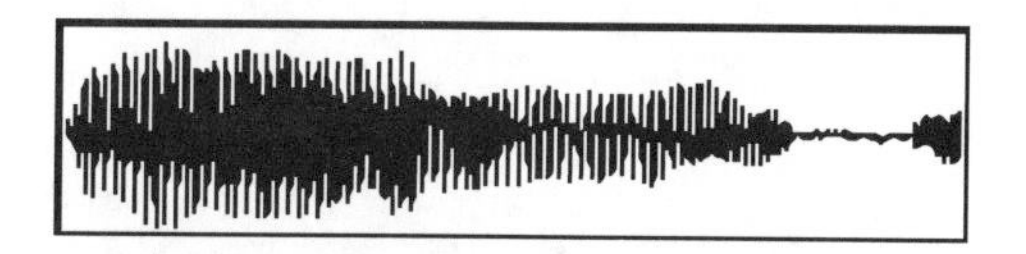

Figure 2–5. A complex waveform

Synthesized and Sampled Sounds

There are two main ways that electronic devices, including the Macintosh, produce sound. One way is to *synthesize* sound. The other way is to *sample* sound.

A device that synthesizes sound is called a *synthesizer.* A device that samples sound is called a *sampler.* Small devices that can record sampled sounds, such as the MacRecorder recording module, are often referred to as *digitizers.*

Synthesizers

A *synthesizer* is an instrument that uses electronic devices called *sound generators,* or *tone generators,* to create complex waveforms. The sounds that are produced in this way can then be combined algorithmically to produce still more complex sounds.

When you create a sound with a synthesizer, you can control the sound's properties—that is, the sound's frequency, amplitude, and timbre—by adjusting the electronic parameters that are used to create the sound.

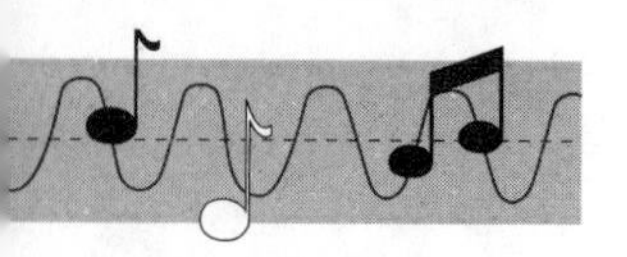

MIDI Synthesizers

Two kinds of synthesizers are commonly used in concerts and in sound studios. A *keyboard synthesizer* is an instrument that uses a pianolike keyboard to produce sound. There are also *rack-mounted synthesizers,* which lack keyboards but can synthesize sounds from signals provided by external keyboards or other signal sources.

Synthesizers contain memory chips and can use both digital algorithms and *program tables* stored in their memories to generate sounds. Many synthesizers in use today can mix digitally synthesized sounds with the waveforms of recorded (or *sampled)* analog sounds to create new and more realistic sounds.

Most of the synthesizers used in concerts and sound studios are MIDI instruments; that is, devices that comply with the MIDI electronic music standard described in Chapter 9.

Macintosh Synthesizers

Two of the three synthesizers built into the Macintosh—the square-wave synthesizer and the wave-table synthesizer—use techniques similar to those employed by MIDI synthesizers to create sounds.

The Macintosh square-wave synthesizer (described in more detail in Chapter 3) generates sounds by synthesizing square waves—simple waveforms that have squared-off corners and sound a bit harsher than sine waves. A square wave, like a sine wave, has one frequency, one amplitude, and no particular timbre. The system alert sound called "Simple Beep," which you can select with the sound control panel, has a sound much like that of a square wave. A square wave has a waveform like the one shown in Figure 2–6.

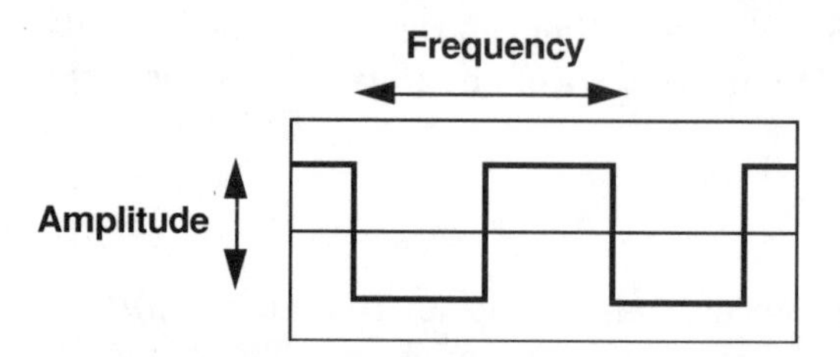

Figure 2–6. A square wave

The Macintosh wave-table synthesizer, like a MIDI synthesizer, can produce sounds from program tables stored in memory. The wave-table synthesizer is a powerful and memory-efficient sound generator, but it is not used by many Macintosh applications.

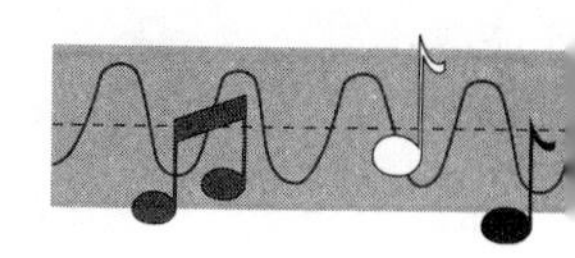

The third Macintosh synthesizer—the sampled sound synthesizer—is the synthesizer that is used by most sound-generating programs. The Macintosh sampled sound synthesizer is covered in detail in Chapter 3.

Despite its name, the sampled sound synthesizer doesn't have much in common with a typical MIDI synthesizer. Instead, it works more like a different kind of MIDI instrument called a *sampler.* A sampler, as you'll see in the next section, is an instrument that can record (or *sample),* and then play back, natural (or *analog)* sounds.

Samplers

A *sampler* is an electronic instrument that can convert a natural (or *analog)* sound into digitized form, can store the sound's digital representation in memory, and can then use that representation to recreate the original sound. When a sampler has recorded and stored a sound, you can edit the sound to make it sound different from the original sound. You can also use various signal-processing techniques to modify the sound by adjusting its electronic parameters, creating new and different sounds.

The samplers used in concerts and sound studios are usually MIDI devices that can be connected to other kinds of MIDI instruments, such as synthesizers and drum machines. Samplers, like synthesizers, come in two main varieties: models with keyboards and rack-mounted models. Rack-mounted samplers, like rack-mounted synthesizers, can generate sounds from signals provided by external keyboards and other kinds of signal-generating devices. MIDI samplers are described in more detail in Chapter 9.

The sampled sound synthesizer that's built into the Macintosh works much like a miniature version of a professional-style MIDI sampler. With a sound-recording device—such as the MacRecorder digitizer or the recording circuitry supplied with some models of the Macintosh—you can record and play back sampled sounds.

Properties of Sound

Every sound has three main characteristics, or *properties:*

- Pitch, or *frequency*
- Volume, or *amplitude*
- Tonal characteristics, or *timbre*

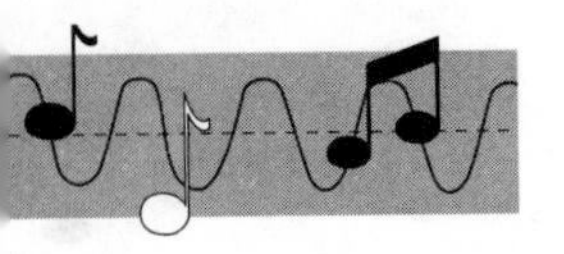

Each of these three properties is described under a separate heading in this section.

Frequency

Some musical tones sound higher than others because every musical sound has a pitch, or *frequency.* The frequency of a sound can be measured in *hertz* (Hz), or cycles per second.

All musical instruments, acoustic as well as electronic, can be tuned to play notes using various frequencies. In concert halls and recording studios, the most widely used tuning procedure is to tune instruments so that the note A in the middle of a piano keyboard has a pitch of 440Hz. Once this pitch has been established, it can be used as a base for tuning every note on a piano keyboard, or every instrument in a band or a symphony orchestra.

If you tune a piano to the "A–440" standard and then play a musical scale going upward, from the 440Hz A note to the A note in the next octave, the frequency of the last A in the scale doubles, to 880Hz. Raise the note another octave, and its frequency doubles again, to 1,760Hz. At this rate of geometric increase, it takes only six octaves for an A note to get from 440Hz to 28,160Hz, a frequency well past the 20kHz frequency that is the upper limit of human hearing.

If you play a musical scale going downward, from middle A on the piano keyboard to the A note in the next lower octave, the frequency of the lower A note is half that of the upper one—220Hz. The A note below that has half of that frequency—110Hz—and so on. In five iterations downward, the frequency of middle A falls to 13.75Hz, below the lower boundary of the audible frequency range.

This algorithm—doubling the frequency of a note each time its octave doubles—works for any two notes that are an octave apart, all the way up and down the frequency range. Going up an octave always doubles a note's frequency, and going down an octave halves the note's frequency.

Since the frequency of a note doubles each time the note goes up an octave, the frequencies of two notes at the high end of the audible spectrum are much farther apart than the frequencies between the same two notes at the low end of the spectrum. For example, the frequency difference between middle A and the A note that is one octave lower is 440Hz minus 220Hz—a 220Hz difference. In comparison, the frequency difference between middle A and the next *highest* A note is twice that much—880Hz minus 440Hz, or a 440Hz difference.

A simpler way of saying all this is that as the notes of the scale ascend, the notes rise arithmetically while their frequencies increase geometrically.

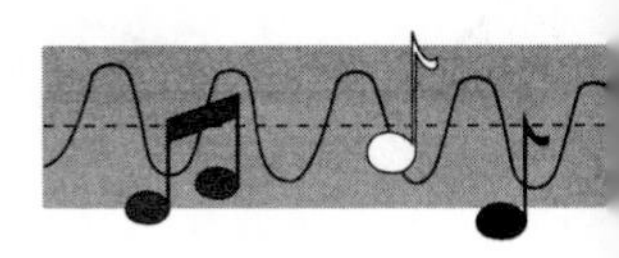

Figure 2–7 shows the differences in frequencies in a range of notes on a piano keyboard. Middle A, with a frequency of 440Hz, is just to the right of center. The note with a frequency of 262Hz is middle C.

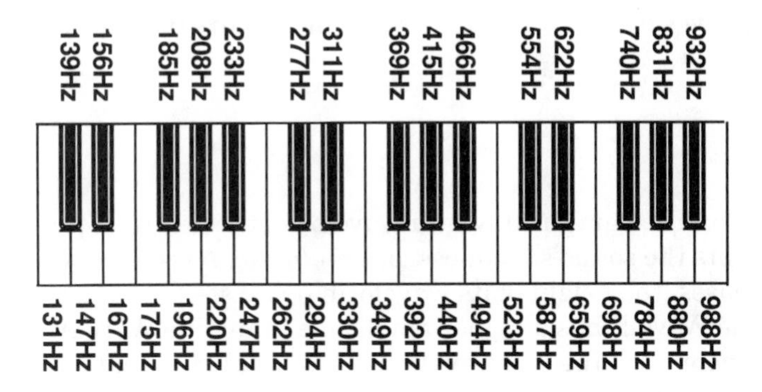

Figure 2–7. Note frequencies

As the pitch of a sound increases, the length of the period between its wave cycles decreases. Thus, in Figure 2–8, Sine Wave B has a higher frequency than Sine Wave A. Count the cycles in the two waveforms, and you'll see that Sine Wave B has twice as many cycle periods as Sine Wave A during the same period of time. That means that the frequency of Sine Wave B is double that of Sine Wave A.

Sine Wave A

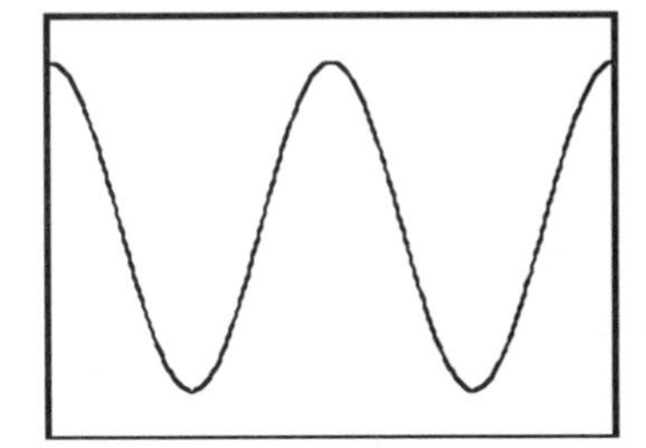

Sine Wave B

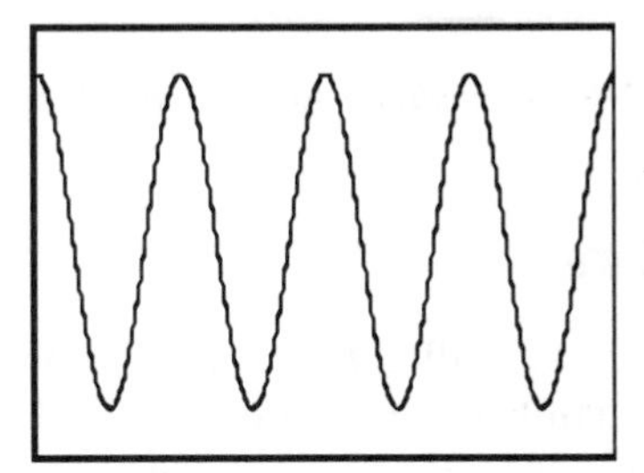

Figure 2–8. Increasing a sound's frequency

The frequency range that is audible to humans is conventionally said to extend from 20Hz to 20,000Hz. One kilohertz (kHz) is equal to 1,000 Hz, so the audible frequency range can also be said to extend from 20Hz to 20kHz.

Although the audible frequency range is considered to extend from 20Hz to 20kHz, high-volume sounds below 20Hz can often be felt, if not

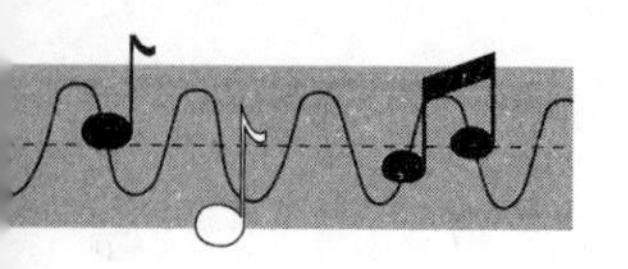

actually heard. And most people—particularly older people—have difficulty hearing sounds as high as 20kHz. However, most waveforms contain subfrequencies, called *harmonics,* that affect the way they sound. And harmonics above 20kHz can affect the audible qualities of a sound, even if the harmonics themselves are too high to hear. Harmonics are described later in this chapter.

Amplitude

When a sound is represented graphically by a waveform, the height of the sound waves represents the sound's loudness, or *amplitude.* As the amplitude of a sound increases, the height of its waveform increases.

In Figure 2–9, Sine Wave B has a higher amplitude than Sine Wave A. If you measured the heights of the two waveforms, you would see that Sine Wave B is twice as high as Sine Wave A. That means that Sine Wave B has twice the amplitude of Sine Wave A.

Sine Wave A

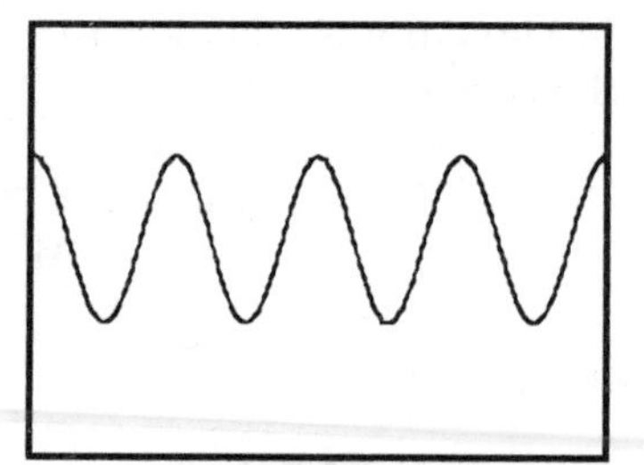

Sine Wave B

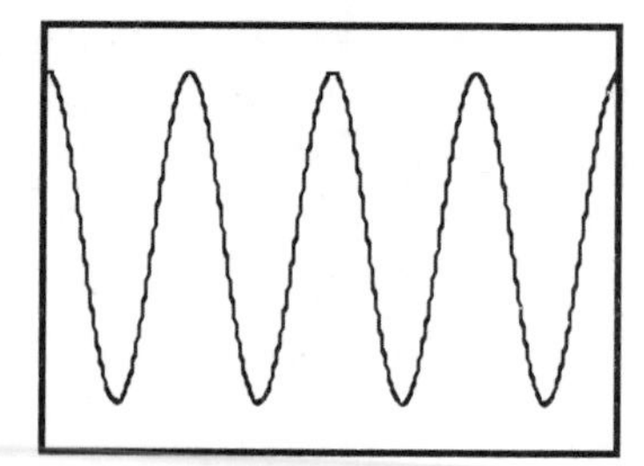

Figure 2–9. Increasing a sound's amplitude

Timbre

Timbre, also called *tone color,* is the distinctive, characteristic quality of a sound. Timbre is the main factor that distinguishes the sound of one instrument from the sound of another. For example, the timbre of a flute is different from the timbre of a violin because the two instruments produce their sound in very different ways. Two sounds may have the same pitch, but if their timbre is different, you can easily tell them apart.

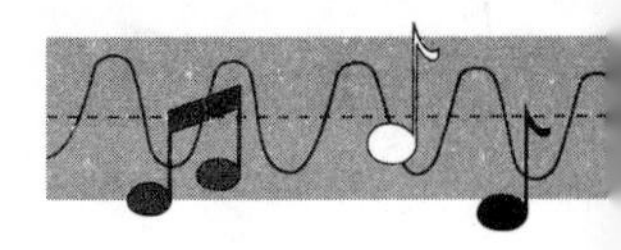

From the standpoint of physics, timbres can be distinguished from each other by their unique and dynamically changing harmonics, or overtones.

Sounds and Waveforms

The peaks and valleys in a sound's waveform reflect not only the sound's amplitude and frequency, but also the general tonal quality, or timbre, of the sound.

No matter how many waveforms you look at, you'll probably never be able to tell exactly what a musical selection will sound like by simply examining its waveform. But if you look at a sound's waveform while you play the sound, it's usually easy to tell when the sound begins and when it ends, and you can often pick out the beginnings and ends of specific segments of the sound.

When you've looked at enough waveforms while listening to the sounds that they generate, you'll probably find that waveforms contain many hints about the tonal characteristics of sounds. With practice, you'll begin to see that waveforms can tell you a great deal about the levels, frequencies, and tonal characteristics of sounds.

ADSR Envelopes

During the life of a musical note, the loudness of the note can be divided into four segments, or phases: *attack, decay, sustain,* and *release*. Audio engineers often represent the four phases in the life of a note with a graphic device called an ADSR envelope.

An ADSR envelope traces variations in the amplitude of a musical note from the time the note begins to the time that it ends. Many electronic musical instruments have controls for adjusting the ADSR envelopes of sounds.

Different kinds of instruments, and different styles of playing, produce different kinds of ADSR envelopes. Figure 2–10 shows the four divisions of an ADSR envelope: the attack, decay, sustain, and release segments of a sound.

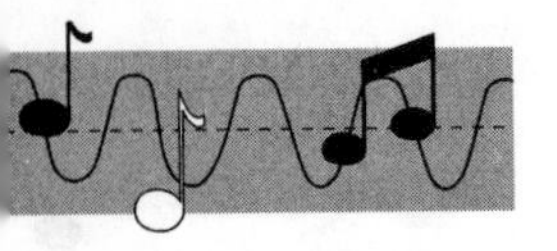

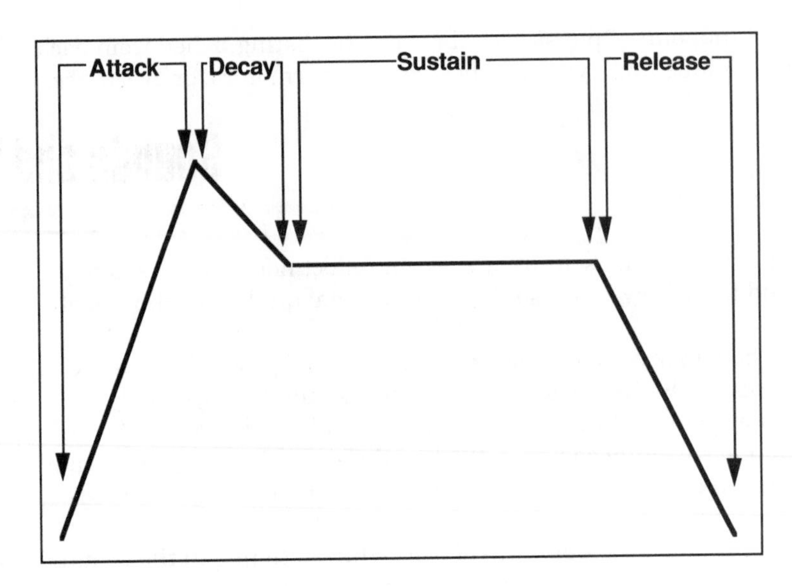

Figure 2–10. ADSR envelope

Attack

The attack phase of a note is the length of time that it takes for a note to rise from silence to its full volume. A note played on an instrument with a fast attack—for example, a trumpet—produces an ADSR envelope with a short attack segment. A note played on a bowed instrument, such as a violin, produces an ADSR envelope that shows a slower speed of attack. The attack phase of a note is also affected by the rhythmic pattern of the music that is being played.

Decay

The decay phase of a note is the stage in which the note drops to a level that can be sustained for a measurable length of time. When you allow a note to "ring"—for example, when you hold down a piano pedal to prevent a note from being damped—you lengthen its decay phase.

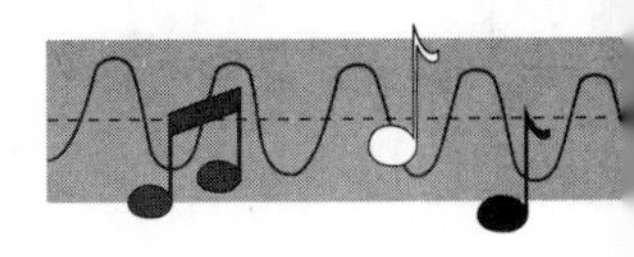

Sustain

After the decay stage of a note is finished, the note is often held at a relatively stable volume for a period of time. This stage in the life of a note is called the note's sustain phase.

Some instruments—for example the trumpet and the flute—give the performer considerable control over the length of a note's sustain phase. By simply holding the note, the performer can lengthen its sustain phase. Other instruments—for example the guitar and the harpsichord—give the performer little or no control over the length of a note's sustain phase.

Release

The release phase of a note's life begins when the performer stops applying the energy that it takes to produce the note. The release phase ends when the note fades to silence. When you play a note on a trumpet, the release phase stops when you stop blowing, and ends almost immediately. When you play a note on a piano, the release phase starts when you release the key, and lasts a little longer.

Kinds of Waveforms

Every waveform, no matter how complex, can be broken down into a combination of sine waves.

As noted at the beginning of this chapter, a sine wave is a gently rolling wave that produces a steady tone. Other important kinds of waveforms include square waves, pulse waves, sawtooth waves, and triangle waves. Each of these waveforms has its own characteristic tone, or timbre, which makes it valuable as a tool for creating music. Finally, complex waves can include features of many other kinds of waves.

Several different kinds of waveforms are shown in Figure 2–11.

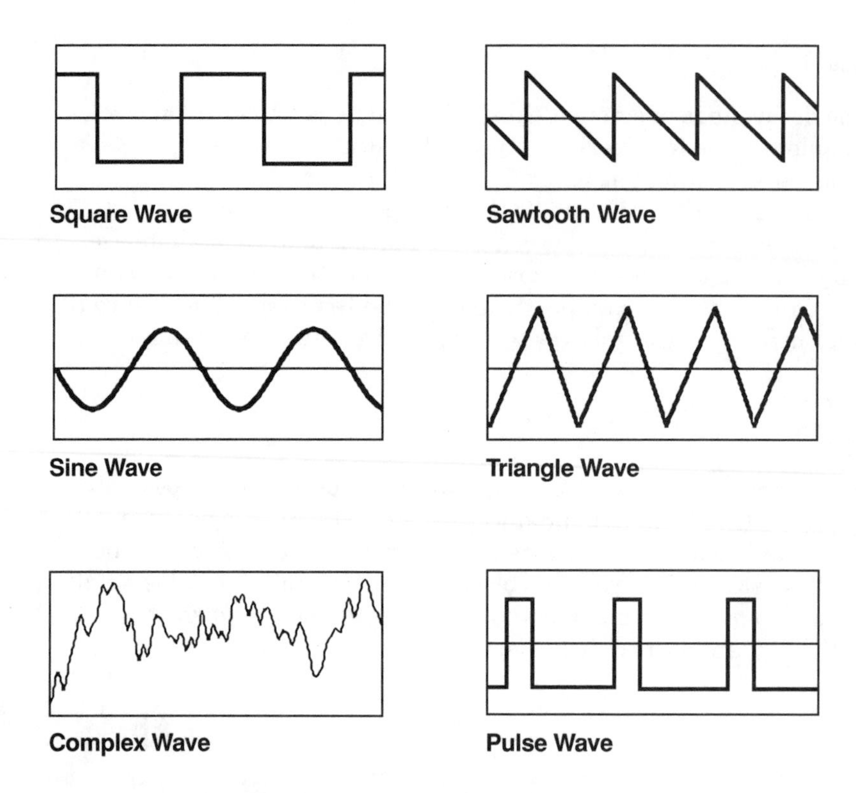

Figure 2–11. Several kinds of sound waves

Table 2–1 lists the general shapes of the sound waves that some popular acoustic instruments produce. When you examine the table, however, remember that things are seldom as simple as they first appear. Actually, because of the existence of harmonics, real acoustic instruments never produce waveforms with edges as perfectly formed as those of a sine wave, or with edges as straight as those of a square wave. Instead, acoustic instruments really produce *complex* waves—that is, waves that contain various wave patterns and various kinds of harmonics.

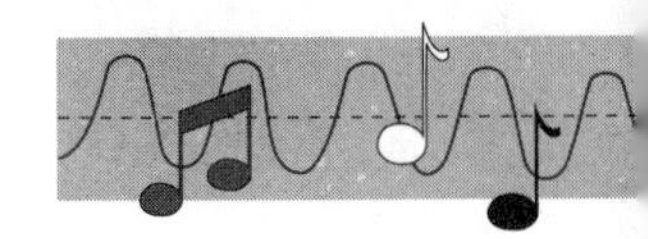

Table 2–1 Waveforms of Acoustic Instruments

Waveform	Instruments
Pulse	Oboe, electric piano, some acoustic pianos, koto, sitar, vibraphone
Sawtooth	Strings, brass, guitar, harmonica
Square	Clarinet, organ, harp, recorder
Triangular	Flute, recorder, whistles
Sine	Flute, pan flute
Noise	Wind and rain, hand clap, jet roar, explosion
Added noise	Flute, pan flute, pipe organ

Sine Waves

The sine wave is the most basic of all sound waves. You can hear what a sine wave sounds like by listening to the time signal on a radio station. You'll find that it sounds smooth, sweet—and boring. It isn't unpleasant to listen to, but it has no personality or character.

Although you probably wouldn't want to spend an evening sitting around listening to sine waves, the sine wave is the most important kind of basic sound wave. In fact, the sine wave is the basic building block of all sound waves. All sounds, no matter how complex, can be broken down into a combination of sine waves.

Adding sine waves to produce more complex waveforms is called *additive synthesis.* Many musicians use additive synthesis to create sounds because it is a simple and flexible technique. Furthermore, you can theoretically synthesize any sound using additive synthesis. However, that can take many steps, and there are often other ways to synthesize sounds more quickly and easily. Additive synthesis is only one of many methods that musicians use for synthesizing sounds.

Figure 2–12 shows how two sound waves can be added to produce a third kind of wave.

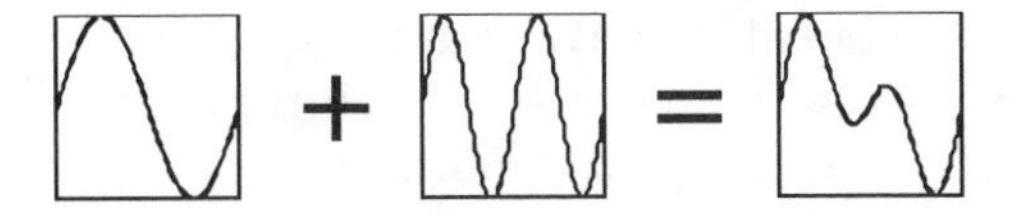

Figure 2–12. Additive synthesis

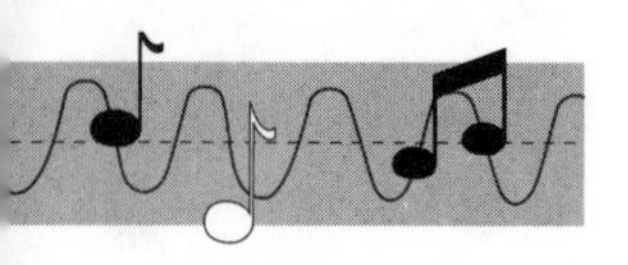

Square Waves

A square wave, as noted earlier in this chapter, is a very simple waveform. Just like a sine wave, a square wave has one frequency, one amplitude, and no harmonics. But unlike a sine wave, a square wave does not have a gently rolling waveform and does not produce a particularly pleasing sound. It abruptly starts and stops many times each second, so it has a harsher sound than a sine wave—brighter, and somewhat raw around the edges.

You can get an idea of what a square wave sounds like by listening to your Mac's "Simple Beep" alert sound.

Other Simple Waveforms

A pulse waveform produces a thin sound. A musical note with a fast attack and a slower decay produces a waveform with a sawtooth appearance. A sound that rises to its highest amplitude at a moderate rate of speed, and then immediately falls to its lowest amplitude at the same speed, produces a triangular waveform, which is often called a bright kind of sound. And a resonant waveform, which you can create by additive synthesis, can produce rich and harmonious tones. A complex waveform can be made up of any combination of simple waveforms.

Pulse Waveforms

When a vibrating object produces a sound, the object is known as a *resonator.* Every acoustic musical instrument has some kind of resonator. The strings of a violin are resonators; so are the strings of a piano or a guitar. The reed of a woodwind instrument is a resonator, and the tube of a brass instrument is a resonator.

If an acoustic instrument has a small resonator, it generally produces a pulse-shaped waveform, which looks something like a square wave but spends more time off than on. For that reason, a pulse wave has a thinner sound than a square. The oboe, the electric piano, the Japanese koto, and India's sitar are all examples of instruments that have small resonators and produce sounds with pulse waveforms. A pulse waveform contains a weak fundamental signal, along with all audible harmonics.

Sawtooth Waveforms

A sawtooth waveform, sometimes called a *ramp* waveform, also contains all audible harmonics. But a sawtooth wave has a stronger fundamental frequency, and weaker harmonics, than does a pulse waveform. Synthesizers

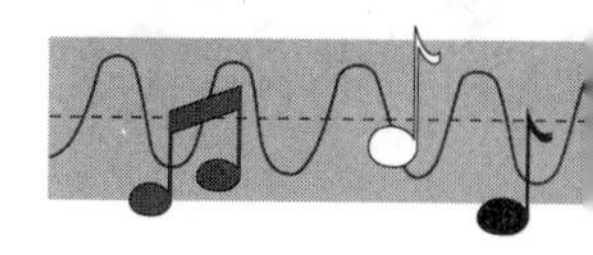

use sawtooth waveforms to synthesize the sounds of various kinds of instruments, including many members of both the string and brass families. String and brass sounds may not seem similar at first glance, but both kinds of instruments produce bright sounds. The main difference between the sound of a brass instrument and a string instrument is that a brass instrument has a sharper attack than a string instrument, and thus tends to have a brighter sound.

Triangular Waveforms

A sound with a triangular waveform is not as bright as a sound with a square waveform. Sounds that have triangular waveforms are produced by flutes, recorders, and whistles.

Complex Waveforms

Theoretically (with techniques that are beyond the scope of this chapter, but are described in some of the books on sound synthesis that are listed in the Bibliography) you can create any kind of wave by simply adding sine waves. When you create a waveform by combining other waveforms that have various frequencies, amplitudes, and timbres, the waveform that results is called a *complex waveform.* Virtually every acoustic sound —that is, virtually every sound that is not produced by an electronic instrument—has a complex waveform. For example, the complex waveform shown in Figure 2–13 was produced by a bullfrog croaking.

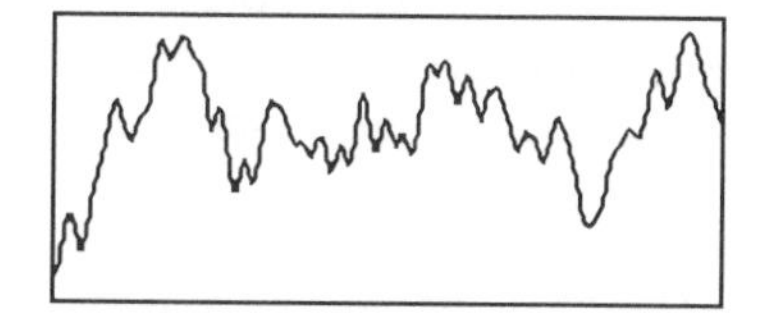

Figure 2–13. A bullfrog waveform

Harmonics

When a musical instrument plays a note that has a certain frequency, the instrument also generates many other frequencies that are exact multiples of that frequency. The main frequency of a musical note is called its *fundamental frequency,* and the frequencies that are generated as side effects are called *harmonics.*

Harmonics have significant effects on the quality of sounds. One reason that different kinds of musical instruments sound different is that they

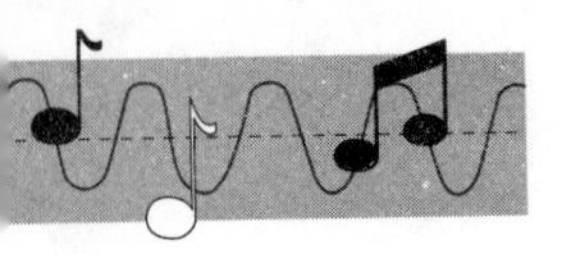

generate different kinds of harmonics. Because of differences in harmonics—as well as differences in the shapes of their waveforms—two musical instruments can sound completely different, even when they are playing the same note.

In mathematical terms, the harmonics of a sound wave are exact multiples of the wave's fundamental frequency. A wave with a frequency of 440Hz has a second harmonic of 880Hz, a third harmonic of 1,320Hz, and so on.

Nonharmonic Sounds

Many sounds contain frequencies that are not harmonically related. One kind of sound that contains nonharmonic components is known—scientifically as well as colloquially— as *noise.*

Metallic sounds, such as the sound of a gong or a bell, also contain nonharmonic components. But those components are not necessarily noise; two musical notes can be musically related, if they are not harmonically related. For example, two notes that are exactly five scale notes apart have a musical relationship known as a *fifth.* However, they have no harmonic relationship, because the higher note in such a pair of notes will never have an exact number of cycles that corresponds exactly to one cycle of the lower note.

Chapters 7 and 8 present more information about the relationship between notes in the musical scale.

Noise

Noise is made up of nonharmonic waveforms that have no fixed pattern. Noise signals contain all audible frequencies, but not necessarily in equal strength. Two kinds of noise—pink noise and white noise—have special uses in the field of audio science.

Pink noise contains all audible frequencies, all played at the same strength. *White noise* also includes all frequencies, but with the frequencies generated in such a way that each *octave* of the audio spectrum has the same signal strength.

White noise—perceived as a high-pitched hissing sound—sounds like the noise you hear on a television set when a channel is not transmitting. White noise is often used to equalize the sound environments in listening rooms and concert halls. If you play white noise through a set of loudspeakers, and measure the sound levels that are generated in various parts of a room, you can correct any imbalances with an equalizer and thus equalize the sound in the room.

Pink noise has less high-frequency content than white noise, and therefore is lower-pitched. It is often likened to ocean surf or gently falling rain.

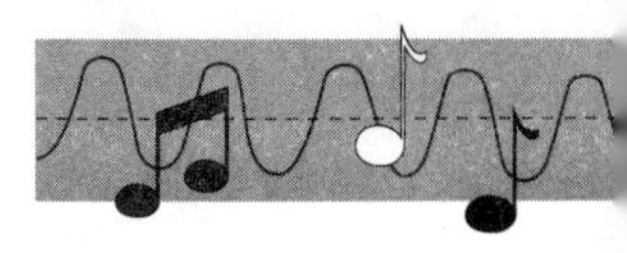

It has more soothing qualities than white noise, which has a relatively energetic sound. Pink noise is sometimes played at low levels through loudspeakers to mask background noise in factories and large, open offices.

In a sampling of white noise, the band of noise that extends from middle A on a piano keyboard to the A note that is an octave lower has the same signal strength as the band of noise that extends from middle A to the A note that is an octave higher. In a sampling of white noise, this loudness ratio is maintained even though the two A notes that span the lower octave cover a 110Hz frequency range, while the two A notes that span the higher octave span a frequency range twice as wide—a range of 220Hz. (Figure 2–7, earlier in this section, shows the differences in the frequencies of notes on the piano keyboard.)

Noise, when used in small amounts, can add subtle characteristics that greatly increase the realism of various kinds of sounds. Synthesizers often use noise as a component of flute sounds, and in sounds such as those produced by pipe organs and drums. Also, noise is often the sole ingredient of synthesized sound effects, such as the sounds of hand claps, jet roars, and explosions.

Metallic Sounds

The strings of stringed instruments and the tubes of brass instruments are long and slender, so they are sometimes called one-dimensional resonators. The longer the effective length of a one-dimensional resonator, the lower is its pitch. The more strongly a one-dimensional resonator is vibrated, the greater is the harmonic content of its sound. One-dimensional resonators produce comparatively simple sounds—sounds that are relatively easy to synthesize.

A gong has a flat surface that resonates in two dimensions—with both width and depth—and is therefore a two-dimensional resonator. A bell is an object with height as well as width and depth, and is therefore a three-dimensional resonator. Two-dimensional and three-dimensional resonators such as gongs and bells do not produce just one fundamental frequency; rather, they produce several fundamental frequencies, along with harmonics of those frequencies, and nonharmonic components as well. Since metallic sounds contain more kinds of components than simpler kinds of sounds, they are more difficult to synthesize.

Because of the musical relationships in their sonic components, metallic instruments often produce rich, harmonious sound. However, they can also produce decidedly discordant sounds if their fundamental tones do not have ear-pleasing musical relationships (for more on musical relationships, see Chapters 7 and 8, which cover melody and harmony).

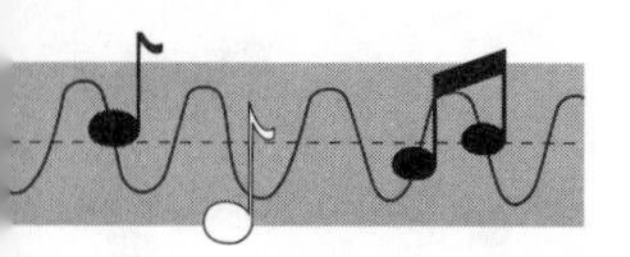

Sound-Processing Techniques

When musicians and audio engineers synthesize sound, they use many techniques to edit sounds and change the characteristics of sounds. With sound-processing programs such as SoundWave and HyperCorder—which are provided on your bonus disk and documented in Chapters 4 and 5—you can perform similar operations on sounds that are produced by your Macintosh. For example, you can do the following:

- Play sounds in loops to conserve memory and disk space or provide continuous background sounds
- Change the sampling rates of sounds to reduce the amount of space they require on disks and in memory
- Reduce disk space and memory requirements by changing the compression ratios of sounds
- Mix sounds together to create new and different sounds
- Use cut-and-paste techniques to move or copy part of a sound's waveform from one place to another, or to insert a portion of one sound's waveform into another sound's waveform
- Add delays to sounds to create echoes and other interesting effects
- Change the volume and speed of sounds
- Turn sounds backward so they play in reverse

Three of these techniques—looping and changing sampling rates and compression ratios—are described briefly in this section. For explanations of the rest of the techniques, and more detailed explanations of those presented here, refer to Chapter 4.

Looping

As you probably know by now, sampled sounds consume vast amounts of memory. One way to have a large collection of sounds on hand, in a relatively small amount of memory, is to use a technique called *looping*.

Looping is often used in musical compositions because musical sound waves are made up of repeatable patterns. Look at the waveform of a musical sound, and you'll usually see that the same pattern repeats itself over and over again.

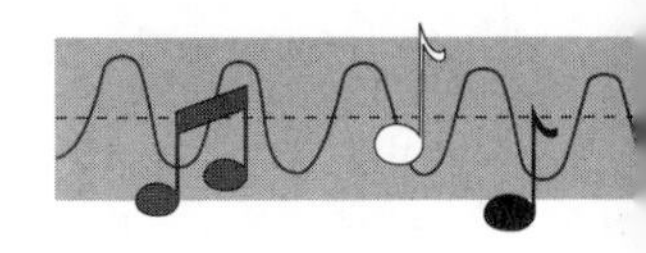

The Sound-Trecker program demonstrates one use for looping: to play a song continuously in the background while other tasks are performed. To experiment with Sound-Trecker's looping capabilities, follow these steps:

1. Open the "Virgin" selection and start playing the song by clicking on the Play button (the button with one arrow).
2. Remove the check mark from the box labeled Repeat.
3. Sound-Trecker responds by playing the Virgin selection continuously —that is, in a loop—until you stop the song manually.

Short Loops

To get an idea of how looping works, suppose that you wanted to play ten seconds of a simple sine wave on the keyboard of a sampler (samplers are described in Chapter 9). You could perform that operation by sampling ten seconds of a sine wave from an analog synthesizer, and then simply playing it back. If your keyboard was capable of ten total seconds of sampling at your selected rate, it would now be full, and you would have no room for other sounds.

You could avoid this waste of memory by creating a loop. Instead of sampling ten full seconds of a sine wave, you could simply sample one cycle. Then you could instruct your sampler to play this single cycle over and over. Each time your sampler reached the end of the waveform, it would jump back to the beginning and start over. This looping continues indefinitely, or at least for as long as you hold down a key. Furthermore, this short loop would require only a fraction of a second of sampling time, leaving you with well over nine seconds of valuable time to sample other sounds.

Best of all, when you create such a loop, you can play your sampled sound for as many iterations as you want—that is, for as long as you like. And you lose nothing by doing this, because every cycle in the waveform of a sine wave is identical.

Long Loops

It isn't quite as economical to loop complex waveforms as it is to loop sine waves. A complex waveform is not made up of one simple sine wave that repeats over and over again. Instead, a complex waveform is made up of many different kinds of sine waves, with various amplitudes, various frequencies, and various harmonic patterns. So, to create a realistic-sounding loop of a complex sound wave, you must use a relatively long sample.

Long loops rely on the fact that most natural sounds have definitive beginnings, but then tend to stabilize over time. For example, a trumpet

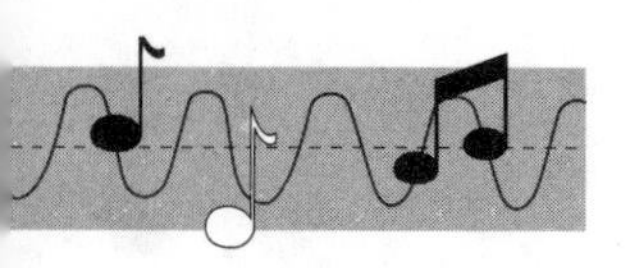

note starts with a sharp attack, but then stabilizes into a tone that doesn't change much more until it starts to die away.

It's true, of course, that there are many different kinds of ways to play a trumpet note. For example, a trumpeter can play a loud note, a soft note, a note that slurs into another, or a tremolo. Furthermore, as any jazz aficionado can tell you, different trumpet players sound very different, and there are many different styles of trumpet playing.

All of these kinds of considerations make looping a challenge. A loop can be as short as one cycle of a sine wave, or as long as a complete symphony played by a symphonic orchestra. To make the best possible use of memory, while creating loops that sound as realistic as possible, you'll have to make some trade-offs and be very creative—but that's what makes sound sampling fun.

Changing Sampling Rates

Sound digitizers such as MacRecorder convert analog sounds into digital sounds by sampling sounds at regular intervals and then storing them in memory as streams of binary numbers. This process does not produce the kind of smooth waveform that an analog sound has. Instead, digitization produces a waveform that can be represented as a series of dots.

Since a digitized waveform is made up of a stream of individual sound samples, you can improve its resolution—and therefore its quality—by using more dots to describe it and spacing the dots closer together. The number of intervals per second that is used to record a sound, and then to represent the sound in memory, is called the sound's *sampling rate*. The higher the sampling rate, the higher the sound quality.

Professional-style MIDI samplers record sounds in words that are 16 binary bits long—that is, in 16-bit samples. Small Macintosh digitizers, such as the MacRecorder module, sample sound in 8-bit words. Because an 8-bit word doesn't have as high a resolution as a 16-bit word, the sound samples that are captured by a MacRecorder-style digitizer produce sound with a lower quality than the sound produced by a higher-resolution MIDI sampler.

Sampling rates are usually expressed in kilohertz, or thousands of cycles per second. A sound recorded at a rate of 22kHz is sampled 22,000 times a second, and a sound recorded at a rate of 5.5kHz is sampled 5,500 times a second. SoundWave, and most other recording programs used with the Macintosh, have a maximum sampling rate of 22kHz. In comparison, the sound on a compact disk is recorded at a sampling rate of 44kHz.

An 8-bit sound sample can store sound with an upper frequency limit of 11kHz, and a 16-bit sample can store sound with a high-frequency limit of 22kHz—approximately the upper limit of human hearing.

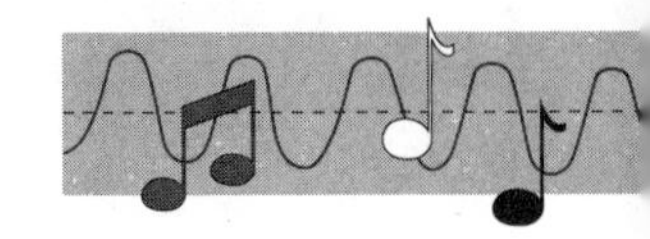

You can experiment with using different sampling rates by launching the Sound-Trecker program. While the song is playing, switch back and forth among the three upper-frequency limits that are listed in the lower right-hand corner of the Sound-Trecker window. As you do that, listen to the results.

You can't increase the frequency range produced by an 8-bit sound sampler, but you can decrease it. And sometimes that's desirable, because the higher you push your sampling rate when you sample a sound, the more space the sound occupies on a disk or in memory.

As you'll quickly learn when you start experimenting with sound, sampled sounds consume huge amounts of memory. For example, one minute of single-channel sound recorded with CD-quality fidelity—that is, at a sampling rate of 44kHz—occupies about 5.3 Mb of disk space. Sound recorded at a 22kHz sampling rate still consumes disk space at a rate of more than 1Mb a minute. Even one minute of telephone-quality speech, recorded at a rate of 11kHz or so, takes up more than half of a megabyte on a disk.

You can adjust the sampling rates of sounds with the SoundWave program introduced in Chapter 4 and the HyperCorder program introduced in Chapter 5. For specific instructions, see those chapters.

Changing Compression Ratios

You can also reduce the amount of disk and memory space that a sound consumes by *compressing* the sound in memory and then decompressing it on playback.

When a sound is compressed, its sampling rate is reduced, but only temporarily; when the sound is played back, various kinds of mathematical formulas are applied to restore the shape that the sound's waveform had before the sound was compressed. Unfortunately, the algorithms that are used to restore the shapes of compressed waveforms aren't perfect; subtle details of waveforms are always lost (or worse, changed) during the compression and decompression process. However, saving memory space by compressing a sound is usually better than lowering the sound's sampling rate. For more details on changing the compression ratios of sounds, see Chapter 4.

Solving Problems

When musicians and studio engineers record and edit sounds, certain problems often arise. Three such problems—aliasing, quantization, and clipping—are described in this section.

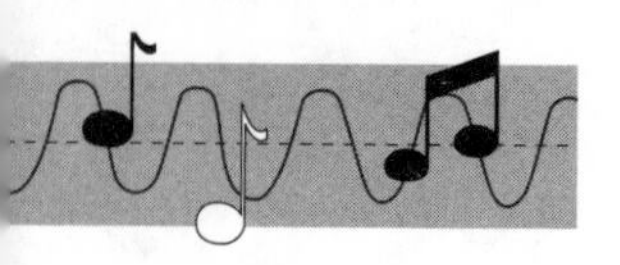

Aliasing

One of the most serious problems that musicians and audio engineers encounter when they sample sounds is a phenomenon called *aliasing*. Aliasing, also called *low-frequency foldover,* occurs when the upper frequencies of a sampled sound are too high for the sampling rate being used. When aliasing occurs, the sound being sampled generates an undesirable lower-frequency image, or *alias,* of itself.

Figure 2–14 is a stylized drawing that illustrates the phenomenon of aliasing. The waveform labeled "Sound wave" is a sound that is being sampled. But the sampling rate is so low that the wave is sampled only at the locations marked by black dots.

Sound wave Alias

Figure 2–14. Aliasing

When the waveform is reconstructed for playback, an undesirable phenomenon takes place: along with the original wave, a second wave shape that can also be described by the black dots is also created and played back. That "shadow" wave is the waveform that is labeled "Alias." When the original sound is played back, the alias wave is also reproduced, and the result is a sound corrupted by aliasing.

The basic rule of aliasing is that any frequency that is above half of the sampling rate will generate a potentially unpleasant and unwanted lower-frequency alias of itself. This phenomenon was discovered by a scientist named H. Nyquist, and is therefore known as the Nyquist effect. You can figure out the foldover frequency in most circumstances by subtracting the output frequency from the sample rate. For example, if a sampling rate is 20 kHz, the upper frequency limit used for recording should be 10kHz. Playing back a sampled frequency that's higher than 10kHz creates a new and possibly noticeable 5kHz alias frequency.

This situation occurs because the sampling rate is too low to describe the original sound with enough resolution to create an accurate waveform. It results in the generation of both the original wave and the alias, which is a new, lower tone.

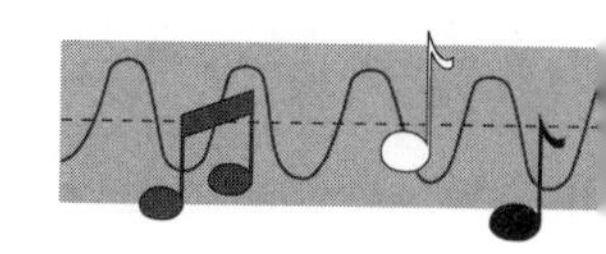

The Wagon-Wheel Effect

An illustration of aliasing that may be easier to understand is the *wagon-wheel* effect that is sometimes seen in movies and on television. Sometimes in a film, when a wagon is moving and its wheels are turning, the spokes in the wheel appear to be stationary, or even going backward. This phenomenon takes place when each frame in the film catches the spokes in the wheel in what appears to be in the same position, or in what appears to be a previous position.

When the wagon-wheel phenomenon occurs, the nonmoving or backward-moving image of the wagon wheel is an alias of the actual image of the wheel. In audio engineering terms, each frame in the film could be considered a visual sample. And the *sampling rate*—or the rate at which the film is shown—is not high enough to avoid the creation of a false image, or alias, of a stationary or backward-moving wheel.

Avoiding the Nyquist Effect

By taking care to avoid the Nyquist effect, engineers can avoid aliasing by limiting the frequency range of a digitized sound to one-half of the sampling rate. Thus, the remedy for aliasing is to make sure that your sampling rate is at least twice as high as the highest frequency you are sampling. If you can't adjust your sampling rate, then you have to adjust the sound you are sampling. This can be done by filtering out all frequencies above half of the sampling rate, which is usually accomplished using an *input sampling filter*.

Because of Nyquist's discovery, the highest frequency that can be sampled at a given sampling rate is called a *Nyquist frequency*. You can figure out a Nyquist frequency quite easily, because it is always equal to half of the sampling rate. If you want to create clean samples that are harmonically true to their source, you must never exceed the Nyquist frequency limit when you sample sounds. That means you must make sure that your sampling rate is at least twice as high as the highest frequency you are sampling.

To avoid aliasing problems, 8-bit digitizers such as the MacRecorder module from Macromedia and the Voice Impact modules from Articulate Systems have built-in anti-aliasing filters that remove frequencies above 11kHz. That means that they can accurately record frequencies up to 10kHz.

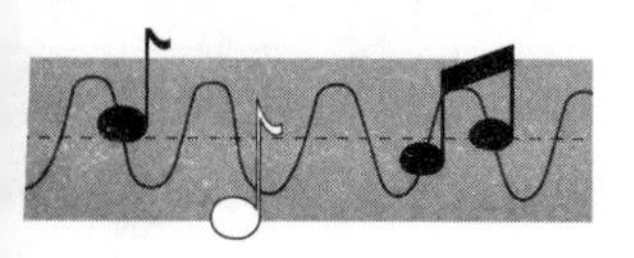

Quantization

Another phenomenon that occurs when sound is digitized is an effect called *quantization.* Quantization is a result of the fact that the amplitude of a sampled sound is restricted to integer values within a limited range. For example, an 8-bit digitizer—such as MacRecorder or the Voice Impact module—uses an integer value between 0 and 255 to represent each sampling of a sound. When a wave sampled using digitization is reproduced, quantization gives the reconstructed waveform a more squared-off shape than it originally had.

When a sound is quantized, a type of noise known as *quantization noise* can denigrate the quality of the sound. The lower the bit resolution of a sample, the higher is the noise level caused by quantization. Therefore, the 8-bit sampling rate used by MacRecorder-type digitizers is more subject to quantization noise than are higher-resolution, 16-bit sampling systems.

Clipping

When the amplitude of a sampled sound exceeds the sound input capabilities of the digitizer being used, a form of distortion called *clipping* occurs. Clipping is what takes place when the volume of a small radio or a portable stereo system is turned up so high that its sound is distorted. A technique for avoiding clipping distortion is provided in Chapter 4.

Using Sound-Trecker

Sound-Trecker is the Macintosh version of a program that was originally written for Commodore and Amiga computers. Sound-Trecker is the only shareware program on this book's bonus disk. If you like it, you're requested to send $30 (for the program and to cover postage) to Frank Seide, Koolbarg 39d, D-2000 Hamburg 74, Germany. Frank will send you the complete Sound-Trecker package, including full documentation and source code. Sound-Trecker may also be downloaded from on-line services.

When you launch Sound-Trecker, the first display that you see is a window like the one shown at the beginning of this chapter in Figure 2–1. If you click the zoom box in the upper right-hand corner, the window collapses, and looks more like the window shown in Figure 2–15.

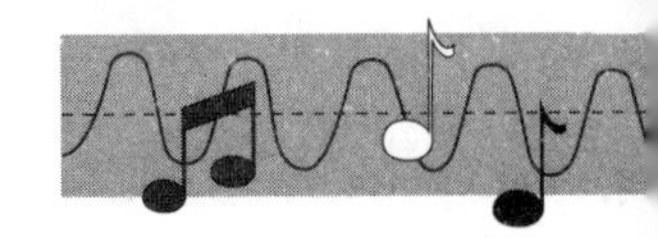

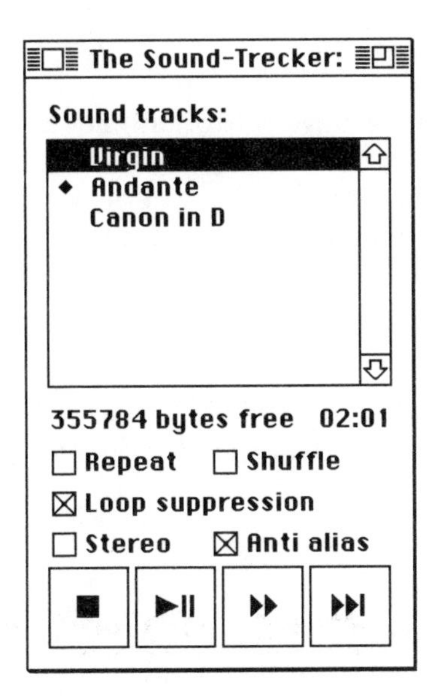

Figure 2–15. The collapsed Sound-Trecker window

Sound-Trecker Music Files

Sound-Trecker plays musical selections that are stored in a very compact file format called the .MOD format. Since the .MOD file format was designed for the Sound-Tracker program, files stored in the .MOD format are sometimes called sound tracks. But when you see a collection of files on a bulletin board service that are labeled .MOD files, those are Sound-Trecker song files.

A sound track file is not a representation of a waveform, but is made up of numbers that represent musical notes. This technique makes it possible to store long musical selections—even selections that are several minutes long—in relatively small files. Generally, sound track files are from 50K to 300K long.

Sound-Trecker and Multitasking

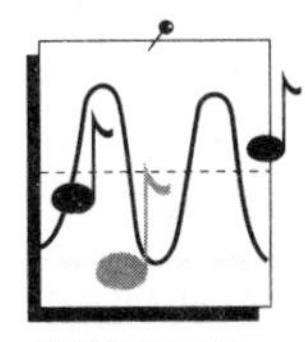

TECH TALK

Although Sound-Trecker supports multitasking, sound-related programs designed to be run under Macintosh System Software earlier than Version 6.0.5 may not work well with Sound-Trecker when Sound-Trecker is being run in multitasking mode. When the Finder issues a Sound Driver call while both Sound-Trecker and certain old programs are running, you may not be able to quit the Finder. This is true, for example, with old versions of the shareware program SoundMaster. ❍

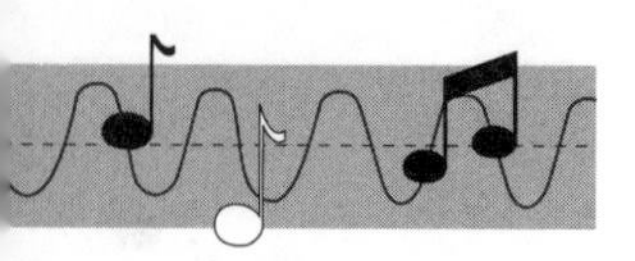

The Sound-Trecker Menu

Most of the controls in the Sound-Trecker window have equivalent menu commands, and most of the program's menu commands have keyboard equivalents. You can find out which controls have menu equivalents by examining the menus and menu items on the Sound-Trecker menu bar.

The Sound Tracks List

To play a song with Sound-Trecker, you must place the song in the Sound tracks list—the list in the upper left-hand corner of the expanded Sound-Trecker window.

Placing a Song in the Track List

To place a song in the Sound tracks list, select the Open command from the File or press the command's keyboard equivalent, Command-O. Sound-Trecker then displays a standard file dialog from which you can choose a song to play. The Open file dialog lists the names of text files, as well as the names of sound track files. That's because Sound-Trecker songs are often uploaded to bulletin boards in the form of text files.

When you choose a text file in the list of files displayed by the Open dialog, a message asks you if you're sure that you want to open the file. If you answer in the affirmative, Sound-Trecker attempts to load the file and play the data that it contains. If the attempt fails, Sound-Trecker displays another dialog window informing you that there's "no sound track" in the file. If the attempt succeeds, Sound-Trecker converts the file to a Macintosh-compatible sound track file and then plays the song that the file contains.

When you open a song, its name is appended to the Sound tracks list. If no song is playing when you open a sound track, Sound-Trecker loads the new sound track and starts playing it. You can start a song that is already in the track list by just double-clicking on its name.

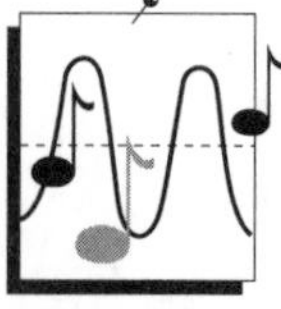

TECH TALK

Selecting Songs with the Finder

You can add a song to the Sound track list by dragging the song's icon into the Sound-Trecker icon in the Finder. You may want to use this method when you want to add many files to the track list; it's faster than using the standard file dialog window that the Open command displays.

If you have System 7, you can drag sound tracks into the Sound-Trecker icon even when Sound-Trecker is running. However, you cannot use this method to load text files that haven't yet been converted to the Macintosh-compatible sound track format. ❍

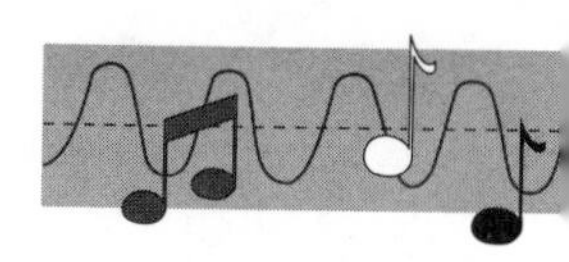

Removing a Song from the Track List

To remove a song from the Sound track list, simply select it and press the Delete (or backspace) key, or choose the Delete command from the File menu. This procedure doesn't remove the file from any disk—just from the Sound track list.

Duplicating a Song in the Track List

You can place the name of a song in the track list as many times as you like by choosing the Duplicate command from the File menu. The song will then play as many times as its name appears in the Sound track listing.

Changing the Position of a Listed Song

You can change the position of a song in the track list by dragging the song to a different position. When you drag a song from one part of the list to another, a dotted line appears around the name that you're dragging. The dotted line disappears when you have placed the song in its new location.

Sound-Trecker Controls

The controls in the Sound-Trecker window are straightforward and intuitive. However, they have many capabilities and many special characteristics that are not immediately obvious. In the remainder of this chapter, these capabilities and characteristics are examined in detail.

Tape Recorder Controls

Below the Sound tracks list in the Sound-Trecker window, there's a control panel that you can operate by clicking tape recorder-style buttons: Stop (a square), Play/Pause (a single arrow), Fast Forward (two arrows), and Next Song (two arrows to the left of a single line).

Stop

Clicking the stop button fades out and stops the song currently being played, and removes the song from memory (but not from the track list).

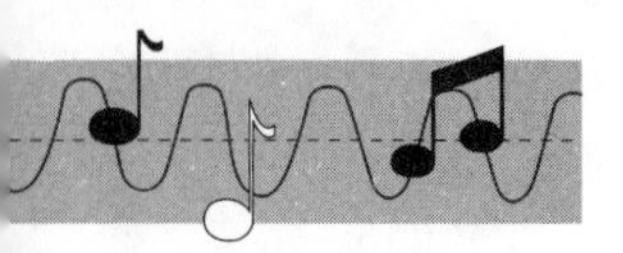

Play/Pause

The Play/Pause button pauses the song currently being played. Clicking this button again restarts the song. If no song is being played, any song that is selected in the Sound tracks list is loaded and starts playing. If the track list is empty, Sound-Trecker automatically executes the Open command.

Fast Forward

The Fast Forward button plays the currently open sound at double speed for as long as the button is held down. If you hold down the Option key, Fast Forward plays the currently open song at four times its normal speed.

Next Song

The Next Song button fades out and then stops the song currently being played. If there's only one song in the Sound tracks list, the Next Song button replays the current song.

Check-Box Controls

Above its tape recorder buttons, Sound-Trecker has five check-box controls: Repeat, Shuffle, Loop Suppression, Stereo, and Anti-Alias. This is how they work.

- **Repeat—**plays the songs in the Sound tracks list in an endless loop. Normally, each program in the track list is played only once. When you check the Repeat box, Sound-Trecker returns to the top song in the list and starts playing the songs again each time.
- **Shuffle—**plays selections listed in the Sound tracks list in random order.
- **Loop Suppression—**prevents certain sound sequences from playing over and over in endless loops. Some sound tracks don't have a specific beginning or end. Instead, they play in an endless loop that repeats the same bars again and again. If Loop Suppression is activated, a sequence that would ordinarily play in an endless loop is faded out and stopped as soon as it starts to replay. Then Sound-Trecker continues with the next song.
- **Stereo—**If your Macintosh is capable of producing stereo sound, you can use this check box to choose between stereo and mono sound.
- **Anti-alias—**lets you choose between two different algorithms for controlling sampling rate conversions.

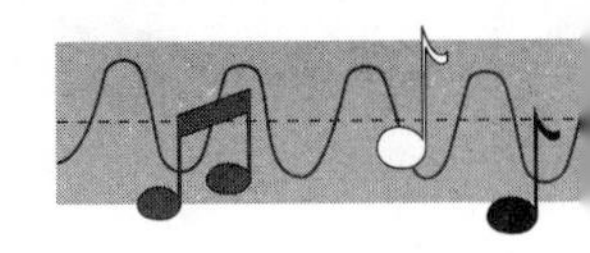

If the Anti-Aliasing check box is not checked, Sound-Trecker plays music using a simple and fast sampling algorithm. This method requires only a small amount of CPU time, but it also produces aliasing distortion that may be noticeable in some songs, especially if you use an external amplifier and speaker or headphones.

If you check the Anti-Aliasing box, Sound-Trecker plays music using a linear interpolation method that produces better sound quality. This algorithm, however, can increase the required CPU time by up to a factor of three.

The Oscillogram/Spectrum Window

As you listen to Sound-Trecker, you can examine two different graphical representations of its output by watching the small window labeled Display. When you click the radio button labeled Oscillogram, Sound-Trecker displays a waveform that represents the sound that is currently playing. When you select the Spectrum radio button, the Sound-Trecker switches to a display that shows the levels of the various frequency bands that make up the sound.

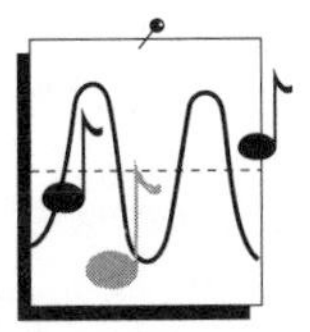

TECH TALK

What the Display Window Displays

In the Sound-Trecker Display window, the generated sound data may be displayed graphically, either as an oscillogram or a frequency spectrum. The display shown in Figure 2–1 is an oscillogram display.

In the display window, the frequency spectrum shows the logarithmic absolute value over the linear frequency axis. The oscillogram display and the spectrum display are generated and shown in real time. However, the spectrum display requires a Fourier transform (FFT). And at 22kHz, with the anti-aliasing control active, the display can be quite slow on a 68020-equipped Macintosh such as a Mac LC. ❍

Volume Controls

If your Macintosh is a model equipped with an MC68020 processor or better, and if you're running System 6.0.7 or higher, Sound-Trecker can play four separate channels of sound. While a selection plays, you can adjust its overall sound level by clicking the mouse inside the thermometer control labeled Total. In the same way, you can individually adjust the levels of each of Sound-Trecker's four channels of sound.

For best results, you should set the master volume control to about 50 per cent, as shown in Figure 2–1. A setting that is much higher than that can result in clipping (a higher volume setting than the system being used can handle), with a significant loss of sound quality. On the other hand, if

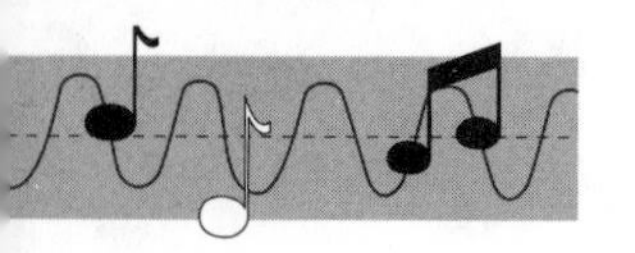

you set the master volume too low, quantization noise becomes more pronounced. If you turn Sound-Trecker's master volume down low, and then turn up the amplifier that you're using to produce audible sound, you may notice more noise.

Frequency Controls

In the lower right-hand corner of the Sound-Trecker window, there is a group of three buttons labeled Frequency. The three buttons are labeled 22, 16, and 11, respectively.

With the three Frequency buttons, you can specify the upper freqency limit of the sound that Sound-Trecker produces. The higher a frequency limit you set, the better the quality of the music that Sound-Trecker plays.

When you select a Frequency button, you determine the freqency at which Sound-Trecker samples sound. Sound-Trecker then adjusts its high-frequency output accordingly. Sampling frequencies are described under the heading "Sound Processing Techniques."

For reasons explained earlier in this chapter, under the heading "Solving Problems," the high-frequency limit of the sound produced by Sound-Trecker is half of the frequency at which the program samples sound. Thus, if you select a sampling rate of 11kHz, the maximum frequency of the sound produced by Sound-Trecker is 5.5kHz, a frequency response that is a little more than telephone quality. If you select a 16kHz sampling rate, Sound-Trecker's sound output is better. If you choose a sampling rate of 22kHz, Sound-Trecker's frequency response extends up to 11kHz—the upper frequency limit of the sound hardware built into the Macintosh.

Fine-Tuning Controls

Below the Frequency buttons, there are three controls in a group that is labeled Fine tuning. This group of controls includes a pair of slide controls labeled Pitch and Speed, and a Reset button.

You can use the two sliders to adjust the playing pitch and the tempo *independently* by plus or minus 50 per cent (approximately). The Reset button returns both sliders to a default setting of about half of their maximum levels.

Playing Collections of Songs

Sound-Trecker can compile a group of songs into a *program*. You can then play the program in the same way that you would play an individual sound.

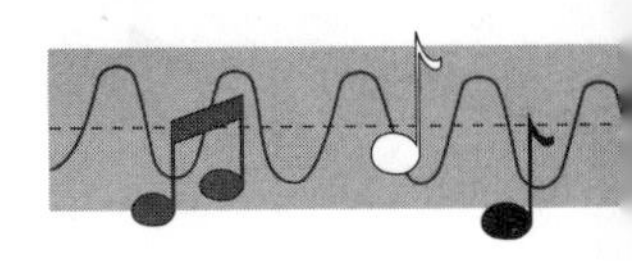

A file that contains a group of songs collected into a program is called a *configuration file.* When you create a configuration file, it contains all songs that are currently in the sound track list, along with all current option settings.

You can create a configuration file by simply selecting either the Save Configuration command or the Save Configuration As command from the File menu. Sound-Trecker then displays a standard file dialog that you can use to save your configuration file in any location and under any name you specify.

You can load a configuration file by selecting either the Load Configuration command or the Open command from the File menu. If you use the Open command to load a configuration file, Sound-Trecker loads the file and starts playing the first selection in the file automatically.

You can also load a configuration file and start the first selection it contains by double-clicking on the file's icon in the Finder. If you have System 7, you can place a configuration file (or a configuration file alias) in the Startup Items folder inside your System Folder. Then, each time you boot or restart your Macintosh, Sound-Trecker will also start and will begin playing music in the background.

Importing Sound-Trecker Music Files

Sound-Trecker music files—that is, files in the .MOD format—are available from many sources, including computer user groups and commercial and public bulletin boards. Sound-Trecker files are also available on disks formatted for non-Macintosh computers—especially for the Amiga, the computer for which Sound-Trecker was designed.

Downloading .MOD Files from Bulletin Boards

Many bulletin boards have a .MOD file department, usually in the Amiga section. After you download and unpack .MOD files for the Amiga, Sound-Trecker can play the files without further modification.

Transferring .MOD Files from PCs to the Macintosh

If you have access to .MOD files stored on an Amiga disk, you can use an Amiga copying utility such as DOS-2-DOS, Cross-DOS, or MSH to copy the files to a IBM PC-compatible disk. Then you can convert the files on the DOS disk to Macintosh format using conversion programs written for the Macintosh. Once you have a disk that a Macintosh can read, Sound-Trecker can play the .MOD files on the disk without any further modification.

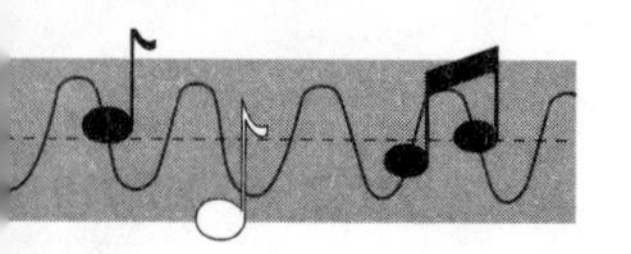

Playing Downloaded or Copied Files

After you download or copy a .MOD file written for the Amiga, it usually has the file type 'TEXT' or '????'. To play such a file, simply launch Sound-Trecker and open the song with the Open menu command. Sound-Trecker can then play the file, and will automatically convert it to a Macintosh-compatible sound track file.

Summary

This chapter introduced some of the basic principles of the science of sound. It also explained some important concepts that can help you understand how electronic instruments, including the Macintosh, produce sound. To help you grasp the fundamentals of audio science, the chapter made use of the Sound-Trecker program.

One important section near the beginning of the chapter explained how synthesizers, samplers, and digitizers generate sounds. That section described the differences and the similarities between professional-style MIDI synthesizers and samplers and the three synthesizers (one of which works more like a sampler) that are built into the Macintosh.

The chapter described the three most important properties of sound—frequency, amplitude, and timbre—and showed how these properties can be illustrated graphically using waveforms. It also described some useful sound-processing techniques that are described in more detail in Chapters 4 and 5, which cover the SoundWave and HyperCorder sound-processing programs.

The chapter also described some problems that are commonly encountered in sound recording, and told where to turn (to Chapters 4 and 5) for tips on how to solve them.

3 Sampled Sound

When you mention the word *synthesizer,* what most people think of is a bank of keyboards played by a long-haired musician, twisting knobs and playing chords and producing all kinds of pounding and wailing and beeping and whooshing sounds.

That may be an accurate description of a synthesizer, but it isn't the only one. From a technical point of view, a synthesizer is simply a device that synthesizes sound. Many of the synthesizers used in music studios don't have keyboards at all, but look like stereo components and are mounted in component racks. And, as you may recall from Chapter 1, there are three powerful electronic synthesizers inside the Macintosh.

The Sound Control Panel, introduced in Chapter 1, produces sound with two of the synthesizers built into the Macintosh. One of these, the square-wave synthesizer, generates a simple beep similar to the one that the Macintosh sounds by default when it displays an alert dialog.

The other synthesizer accessed by the Sound Control Panel is called a sampled sound synthesizer. It generates all of the custom sounds that you can choose as a system alert by using the Sound Control Panel.

The Sound Control Panel doesn't access the third Macintosh synthesizer: the wave-table synthesizer, which produces sounds from short waveforms stored as tables in RAM.

In this chapter, you'll get a chance to experiment with all three of your computer's built-in synthesizers. You'll have an opportunity to put all three through their paces with an entertaining and instructional piece of sound software on your bonus disk called SoundApp.

About SoundApp

SoundApp was written by Jim Reekes, a Sound Manager expert at Apple, and it is used by the Developer Technical Support group at Apple to show

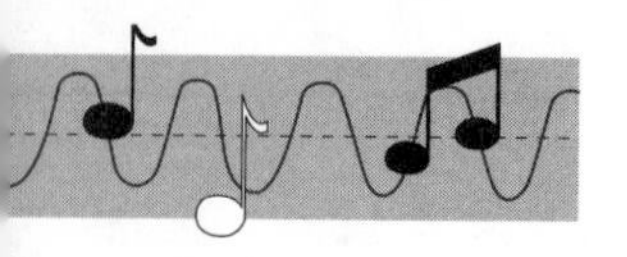

developers of Macintosh how to write sound software. As a side benefit, it can really show off the sonic power of your Macintosh.

If your Macintosh has sound-recording hardware, you can use SoundApp to record sounds (although, for practical purposes, it makes more sense to record sounds with a program that has more features, such as the SoundWave program introduced in Chapter 4 or the Audio Palette HyperCard tool covered in Chapter 5). If your Mac is not equipped for recording, you can still use SoundApp to play any of the sounds that are on this book's bonus disk (although you'll have to convert some of them from a file format to a resource format first. You can convert sound files to sound resources with the SoundWave program introduced in Chapter 4; for more about sound resources, see Appendix F).

An enormous variety of other sounds that you can play with SoundApp are available from public-access bulletin boards, Macintosh user groups, and commercially distributed disks and CD-ROMs. The addresses of some companies and groups that distribute sounds on disks and CD-ROMs are listed in Appendix B.

The SoundApp program can play notes, scales, and melodies, and it can play them in various timbres that imitate various kinds of musical (and not-so-musical) instruments. SoundApp can even demonstrate how "Pictures at an Exhibition" by Mussorgsky would sound if it were sung by a howling cat—or by a Saint Bernard—as you'll see later in this chapter.

From a technical point of view, SoundApp demonstrates the three synthesizers that are built into the Macintosh: the square-wave synthesizer, the wave-table synthesizer, and the sampled sound synthesizer. As you experiment with SoundApp, you'll learn what those three synthesizers are, how they work, and what they do.

Launching SoundApp

SoundApp is one of the software programs on the bonus disk that comes with this book. If you've decompressed the programs on your bonus disk (instructions are presented in Chapter 1), you can launch SoundApp by following these steps:

1. If you have a sound-recording module, ensure that it's connected to the modem or printer port of your Macintosh before you turn on your computer; it's always best to have your computer turned off when you connect peripherals.
2. Find the SoundApp folder that you copied from your bonus disk. The folder is named 03–SoundApp. Open the folder.

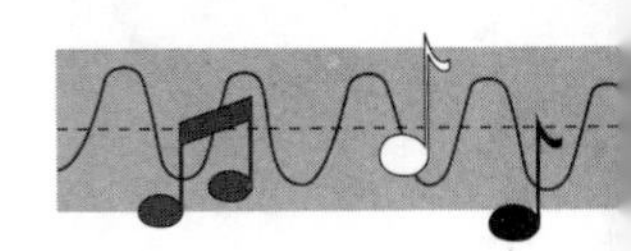

3. Double-click on the file labeled Example Sounds. If you forget and launch SoundApp by clicking on its application icon, the application opens but doesn't immediately display a window. That's no problem; you can still open the Example Sounds window by choosing Open from the File menu and then selecting the file named Example Sounds.
4. SoundApp now opens its main window, and you can start experimenting with the program. You don't have to know how SoundApp works to listen to some sounds. Just select a sound or two from the list of sounds displayed in the SoundApp window, and press some of the play buttons. You might be surprised at some of the things you hear.

Sound Files and Sound Resources

To understand how the SoundApp program works, it helps to have a basic understanding of how the Macintosh stores sounds on disk and in memory.

When you create a sound with your Macintosh, you can store it on a disk in one of two ways: as a sound file or as a sound resource. The SoundApp program works only with sound resources, but many other sound-related programs—such as SoundWave, which is introduced in Chapter 4—can be used with both sound files and sound resources.

What Are Sound Resources?

A sound file is a data file like any other Macintosh data file; it's a block of data that has an icon and can be placed inside a folder on the Macintosh desktop. A resource is a block of information that can be stored in a special way inside a Macintosh file.

Since resources are only pieces of files, they are normally invisible to the Macintosh user. They don't normally show up as Finder icons on the desktop. However, when you start creating, editing, and playing Macintosh sounds, it's helpful to know something about resources, since a sound can be stored on a disk as a resource tucked away inside a file.

Although the Macintosh-using public is mostly unaware of the existence of resources, almost every Macintosh application contains a large number of resources. For example, most commercial Macintosh programs create their dialog boxes, icons, and text strings from information that is stored in the form of resources. And, as mentioned a few paragraphs back, data files can also contain resources.

Why Sounds Are Stored as Resources

Sounds are stored in two formats because sound files and sound resources each have their advantages and disadvantages.

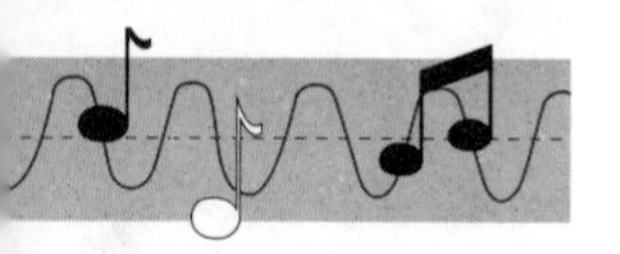

Sound resources take up less memory and can be used in HyperCard stacks. Also, *applications* can manipulate sound resources quite easily. But sound files are easier for Macintosh *users* to manipulate, since the Macintosh operating system treats a sound file like any other kind of file.

Because sound files are easier for Macintosh users to handle than sound resources are, sound-editing programs—such as SoundWave, which is introduced in Chapter 4—are designed primarily for use with sound files. However, since HyperCard stores sounds as resources, the HyperCorder program, introduced in Chapter 5, works more efficiently with sound resources than with sound files.

Varieties of Sound Files and Sound Resources

There are many kinds of sound files, and there are several kinds of sound resources. As you gain experience in working with Macintosh sound, you may find that you need to know more about the various kinds of sound files and sound resources that the Macintosh uses, because some sound-related programs are compatible with some kinds of sound formats, while other programs are compatible with other formats. For more information on sound files and sound resources, you can refer to Appendix F.

The SoundApp Window

If you don't have a sound input driver installed in your System Folder, then the window that SoundApp opens is similar to the window shown in Figure 3–1. If no sound driver is installed, or if SoundApp can't find one, the SoundApp window has buttons for playing and stopping sounds, but no buttons for recording. (For instructions on installing sound drivers, see Chapter 1.)

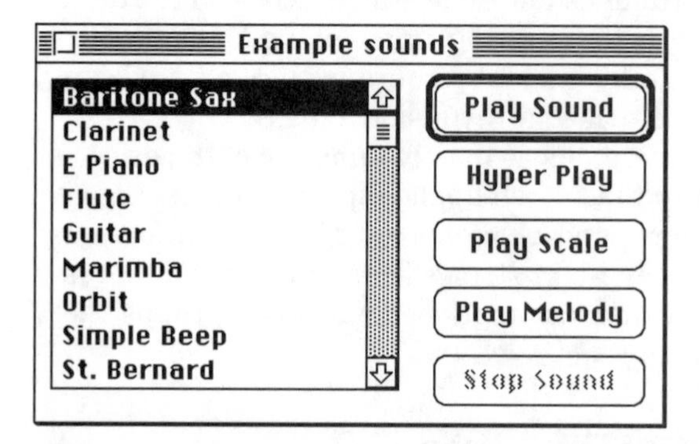

Figure 3–1. The SoundApp window with no sound driver installed

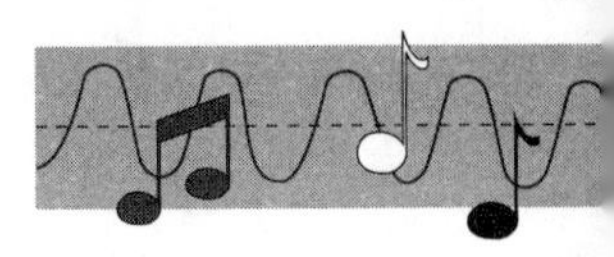

If your System Folder contains a sound input driver, and you have a recording module plugged into your computer's modem or printer port, the SoundApp window looks more like the expanded window shown in Figure 3–2. The expanded SoundApp window has a button for recording sound, as well as buttons for playing and stopping sounds.

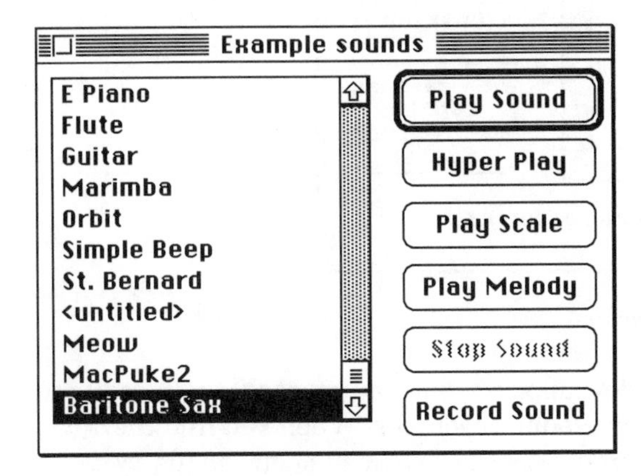

Figure 3–2. The SoundApp window with a driver installed

SoundApp Menus

Once SoundApp is running, you can put the program through its paces by selecting menu items and clicking buttons in the SoundApp window. The commands under the SoundApp File and Edit menus work much like standard Macintosh menu commands, but are specially designed to be used with sound resources and with files that contain sound resources. By choosing from among SoundApp's File menu commands, you can create new sound files, open and close sound files, and quit SoundApp. With the commands under the Edit menu, you can cut, copy, paste, and clear sound resources from the currently open file.

When you select Open, SoundApp displays a standard dialog window like the one shown in Figure 3–3. From that dialog you can open any user-accessible file. If you check the box labeled *Show only files with sound resources,* only the names of files that contain sound resources are displayed. The check box is provided because SoundApp can't play sound files; it can only play sound resources. Therefore, if you're looking for a sound for SoundApp to play, you can put a check in the box and then you won't have to look at the names of files that SoundApp can't use. (For more information about the differences between sound files and sound resources, see Appendix F.)

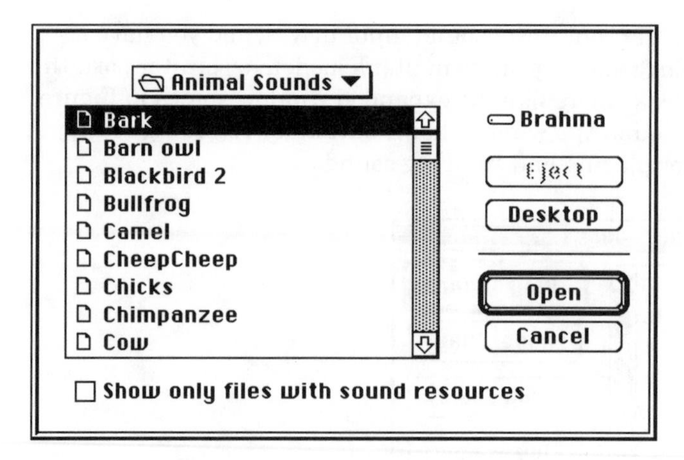

Figure 3–3. The SoundApp Open dialog

When the Open dialog window appears, you can move freely from file to file, looking for files that contain sound resources. When you find the name of a file that contains sound resources, you can open the file by selecting its name and then clicking on the Open button. The Open dialog then disappears, and the main SoundApp window becomes the active window. At that point, if the file that you have selected contains any sound resources, their names are listed in the SoundApp window.

When the SoundApp window is displayed, you can remove a sound from the window's list of available sounds by choosing either Cut or Clear from the Edit menu. Be careful, though; if you delete a sound using Cut, or clear a sound and then quit SoundApp, the sound is gone forever.

The most interesting menu commands that SoundApp offers are those under the Demos menu. The commands under the Demos menu can play notes, scales, and melodies with two of the synthesizers built into the Macintosh: the square-wave synthesizer and the wave-table synthesizer.

The third synthesizer inside the Macintosh—the sampled sound synthesizer—is not on the SoundApp menu. But you can demonstrate that one by clicking on the buttons in the SoundApp window.

Using SoundApp

Although SoundApp was designed primarily to demonstrate Macintosh sounds, you can also use the program to move sound resources from one location to another. (Since SoundApp works only with sound resources, if

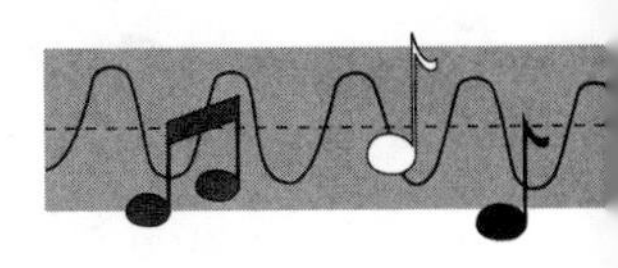

you want to move sounds that are stored as files, you must use some other program—such as SoundWave, which is introduced in Chapter 4.) For example, to move a sound from the SoundApp folder on your bonus disk to another folder, these are the steps to follow:

1. From the Finder, locate the folder that contains the files you have extracted from your bonus disk. Open the folder labeled Sounds and Music. Then launch SoundApp by opening the folder labeled 03–SoundApp and clicking on the icon labeled Example Sounds. SoundApp responds by opening its application window—either a short window like the one shown in Figure 3–1, or a long window like the one shown in Figure 3–2. The window is titled Example Sounds.

   If you forget and open SoundApp by double-clicking on its application icon instead of double-clicking on the Example Sounds icon, the Finder opens SoundApp but doesn't immediately open a SoundApp window. You can then open a SoundApp window manually by selecting Open from the File menu.

2. From the list of sounds displayed in the SoundApp window, select the Banjo sound. (Before you copy the Banjo sound, you might want to press the Play Melody button and listen to what happens.)
3. Select the Copy command from the Edit menu. SoundApp responds by copying the sound to an internal clipboard.
4. Select Open from the File menu. A dialog like the one in Figure 3–3 now appears on your screen.

   Notice the check box at the bottom of the Open dialog that says, *Show only files with sound resources.* If you check that box, only the names of files that have resources are listed in the dialog window.

5. Using standard Macintosh procedures for opening files (see your computer's documentation for details), find the folder labeled Sounds and Music. Double-click on the file name Sound Resources. SoundApp then opens a second window, titled Sound Resources.
6. When the Sound Resources window appears, select the Paste command from the Edit menu. SoundApp then pastes the Banjo sound resource into the Sound Resources file.

Inside Macintosh Sound

SoundApp's main purpose is to demonstrate the three sound synthesizers that are built into the Macintosh: the square-wave synthesizer, the

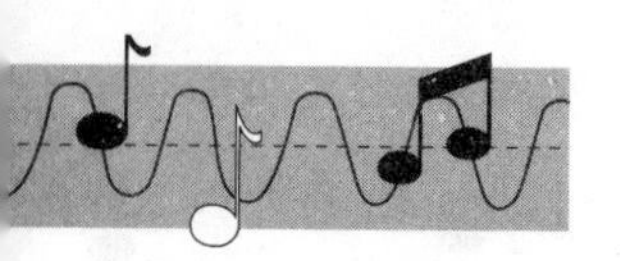

wave-table synthesizer, and the sampled sound synthesizer. To understand what SoundApp does, and how the Macintosh produces sound, it helps to know something about how these three synthesizers work.

This section tells how the Macintosh produces sound. It describes the three synthesizers built into the Macintosh, and tells how SoundApp demonstrates them. As you read this section, you'll get a chance to experiment some more with SoundApp, and to listen to the synthesizers hiding inside your Macintosh.

How the Macintosh Makes Sounds

When Apple unveiled the Macintosh in 1984, the new computer already had the most advanced sound capabilities of any personal computer on the market. It generated sound with an audio chip manufactured by Sony, and it accessed the Sony chip with a Sound Driver that was built into the computer's system software.

With each passing year, Apple has added new improvements to the sound capabilities of the Macintosh. Today, every Macintosh has not one, but two Sony sound chips, as well as an Apple Sound Chip (ASC) that is manufactured by Apple. With this new circuitry, the Macintosh can process sound faster, can reproduce it better, and can offer more new sound capabilities with the introduction of each new model and with each new software upgrade. Recent improvements in Macintosh sound include the ability to record multiple channels, the ability to play sounds continuously from a disk while the CPU performs other tasks, and the ability to play more natural-sounding sounds.

The Sound Manager

One of the most important advances in Macintosh sound accompanied the introduction of System 6. With the unveiling of System 6, Apple replaced the Macintosh Sound Driver with a new Toolbox manager called the Sound Manager. The Sound Manager had many new and improved features. It could process sound much better and faster than the Sound Driver, but it could still run programs written for the Sound Driver—provided they were written in accordance with Apple's Human Interface Guidelines.

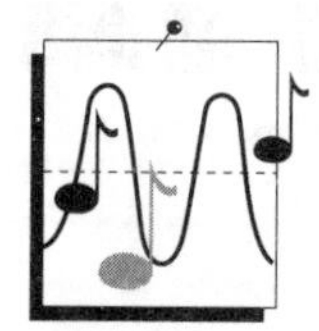

TECH TALK

How Internal Routines Use the Sound Manager

Macintosh Toolbox managers are prewritten software routines that are supplied as part of the Macintosh system software. Application programs can use Toolbox managers to perform many kinds of common tasks, such as managing the opening and closing of windows and drawing shapes on the screen. Apple encourages developers of Macintosh applications to use Toolbox managers when they can rather than

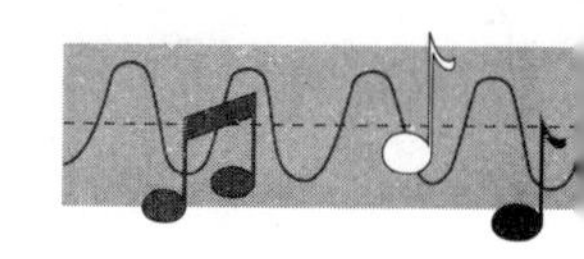

writing their own routines that access the computer's hardware directly. Thus, developers of applications that generate sound are encouraged to use the Sound Manager in their programs whenever possible.

When a routine that is part of the Macintosh Toolbox or operating system needs to produce a sound, it calls the Sound Manager, just as application programs are encouraged to do. For example, the SysBeep procedure, once documented as an operating-system utility, is now a Sound Manager routine.

The Macintosh Toolbox, officially titled the Human Interface Toolbox, is documented in Inside Macintosh. *Additional information about programming the Toolbox is provided in* Extending the Macintosh Toolbox, *written by John C. May and Judy B. Whittle, and published by Addison-Wesley.* ❍

The Enhanced Sound Manager

When System 6.0.7 made its debut, Apple improved the Sound Manager by adding new routines for sound input, continuous play-from-disk capabilities, sound-channel mixing, and audio compression and expansion. The Sound Manager was enhanced so much with the release of System 6.0.7 that Apple started calling it the enhanced Sound Manager. The enhanced Sound Manager was improved still more for System 7, and it continues to be upgraded in maintenance releases of Macintosh system software.

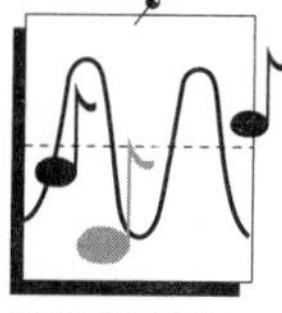

TECH TALK

Using the Sound Manager

Apple strongly suggests that developers of sound-related Macintosh software use the Sound Manager rather than accessing the computer's sound hardware directly. By using the Sound Manager, application developers can ensure that software they write for current Macintosh models will also work with future models.

QuickTime, a utility created by Apple to help application developers make Macintosh movies, is a shining example of how applications can take advantage of the capabilities of the Sound Manager. According to engineers at Apple, QuickTime generates sound in the officially endorsed manner: by using the Sound Manager instead of addressing the Macintosh sound hardware directly. Furthermore, according to Apple engineer Jim Reekes, who wrote SoundApp, the programmers who wrote QuickTime didn't do anything extraordinary with the Sound Manager to make it work with QuickTime. They just wrote good code that made ordinary Sound Manager calls within the scope of Apple's Human Interface Guidelines. ❍

A Tale of Three Synthesizers

The enhanced Sound Manager does its work with the help of the three sound synthesizers that are built into the Macintosh. Each synthesizer uses a different principle to generate sound, and each produces sound in a different way.

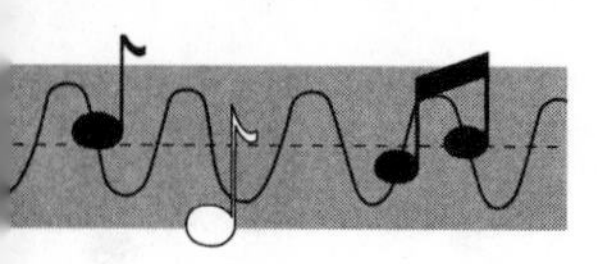

When an application program needs to generate a sound, it can activate any of the three synthesizers built into the Macintosh by making a call to the Sound Manager. The Sound Manager then uses whatever hardware is needed to produce the specified sound.

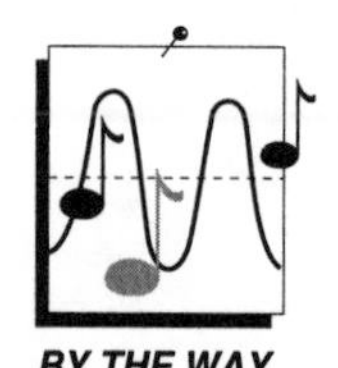

BY THE WAY

Speech and MIDI Synthesizers

As this book went to press, Apple was putting the finishing touches on a fourth synthesizer: a **speech synthesizer,** *which can generate speech sounds. The speech synthesizer will replace a system extension called MacinTalk, a speech synthesizer covered in Chapter 6.*

In addition to the internal Macintosh synthesizers, external MIDI synthesizers can be connected to the computer's modem or printer port. MIDI, an acronym for Musical Instrument Digital Interface, is a worldwide standard for interfacing electronic musical instruments such as synthesizers, samplers, and drum machines.

With an external MIDI interface unit, you can connect the Macintosh to many different kinds of musical instruments and electronic devices. You can then use the Macintosh as a central control panel for a sophisticated sound studio. In fact, many professional musicians and sound engineers have electronic sound studios that are centrally controlled through Macintosh computers. MIDI instruments and MIDI software are covered in much more detail in Chapter 9. ❍

The Square-Wave Synthesizer

A square wave, as you may remember from Chapter 2, is a square-shaped waveform. The Macintosh square-wave synthesizer, as you might guess from its name, generates sounds with waveforms known as square waves.

Listening to a Square Wave

If you're running the SoundApp program, the Demos menu provides three commands that can demonstrate the square-wave synthesizer. These commands, and their functions are as follows:

- **SquareWave Snth Scale—**plays a scale
- **SquareWave Snth Melody—**plays a segment of "Pictures at an Exhibition" by Mussorgsky through the square-wave synthesizer
- **SquareWave Snth Timbres—**demonstrates various tonal qualities, or timbres, of square waves

Looking at a Square Wave

When a sound's waveform is displayed graphically, the height of the waveform represents the sound's volume, or amplitude, and the width of the waveform represents the sound's pitch, or frequency. Thus, you can some-

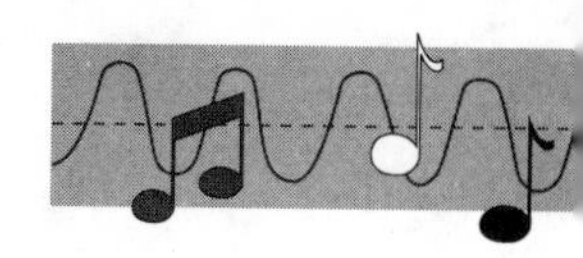

times get a fair idea of what a waveform sounds like just by looking at its shape. For example, a square wave starts at a given volume, plays at the same volume for a given period of time, and then stops. Because a square wave starts and stops so abruptly, a sound represented by a square wave has a bright, harsh sound.

Figure 3–4 shows the waveform of a square wave.

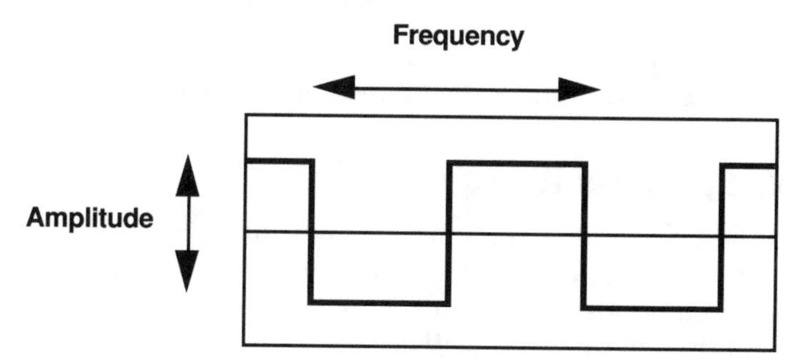

Figure 3–4. A square wave

Limitations of the Square Wave Synthesizer

The square-wave synthesizer is the simplest—and the most limited—of the three sound synthesizers built into the Macintosh Sound Manager. The only kind of sound that it can produce is a simple beep. However, by generating sequences of square waves with varying pitches and durations, you can make the square-wave synthesizer play tunes. You can also instruct the Sound Manager to generate square waves that have subtly different tonal qualities, or *timbres*.

Despite its limitations, the square-wave synthesizer does have some advantages: it uses little CPU time, and it is easy for applications to use.

The Wave-Table Synthesizer

When the Sound Manager needs to produce more complex sounds than the square-wave synthesizer can manage to produce, it can use the wave-table synthesizer. The wave-table synthesizer, as its name implies, generates sounds from a *wave table:* a sequence of bytes that are stored in memory as an array.

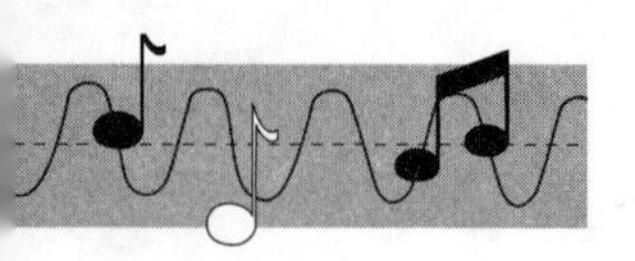

Demonstrating Wave-Table Synthesis

The SoundApp Demos menu has three commands that demonstrate the wave-table synthesizer. Those commands, and their functions, are as follows:

- **Wave Snth Scale—**plays a scale through the wave-table synthesizer
- **Wave Snth Melody—**plays a wave-table synthesis version of—wouldn't you know it?— "Pictures at an Exhibition" by Mussorgsky
- **Wave Snth Counterpoint—**plays a multichannel version of a German oldie, "Schaut, ihr Sünder" by Löwenstern, arranged by Bach

How Wave-Table Synthesis Works

The wave-table synthesizer—unlike the square-wave synthesizer—can generate sounds that have complex waveforms. So it can easily produce sounds that have different kinds of tones, or *timbres*—far more timbres than you can get with the square-wave synthesizer.

You can create a wave table by recording a sound and then measuring its amplitude at fixed intervals. Then you can store your wave table on a disk or in RAM in the form of bytes. Each byte in a wave table contains a value from 0 to 255, or from $00 to $FF in hexadecimal notation.

When you want to reproduce the sound that you have recorded, you can call the Sound Manager. The Sound Manager can then reproduce that sound by passing the wave table's address to the wave-table synthesizer.

How Wave Tables Are Stored

When a sound is represented as an array of bytes, the closer together in time the bytes are, the higher is the quality of the sound. An application can use any number of bytes to create the sequence of amplitudes that make up the waveform, but 512 is the recommended number. If an application describes a wave table using any number of bytes other than 512, the Sound Manager resizes the wave table to 512 bytes. To keep the waveform accurate, it's best to create a 512-byte wave table in the first place. Thus, the Sound Manager can convert a wave table into a sound by measuring the value of the wave's amplitude at every $1/512$ interval of the wave and then sending those measurements to the sound hardware inside the Macintosh.

Because a wave table can be no more than 512 bytes long, it cannot represent a very long sound. Therefore, a wave table is generally used to store only one cycle of a sound wave (for an explanation of what a cycle is, see the section "What Is Sound?" in Chapter 2). When the wave-table synthesizer plays a sound stored as a wave table, it plays the wave cycle stored

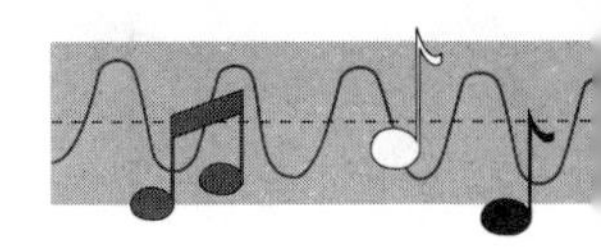

in the wave table as many times as necessary, looping over and over through the wave table for the duration of the sound.

Advantages of the Wave-Table Synthesizer

The wave-table synthesizer is an efficient sound generator that not many applications use, but that more application developers should investigate. It stores sounds quite economically, since each wave table that it uses takes up only 512 bytes.

The wave-table synthesizer is so memory-efficient because each waveform that it uses can generate several frequencies of sound. Once you have stored a sound as a wave table, the Sound Manager can play it back at any desired frequency, any desired amplitude, and any desired duration.

Since the Sound Manager can loop over and over through a wave table to extend the duration of a sound, you can change the length of a wave-table note without changing its pitch; you can extend it without making it turn into a bass note, and you can shorten it without making it sound like a chipmunk. Thus, you can use the same waveform to play long or short sounds.

You can also make changes in the pitch of a wave-table note without changing the character of the note—as long as the changes aren't too drastic. If you raise or lower a note a tone or two, the change in the note's timbre is not usually noticeable. But if you change the note's pitch by more than a couple of tones, it can begin to sound odd, because most instruments —particularly the human voice—produce sounds of different pitches in different ways.

For example, imagine how it would sound if you tried to make the voice of a bass singer sound like the voice of a soprano just by speeding up a phonograph record. That wouldn't work very well, because pitch is not the only difference between a bass singer's voice and a soprano's voice. When you try to change a sampled sound in this way, and your effort doesn't work very well, the result is an effect sometimes referred to as "Munchkinization."

The Sampled Sound Synthesizer

Sounds that occur in nature are called *analog* sounds. The only kind of sound that the human ear can perceive is analog sound. The process of recording analog sound on an analog record or tape is known as *analog recording.*

When you convert a sound into a sequence of numbers so that you can store its waveform as a series of bytes, it is called a *digitized* sound. The process of recording digitized sounds on a digital tape or a digital compact disc is called *digital recording.*

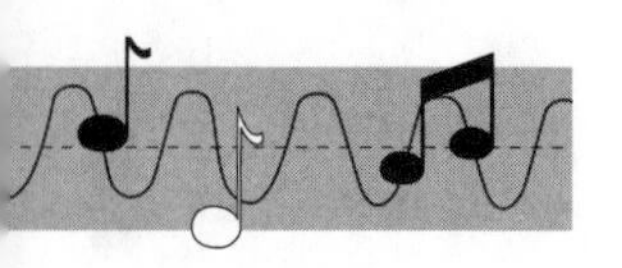

When you record a sound through a plug-in recording module, the sound circuitry inside your computer or inside your recording module converts the sound of your voice from an analog sound to a digitized sound. Therefore, a plug-in recording module is often referred to as an analog-to-digital (A/D) converter—or, more simply, as a *digitizer.*

When you record a digitized sound, the Sound Manager stores the waveform of the sound as a series of binary numbers; that is, by *sampling* the sound at evenly spaced intervals. The bytes that make up a sampled sound are similar to the individual frames that are linked to create a motion picture.

A sampled sound, like a wave-table sound, can be stored on a disk or in memory as a series of bytes. Unlike a wave-table sound, however, a sampled sound does not represent a single cycle of a sound wave. Rather, a sampled sound is an actual recording of a sequence of sounds. And a sampled sound can be a sound sequence of virtually any length—depending, of course, on how much disk or memory space is available.

When you record a sound with the sampled sound synthesizer, a complete sound sequence—from beginning to end—is stored in memory. To play the sound, the Macintosh reconstructs the original waveform by reconnecting the sound samples.

How the Sampled Sound Synthesizer Works

When you record a sound with a sound digitizer, the Sound Manager plays back the sound by accessing the sampled sound synthesizer. Although the sampled sound synthesizer usually plays back sampled sounds—as you would expect from its name—it can also play sounds that are *synthesized*, or artificially produced, either before playback or at playback time.

Although sampled sounds consume enormous amounts of disk space and memory, the sampled sound synthesizer is the synthesizer most used in Macintosh applications. It is useful for reproducing prerecorded sounds such as speech or sound effects, and since it usually plays back real sounds that have been recorded, it produces natural-sounding sounds.

Demonstrating Sampled Sounds with SoundApp

The most interesting feature of the SoundApp program is its ability to handle sampled sounds. Turn back to Figures 3–1 and 3–3, which show the SoundApp window, and you'll see that the window contains a list of sampled sounds.

It's easy to demonstrate the sampled sound synthesizer with SoundApp. Here's how: To select a sound that you'd like to hear, simply click on the name of the sound in the list of sounds that are available.

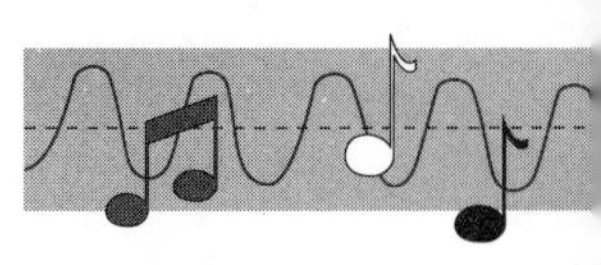

When you have selected a sound, you can listen to it by clicking on the buttons in the SoundApp window. The buttons have the following functions:

- **Play Sound—**simply plays the selected sound.
- **Hyper Play—**plays the same sound using a special algorithm that HyperCard uses to play sampled sounds (for more information on HyperCard sounds, see Chapter 5).
- **Play Scale—**presents a multioctave scale played with the sound that you have selected.
- **Play Melody—**plays a famous classical selection (you guess the name this time) using the sound you have selected. For a real treat, listen to the Saint Bernard and the cat on the fence belting out this timeless classic.
- **Stop Sound—**terminates any sound that is playing. This is the button to select when you hear the pounding on the ceiling.

If your Macintosh is equipped with recording hardware, and if a sound driver is installed in your System folder, then your SoundApp window has a sixth button:

- **Record Sound—**lets you record sounds and install them in SoundApp. When you have recorded a sound, you can save it, and its name then appears in the list of available sounds in the SoundApp window.

Summary

This chapter explained how the Macintosh produces sound. It also documented the SoundApp program, an application which Apple's Developer Technical Support group provides to developers to demonstrate the three sound synthesizers built into the Macintosh. These three synthesizers are the square-wave synthesizer, which can generate beeps and play melodies using simple square waves; the wave-table synthesizer, which can produce tunes by playing short waveforms at varying pitches and durations; and the sampled sound synthesizer, which can play longer sounds and sound sequences made up of complex waveforms.

This chapter introduced one free software program that's on this book's bonus disk: SoundApp, which can really put the Macintosh Sound Manager through its paces.

4
Sound Processing

There's more to making a recording than talking into a microphone. In today's world of samplers, synthesizers, and lip-synched concerts, it's just as routine to edit a sound as it is to record one. In fact, many CDs are recordings of performances that never took place; they contain more synthesized sound than music that was recorded in a concert or a studio.

The SoundWave Program

In Chapters 1 and 2, you learned how the Macintosh generates sound, and you got an inside look at your computer's three built-in synthesizers. In Chapter 3, you got a chance to experiment with SoundApp, which was designed by engineers at Apple to demonstrate the sound capabilities of the Macintosh.

In this chapter, you'll learn how to edit sounds, and how to add special effects to sounds, with a powerful sound-editing program called SoundWave. SoundWave is an application program that lets you edit and play back sampled sounds. Sampled sounds, sometimes called digitized sounds, are sounds that have been converted into streams of binary numbers so they can be stored on a computer disk or in a computer's memory. Sampled sounds are described in more detail in Chapters 2 and 3.

SoundWave works with 8-bit digitized sounds—the kind of sounds that you can record with the microphones that come with some models of the Macintosh, or with 8-bit sound digitizers such as the MacRecorder from Macromedia. If your Macintosh doesn't have a microphone and you don't have a voice digitizer, you can use SoundWave to edit prerecorded sounds. You can get 8-bit sounds in almost unlimited numbers from Macintosh user groups, computer software companies, and from public and commercial

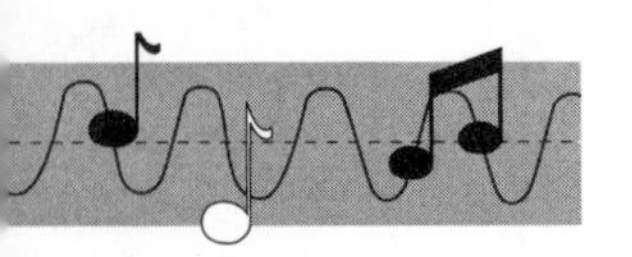

computer bulletin boards. Appendix B lists the addresses and telephone numbers of many companies and organizations that can provide you with prerecorded sounds.

What SoundWave Can Do

SoundWave is a sound-processing program: an application that lets you edit sounds by copying, cutting, and pasting waveforms in much the same way that you can copy, cut, and paste segments of text when you're using a word processor. If your Macintosh has a built-in or plug-in microphone, you can also use SoundWave to record sounds, and to edit and save sounds that you record. You can display waveforms of sounds, and you can examine two-dimensional and three-dimensional spectral images of sounds.

You can listen to selected portions of sounds; mix sound segments from the same sound file or different sound files; change the volume and speed of a sound; balance frequency bands with an on-screen equalizer; add delay effects to sounds; and fade sounds in or out with on-screen volume controls. You can even turn a sound backward so that you hear it in reverse on playback.

Working with Sound Files and Sound Resources

Sounds can be stored on disks and in memory in two formats: as data files or as sound resources. With SoundWave, you can load and process sounds that have been stored in either format. Also, SoundWave can save sounds as either sound files or sound resources. Therefore, you can use SoundWave to convert files from one format to another. You can load a sound that has been stored as a resource, and then save it as a data file—or you can load a sound resource and save it as a sound file. (You can do the same thing with the HyperCorder program introduced in Chapter 5.)

The file-translation capabilities of SoundWave (and HyperCorder) are important because some sound-related applications store sounds in data files, while other programs store sounds as resources. To make things even more complicated, there are many kinds of sound files, and there are several kinds of sound resources. For example, sounds recorded with the MacRecorder digitizer are usually stored in files known as 'AIFF' data files, whereas the popular Super Studio Session musical format stores sounds as type 'XSNG' files. In contrast, HyperCard sounds and Macintosh system alert sounds are generally stored as either Format 1 or Format 2 resources.

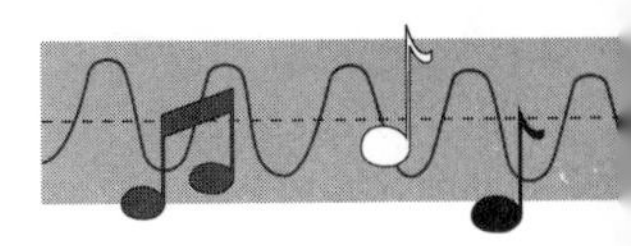

The formats of sound files and sound resources are beyond the scope of this chapter, but are covered in more detail in Appendix F. Figure 4–1 shows the icons of some of the more popular kinds of Macintosh sound files.

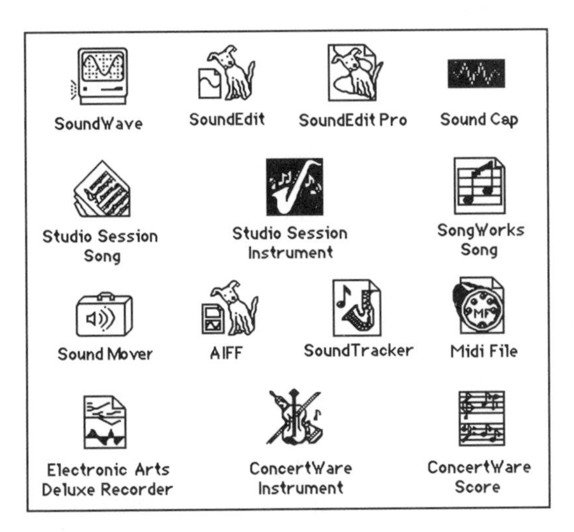

Figure 4–1. Types of sound files

Editing Sounds and Adding Special Effects

SoundWave has controls and menu commands that you can use to edit sounds and add special effects. With SoundWave's editing and special-effects features, you can do the following:

- Cut and paste sounds, just as you would cut and paste pictures or text in a word processor or a graphics program
- Copy or move sounds within the same file, or from one file to another
- Adjust the amplitudes of the frequency bands in sounds using a dialog window that works like a graphic equalizer
- Delay sounds to create echoes and other interesting effects
- Change the volume and speed of sounds
- Turn sounds backward so they play in reverse
- Add silent segments to sounds
- Average out the amplitude variations in sounds by smoothing out changes in volume

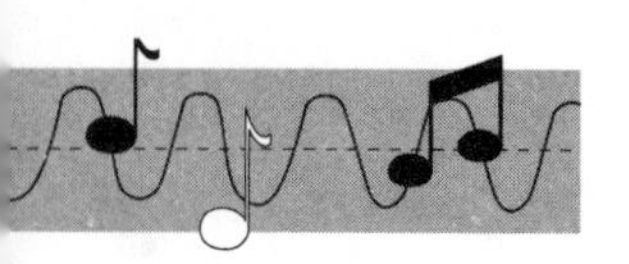

- Change the sampling rates of sound files (the number of bytes per interval used to store sounds in memory; sampling rates are described under the next heading)
- Change the compression ratios of sound files (compression methods are sometimes used to save memory when sounds are stored; compression ratios are described under the next heading)

You'll get a chance to try out many of these special effects as you read the rest of this chapter.

Using SoundWave

SoundWave is a state-of-the-art application for making, playing back, and editing digital recordings. SoundWave is part of the Authorware Professional package, a powerful software kit manufactured by Authorware, Inc., for writing multimedia software. Authorware is now part of Macromedia.

Authorware Professional for the Macintosh won the prestigious Eddy award for best multimedia software in 1990. SoundWave is a sound-recording and sound-editing module that is included in the Authorware Professional system.

Many companies use components of the Authorware Professional system in their products. For example, when you buy the Voice Impact Pro recording package from Articulate Systems, the main recording and editing program that you get with the package is SoundWave—the same SoundWave program that's included on the bonus disk that comes with this book. (Interestingly, Articulate Systems doesn't ship SoundWave with its basic, low-end Voice Impact digitizer—only with its high-end, more expensive Voice Impact Pro recording package.)

Since Articulate Systems holds a nonexclusive license to distribute SoundWave, Addison-Wesley was able to obtain a license to distribute the SoundWave program with this book. Furthermore, the program that's on this book's bonus disk is not a stripped-down demonstration version of SoundWave. It's the real thing: a 100 percent intact, fully working version of the Authorware Professional SoundWave program.

In this section, you'll have a chance to launch SoundWave and load a sound file. If you have recording hardware, you'll also get an opportunity to make and save sounds of your own. If your Macintosh doesn't have a built-in microphone, and you don't have a plug-in digitizer, you can't record sound, but you can do everything else described in this section. Later in the chapter, you'll edit sound. You'll also learn more about adjusting sampling rates and compressing sounds.

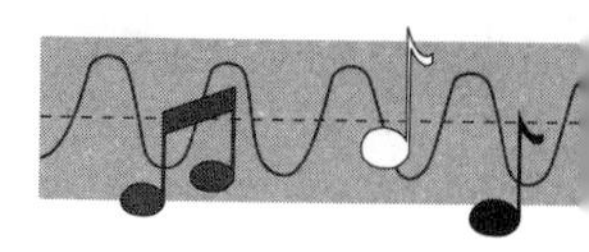

Launching SoundWave and Playing a Sound

SoundWave has many sophisticated features that you must learn if you want to use the program effectively. However, it's easy to launch SoundWave and experiment with it. Just follow these steps:

1. If you have a sound digitizer, make sure you have connected it to your computer's modem or printer port before you turn on your Macintosh.
2. Find the folder that contains the files you copied from your bonus disk. Then find and open the folder labeled Sounds and Music.
3. Double-click on the sound file titled Melodrama. Two things now happen. First, the Finder launches the SoundWave program. Next, SoundWave opens its main window, which is called the sound window, and opens the Melodrama sound file. SoundWave displays the Melodrama file in the sound window, as shown in Figure 4–2.

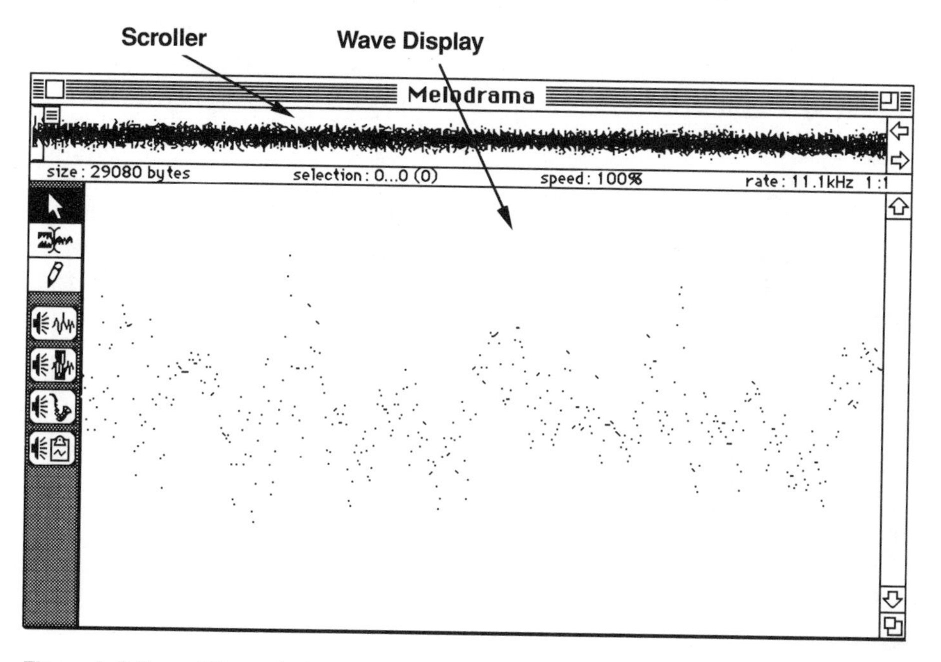

Figure 4–2. SoundWave window

If you forget and launch SoundWave by clicking on its application icon, the application opens but doesn't immediately display a window. That's no problem; you can still open the sound window by choosing Open from the File menu, and then finding and selecting the Melodrama file.

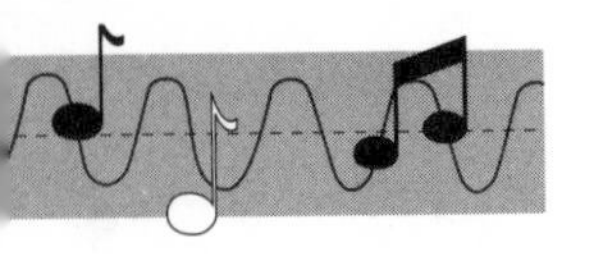

You can also open a new sound file by selecting New from the File menu. The New command opens an empty window, but for now, I'll assume you've selected the Open command and opened the Melodrama sound file.

In Figure 4–2, the Melodrama sound's waveform is displayed in two places: in a ribbon called a *scroller,* just below the sound window's title bar, and in the main section of the window, an area called the *wave display.* The scroller and the wave display are labeled in the illustration.

The scroller provides an overall view of a complete sound file, and the wave display provides a magnified view of a small part of the file. You'll learn to manipulate these two views later in this chapter. Meanwhile, just note that while the waveform shown in the scroller looks like you might expect a waveform to look, the waveform in the display is made up of tiny dots, as shown in Figure 4–2. Those dots show how the sound is stored in memory; they describe a bit-by-bit sampling of the sound, representing each bit by a single dot.

4. You can connect the dots in the wave display so that they form a display that is more recognizable as a waveform. Just select the command labeled Connect the Dots from the Display menu, and SoundWave joins the dots, creating a display like the one shown in Figure 4–3.

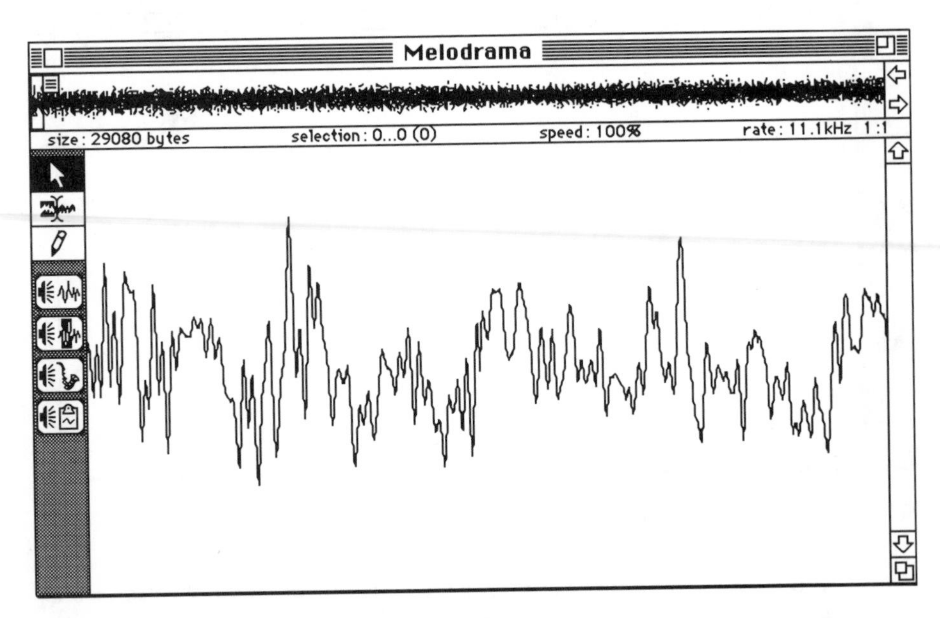

Figure 4–3. Sound window with dots connected

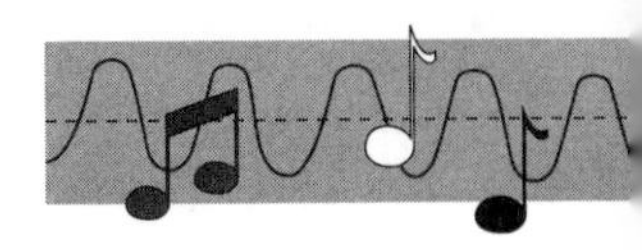

Notice that Connect the Dots is a toggle command. When you select Connect the Dots in the Display menu, a check mark appears beside the command. Until you select Connect the Dots again, all files opened by SoundWave are shown in the wave display with their dots connected.

5. To play the Melodrama sound, just click on the Play Sound icon in the SoundWave tools palette. The tools palette is the horizontal palette on the left-hand side of the sound window. Figure 4–4 shows the tools palette, with its parts labeled.

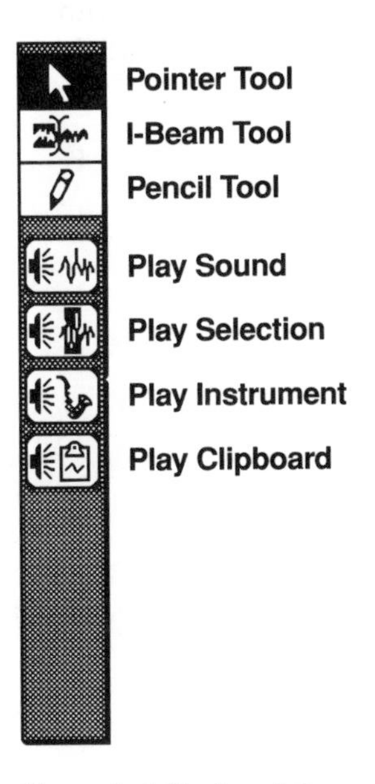

Figure 4–4. Tools palette

Recording Sound

The following paragraphs are a tutorial guide to recording sound with SoundWave. If you don't have a sound digitizer, and you aren't interested in SoundWave's recording features, feel free to skip these steps.

Preparing to Record a Sound

Before you can record a sound with SoundWave, you must create a sound file. Alternatively, if you want to edit an existing sound file, you can open the file by choosing the Open command under the File menu. To open a new file and record a new sound, these are the steps to follow:

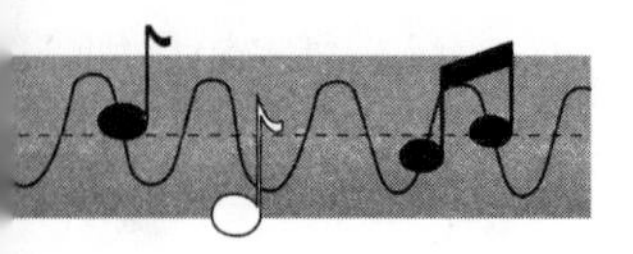

1. If you have finished listening to the Melodrama sound file, close the Melodrama file by clicking on the sound window's close box.
2. Open a new sound file by selecting Record from the File menu. When you select Record, SoundWave opens a Record dialog window. The kind of dialog window that SoundWave opens depends on the kind of sound hardware and software that you have installed in your system.

   If you're using the MacRecorder sound driver with a version of system software earlier than System 6.0.7—or if you're using a sound driver that can't automatically find your digitizer—then SoundWave displays a basic Record dialog box like the one in Figure 4–5.

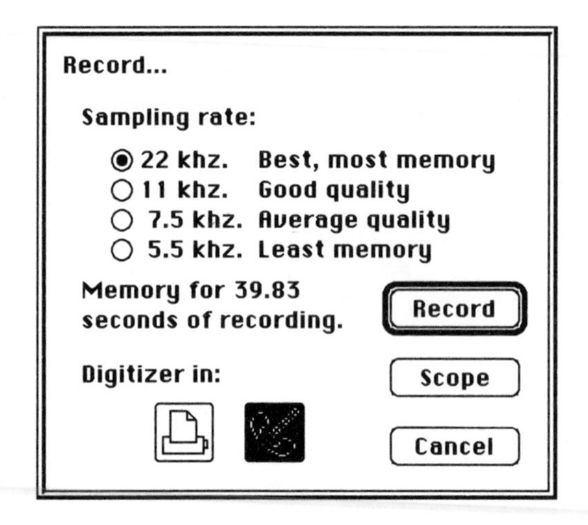

Figure 4–5. Basic Record dialog box

The basic Record dialog box contains a pair of icon buttons that you can click to specify whether your recording module is connected to your modem port or your printer port. The dialog also provides a set of radio buttons that you can click to specify a sampling rate (the number of bytes per interval that are used to record and store a sound).

In addition, the basic Record dialog box contains a button labeled Scope that can display the SoundWave scope window. With the scope window, you can set your recording level, as explained later in this chapter.

If you're using System 6.0.7 or later, and you have a sound driver that can automatically figure out what it needs to know about your sound hardware, then SoundWave displays a more elaborate Record

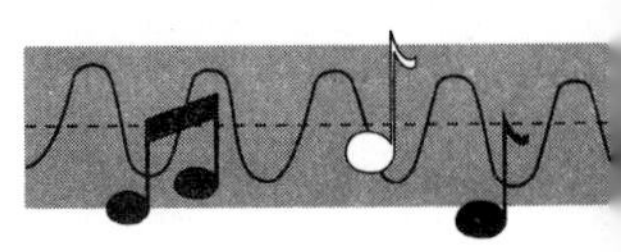

dialog window when you select the Record menu command. This deluxe Record dialog box is shown in Figure 4–6.

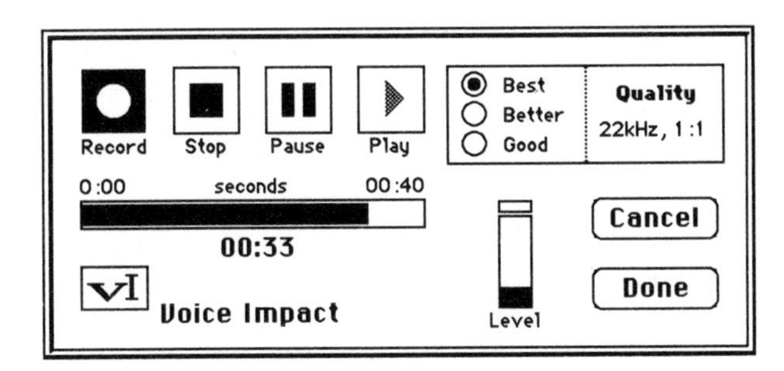

Figure 4–6. Deluxe Record dialog box

The deluxe Record dialog box contains four tape recorder–style controls: Record, Play, Pause, and Stop. Also, there are three buttons that you can use to adjust your sampling rate: Good, Better, and Best. A horizontal bar meter shows elapsed recording time, and a vertical thermometer bar displays your current recording level.

3. When recording is finished, SoundWave opens a new Untitled window containing the sound you have recorded.

Using the Basic Record Dialog Box

If SoundWave displays the basic Record dialog box with your sound-recording system, these are the steps to follow to record a sound:

1. **Choose a sampling rate:** By selecting one of the radio buttons in the Record dialog, you can set a sampling rate for the recording you are about to make. As you can see by looking at the basic Record dialog box shown in Figure 4–5, SoundWave can record with four sampling rates. The rates range from 22kHz, which produces the best sound but requires the most memory, down to 5.5kHz, which produces the poorest sound but requires the least memory. (For more on sampling rates, see the section "Using SoundWave.")

   For the moment, you aren't going to record very much sound, so you might as well choose the best-sounding sampling rate: 22kHz.

2. **Select a digitizer port:** The basic Record dialog contains two icons: a printer icon that represents your computer's printer port, and a telephone-receiver icon that represents its modem port. Choose the port to which your digitizer is connected.

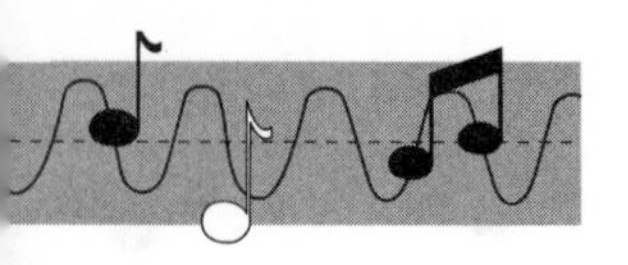

3. **Adjust the input level:** Each of the digitizers described in this book is equipped with an input-level control, or gain control. On some digitizers, the volume control must be at least partly turned on before the digitizer can operate. Also, on some digitizers, a small light comes on when the digitizer is switched on and flashes with varying intensity when the module is recording, so that you can see when the digitizer is on and when it is recording. Both Voice Impact Pro and the SID digitizers have on-the-air LEDs.

   When you have located your digitizer's volume control, click on the button labeled Scope in the basic Record dialog. SoundWave then displays a window that resembles an oscilloscope. When the scope window appears, speak into your digitizer's microphone. A waveform generated by the sound of your voice appears on the screen.

   As you speak, adjust your digitizer's input level and watch the height of the sound wave in the scope display change. To prevent an unpleasant form of distortion called clipping, which occurs when a waveform's top and bottom edges are cut off, adjust the input level until the wave on the screen fills about 80 percent of the window in which it appears.

   When you have finished adjusting the input level, click your mouse button. The scope window then disappears, and the basic Record window becomes active again.

4. **Record a sound:** To close the basic Record window and start recording, simply click on the button in the Record dialog labeled Record. SoundWave then displays a small Recording window similar to the one in Figure 4–7.

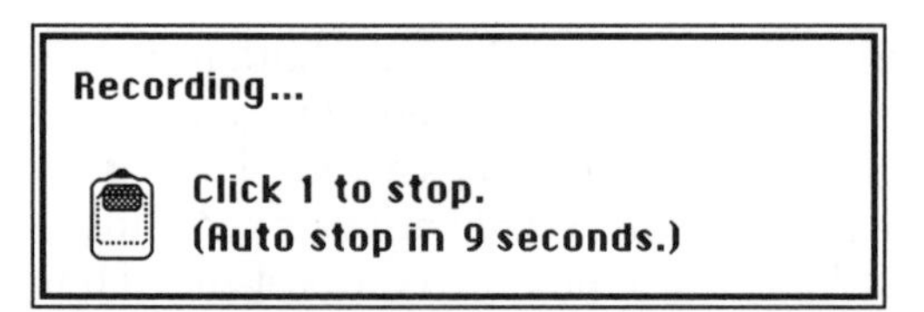

Figure 4–7. Recording window

5. **Close the Recording window:** While the Recording window is open and you are recording, make sure that you don't move the mouse or click on the mouse button, because that will terminate your recording. When you have finished recording, you can stop the recording operation by either moving the mouse or clicking on the mouse button. The Recording window then disappears, and the main SoundWave window appears on the screen.

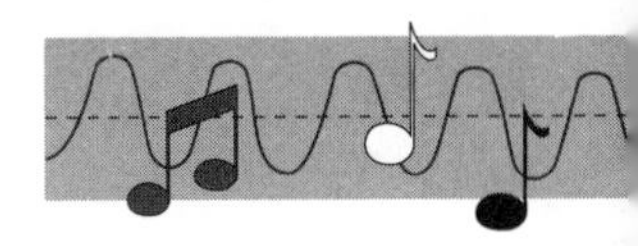

6. **Save your sound:** To save your sound, choose Save or Save As from the File menu. SoundWave then displays a Save dialog window that looks like the one in Figure 4–8.

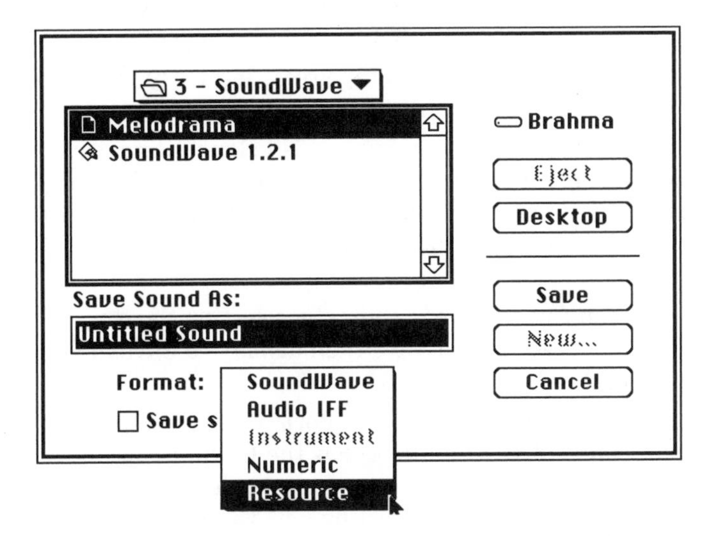

Figure 4–8. SoundWave Save dialog box

One special feature of the SoundWave Save window is a pop-up menu labeled Format. The Format menu lets you save a sound in any one of the five formats shown in Figure 4–8. Below the Format pop-up menu, there's a check box—partly obscured in the illustration —that allows you to save only a selected part of a sound. For more information on selecting parts of sounds, see the heading "Editing a Sound" in the section "Using the SoundWave Tools."

Using the Deluxe Record Dialog

If you're using the deluxe Record dialog, you can make a recording by following these steps:

1. **Choose a sampling rate:** By selecting one of the three radio buttons in the deluxe Record dialog shown in Figure 4–6, you can set a sampling rate for the recording you are about to make. For this exercise, choose the best-sounding sampling rate: 22kHz (for more information on how to make that choice, see the section "Using SoundWave").
2. **Adjust the recording level:** When you're using the deluxe Record dialog, you can adjust the recording level by observing the horizontal sound-level meter. Notice that there is a small horizontal rectangle

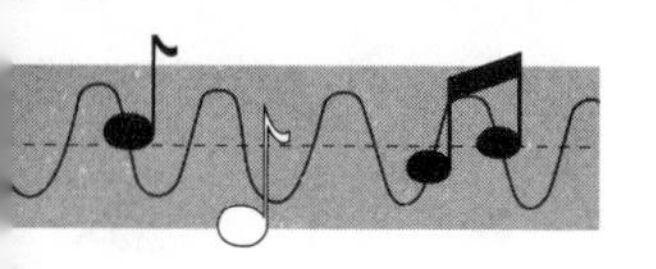

above the recording-level meter. If that rectangle becomes filled in, your sound level is too high, and your recording may be distorted. If your digitizer has a recording-level control, you can adjust whatever gain controls are available to cut back on your recording level.

3. **Record a sound:** With the deluxe Record dialog, you can record sounds in the same way you would on a tape recorder: by simply clicking on the Record, Stop, Pause, and Play buttons.
4. **Close the Record dialog:** When you have finished recording, you can halt the recording operation and close the Record dialog by clicking on the button labeled Done. The deluxe Recording dialog window then disappears, and the main sound window (shown earlier in Figure 4–2) appears on the screen.
5. **Save your sound:** You can save your sound by selecting Save or Save As from the File menu. SoundWave then displays a Save dialog like the one shown earlier in Figure 4–8.

   The Save dialog has a pop-up menu labeled Format that lets you save a sound in any one of five formats. Below the Format pop-up menu, there's a check box that lets you save only a selected part of a sound. For more information on selecting parts of sounds, see "Editing a Sound" in the section "Using the SoundWave Tools."

Adjusting Sampling Rates with SoundWave

The SoundWave program can sample sound at four rates:

- **22kHz—**produces the best sound but requires the most memory
- **11kHz—**produces good sound and requires less memory
- **7.4kHz—**produces fair sound quality and uses still less memory
- **5.5kHz—**produces sound that may be suitable for voice and certain sound effects, and uses the least memory

Table 4–1 shows how much disk space (or RAM) is required to store three sizes of sounds at two different sampling rates.

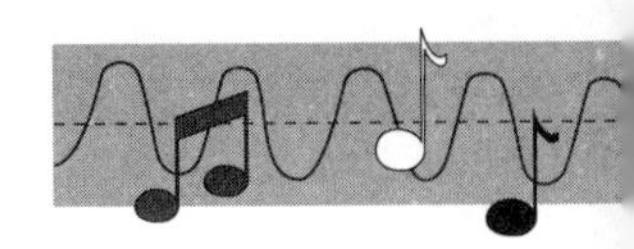

Table 4–1 The Effects of Sampling Rates on Sound Storage Requirements

Period	Rate	Memory
1 sec.	22kHz	22K
30 sec.	22kHz	660K
1 min.	22kHz	1,320K
1 sec.	11kHz	11K
30 sec.	11kHz	330K
1 min.	11kHz	660K

Sampling Rates and Word Size

The quality of a digitized sound is determined not only by the rate at which it was sampled, but also by the *word size,* or resolution of the equipment used to sample the sound. The resolution of a sound depends upon the length of the binary numbers into which the sound is converted. Digitizers used with the Macintosh store sound values as 8-bit numbers—that is, as numbers ranging from 0 to 255. Therefore, Macintosh digitizers are said to have an 8-bit resolution. In contrast, an audio compact disc stores sound values as 16-bit numbers, or as numbers ranging from 0 to 65,535. Thus, sound on a compact disc has a 16-bit resolution.

Choosing a Sampling Rate

The sampling rate you should choose depends both on how good you want your sampling to sound and how much storage space you have available. The best way to find out what sampling rate you want to use is to listen to sounds that are sampled at each rate, and then decide. Generally speaking, you need higher sampling rates to make music sound good, but lower sampling rates are fine for many kinds of sound effects and for most voice recordings.

You can use the Resample and Assume Rate commands on the Wave menu to change the sampling rates. See the section "SoundWave Menus" later in this chapter.

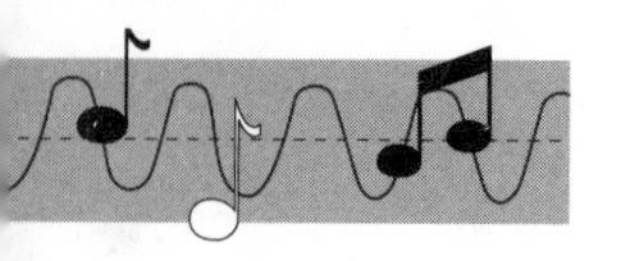

Compressing Sounds

SoundWave can compress sounds using two ratios: 3 to 1 or 6 to 1. As you might guess, a sound compressed at a 3:1 ratio consumes one third of its original memory, and a sound compressed at a 6:1 ratio takes up one sixth of its original space.

The Built-in recording program, which Apple provides with microphone-equipped models of the Macintosh, also provides two compression ratios: 3:1 and 6:1. However, the Built-in program offers only a 22kHz sampling rate.

Other recording and sound-editing programs offer different sampling ratios. For example, the SoundEdit Pro application from Macromedia can compress sounds at ratios of 8:1, 6:1, 4:1, and 3:1.

When you record a sound with SoundWave, you can compress the sound by choosing the Compress command under the Wave menu. SoundWave then displays a dialog window in which you can specify a compression ratio of 3:1 or 6:1. Unless you choose the Compress command and specifically set a compression ratio, SoundWave doesn't apply compression when it records or plays a sound.

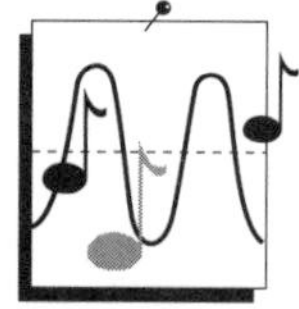

TECH TALK

The MACE Compression System

The enhanced Sound Manager, which Apple introduced with System 6.0.7, includes a set of sound-compression software routines known collectively as Macintosh Audio Compression and Expansion (MACE).

A MACE kit is available as a separate product from APDA (the Apple Programmer's and Developer's Association). APDA's address is 750 Laurel Wood Drive, Santa Clara, CA. The telephone number is 800-282-2732.

MACE, like SoundWave, can compress sampled sound in two ratios: 3:1 or 6:1. Thus, SoundWave can decompress and play back sounds that have been compressed with the MACE system.

Applications that use MACE to compress sampled sounds can decompress the sound and play it back in two different ways. An application can decompress the sound in real time, as it is being played back, or it can decompress the sound, store it in a buffer, and then play it back from the buffer. That means that sound can play in the background while the Macintosh's central processor carries out other tasks. Therefore, applications that perform screen updates or accept user input—particularly animation and multimedia applications—should expand and play back sound using the buffered method. ❍

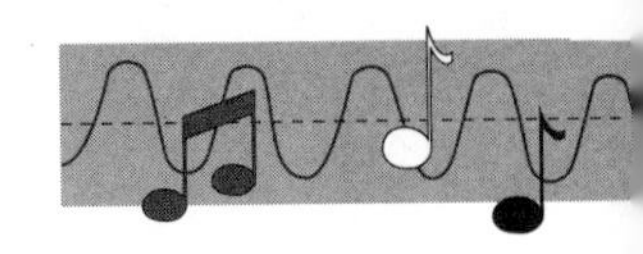

Compression Trade-Offs

When you compress a sampled sound, there are trade-offs, of course—the more a sound is compressed, the lower is its fidelity. When SoundWave compresses sound at a ratio of 3:1, a small amount of hiss is added when the sound is decompressed and played back. This hiss is not too noticeable when sound is played back through the small internal speaker built into the Macintosh.

When sampled sound is compressed at a 6:1 ratio, the loss in quality is much more noticeable; in fact, the frequency response of a sound is cut in half when it is compressed at a ratio of 6:1 and then decompressed at playback time. Still, a 6:1 compression ratio can be useful for recording voice and sound effects in situations where extremely high-quality sound is not required.

Calculating the Results of Compression

You can calculate the approximate amount of disk space that is needed to save a compressed sound. Just multiply the duration of the sound by the sampling rate, and divide the result by the compression ratio. This is the formula:

$$\frac{\text{Seconds of Sound} \times \text{Sampling Rate}}{\text{Compression Ratio}} = \text{Storage Space}$$

As an illustration of how this formula works, a 30-second sound recorded at 22kHz and saved with a 3:1 compression ratio consumes 220K of disk space. Or, in mathematical terms:

$$(30 \times 22\text{kHz}) / 3 = 220\text{K}$$

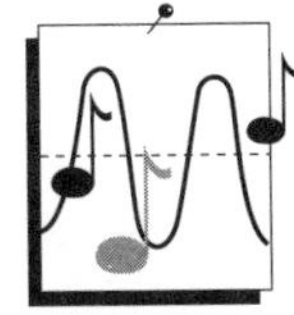

BY THE WAY

Compact Pro Doesn't Hurt Sounds

The data on the disk that comes with this book wasn't compressed with a sound-compression system, so it hasn't been subjected to any degradation. It was compressed using the Compact Pro application, which compresses data and then restores it to exactly the same contents that it had when it was compressed. Some of the sampled sounds on your bonus disk have been compressed using sound-compression systems, but none of the data on the disk has been degraded in any way by compressing it with Compact Pro. ❍

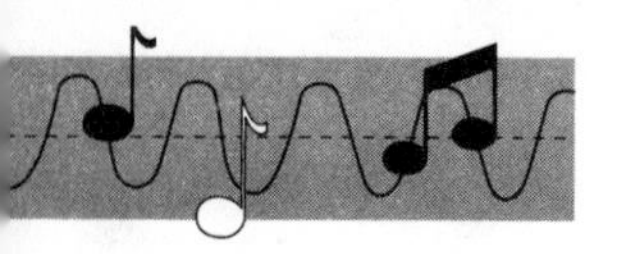

Alternatives to Compression

No matter how much you increase the compression of your sounds and lower their sampling rates, you may still sometimes find that you don't have enough RAM available to store the sounds you need. In case you encounter that problem, here are some suggestions for making the best use of the memory you have available:

- If you're not using System 7, turn MultiFinder off.
- Allocate more memory to SoundWave, HyperCard, or other programs that you use to record, edit, and play sounds. For details on how to do that, see the documentation that came with your Macintosh.
- Turn the RAM cache off in your control panel.
- If you have a color monitor, open your Monitors control and switch to the black-and-white monitor setting.

For more tips on conserving memory, consult the documentation that came with your Macintosh.

The Sound Window

SoundWave can display three kinds of windows:

- **Sound windows**—in which sounds are displayed and edited
- **Scope window**—can help set sound levels prior to a recording session
- **Spectrum windows**—which can display a three-dimensional or two-dimensional spectrum analysis of a sound

The sound window, shown in Figure 4–2 at the beginning of this chapter, is SoundWave's main window. The other SoundWave windows are described under their own headings later in this chapter.

SoundWave can open up to four sound windows at once, with a separate sound displayed in each window. When multiple sound windows are open, you can move them around freely and view them in the conventional Macintosh "front window active" fashion. You can also place them in tiled or stacked arrangements by selecting the Stack Windows command or the Tile Windows command from the Display menu.

The sound window is a standard Macintosh document window with a standard set of window controls: a title bar, a close box, a zoom box, and a resizing box. All of the controls work in the standard ways, and there are

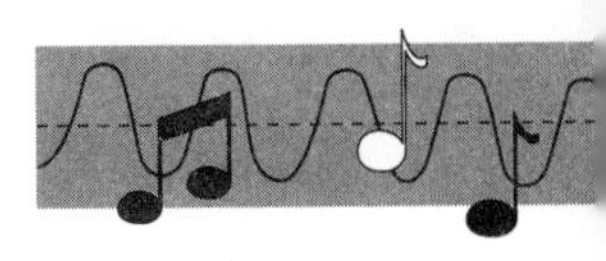

also some extra features. Just below the title bar, there's a long, ribbon-shaped rectangle called a scroller. Just below the scroller, there's another rectangle called the information bar, which is labeled in Figure 4–9.

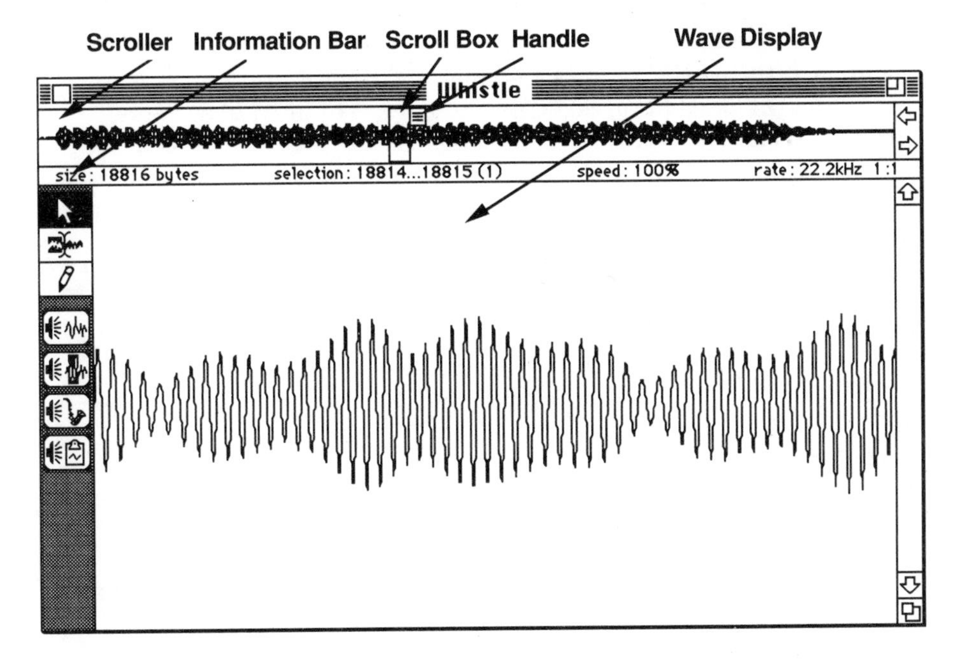

Figure 4–9. Sound window components

The sound window's content region—the large rectangle that fills most of the window's space—is called a wave display. As Figure 4–9 shows, both the scroller rectangle and the wave display region contain images of sound waves.

The Scroller, Scroll Box, and Handle

When you open a sound file with SoundWave, a waveform that represents the entire file is displayed in the scroller. Part of the waveform is magnified and shown in the wave display—either in the form of dots, as shown earlier in this chapter in Figure 4–2, or in the form of a continuous wave, as shown in Figure 4–9. Information about the currently open sound file is displayed in the information bar.

You can't adjust the width of the scroller ribbon or the width of the wave display. The scroller always displays a complete sound, and the wave display shows whatever part of that sound can be magnified and placed inside the wave display rectangle. Therefore, SoundWave always calculates the

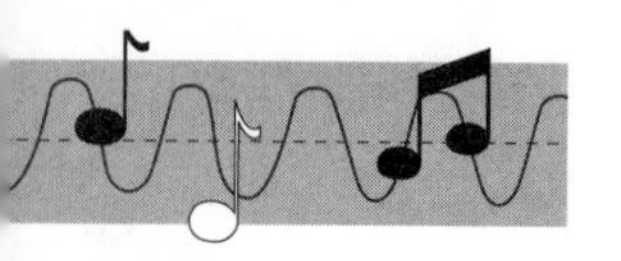

contents of the scroller and the wave display automatically, depending upon how long the active sound sequence is, and upon how much of the sound's waveform fits inside the wave display.

Inside the scroller ribbon, there's a smaller outlined area called the *scroll box.* The portion of the open sound file that you see in the scroll box is the same as the portion of the sound file that's shown in the wave display.

If the active sound file is small, the scroll box is comparatively large, because a relatively large portion of the total sound found can be displayed in the wave display. If the active sound file is large, the wave display can show only a small portion of the complete sound, so the scroll box is shown in a smaller size; it can even show up as just a line, if the sound file is very large.

The small rectangle next to the upper right-hand corner of the scroll box is called a *handle.* With the handle, you can drag the scroll box back and forth along the scroller ribbon.

There are three ways to move the scroll box: by dragging the scroll box itself; by dragging its handle; or by clicking on the scroll arrows at the right-hand end of the scroller.

The scroller ribbon serves two purposes:

- With the mouse, menu commands, or keyboard commands, you can select all or part of the sound displayed in the scroller. Then you can cut, paste, or copy the part of the sound that you have selected, in the same way that you would cut, paste, or copy text using a word processor. You can copy your selection from one part of a sound file to another, or to a completely different sound file.
- By dragging the scroll box back and forth inside the scroller, you can change the portion of the currently active sound file that is shown in the wave display. You can drag the scroll box by its handle, or you can move it by clicking on the small arrows to the right of the scroller.

There are two command-key equivalents for mouse operations in the scroller:

- **Command-B—**scrolls to the beginning of the current selection
- **Command-E—**scrolls to the end of the current selection

The Wave Display

The large rectangle that appears below the scroller—and occupies most of the space in the sound window—is called the *wave display.* The wave display shows a magnified view of the part of the active sound file that is enclosed by the scroll box inside the scroller. Each byte of sound in the sound wave—stored in memory as a number from 0 to 255—is displayed as a single dot in

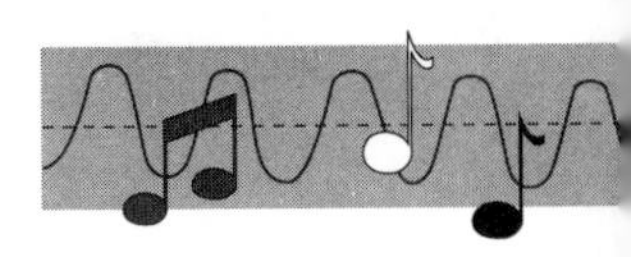

the wave display. But by toggling the Connect the Dots command under the Display menu, you can join the dots that make up the wave display so that they describe a recognizable waveform, as shown in Figure 4–9.

The Information Bar

The long horizontal rectangle between the scroller and the wave display is called the *information bar.* It contains information about the currently active sound file: the size of the file in bytes, the location and length of any currently selected sound segment, the playback speed, and the sampling rate.

The Tools Palette

To the left of the sound window's wave display, there is a palette of tools that you can use to play and edit sounds. The tools in the tools palette, and their names, are shown earlier in this chapter in Figure 4–4.

The Pointer

The pointer tool, shaped like an arrow, works much like the pointer in Macintosh applications such as MacPaint, MacDraw, and the Finder. You can use it to operate scroll bars, select menu commands, and choose options in dialogs.

The I-Beam

The I-beam tool, as you have seen, works like the I-beam tool in word-processing applications such as MacWrite and Microsoft Word. You can select waveforms or portions of waveforms by placing the I-beam tool on the waveform in the scroller of the wave display, holding down the mouse button, and dragging the mouse. Then you can perform various operations on the selection you have made. You can cut, copy, and clear sounds; move sounds from one part of a file to another or between files; and apply special effects to sounds.

When you have selected a sound or part of a sound, you can play the portion of the sound that you have selected by clicking on the Play Selection tool in the tools palette.

When you have made a selection with the I-beam tool, you can use the Copy command from the Edit menu to copy your selection to the SoundWave clipboard. Then you can use still another tool, the Play Clipboard tool, to play the segment you have copied to the clipboard. When you have copied a sound to the clipboard, you can place an insertion point inside the scroller or the

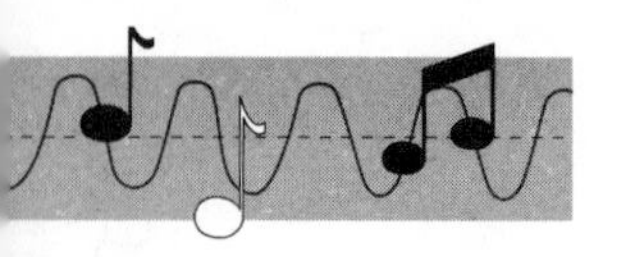

wave display and paste your selection back into the currently active sound file. You can use the same technique to paste your selection into another sound file.

To select a segment of the currently active sound file without dragging the mouse, you can click on the I-beam tool in the tools palette, and then Shift-click at either the beginning or end of the sound segment that you want to select. Shift-clicking is a handy method for selecting part of a sound when the whole sound is too long to fit inside the wave display window.

If you are making a selection in the wave display, and you move the mouse outside the left or right border of the wave display, the display scrolls automatically to follow the movement of the mouse. When you have placed the insertion point where you want it, you can select the segment by dragging the I-beam across the waveform. Alternatively, you can click the mouse at one end of your selection and then Shift-click at the other end, to select all of the waveform in between.

When you are using the I-beam tool, you can substitute the following command-key operations for mouse operations:

- **Command-H**—moves the left edge of the selection slightly to the left
- **Command-J**—moves the left edge of the selection slightly to the right
- **Command-K**—moves the right edge of the selection slightly to the left
- **Command-L**—moves the right edge of the selection slightly to the right

The Pencil

The pencil tool works much like the pencil tool in graphics programs such as MacPaint. The pencil tool is handy for making minor modifications to sounds. With it, you can make changes in a sound wave by displaying the wave in the sound window and then sketching in your changes. Your penciled-in changes actually change the way the waveform sounds. If you move the pencil past the left or right edge of the wave display when you are editing in changes, the display scrolls as the pencil tool moves.

You can't use the pencil tool in the scroller ribbon, or when you're working with a compressed sound.

The Play Sound Tool

The Play Sound tool plays the complete sound displayed in the scroller window from beginning to end, no matter where the insertion point is placed.

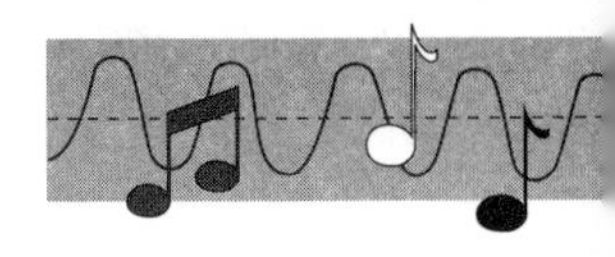

The Play Selection Tool

The Play Selection tool plays any sound segment that you have selected. If you haven't selected a portion of a sound, Play Selection plays the complete sound displayed in the scroller window.

The Play Instrument Tool

The Play Instrument tool can play a sound stored as a Studio Session file, provided the sound was recorded at a sampling rate of 11kHz with no compression. Also, the sound must be more than 1480 bytes long and no longer than 32,767 bytes. You can check to see whether a sound meets these specifications by examining the information bar. Studio Session files are described in more detail in Appendix F. For more information on compression ratios, see the section "Using SoundWave."

The Play Clipboard Tool

The Play Clipboard tool shows the sound segment most recently copied or clipped to the SoundWave clipboard, if there is one. With the Play Clipboard tool, you can listen to sounds copied to the clipboard before you paste them into other sounds.

Using the SoundWave Tools

At the beginning of this chapter, in the section "Using SoundWave," you learned how to open and play a sound called Melodrama. In the remainder of this section, you'll get a chance to open and edit some other prerecorded sounds.

Opening a Sound Resource

Before you can use the tools in the tools palette, you must have a sound resource or a sound file to work on. (SoundWave can open sounds stored as sound resources, as well as sounds stored as sound files. For more information about the various formats of sound resources and sound files, see Appendix F.)

To open a sound resource to edit, follow this list of steps:

1. Launch SoundWave (if it is not running already) and choose Open from the File menu.
2. Open the folder that holds the files you have copied from your bonus disk, and then open the Sounds and Music folder.

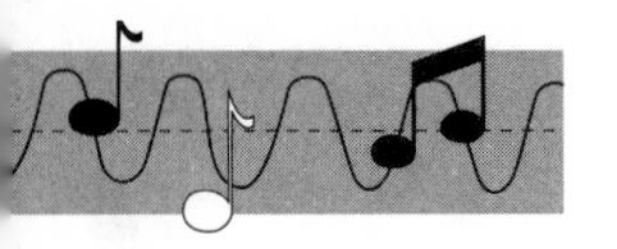

3. When SoundWave's Open dialog box appears, select Resource from the pop-up menu labeled Format. Then open the Sound Resources file.
4. From the list of sounds in the Sound Resources file, choose the sound 1–2–3–4.
5. If you like, you can play the sound by clicking on the Play Sound tool.

Cleaning up a Sound

The 1–2–3–4 sound is a series of four percussion sounds built into the Yamaha PSR-400 electronic keyboard instrument. The sound was recorded through the line input of a MacRecorder digitizer.

When you play the sound sequence, you may notice a small click at the end, just after the word *four.* In Figure 4–10, the click is labeled; it is a small dot near the right-hand end of the scroller ribbon.

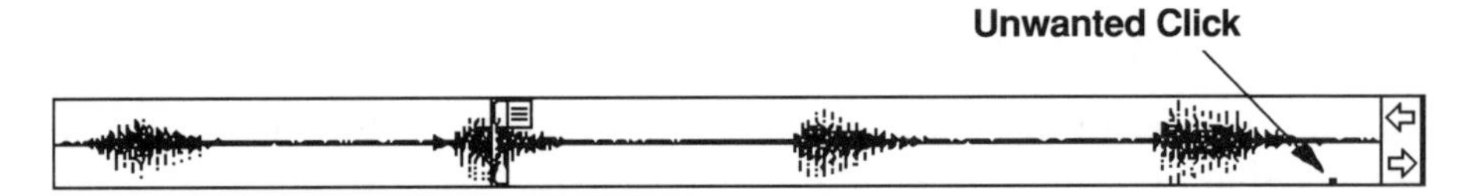

Figure 4–10. Unwanted click in scroller

You can easily eliminate the click in the 1–2–3–4 sound by using SoundWave's Cut command. Here's how:

1. Choose the I-beam cursor from the tools palette.
2. In the scroller display, hold down the mouse button and move the mouse to select the portion of the sound that contains the click, as shown in Figure 4–11.

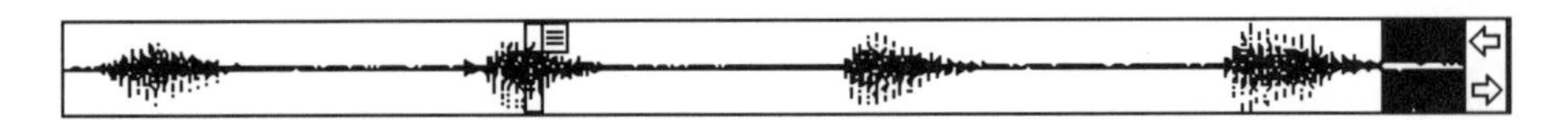

Figure 4–11. Selecting click in scroller

3. To make sure that you have selected the correct sound segment, play the portion of the sound that you have selected by clicking on the Play Selection tool.
4. If there is anything wrong with your selection, repeat step 3. When you are satisfied with your selection, choose Cut from the Edit menu or type the command's keyboard equivalent, Command-X. The portion of the sound you have selected then disappears.

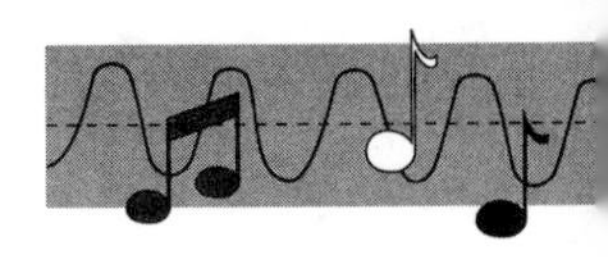

5. Play the 1–2–3–4 sound again by selecting the Play Sound tool. The click is now gone. As a side benefit, you have also saved a few bytes of memory by eliminating some unneeded silence at the end of the sound.
6. If you want to save the sound in its new, cleaner form, choose Save or Save As from the File menu and save your sound. If you don't see any need to keep the original sound file, you can write over the old file by choosing Save. If you want to preserve the old file as well as copying it into a new version, use the Save As command.

Editing a Sound

You can also use SoundWave's Cut, Copy, and Paste commands to make some more substantial changes in the 1–2–3–4 sound file. For example, by following these steps, you can change the order of the words that make up the file:

1. In the scroller, select the third burst of sound in the file—the word *three*—as shown in Figure 4–12.

Figure 4–12. The word* three *selected

2. Before you delete the sound segment that you have selected, listen to it by clicking on the Play Selection tool. You should hear the word *three.* If you hear something else, try step 1 again.
3. Select Cut from the Edit menu, or type Command-X. The selected sound segment disappears.
4. Move the SoundWave insertion point to a point halfway between the first two sound bursts—the words *one* and *two.*
5. When the insertion point is in the correct place, paste the word *three* into its new location by selecting the Paste command or by typing its keyboard equivalent, Command-V. The sound segment that you have cut now appears in its new location, as shown in Figure 4–13.

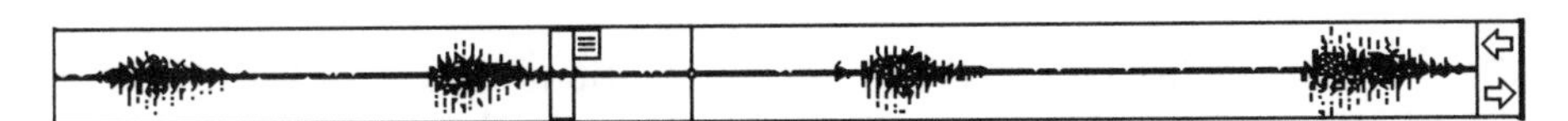

Figure 4–13. The word* three *reinserted

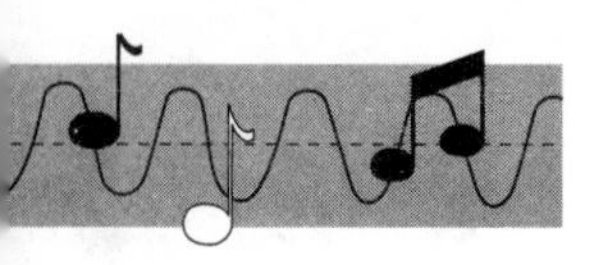

6. Play the edited sound by clicking on the Play Sound command. The digitized voice now says, "1–3–2–4."
7. By moving the word *three* to a new location, you may have disturbed the rhythm of the sound sequence 1–2–3–4. If that has happened, you can adjust the periods of silence between the sounds until you have corrected the rhythm of the sound segment.

   You can substitute silence for a segment of a sound by selecting the section of the sound that you want to silence and then choosing the Silence command under the Wave menu. Alternatively, you can use the Copy menu command to copy a segment of sound that is already silent to the clipboard. Then you can use the Paste command to paste the segment of silence that you have copied into another part of the sound that you are editing. This is a tricky procedure, so be sure to save your work often, and remember that practice makes perfect (sometimes).
8. When you have finished editing the 1–2–3–4 sound, you may want to save it under a new name by choosing the Save As command under the File menu. Remember that if you simply save it with the Save command, you'll write over the original sound, which says "1–2–3–4" in the correct order. Fortunately, assuming you have extracted the files on your bonus disk in accordance with the instructions in Chapter 1, you'll always have a backup copy of the 1–2–3–4 sound on your bonus disk, even if you inadvertently destroy the extracted sound.

SoundWave Menus

When a sound window is open, the SoundWave menu bar contains five menus: File, Edit, Wave, Display, and Custom. Under the headings that follow, the SoundWave menu commands are examined in some detail. There's additional information about some of the menu commands you have used, and there's new information about the commands you haven't yet had a chance to try.

The File Menu

The SoundWave File menu contains the traditional Macintosh File commands, plus a Record command that's used in sound recording.

Record

The Record command, as you have seen, opens a Record dialog so you can record a sound. Record then creates a new Untitled window that you can use to record a new sound.

New

The New command opens a new Untitled sound window. You can then copy prerecorded sounds from other sources into your new Untitled window.

Open

The Open command displays a dialog window that you can use to select and open a sound file or a sound resource. (You can store sounds on disks in two formats: as sound resources or sound files. SoundWave can load, save, and process sounds stored in both formats. For more information about the various kinds of sound resources and sound files that the Macintosh uses, see Appendix F.)

When you select the Open menu command and SoundWave displays the Open dialog box, you can specify the kind of sound that you want to open by clicking on a pop-up menu labeled Format. With the Format pop-up menu, you can instruct the Open dialog box to list only the names of files or only the names of resources.

When you choose a file or a resource and click on the Open button, SoundWave opens a sound file and displays the sound's waveform in the scroller and wave display windows.

Close

The Close command closes any currently active SoundWave window.

Save

The Save command displays the Save dialog window shown earlier in Figure 4–8. You can then save the currently active sound file. By selecting commands from the pop-up menu labeled Format, you can save a sound file in any one of five formats: SoundWave, Audio AIFF, Sound Studio Instrument, Numeric, and the sound Resource format. Figure 4–1, at the beginning of this chapter, shows the icons of several popular kinds of sound files. For more on the formats of sound resources and sound files, see Appendix F.

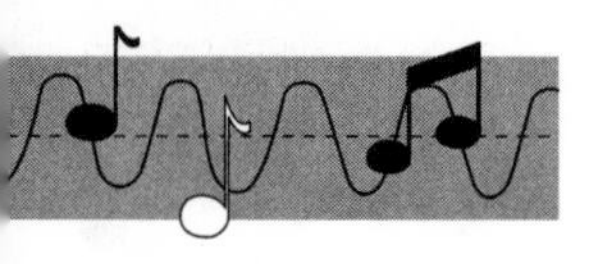

When you save a sound file with the Save command, it's important to remember that SoundWave saves the file in its current form, and that any previous versions of the sound are lost. Therefore, it's safer to save files using the Save As command, which is described under the next heading.

Save As

The Save As command also opens the Save dialog window. You can then save the currently active sound file at a destination you choose and under a name you choose. If you select a portion of a sound and then choose Save As, the Save As dialog displays a check box that you can use to save only the portion of the sound file that you have selected.

Get Info

The Get Info menu command displays important information about the currently active sound file in a dialog like the one shown in Figure 4–14. The dialog shows the title of the active sound window, the sampling rate used for recording, the compression ratio, the sound's size in relation to free memory, the amount of memory that is free, the length of the selected sound segment (if any), and the contents of the SoundWave clipboard.

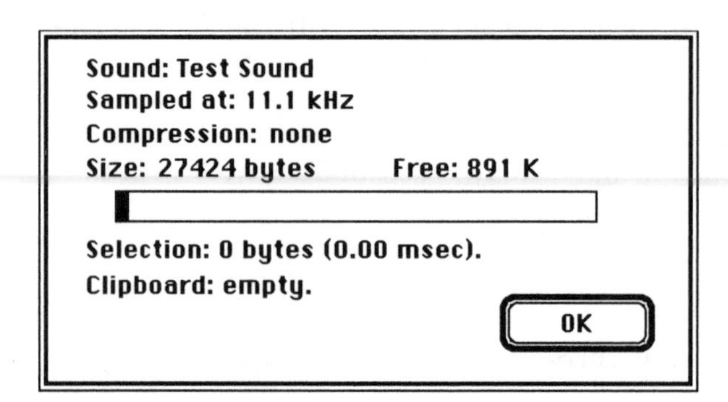

Figure 4–14. Info dialog

Page Setup, Print Options, Print, and Quit

The Page Setup, Print Options, and Print commands set up your printer and a sound file for printing, and then print the file.

The Page Setup command displays a standard Macintosh Page Setup dialog that you can use to set printer and page options.

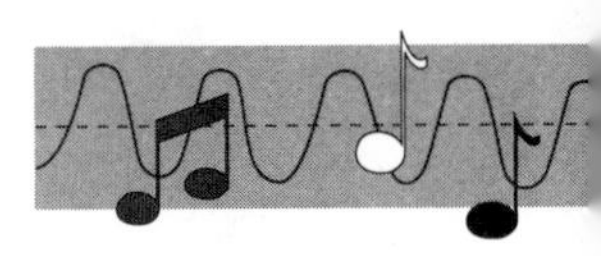

The Print Options command, shown in Figure 4–15, displays a dialog that provides special options for printing SoundWave files. The scaling options in the Print Options dialog allow you to scale your printout so that it prints a specified amount of sound on each page. The dialog also contains a Print Selection Only button, which you can use to print only a portion of sound that you have selected in the SoundWave scroller or the wave display window.

Print Options

Horizontal Scaling: ◉ 1:1 ○ 2:1 ○ 4:1

Vertical Scaling: ◉ 1:1 ○ 2:1 ○ 4:1

☐ Print Selection Only

Cancel OK

Figure 4–15. Print Options dialog

When you have set your printing preferences with the Print Options menu, you can select the Print command to print sound files.

The Quit menu command quits the SoundWave application.

The Edit Menu

The SoundWave Edit menu includes all of the standard editing functions —Cut, Copy, Paste, Clear, and Undo—as well as several special sound-related commands.

Undo, Cut, Copy, Paste, and Clear

These are standard commands that perform standard Macintosh operations. Before you can use a Cut, Copy, or Clear command, you must select a portion of a waveform in either the SoundWave scroller or the wave display window. You can make selections with the I-beam tool, the SoundWave menu, or keyboard commands. When you have selected a sound or a portion of a sound, you can cut your selection, clear it, or copy it to the SoundWave clipboard.

When you have cut or copied a sound, you can paste it back into the same file it came from, or into a different file. The SoundWave Edit menu is a powerful tool for editing sounds.

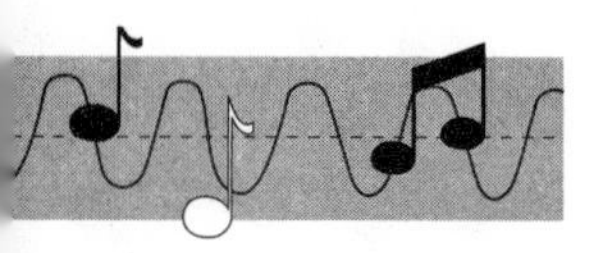

Mix

With the Mix command, you can mix a sound on the SoundWave clipboard with a sound in a SoundWave window. The Mix command displays a dialog window like the one shown in Figure 4–16.

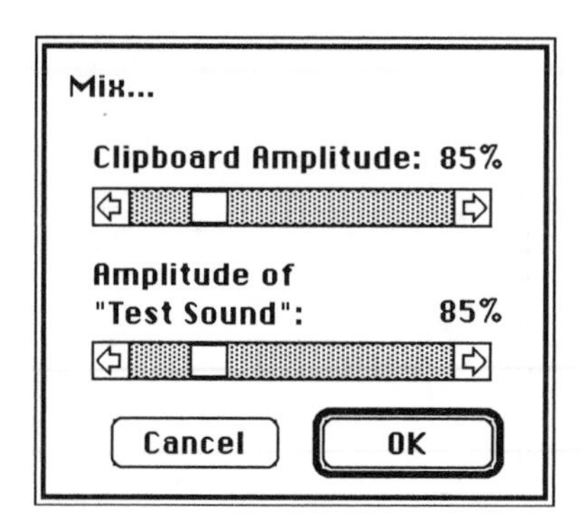

Figure 4–16. Mix dialog

When you mix sounds, they blend together, starting at a specified insertion point and continuing for the duration of the sound. To mix one sound with another with SoundWave, these are the steps to follow:

1. Open a sound by selecting Open under the File menu.
2. Using the I-beam tool, select the part of the sound that you want to mix.
3. Select the Copy command from the Edit menu. That copies your selection to the SoundWave clipboard.
4. Open another sound by selecting Open under the File menu.
5. In the wave display or the scroller window of the newly opened sound, use the I-beam tool to select the part of the sound you want to mix.
6. Choose the Mix command from the Edit menu. SoundWave mixes the two sounds and displays the waveform of the mixed sound in the scroller and wave display windows of the currently open sound.
7. With the slide controls in the Mix dialog, adjust the amplitude of each sound you are mixing (the sound on the clipboard and the currently open sound) until the sounds blend in the way you want them to.
8. When you have mixed a sound, audition it by clicking on the Play Selection button in the tools palette.
9. If you aren't satisfied with your sound, undo your mix by selecting the Undo command from the Edit menu. Then choose the Mix menu command again to remix the sound.

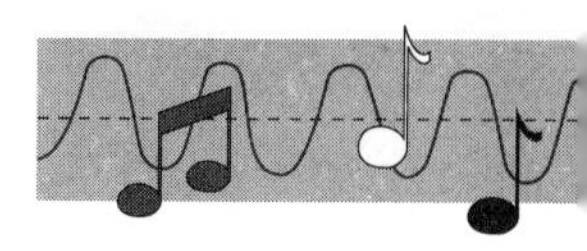

Play Options

The Play Options command displays a dialog window that allows you to set four options for the playback of your sound. The Play Options dialog is shown in Figure 4–17.

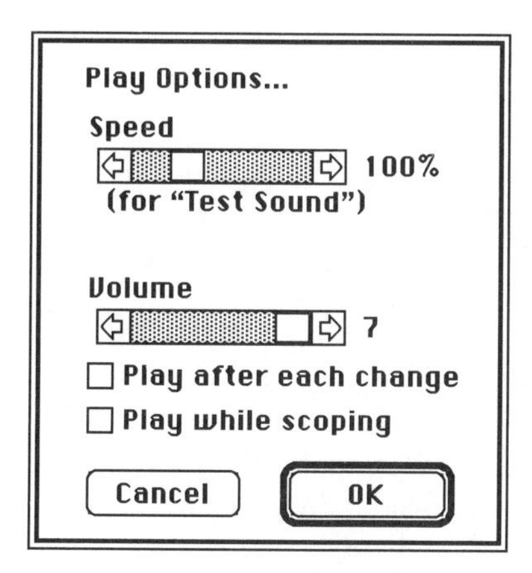

Figure 4–17. Play Options dialog box

By adjusting the slide controls in the Play Options dialog window, you can play the currently active sound file, or any portion of that file, at a specified speed and volume. The Play Options dialog box doesn't make any permanent changes in a sound file; it affects only the way the sound is played back. Thus, you can use Play Options to hear how various alterations would affect a sound. You can then use other commands to make permanent changes in the sound.

With the Play Options command, you can speed up or slow down the playback of sound, and you can play a sound louder or softer than the volume at which it was recorded.

Note that when you change the speed of a sound with the Play Options dialog, its pitch also changes; the effect of changing the speed of a sampled sound is similar to the effect you get when you speed up or slow down an analog record or a tape recording. But these changes aren't permanent; even if you make a change in a sound and then save the sound, your changes do not affect the sound file.

The Play Options window also contains two check boxes. If you check the box labeled *Play after each change,* SoundWave plays the currently active file anytime you make a change in it.

If you check the box marked *Play while scoping,* SoundWave plays any sound that is being adjusted using the scope window. The sound plays

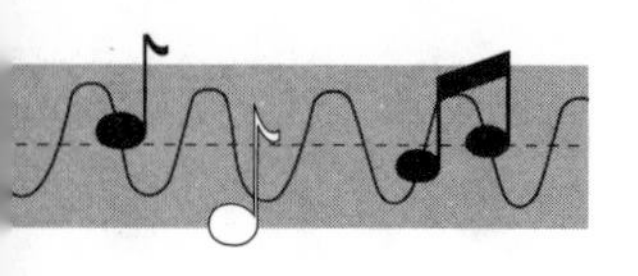

through the Macintosh speaker at the same time it is being recorded. (Procedures for using the scope window are listed earlier in this chapter, in the section "Using SoundWave.")

The Play while scoping option can be useful when you are recording sounds through a line input rather than through a microphone.

Studio Options

The Studio Options command allows you to set options affecting the playback of sounds stored in Studio Session files. When you select Studio Options, SoundWave opens a dialog that lets you specify what note you want played and what octave the note should be in. You can also specify whether you want the sound to play only once or whether you want it to play in a loop that lasts for as long as the mouse button is held down.

By storing a note in an Instrument file, you can save a considerable amount of memory, since a single note can be played at many different pitches and for many different lengths of time. However, to use these capabilities to their best advantage, you must play Instrument files using Studio Session from Bogas Productions, the application for which they were designed.

Select All

The Select All command selects the entire active sound file. It's an alternative to selecting a file by dragging or Shift-clicking. The keyboard equivalent of the Select All command is Command-A.

Show Beginning

The Show Beginning command moves the scroll box in the scroller to the beginning of any sound segment that is selected in the scroller or in the wave display. If no sound segment is selected, but there is an insertion point in either the scroller or the wave display, Show Beginning moves the scroll box to the insertion point. Command-B is the keyboard equivalent of the Show Beginning command.

Show End

The Show End command moves the scroll box in the scroller to the end of any sound segment that is selected in the scroller or in the wave display. If no sound segment is selected, but there is an insertion point in either the scroller or the wave display, the Show End command moves the scroll box to the insertion point. Command-E is the keyboard equivalent of the Show End command.

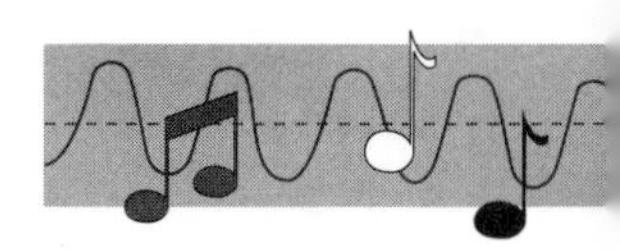

The Wave Menu

You can change the characteristics of a sound, or add special effects to a sound, by choosing commands from the Wave menu.

Most Wave menu commands act only on portions of a sound that are selected. Therefore, to add an effect that lasts through a complete sound, you should select the entire sound before executing the command. An easy way to do that is to choose the Select All command from the Edit menu.

The first six commands under the Wave menu—Filter, Delay, Amplify, Reverse, Silence, and Smooth—can change the amplitude of sounds and alter their waveforms to change their characteristics in various waves. The last three commands —Resample, Assume Rate, and Compress—change the sampling rates and compression ratios of sounds to save memory, and to correct the reproduction of sounds recorded with other applications.

It isn't difficult to understand how the first six Wave commands work. With a little experimentation, you can see and hear for yourself how these commands affect sounds.

However, to understand how the last three menus under the Wave menu work, it helps to have an understanding of sampling rates and compression ratios (see the section "Using SoundWave" earlier in this chapter).

Filter

The Filter command displays a dialog window that looks like a graphic equalizer, as shown in Figure 4–18. With the Filter command, you can equalize the amplitudes of the frequency bands in a sound or a portion of a sound by moving slide controls in the Filter dialog window.

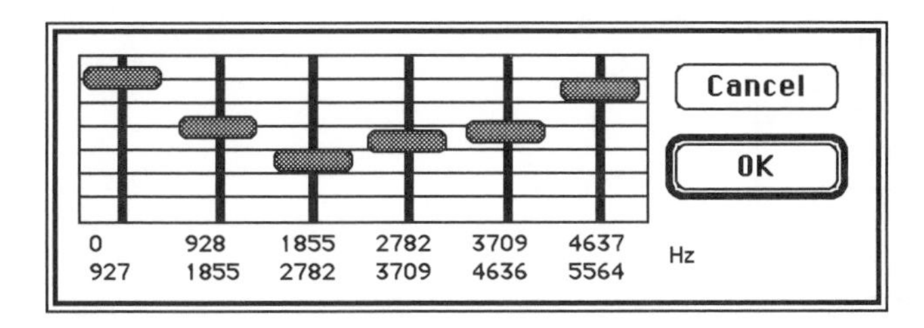

Figure 4–18. Filter dialog box

The slide controls in the Filter dialog work just like the slide controls on a graphic equalizer; each slider is a volume control for the frequency band labeled below it. The controls in the Filter dialog can amplify each frequency band shown from 0 percent to 200 percent.

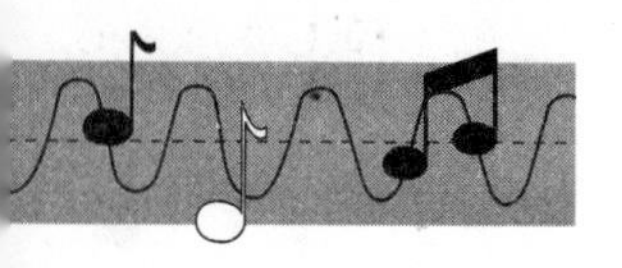

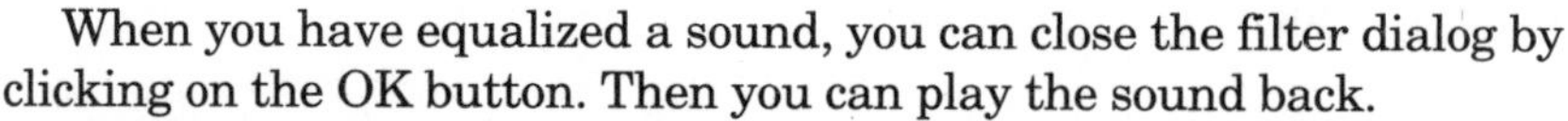

When you have equalized a sound, you can close the filter dialog by clicking on the OK button. Then you can play the sound back.

If you aren't pleased with the sound, you can select the Undo command from the Edit menu, choose the Filter command again, and reequalize the sound.

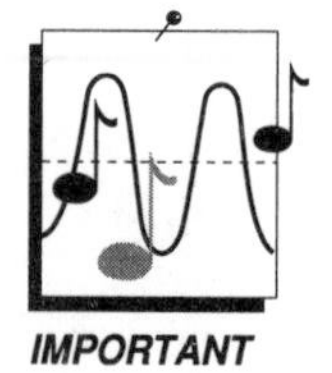

IMPORTANT

What Undo Can't Undo

Although the Undo command under the File menu can come in handy, you shouldn't put too much confidence in it. Remember that the Undo command reverses the effects of **the last command that was executed.** *You can't back it up any farther than that, so be careful.* ❍

Delay

The Delay command can create echo effects and other interesting sounds. When you add a delay to a waveform with the Delay command, a copy of the waveform is slightly delayed and then mixed with the original waveform. Then, when you play back the sound, you hear the original sound mixed with the delayed sound.

When you select a sound or a segment of a sound and execute the Delay command, SoundWave displays a dialog box like the one shown in Figure 4–19. You can then select the following:

- The amount of time delay that you want SoundWave to use
- The amplitude of the delayed sound
- The amplitude of the original sound

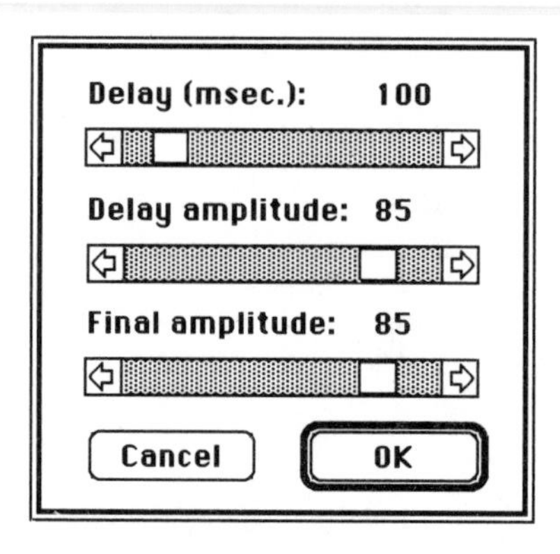

Figure 4–19. Delay dialog box

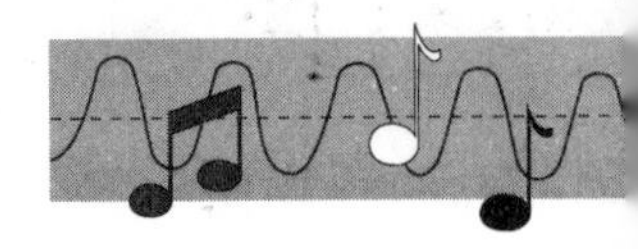

When you have added a delay to a sound, you can close the Delay dialog, audition the sound, and then save it. If you aren't satisfied with the sound, you can select Undo from the File menu, choose the Delay command again, and give it another try.

Amplify

You can adjust the amplitude of a sound or a selected sound segment with the Amplify command. You can increase the amplitude of the entire sound, or you can use the Amplify command to fade the sound in or out.

When you select Amplify, SoundWave displays a dialog like the one in Figure 4–20. The Amplification slide control, using the original amplitude of the sound as a guide, amplifies the sound at a level ranging from 1 percent to 400 percent of its original amplitude.

Amplification: 100%

Don't fade
Fade in
Fade out
Cancel
OK

Figure 4–20. Amplification dialog box

The radio buttons under Amplification Control are labeled *Don't fade, Fade in,* and *Fade out.* With these three buttons, you can increase the amplitude of your selection evenly from start to finish; fade the sound in to its specified amplitude; and fade the sound out to its specified amplitude.

Reverse

The Reverse command reverses the storage order of a selected sound file or sound segment. When you execute the Reverse command and then play back the sound, your selection plays backward. If you execute Reverse again, SoundWave restores your original sound.

Silence

With the Silence command, you can replace a selected sound segment with dead silence. If you make a mistake, you can undo your action by selecting Undo from the Edit menu.

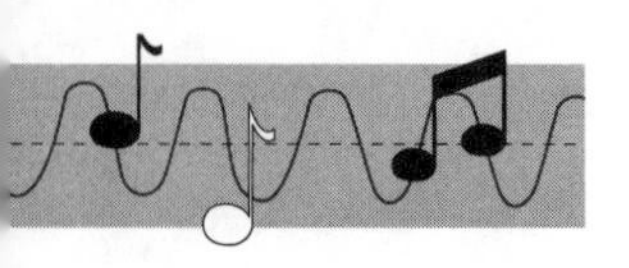

Smooth

The Smooth command averages out the amplitude variations in a sound or a segment of a sound by smoothing out changes in volume. When you smooth out a sound and play it back, it's less harsh around the edges than the original sound. You can undo the effects of the Smooth command by selecting Undo from the Edit menu.

Resample

SoundWave can sample sounds at four different rates: 22,000, 11,000, 7,400, and 5,500 bytes per second. With the Resample command, you can change the sampling rate of a selected sound from its original rate to a lower rate, but you can't raise it. When you resample a sound at a lower rate, it consumes less memory but its quality suffers. (For more about sampling rates, see the section "Using SoundWave" earlier in this chapter.)

The Resample command, unlike most of the commands under the Wave menu, affects the entire active sound file—not just a selected portion of the sound.

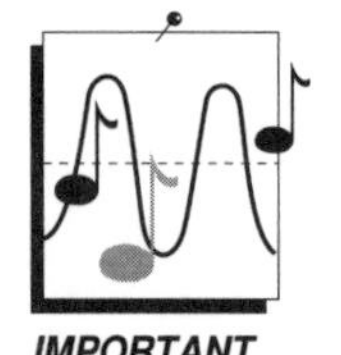

IMPORTANT

Warning: You Can't Undo the Resampling Command!

Resample is a menu command that you should use with caution. **The Undo command does not work with Resample, as it does with most other SoundWave menu commands.** *Furthermore, if you resample a sound at a lower rate and then save it—replacing the sound from which it came—you'll never be able to resample it at its original rate and restore its original quality.* ❍

Assume Rate

With the Assume Rate command, you can adjust the sampling rates of sounds not recorded with SoundWave so that they play back properly. Assume Rate doesn't change the contents of a sound file—just the way that it is interpreted.

The Assume Rate command affects the entire active sound file, not just a selected segment of a sound.

Compress

When you select the Compress command, SoundWave displays a dialog box like the one in Figure 4–21. You can then click on the 3:1 button to compress the open sound at a 3:1 ratio, or you can click on the 6:1 button to compress the sound at a 6:1 ratio. If you click on Cancel, or if you don't

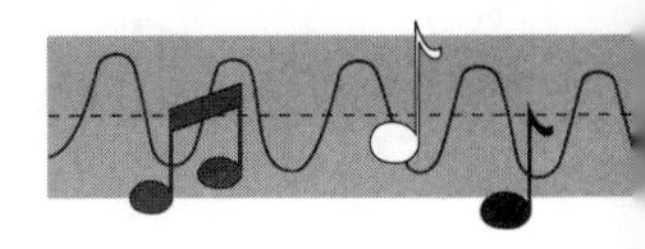

use the Compress command, SoundWave records and plays sounds with no compression.

A warning: Use the Compress command with caution. When you've compressed a file and saved it, you can't restore it to its decompressed form. The safest way to use the Compress command is to save a copy of the file under a new name, and then compress the *copy*, not the original file.

Compress "Woop Woop" at:

◉ 3:1 ○ 6:1

Cancel OK

Figure 4–21. Compression dialog box

The Display Menu

The commands under the Display menu give you control over the windows that SoundWave displays and over the appearance of the waveforms shown in the windows.

Spectrum

The Spectrum window displays a two-dimensional or three-dimensional spectrum analysis of the currently active sound file. For more details on the Spectrum window, see the heading "The Spectrum Window" later in this chapter.

Connect the Dots

When SoundWave opens the sound window, the waveform shown in the wave display window is made up of dots that represent the actual bit-by-bit sampling of the sound. By selecting the Connect the Dots command, you can join the dots in the Display window. Then you can see the waveform display that the dots describe.

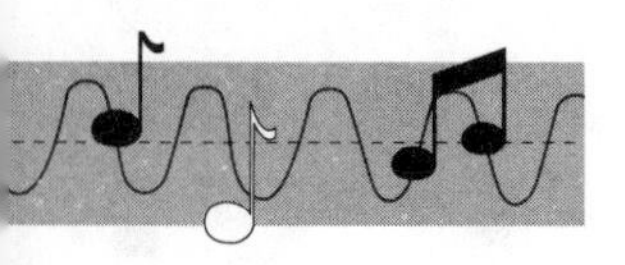

Stack Windows

The Stack Windows command stacks all the open sound windows, one on top of the other, offsetting them slightly from the upper left-hand corner of the screen.

Tile Windows

The Tile Windows command arranges all the open sound windows side by side on the screen.

The Window List

When you are using SoundWave and have one or more windows open, SoundWave lists the names of all open sound and spectrum windows under the Display menu, just below the Stack Windows and Tile Windows commands. If you select a window from this window list, it becomes active and is brought to the front of your desktop.

The Custom Menu

SoundWave is part of the Authorware Professional, a program created by Authorware, Inc., for designing multimedia applications. When you design an Authorware application that makes use of SoundWave, you can add custom commands to SoundWave and place them under the Custom menu. To add customized commands to the SoundWave program that comes with this book, you must own the Authorware Professional program.

In the version of SoundWave that comes with this book, two Custom commands are defined: About Custom, which displays an About box, and a Tone Generator command.

Tone Generator

The Tone Generator command generates sine waves. As you may recall from Chapter 2, a sine wave is a simple waveform generated by a sound with just one frequency and one amplitude.

When you select the Tone Generator command, SoundWave displays a dialog box like the one shown in Figure 4–22. By filling in the text boxes in that dialog, you can generate up to four sine waves with different frequencies and amplitudes. Then you can display them in the sound window and save the file if you like.

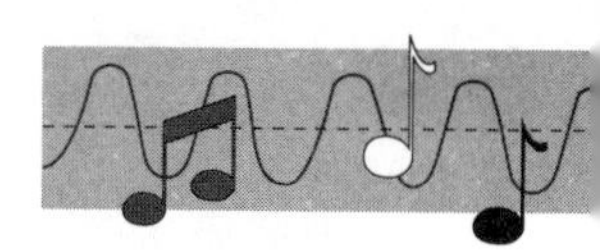

Tone Generator

This utility will generate up to four sine waves of different frequency and amplitude.

Length is entered in bytes. A value of 22255 produces one second of sound.

Period is entered in bytes. Twenty-two bytes gives a 1 kHz tone.

Amplitude should be from 0 to 127.

Length 2225

Wave	period	amplitude
1	44	117
2	1	0
3	1	0
4	1	0

Cancel OK

Figure 4–22. Tone Generator dialog box

You can enter the length, in bytes, of each sound you want generated. A value of 22kHz produces one second of sound.

You can also enter the period, in bytes, of each sound you want generated. A value of 22 bytes produces a 1kHz tone.

Finally, you can set the amplitude of each sound you want generated, using a value ranging from 0 to 127.

If you use the Tone Generator command to create more than one tone, SoundWave mixes the sounds you have created. You can then listen to the harmonics that make up the sounds.

Using the Tone Generator Command

With the Tone Generator command, you can display a sine wave in the SoundWave program's sound window by following these instructions:

1. Open a sound window by selecting the New command from the File window.

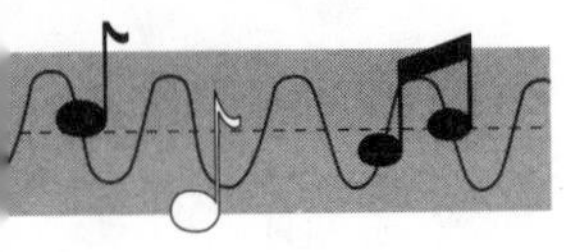

2. Select the Tone Generator command from the Custom menu. When the Tone Generator dialog box appears, type in the numbers that are shown in Figure 4–22. Then close the dialog window by clicking on the OK button. SoundWave responds by opening the sound window and presenting the display shown in Figure 4–23.

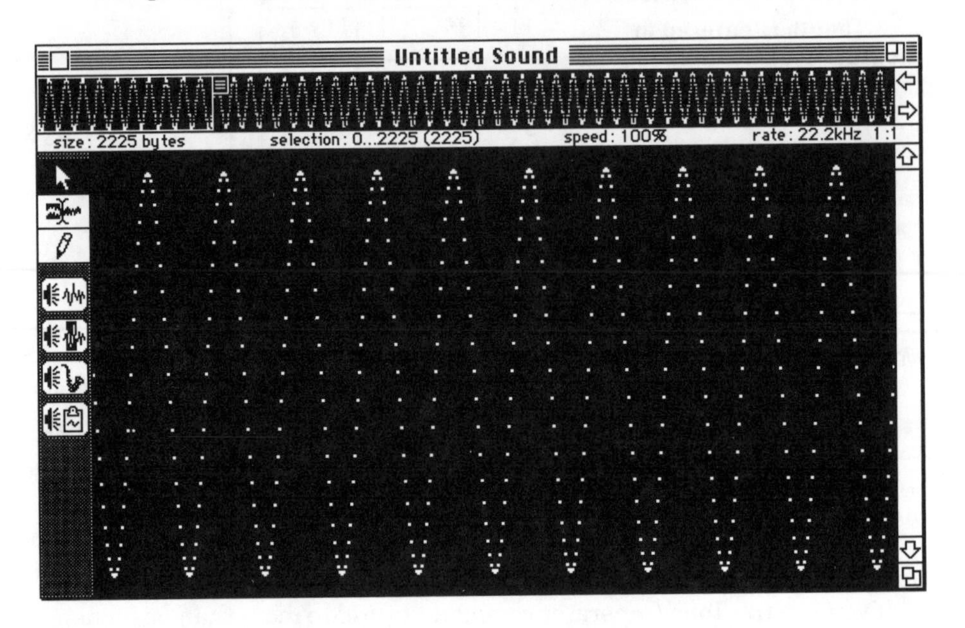

Figure 4–23. Tone-generation waveform

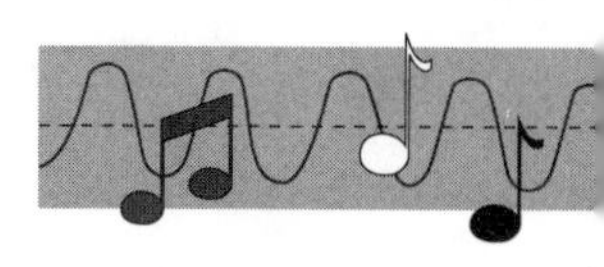

3. If the scroller window and the wave display are darkened—as they are in Figure 4–23—that is because the entire waveform in the wave display is currently selected. You can deselect the displayed waveform by clicking on the I-beam tool and then clicking anywhere within the large sound window. The sound window should then lighten up, like the window shown in Figure 4–24.

Figure 4–24. Deselected sine wave

4. To connect the dots in the wave display window so that you can see the waveform of the displayed sound, choose the Connect the Dots command from the Display menu. SoundWave then completes its drawing of the waveform, as shown in Figure 4–25.

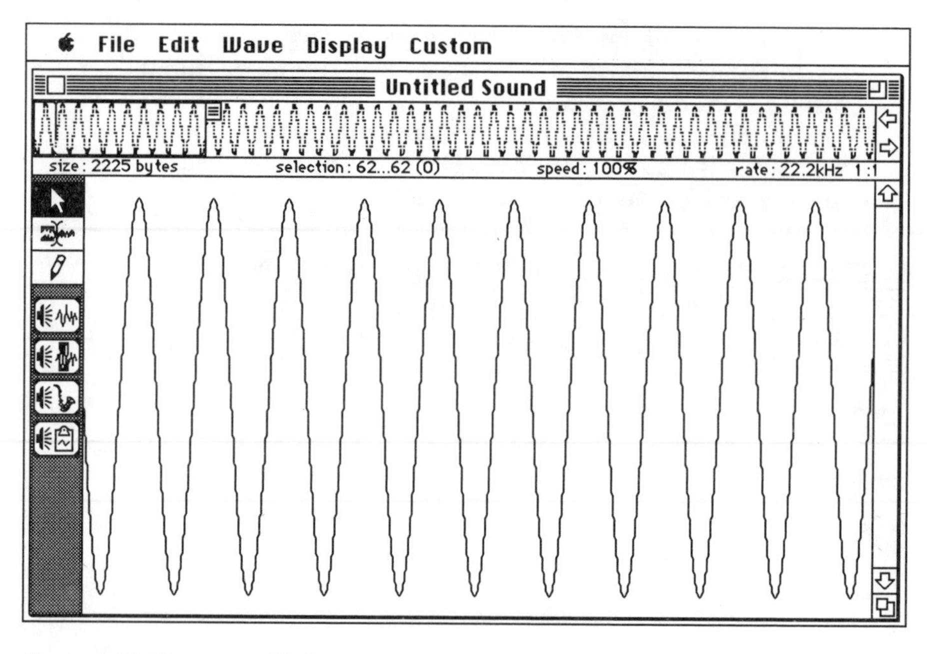

Figure 4–25. Sine wave with dots connected

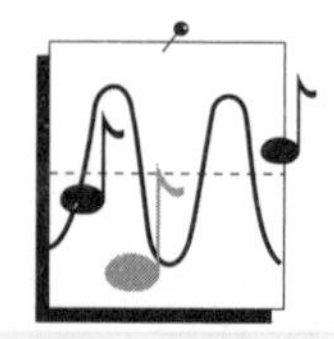

TECH TALK

Sine Waves

*A **sine wave,** as you might guess from its name, a wave with a form that describes a geometrical figure called a **sine.** A sine wave is a smooth, gently rolling wave with a pure and pleasing—if somewhat boring—sound.*

Mathematically, a sine is the ordinate of the endpoint of an arc of a unit circle centered at the origin of a Cartesian coordinate system. And a sine curve is the graph of the equation $y = \sin x$.

A sine wave is one of the simplest kinds of sound waves, but also one of the most important. You can synthesize any kind of sound wave by combining sine waves that have various frequencies and amplitudes. ❍

The Spectrum Window

As mentioned earlier in this chapter, SoundWave can display three kinds of windows: sound windows, scope windows, and spectrum windows. Spectrum windows can display a three-dimensional or two-dimensional spectrum analysis of a sound.

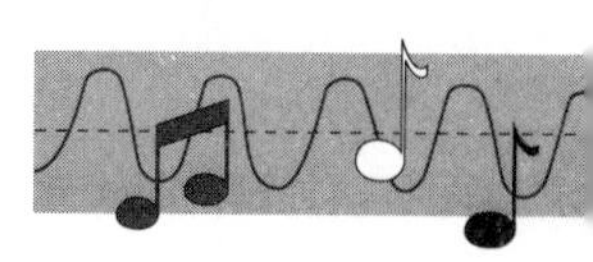

Spectrum Analysis

Every sound wave has a particular *spectrum* that is defined by the harmonics that make it up.

To examine the spectrum of a sound wave, audio engineers sometimes use a device called a *spectrum analyzer*. A typical spectrum analyzer is a small box with an array of LEDs on the front panel. When you feed a signal into a spectrum analyzer, its LEDs light up to show how much sound of various frequencies the signal contains. Some spectrum analyzers can produce a spectrum analysis in printed form.

A spectrum analysis can describe a sound wave in two domains: the time domain and the frequency domain. An analysis of a sound wave in the *time domain* shows the amplitude of the waveform at various points in time. An analysis of a sound in the *frequency domain* maps the comparative levels of the various frequencies that make up the sound.

Both of these kinds of views have both advantages and shortcomings. A time domain analysis shows what a sound is doing over a period of time, but offers little insight into the dynamic activity of a sound's harmonics during that period.

A frequency domain analysis provides more detailed information about a sound's harmonic content, but it is usually only a snapshot that represents a single instant in time. For simple waves, such as a sine wave or a sawtooth wave (which doesn't change much over a period of time), a snapshot often suffices. But for more complex sounds, a one-shot spectrum analysis is far too limited.

The most flexible way to look at sound is to consider both the time and frequency domains. The SoundWave spectrum window—which you can view by simply selecting a menu item—provides a detailed 3-D or 2-D picture of any sampled sound in both the time domain and the frequency domain.

Spectrum Window Features

As you may recall from Chapter 2, a waveform is a graphic representation of a sound's amplitude and frequency. The height of a waveform represents a sound's volume, or amplitude, and the width of the waveform represents the sound's pitch, or frequency. In addition, the length of a waveform represents the length of a sound. In other words, the length of the waveform is a representation of the sound's time domain.

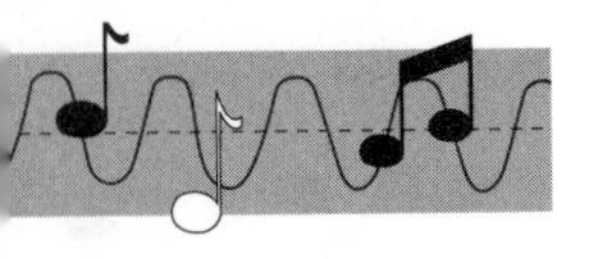

Figure 4–26 shows a 2-D image of a sound wave displayed in the SoundWave spectrum window. The diagram shows the comparative amplitudes of the frequencies that make up the sound at a single instant in time. The time that is shown is the time that the sound begins.

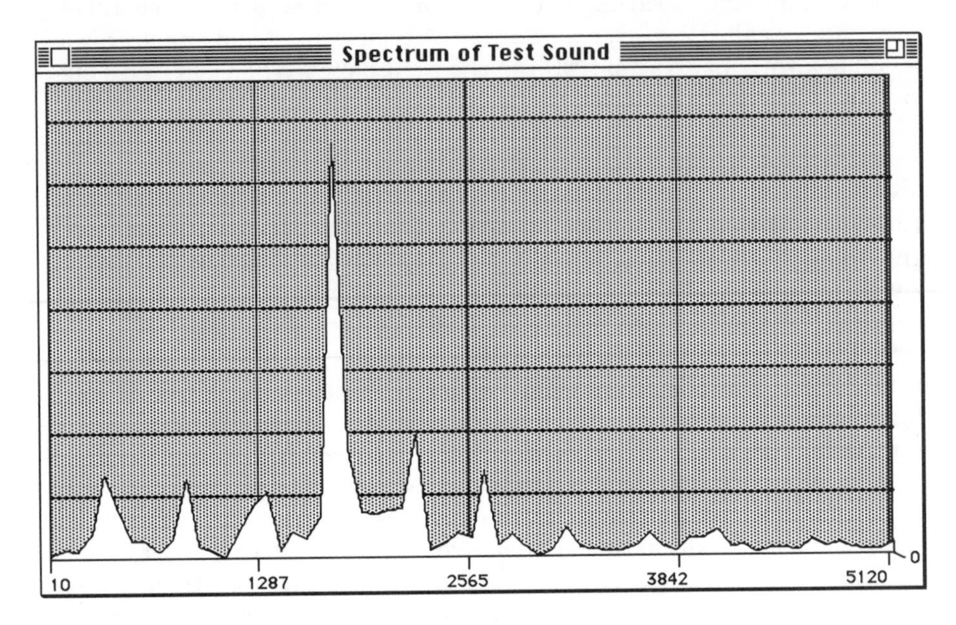

Figure 4–26. 2-D spectrum window

Figure 4–27 is a 3-D spectrum analysis of the same sound. A time domain analysis, expressed in milliseconds and showing the amplitude of the waveform at various points in time, is shown in the lower right-hand corner of Figure 4–27. An analysis of the same sound in the frequency domain extends across the bottom of the diagram. It maps the comparative levels of the various frequencies that make up the sound.

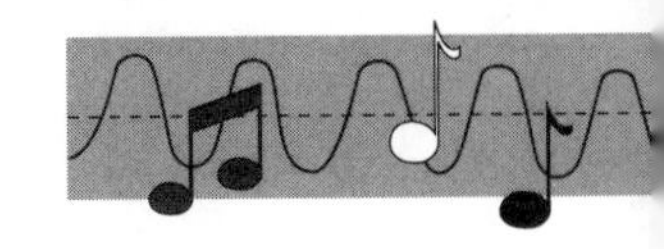

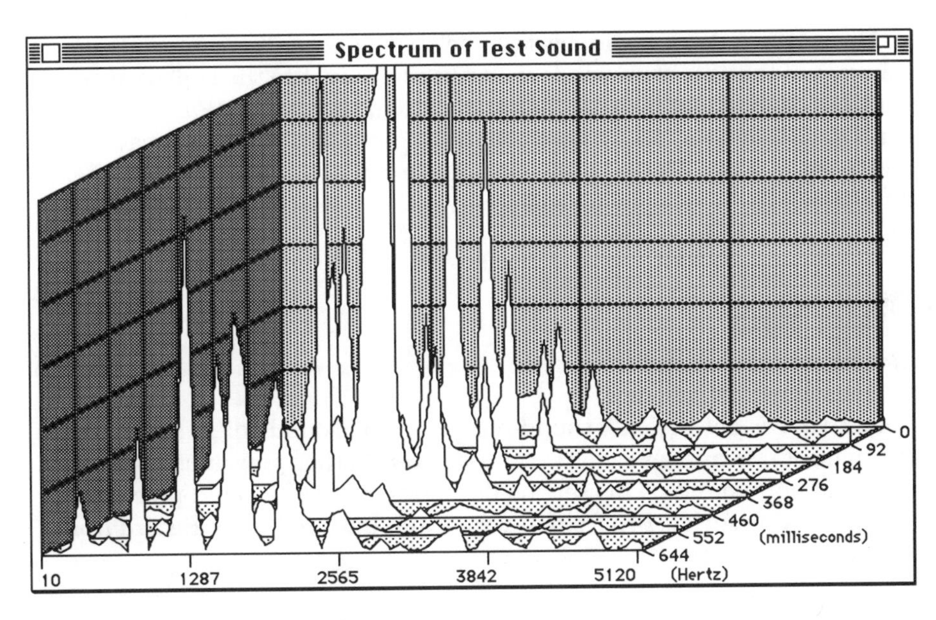

Figure 4–27. 3-D spectrum window

Opening the Spectrum Window

You can display the spectrum window by placing a waveform in the wave display window and choosing the Spectrum command under the Display menu. SoundWave then displays a dialog window that allows you to select the range of frequencies that will be displayed, and to specify whether you want a 2-D or a 3-D analysis. When you have made your choices, a spectrum window is created and displays a spectrum analysis of the sound shown in the sound window.

A spectrum window has no resizing box, but you can resize the window by placing the mouse on the lower right-hand corner of the window, holding down the mouse button, and dragging the corner of the window, just as if a resizing box were displayed.

The SoundWave spectrum window shows the amplitude of frequencies in a series of 1K segments of sound. Starting at the beginning of the sound segment selected, the spectrum window breaks the sound down into slices of 1,024 bytes each. When a new spectrum window is created, the frequencies of the first slice are plotted with their relative amplitudes. If a 3-D spectrum is displayed, the next slice is plotted in a position that is offset from the one before it to show how the frequencies that make up the sound have changed over time. If there's enough sound, eight slices are plotted. The starting time of each sound is shown in milliseconds.

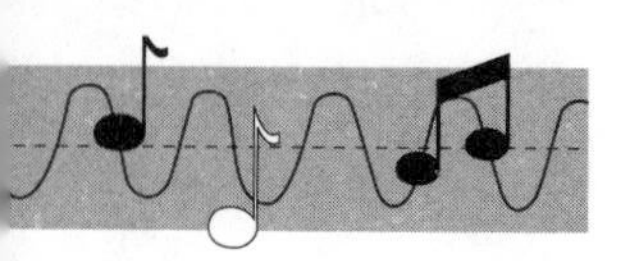

Up to four spectrum windows can be open at once. You can print the contents of the spectrum window, or you can copy it to the clipboard so that you can paste it into another application, such as MacPaint or MacDraw. However, you cannot use menu commands to load or save a spectrum window. That's because a spectrum window is merely an alternate view of a waveform. To load or save the waveform, you must use SoundWave's main window.

Other Sound Programs

SoundWave is not the only sound-recording and sound-editing program on the market. Macintosh owners can use several other programs to record, edit, and play sounds. This section describes two other sound-processing programs: SoundEdit Pro from Macromedia, Inc., and Voice Record from Articulate Systems.

SoundEdit Pro

SoundEdit Pro, from Macromedia, is the successor to the popular SoundEdit recording and editing program from Farallon. With SoundEdit Pro, you can edit and save high-fidelity 16-bit sound as well as 8-bit sound recorded with digitizers such as MacRecorder. Also, SoundEdit Pro can record sounds at any sampling rate up to 48kHz.

SoundEdit Pro can record and play back sounds containing multiple tracks, and it can manipulate tracks either individually or in groups. The program has a sound-recording window with tape recorder–style controls, and it offers a new, easy-to-operate mixing system.

Figure 4–28 shows the main SoundEdit Pro window, with two tracks displayed; the controls window; and a selection palette. The selection palette is a movable, floating window containing information about the location of the current selection or insertion point.

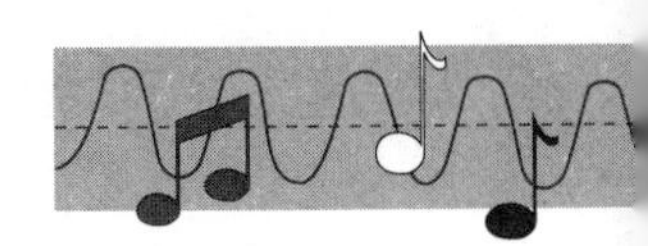

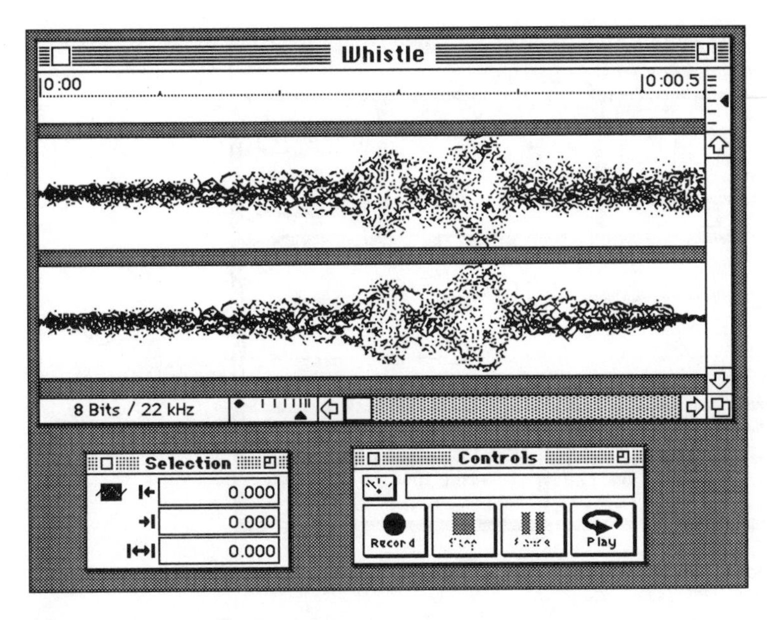

Figure 4–28. SoundEdit Pro display

Voice Record

Voice Record is a recording and sound-editing program that comes with the Voice Impact and Voice Impact Pro digitizers manufactured by Articulate Systems. Voice Record is also supplied with Voice Navigator, a voice-recognition system from Articulate Systems.

The Voice Impact Pro and Voice Navigator packages also include the SoundWave recording and editing system. Figure 4–29 shows the recording window displayed by Voice Record.

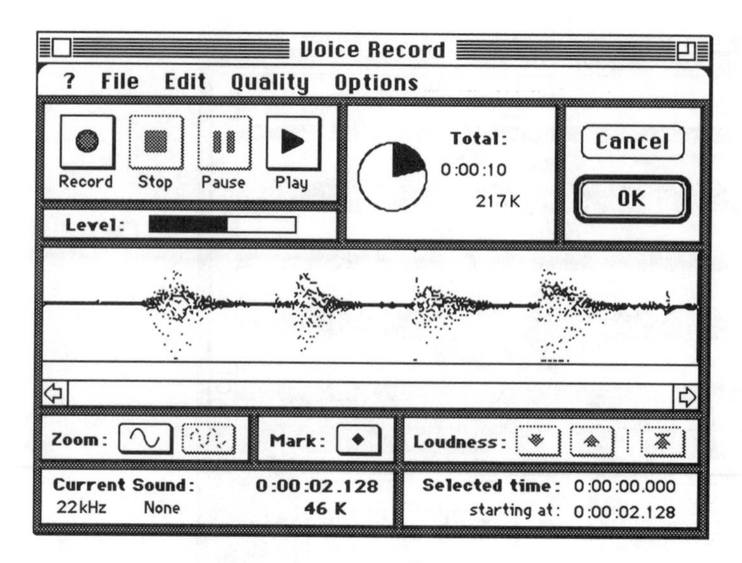

Figure 4–29. Voice Record window

The Voice Record program combines sound-recording and sound-editing capabilities in one integrated window that can be accessed directly from within many applications that support sound input, including Microsoft Word, Microsoft Excel, and QuickMail. Furthermore, when you buy an Articulate Systems product, you get a Voice Record desk accessory as well as a stand-alone Voice Record application.

Another software package that comes with Articulate Systems products is Voice Bandit, a system extension that substitutes the Voice Record dialog box for the standard Apple voice-recording dialog box in sound-aware applications and desk accessories.

Summary

This hands-on chapter documented the SoundWave program, a powerful application that is supplied on the bonus disk that comes with this book. With SoundWave, you can record, edit, and play back sound; load and save prerecorded sounds or sounds that you have created or edited; and add special effects to sounds. By loading a sound file that has been stored in one format, and then saving it in another format, you can also use SoundWave to convert sound files and sound resources from one format to another.

Another sound-processing program—HyperCorder, designed for use with HyperCard—is introduced in Chapter 5.

5 HyperCard Sound

HyperCard is the Macintosh utility that made programmers out of the rest of us. With HyperCard, even if you don't know a programming language, you can make your Macintosh do some pretty impressive things. Without writing a line of program code, you can create stacks, cards, fields, and buttons that can do many of the same things that objects in conventional applications can do. And the newest versions of HyperCard—like the newest versions of the Macintosh—contain new tools and new features that make it easier for HyperCard owners and developers to design powerful sound-related programs.

Many software manufacturers now publish sound programs for HyperCard, and many amateur programmers have designed sound-related HyperCard stacks that you can download from telecommunications services and computer bulletin boards or obtain from Macintosh user organizations. Some telecommunications services and Macintosh user groups are listed in Appendix B.

This chapter demonstrates the sound power of HyperCard with a program called HyperCorder, which is included on the bonus disk that comes with this book. HyperCorder—written exclusively for this volume—is similar to the SoundWave program introduced in Chapter 4, but it is designed to be used in a HyperCard environment.

With HyperCorder, you can cut, copy, and paste the waveforms of sounds, using standard Macintosh cut-and-paste techniques. HyperCorder can also move sounds from one HyperCard stack to another, move sounds back and forth between HyperCard stacks and sound files, and convert sounds from one format to another. With HyperCorder, as with the SoundWave program introduced in Chapter 4, you can convert sound resources to sound files, and vice versa.

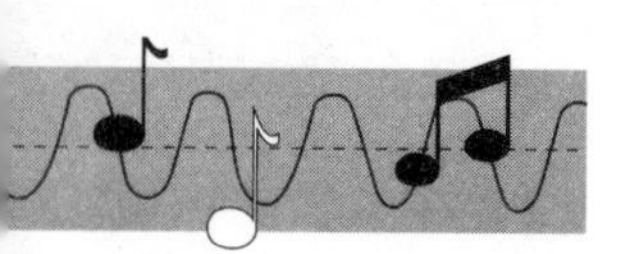

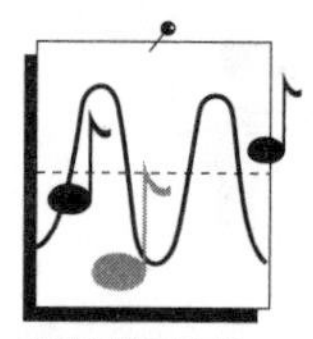

TECH TALK

HyperCard Programming

You can create impressive HyperCard stacks without writing a line of code. You can do even more if you're willing to devote a little time and effort to learning HyperTalk, HyperCard's programming language.

HyperTalk is much easier to learn than more conventional languages, such as C and Pascal. Yet because it was designed specifically to support the sophisticated graphics features of the Macintosh, HyperTalk is extremely powerful. With HyperTalk, a programmer can create an application in a fraction of the time it would take if the program were written in a more conventional language such as Pascal or C.

Unfortunately, you can't write HyperTalk programs with the version of HyperTalk that is shipped with current models of the Macintosh. To write HyperTalk programs, you must buy a developer's version of HyperCard, which is published by Claris and available from your Apple software dealer. The developer's version of HyperCard includes the HyperTalk programming language and the documents that you need to write HyperCard programs. ❍

The HyperCorder Program

The HyperCorder program is a sound processor designed to work in a HyperCard environment. HyperCorder, like the SoundWave program covered in Chapter 4, displays sounds as waveforms that you edit by clicking and dragging the mouse or by selecting menu commands.

The sound engine of the HyperCorder program is the Audio Palette, a sound-editing utility that was created by Apple and is now marketed by Claris. When you launch HyperCorder, the Audio Palette is displayed as a floating window, or *windoid,* like the one shown in Figure 5–1.

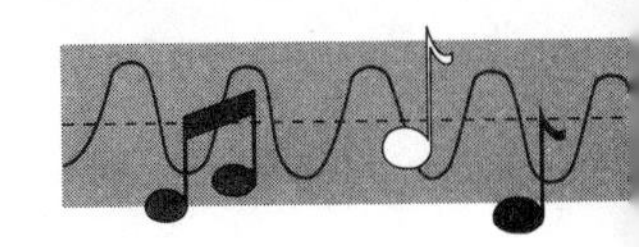

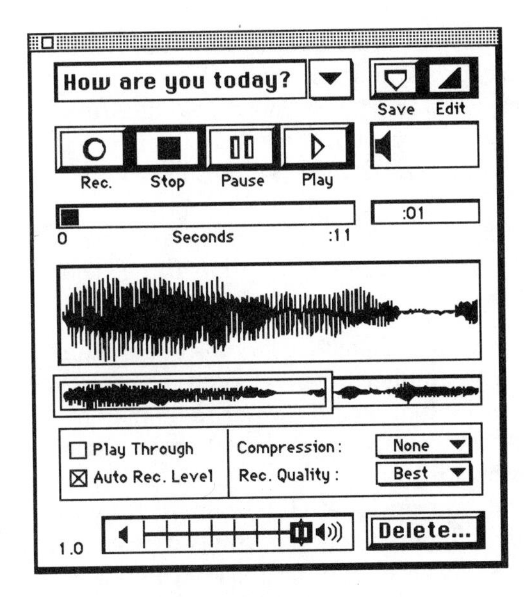

Figure 5–1. The Audio Palette window

As Figure 5–1 shows, the Audio Palette window resembles the sound window of the SoundWave program. And the Audio Palette window works much like SoundWave's sound window, too. The Audio Palette, like the SoundWave program, displays sounds as waveforms that can be cut, copied, pasted, and even moved from one sound file to another.

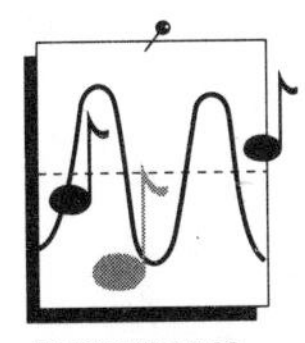

TECH TALK

The Audio Palette XCMD

If your Macintosh is a model that came with a plug-in microphone and built-in recording circuitry, you may already be familiar with the Audio Palette. That's because the Audio Help stack, which comes with mike-equipped Macs, uses the Audio Palette as a sound-editing utility.

Up to now, the only way to obtain a copy of the Audio Palette was to buy a Macintosh equipped with a microphone. Now there's another way: The Audio Palette has been licensed from Claris for use with this book, and it is included in the copy of HyperCorder that's on your bonus disk.

Technically, the Audio Palette is an **XCMD** *(pronounced X-command): an executable code resource that is written in a conventional programming language (such as C, Pascal, or assembly language) and is stored as a HyperCard stack resource. When a software designer writes an XCMD and attaches it to a HyperCard stack, the utility created by the XCMD becomes a part of the stack in which it is stored. (For more information about resources, see Appendix F.)*

If you're a HyperCard programmer, you can also use the Audio Palette in other stacks. Use ResEdit to copy the Audio Palette resource from the HyperCorder program. Then you can use the Audio Palette to add sound-recording and sound-editing capabilities to your own HyperCard stacks. Procedures for doing that are provided at the end of this chapter. ❍

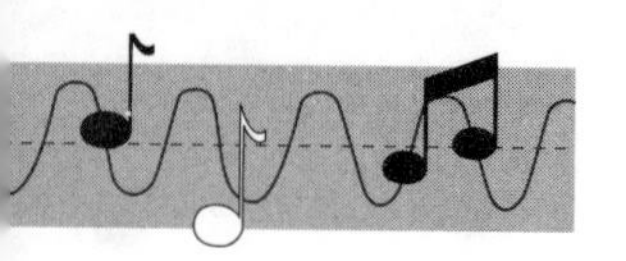

One of the most useful features of HyperCorder is its ability to convert sound files into HyperCard sound resources, and vice versa. With HyperCorder, you can convert SoundWave, SoundEdit, and Sound Cap files to HyperCard resources. Going in the other direction, HyperCorder can translate HyperCard resources back into SoundWave, SoundEdit, and Sound Cap files.

Translating sound files is a useful capability, but HyperCorder is much more than a sound-conversion program. Here are a few other things that you can do with HyperCorder:

- You can cut, copy, and paste sounds and parts of sounds using standard Macintosh cut-and-paste techniques. HyperCorder is a sound-processing program. HyperCorder, like SoundWave, can display a sound as a waveform. You can then select any segment of the sound by dragging, shift-clicking, or clicking button controls. When you have selected part of the sound, you can delete the segment from the sound or copy it to the clipboard. Then, if you like, you can paste the segment into another location—either in another part of the same sound sequence, or into an entirely different file.
- You can adjust the volume of sounds, adjust the sampling rate of sounds, and even compress sounds. When you have changed the characteristics of the sound, you can save it in three different ways: as a HyperCard sound resource, as a resource in a non-HyperCard file, or as a stand-alone sound file.
- One of the neatest features of HyperCorder is that it lets you link sounds to HyperCard buttons. When you associate a sound with a button, you can click on the button, and HyperCorder makes the corresponding sound.
- Also, you can assign any icon you like to each sound button you create, so that the picture on the button matches your sound. When you have assigned a sound to a button, you can copy that button to any card, or even to any stack. And when you copy a sound button to another stack, the button's sound also gets copied! So you can create sounds and sound buttons for your own HyperCard stacks; likewise, you can create HyperCard stacks that have their own sound buttons and their own sounds!
- Finally, if you have a sound digitizer—such as MacRecorder, one of the Voice Impact modules, or SID—you can use HyperCorder to record, edit, and play back your own sounds.

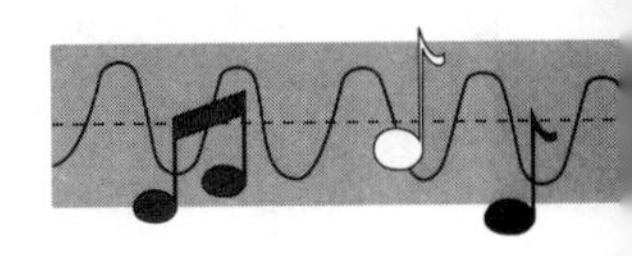

The best way to see how the Audio Palette works—and to become familiar with the overall operation of HyperCorder—is to do some experimenting with the HyperCorder program. Although HyperCorder has many capabilities that you might not know about until you finish this chapter, you don't have to understand the many features of HyperCorder to start using the program. The program is so intuitive that the best way to start using it is simply to launch it and dive right in. While you're reading this chapter, feel free to do that at any time. Then, if you like, you can return to the text and continue learning more about the subtleties of the HyperCorder program.

What You Need to Use HyperCorder

To use HyperCorder, you need the following:

- A Macintosh Plus or better with at least 2Mb of RAM
- At least 1,000K of free RAM that you can allocate to HyperCard
- System 6.0.5 or later
- A hard disk with at least 500K of free space
- HyperCard 2.0 or later

Launching HyperCorder

If you have extracted the compressed files on your bonus disk, find the folder labeled 04–HyperCorder. Open that folder and copy the HyperCorder stack into your HyperCard folder.

To use the Audio Palette, you must allocate at least 1,000K of RAM to HyperCard. Allocating 1,500K to HyperCard is even better.

To allocate the necessary space to HyperCard, select the HyperCard icon in the Finder and then select the Get Info command from the File menu. When a window titled HyperCard Info appears, find the text box labeled *Current size* in the lower right-hand corner of the window. If your computer system has 2Mb of RAM or less, type the number **1,000** in that text box. If you have more than 2Mb of RAM, type the number **1,500.** Then close the HyperCard Info window.

If you have difficulty with this procedure, refer to the documentation that came with your Macintosh.

When you have allocated HyperCard the space that it needs to run the Audio Palette, launch HyperCorder from the Finder by double-clicking on the HyperCorder icon. HyperCard should then open the main HyperCorder window, as shown in Figure 5–2.

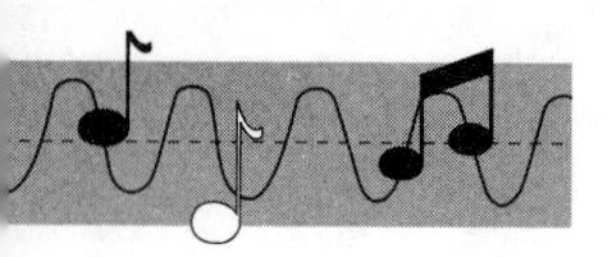

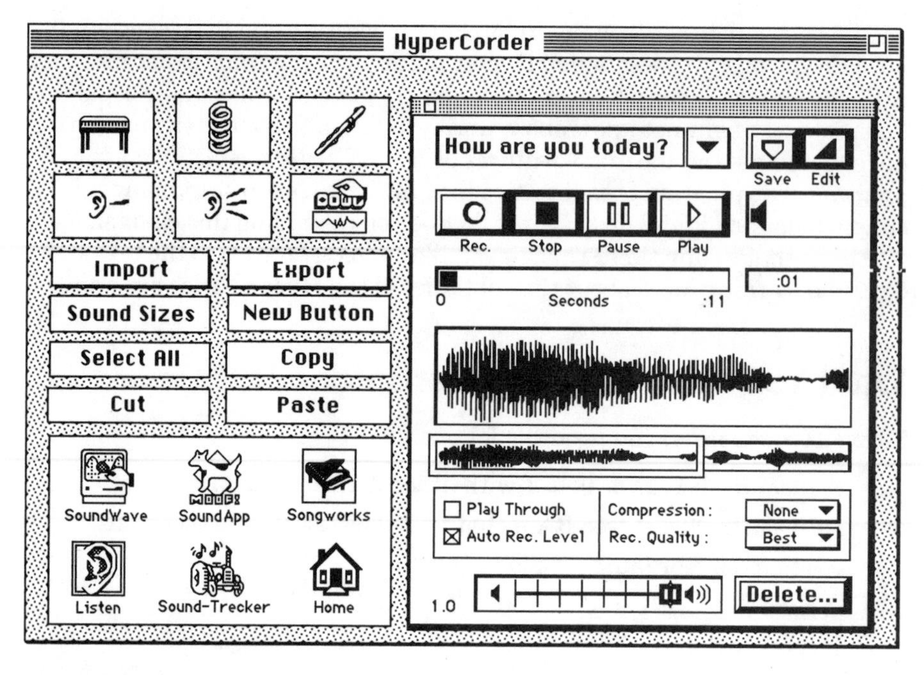

Figure 5–2. The HyperCorder window

Using the Audio Palette

When you open HyperCorder, the Audio Palette, as shown in Figure 5–3, occupies the upper right-hand quarter of the HyperCorder window.

Figure 5–3. Collapsed Audio Palette window

You can expand the Audio Palette to cover the whole right-hand side of the HyperCorder window by clicking on the button labeled Edit in the upper right-hand corner of the Audio Palette, or by clicking on the push-

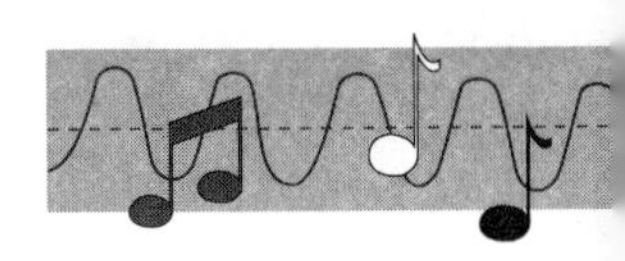

button button—the rightmost control in the second line of buttons to the left of the Audio Palette window, shown in Figure 5–4. The Audio Palette then expands to its full size and covers the whole right-hand half of the HyperCorder window, as shown earlier in Figure 5–2.

Figure 5–4. The pushbutton button

The Audio Palette is a movable windoid with a close box in the standard place: at the left-hand end of the title bar. You can move the Audio Palette around by dragging its title bar, and you can even close the Audio Palette window by clicking on the close box at the left-hand end of the palette's title bar. Fortunately, however, when the Audio Palette goes away under HyperCorder, it doesn't go far. When you have closed the Audio Palette, you can reopen it quickly and easily by simply clicking on the push-button button shown in Figure 5–4. You can also reopen the Audio Palette by simply moving the HyperCorder window. You can move the Audio Palette by dragging the bar that contains the close box; that is, the bar that's in the traditional location of a title bar.

Playing a Sound

When you launch HyperCorder, the word *Untitled* appears in a name box near the top of the Audio Palette panel. That name box is part of a pop-up menu called the Sound pop-up menu; when the word *Untitled* appears in the name box, it means that no sound is currently open. To open a sound with the Audio Palette and play it, these are the steps to follow:

1. Select a sound from the Sound pop-up menu. The Sound pop-up menu lists, in alphabetical order, the names of all sounds that are currently available to HyperCorder. They include all sounds in the current stack; all sounds in stacks that are currently open; and all sounds in the HyperCard Home stack.
2. Choose one of the sounds listed and release the mouse button. The name of the sound you have selected then appears in the Sound pop-up menu's name.
3. To play the sound, click on the Play button below the title window. To stop the playing of the sound temporarily, click on Pause. To resume the playing of the sound, click on Pause again.

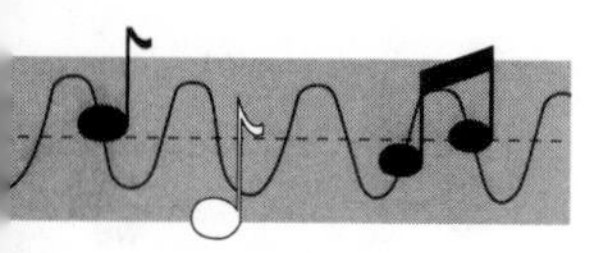

Recording a Sound

If you have a digitizer installed in your computer system, you can record a sound with the Audio Palette. To record a sound, follow these steps:

1. Select the word *New* from the Sound pop-up menu. If another sound is open and has not been saved in its current form, the Audio Palette displays a message asking you if want to save the open sound. Save the open sound if you like. When you have made that choice, the Audio Palette closes the open sound, and the word *Untitled* appears in the name box of the Sound pop-up menu. The Audio Palette is then ready for you to record a new sound.
2. To record a sound, click on the Record button below the name box.
3. Next to the Audio Palette's Play button, there's an icon shaped like a loudspeaker. When you speak into the microphone connected to your Macintosh, lines representing sound waves appear to come from the speaker icon. There are seven waves in all, and the biggest one—the one that's farthest to the right—is shaded.

   When you record a sound, the speaker icon works like a recording-level meter. The shaded sound wave is like the red light on a level meter; it shouldn't flash very often or for very long, and certainly shouldn't stay on continuously.

   When you're recording, you can control the level of your sound by adjusting the recording-level control on your digitizer. Also, if you're using a microphone, you should place it 9 to 12 inches from the source of the sound. You can adjust the recording level by moving the microphone closer to or farther away from the sound source.
4. When you're ready to start recording, click on the button labeled Rec.
5. Below the Rec. button, there's a bar-shaped elapsed-time meter. The figure shown under the right-hand end of the meter is the amount of recording time that you have left when you're making a recording. The amount of time displayed depends upon the amount of RAM currently available to HyperCard.

   As you record a sound, the bar meter fills and the amount of time that you have left to record decreases. When the bar is full, you have run out of recording time.
6. If you want to stop recording temporarily, click on the Pause button. To resume recording, click on Pause again.
7. When you finish recording, click on the Stop button. To listen to the sound you have recorded, click on Play.
8. If you're not satisfied with recording, you can click on the Rec. button and record your sound again.

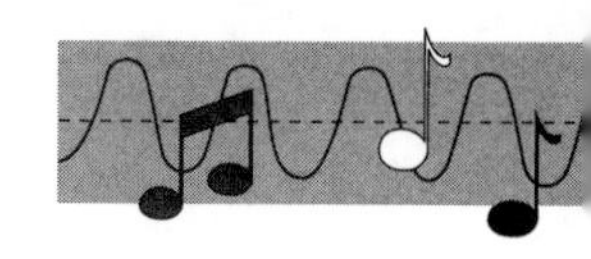

9. When you're satisfied with your recording, you can give your sound a name. With the mouse, just select the text in the Audio Palette's name box (which should be the word *Untitled* if you're recording a new sound) and type in a name.

The Expanded Audio Palette

HyperCorder uses the Audio Palette to display sounds as waveforms, and when the Audio Palette is displayed, you can cut, copy, and paste sounds by using standard Macintosh techniques.

Sound waves are displayed in the lower half of the Audio Palette window. Therefore, before you can edit a sound, you must expand the Audio Palette to its full height. When the Audio Palette is shown at its full height, it covers the right-hand half of the HyperCorder window.

As mentioned previously, you can expand the Audio Palette to its full height by clicking on the Edit button in the upper right-hand corner of the Audio Palette window. Or you can toggle back and forth between a collapsed Audio Palette and an expanded Audio Palette by clicking on the push-button button, illustrated earlier in Figure 5–4.

The Audio Palette's Controls

When the Audio Palette is extended to its full height, you can change the sampling rate and compression ratios of sounds by selecting options from the pop-up menus labeled Rec. Quality and Compression. If your digitizer has automatic recording-level and play-through features, you can select those features by checking the boxes labeled Auto Rec. Level and Play Through.

At the bottom of the Audio Palette window, there's a slide that adjusts playback volume. To the right of the volume control slide, there's a Delete button that you can use to delete sounds from the HyperCorder stack and all other open stacks.

The Wave Display Window and the Scroller Window

HyperCorder, like SoundWave, displays the waveforms of sounds in two places: a main wave display window and a scroller window. In SoundWave, you may recall, the scroller window is at the top of the display, and the wave display window is below it. In HyperCorder's Audio Palette, however, those positions are reversed, as illustrated in Figure 5–5.

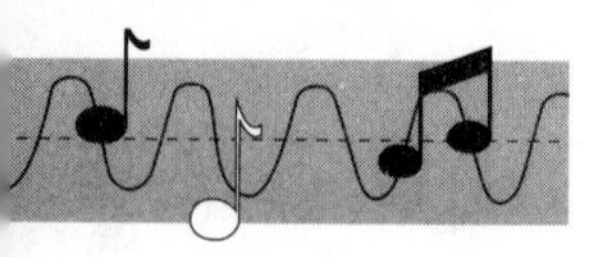

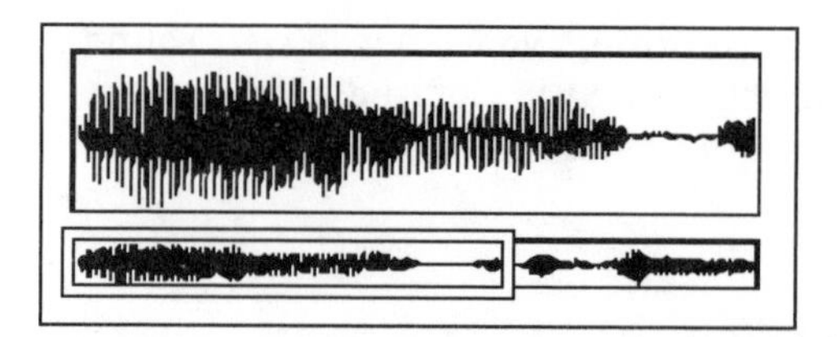

Figure 5–5. The HyperCorder wave and scroller displays

Despite this minor difference, the wave display window and the scroller window in HyperCorder work much like the wave display window and the scroller window in SoundWave: The scroller shows a complete sound file, and the wave display shows a magnified view of a part of the file.

In HyperCorder, as in SoundWave, a frame encloses part of the scroller display. When you place the cursor over the frame, the cursor becomes a hand, as shown in Figure 5–6. Then, by holding down the mouse button while you move the cursor, you can slide the frame back and forth along the scroller. As you do so, the part of the waveform that's inside the wave display window expands and shrinks to match the portion of the waveform that's inside the scroller frame.

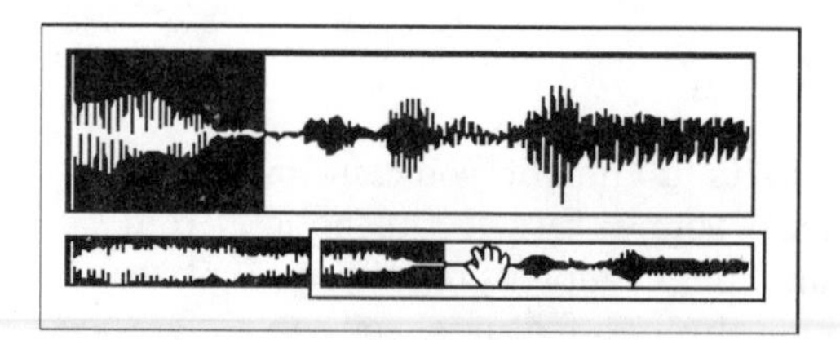

Figure 5–6. Moving the scroller frame

When you place the cursor over the scroller frame, the cursor becomes a pointing finger, as illustrated in Figure 5–7. Then, by holding down the mouse button while you move the cursor, you can adjust the size of the scroller frame.

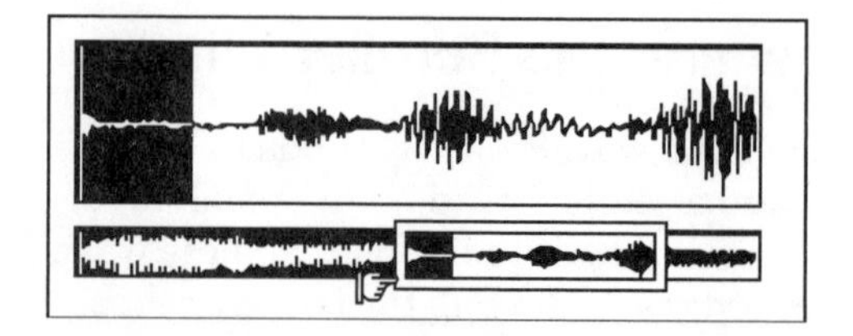

Figure 5–7. Adjusting the size of the scroller frame

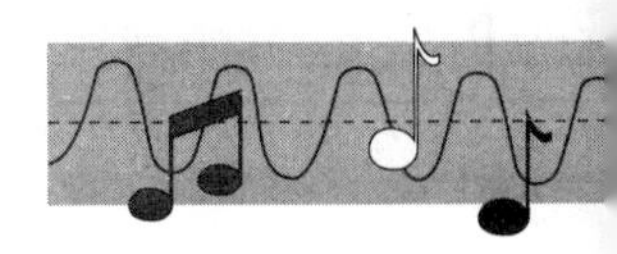

Selecting a Sound Segment

You can place an insertion point in the wave display window by simply clicking on the mouse inside the wave display. Alternatively, by dragging the mouse, you can select any part of the sound segment that's shown in the wave display window. You can select a complete sound by dragging the mouse from one end of the sound to another.

When you select part of a sound in the wave display, you can play your selection by clicking on the Audio Palette's Play button. In Figure 5–8, for example, the question "How are you today?" is the active sound. However, only the first part of the sound—"How are you . . ."—is selected in the sound that is shown in the wave display window. Below the wave display, in the small scroller window, the same part of the sound is selected.

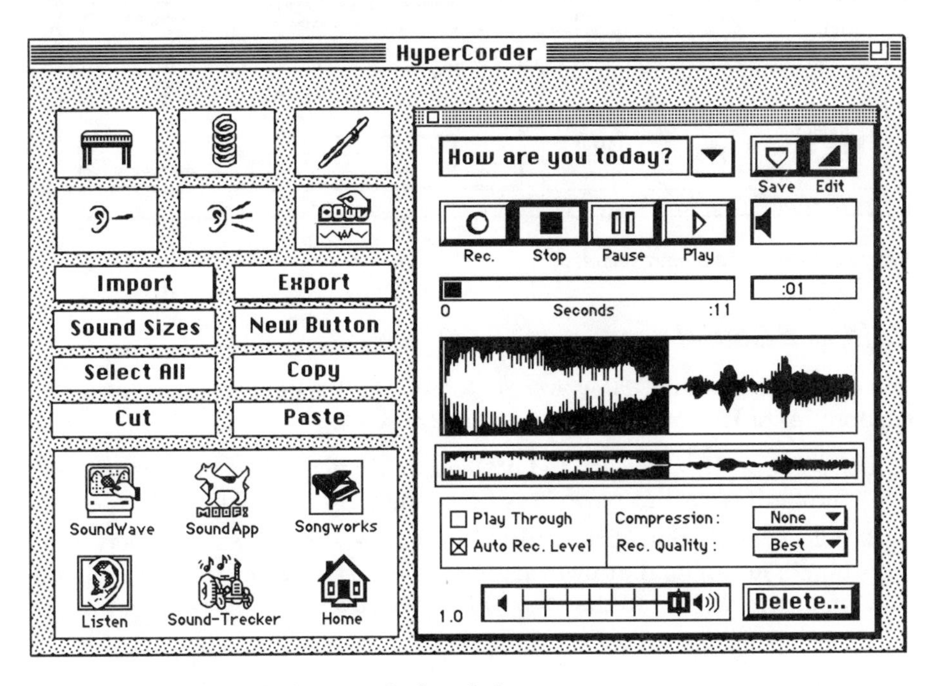

Figure 5–8. A selection in the wave display window

You can see how the wave display window and the scroller window work by creating the display shown in Figure 5–9. First, launch HyperCorder and open the sound "How are you?". When you have done that, select the words "How are you . . ." as shown in Figure 5–9. Then click on the Play button. In response, HyperCorder should speak the words "How are you . . ."

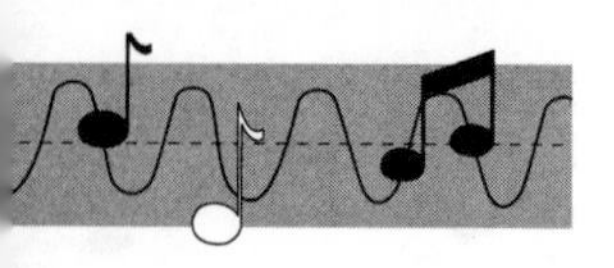

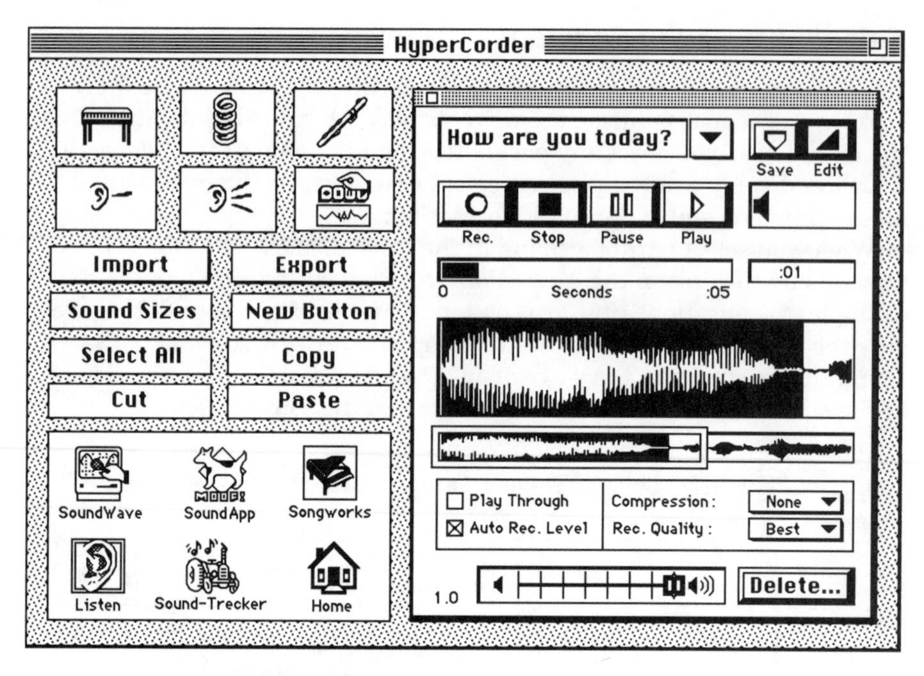

Figure 5–9. Part of a sound selected

Editing a Sound

You can use the sound "How are you today?" to demonstrate the editing capabilities of HyperCorder. Just follow these steps:

1. Open the "How are you today?" sound. Do not adjust the size of the scroller frame, but move it as far to the right as it will go.
2. Select the portion of the sound that appears in the wave display window. You can do that by dragging the insertion point from one end of the wave display to the other. Figure 5–10 shows the result of this operation.

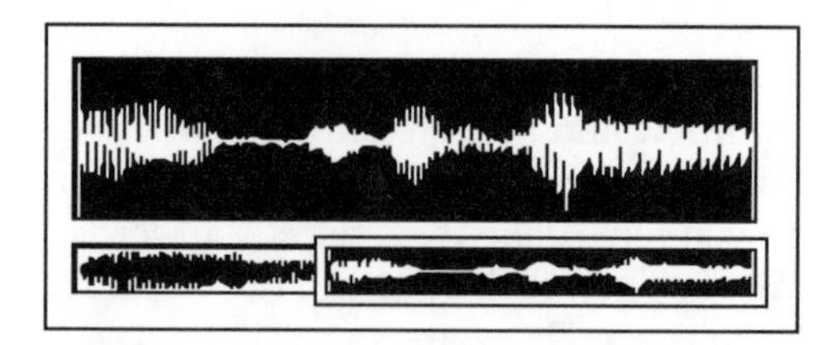

Figure 5–10. Dragging the insertion point

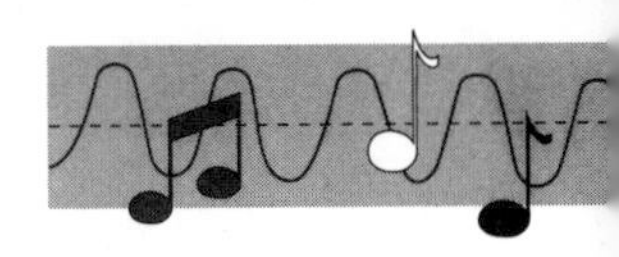

3. Play the sound segment that you have selected. The segment should consist of the words ". . . you today?"
4. Copy your selection to the clipboard by clicking on the Copy button in the middle row of buttons to the left of the Audio Palette.
5. Place the cursor over the scroller frame. When the cursor changes to a pointing finger, use the finger to stretch the scroller frame to its full length, as in Figure 5–11.

Figure 5–11. Stretching the scroller frame

6. Click on the mouse inside the wave display window to deselect the portion of the sound that is selected. Then place the insertion point at the far right end of the wave display window and click on the Paste button in the middle group of buttons to the left of the Audio Palette. HyperCorder should respond by pasting a second copy of the words ". . . you today?" at the end of the phrase "How are you today?"
7. Check to see whether your pasting operation has worked by clicking on the Audio Palette's Play button. HyperCorder should then say, "How are you today . . . you today?"
8. At this point in the experiment, it may seem that there isn't enough silence between the first and second ". . . you today?" segment. You can insert more silence between *you* and *today* by clicking on the Copy button, and pasting the silence between the two ". . . you today?" segments. If you do that, your sound wave—stretched to its full length—will look something like the one in Figure 5–12.

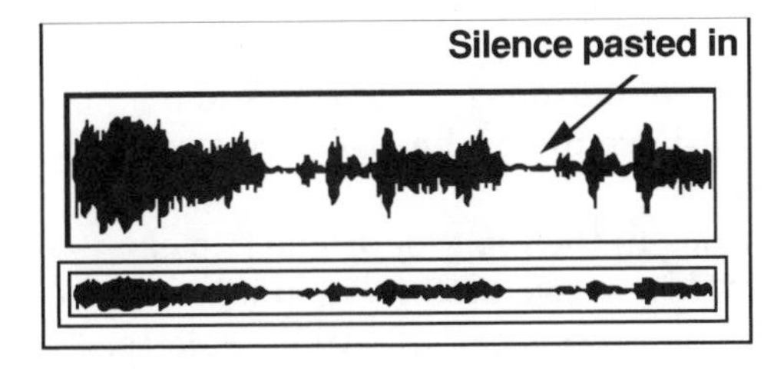

Figure 5–12. A moment of silence

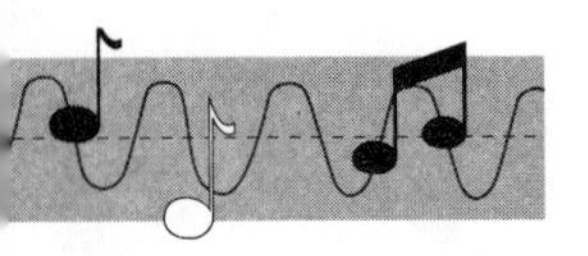

9. Now select the second "... you today?" segment, copy it to the clipboard by clicking on the Copy button, and paste a third "... you today?" segment at the end of the sound. Then play your sound by clicking on the Play button, and you should hear Maxine Headroom (remember Max?) saying, "How are you today ... you today ... you today?"
10. You can save the sound you have edited by clicking on the Save button near the top of the Audio Palette window.
11. Your edited sound should resemble the "How RU3X" sound that comes with HyperCorder. You can play both the "How are you?" sound and the "How RU3X" sound by clicking on the two ear buttons in the top group of buttons next to the Audio Palette window. Click on the second ear button—the one next to the three sound waves—and you can grade yourself on how well you did with your editing.

The Other Half of HyperCorder

In the left-hand panel of the HyperCorder window—the half not covered by the Audio Palette—are three groups of buttons. These buttons are not part of the Audio Palette, but are specific to the HyperCorder stack.

The first five buttons in the top group of buttons play some interesting sounds, and the sixth button—as you have seen—controls both the presence and the size of the Audio Palette.

The buttons in the middle group move sounds back and forth between stacks and files, and provide some editing features that the Audio Palette lacks. With the bottom group of buttons, you can navigate to other sound programs that are provided on your bonus disk.

Before you can use the bottom group of buttons, you must tell HyperCorder where the other programs from your bonus disk are. For instructions on how to do that, see the heading "Navigation Buttons" later in this chapter.

Buttons That Play Sounds

The first three buttons in the top group of buttons next to the Audio Palette play HyperCorder's three built-in sounds: a harpsichord sound, a boing sound, and the sound of a flute.

You've tried the second line of buttons in the top group: The two ear buttons play the original and edited "How are you today?" sounds, and the push-button button controls the size and presence of the Audio Palette.

Command Buttons

With the middle group of buttons on the left side of the HyperCorder window, you can do the following:

- Copy Sounds to and from other HyperCard stacks and to and from stand-alone sound files. When you copy sounds with HyperCorder, the program performs all necessary file translations automatically.
- Determine the sizes of the sound resources currently stored in the HyperCorder stack.
- Create customized buttons for sounds.
- Cut, copy, and paste sounds.

One of the most interesting features of HyperCorder is that it can link HyperCard buttons to sounds. When you have created a button and have linked the button with the sound, you can copy the button—and the sound that goes with it—to any HyperCard stack. Furthermore, the process of copying sounds and buttons from stack to stack is easy; all you have to do is select and drag icons, and click on controls.

Importing a Sound

With the Import pop-up menu, shown in Figure 5–13, you can copy a sound to the HyperCorder stack from:

- Any other stack
- Any file in which sounds are stored as resources
- Any stand-alone sound file of type 'FSSD'; that is, any SoundWave, SoundEdit, or Sound Cap file

Figure 5–13. The Import pop-up menu

The Import menu, as Figure 5–13 shows, is a hierarchical pop-up menu. The first sublevel of the Import menu has two items:

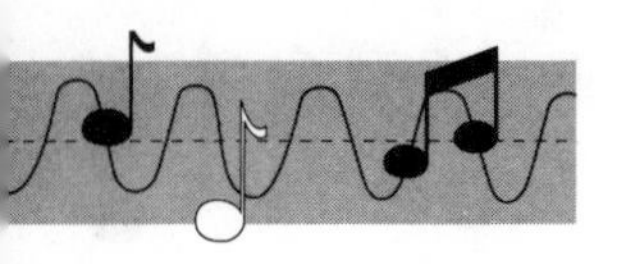

- **From Stack—**instructs HyperCorder to import a sound from another stack
- **From File—**instructs HyperCorder to import a sound from a stand-alone sound file

If you select the menu item From Stack, HyperCorder displays a standard file dialog that you can use to find and open the stack that contains the sound you want to import.

If you choose the menu item From File, you must use the second sublevel of the menu to tell HyperCorder whether you want to import the sound from a sound file or from any file. To import a sound from a stand-alone sound file (a file of type 'FSSD'), select Sound File from the second sublevel of the menu. To import a sound from a file that stores sounds as resources—for example, from your System file or from a Sound Mover suitcase—choose the menu item Any File.

When you have told HyperCorder what kind of source file you have in mind, HyperCorder displays a dialog that you can use to select a sound from the kind of file you have specified.

Exporting a Sound

The Export pop-up menu, shown in Figure 5–14, lets you copy a sound from the HyperCorder stack to:

- Any other stack
- Any file in which sounds are stored as resources
- Any stand-alone sound file of type 'FSSD'; that is, any SoundWave, SoundEdit, or Sound Cap file

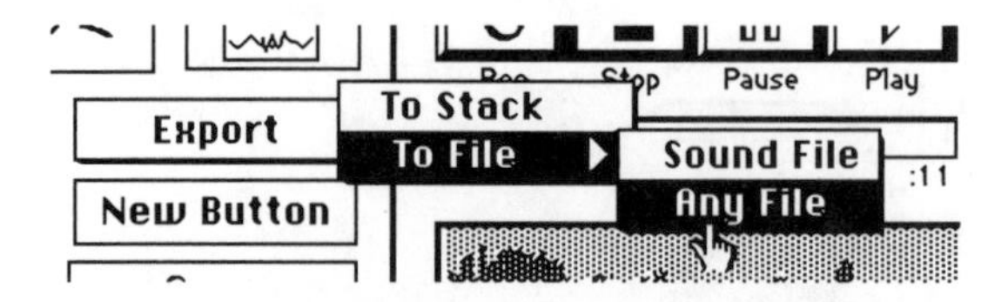

Figure 5–14. The Export pop-up menu

When you use the Export pop-up menu to copy a sound from HyperCorder to another stack, HyperCorder also copies any button that may be linked to the sound. In other words, the Export pop-up menu copies buttons as well as sounds!

The Export menu, like the Import menu, is a hierarchical pop-up menu. From the first sublevel of the Export menu, you can choose from two items:

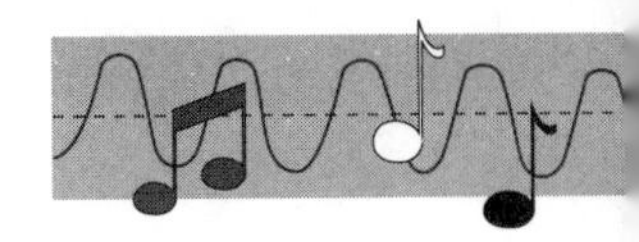

- **To Stack**—exports a sound from the HyperCorder stack to another stack.
- **To File**—exports a sound from HyperCorder to a file. By selecting the To File menu item, you can convert a HyperCard sound to a stand-alone file of type 'FSSD', and you can then export that sound file to any directory you choose. Alternatively, you can copy a sound resource from the HyperCorder stack to any file in which sounds can be stored as resources.

Exporting a Sound to Another Stack

To export a sound from HyperCorder to another HyperCard stack, select the item To Stack from the first sublevel of the Export menu and follow these steps:

1. When you select the menu item To Stack, HyperCorder displays a file dialog that you can use to open any HyperCard stack you choose.
2. When you open a stack with the file dialog, HyperCorder displays the first card of the stack you have selected and creates a sound button on the card. If the sound you have selected has a customized icon button, HyperCorder copies the sound button's icon to the stack that you have opened and creates a new sound button that has the appropriate icon. If the sound has no custom button, HyperCard creates a button with a generic sound icon like the one shown in Figure 5–15.

Figure 5–15. Generic sound button icon

3. When the new sound button appears, the cursor changes from its pointing-finger shape to a cross shape. HyperCorder then displays a message box asking you to drag the button where you want it. When you move the new button to its final location, HyperCard pastes the button in the location you have chosen. (This procedure is similar to the procedure for creating a new sound button, which is described later in this section.)
4. When you have selected a location for your new sound button, HyperCorder displays a dialog asking whether you want to keep your destination stack open or return to HyperCorder. When you have made that choice, the exporting operation is complete.

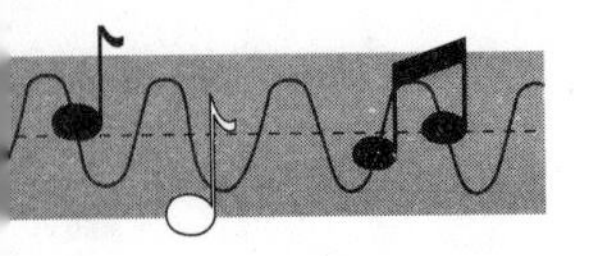

Exporting a Sound to a File

If you choose the To File menu option, you can use the second sublevel of the Export pop-up menu to specify whether you want to export the sound to a sound file or to any file. To export a sound to a stand-alone sound file (a file of type 'FSSD'), select Sound File. To export a sound to a file that stores sounds as resources—for example, your System file or a Sound Mover suitcase—choose Any File.

When you select the Sound File item, HyperCorder displays a standard file dialog window that you can use to select and open a destination folder. HyperCorder then translates the sound you have selected into a sound file, and stores the file in the folder you have specified.

When you select the Any File item, HyperCorder displays a standard file dialog window that you can use to select a destination file, and it then stores the sound you have chosen as a sound resource in the file you have specified.

Sound Sizes

Click on the Sound Sizes button to find out the size (in bytes) of each sound in the stack.

Creating a Button for a Sound

With the HyperCorder button labeled New Button, you can create customized buttons for sounds. These are the steps to follow:

1. Select a sound from the Audio Palette's Sound pop-up menu.
2. Click on the New Button button.
3. In response, HyperCorder opens a window that offers you a choice of sound icons. Select an icon and click on the OK button.
4. The icon window then closes, and HyperCorder returns to its main window.
5. When the main window opens, the cursor changes from its pointing-finger shape to a cross shape. HyperCorder then displays a message box asking you to drag the button where you want it. When you move the new button to its final location, HyperCorder pastes the button in the location you have chosen.

If you like, you can place your button in the space in the lower right-hand corner of the HyperCorder window. That space, labeled *Put your sound buttons here,* is visible only when the Audio Palette window is collapsed.

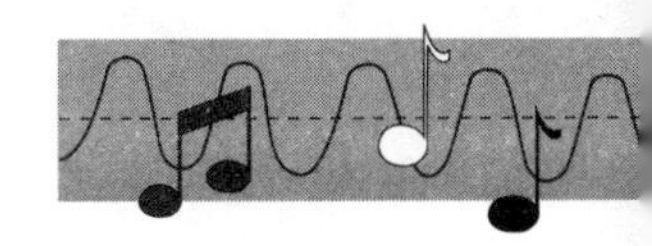

See the section "Special Operations" later in this chapter for tips on moving and removing custom buttons.

Selecting All of a Sound

You can select the complete sound shown in the scroller window. You can click on the Cut, Clear, or Paste buttons or their keyboard equivalents to cut, clear, or replace the sound.

Copying a Selection

The Copy button copies any portion of sound that has been selected to the clipboard. You can then paste that selection into another sound by clicking on the Paste button. The keyboard equivalent of the Copy button is Command-C.

Cutting a Selection

The Copy button deletes any portion of sound that has been selected, and saves that selection to the clipboard. You can then paste that selection into another sound by clicking on the Paste button. The keyboard equivalent of the Cut button is Command-X.

The Paste Button

The Paste button pastes into the currently active sound any portion of a sound that has been saved to the clipboard. If a part of the active sound has been selected, Paste replaces the selected part of the sound with the sound that has been saved to the clipboard. Otherwise, the Paste button pastes the saved sound into the active sound at the current insertion point. The keyboard equivalent of the Paste button is Command-V.

Navigation Buttons

In the lower left-hand corner of the HyperCorder window, there are six buttons that can take you quickly to five other sound-related applications included on your bonus disk or to the Home card. Before you can use these navigation buttons, you must extract the applications shown from your bonus disk and store them on a hard disk.

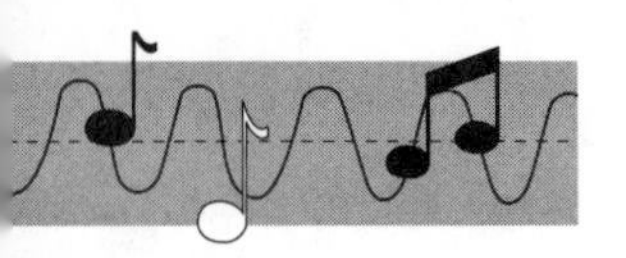

When you click on a navigation button for the first time, HyperCard displays a message box asking you the location of the application you have selected. When you have informed HyperCard of the locations of all five applications, you can click on any of the buttons, and HyperCard will take you immediately to the program you have chosen.

The HyperCorder Menu Bar

When you open the HyperCorder stack, HyperCorder adds two items—Audio and HyperCorder—to the HyperCard Edit menu. From that point on, from any HyperCard stack that is open, you can do the following:

- Open the Audio Palette by selecting the Audio command
- Open the HyperCorder stack by selecting the HyperCorder command

As noted at the beginning of this chapter, you don't have to run HyperCorder to use the Audio Palette. When you open the HyperCorder stack, HyperCorder adds an Audio item to the Edit menu. From that point on, from any HyperCard stack that is open, you can open the Audio Palette by selecting the Audio command. Then, if the open stack contains any sound resources, you can play them and edit them by using the Audio Palette.

Special Operations

Two of HyperCorder's features are so well hidden that you wouldn't know what they are if someone didn't tell you. Here are the secrets:

- **Moving a button—**when you have created a custom button with the New Button control, you can move the button to another location by holding down the Option key while you drag the button. This procedure works with any custom button, whether it is installed in the HyperCorder stack or in another stack.
- **Removing a button—**you can delete a custom sound button from the HyperCorder stack or from another stack by holding down the Command key while you click on the button with the mouse. HyperCorder then displays a dialog asking if you really want to delete the sound. If you answer yes, HyperCorder deletes the sound —and the button.

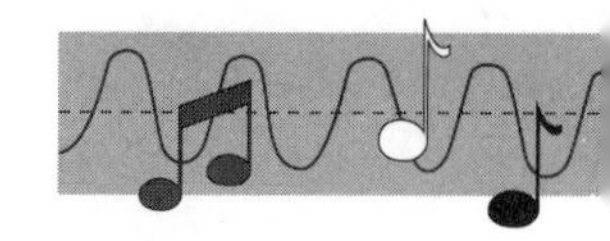

Using the Audio Palette in HyperCard Programs

Since the Audio Palette is written as an XCMD, you can copy it (and its supporting resources) into any stack using ResEdit. Then, in any HyperCard script you write, you can invoke the Audio Palette XCMD in the same way that you would call a message handler: Simply execute the command

```
AudioPalette
```

from your script.

You can activate the Audio Palette but make it invisible by typing the command

```
AudioPalette invisible
```

When the Audio Palette is active but invisible, you execute sound commands from a HyperCard script in the same way that you would if the Audio Palette were visible, even though it cannot be seen on the screen.

You can also show and hide the Audio Palette by executing these HyperTalk statements:

```
Hide Window AudioPalette
Show Window AudioPalette
Close Window AudioPalette
```

Sending Messages to the Audio Palette

The Audio Palette responds to fourteen messages in the same way that it would respond to a user clicking on a button. For example, if you send the message Play to the Audio Palette from a HyperTalk script, the Audio Palette responds by playing the sound that is currently displayed in the Sound pop-up menu.

To send a message to the Audio Palette from a HyperCard script, this is the syntax to use:

```
Send [message] to window AudioPalette
```

For example, to send a Play message to the Audio Palette, you could execute this statement:

```
Send play to window AudioPalette
```

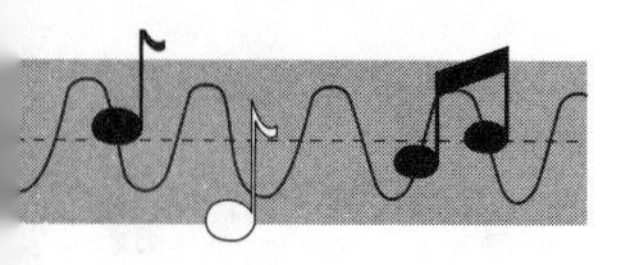

All fourteen messages that you can send to the Audio Palette in this manner are listed in Table 5–1.

Table 5–1. Audio Palette Messages

Clear	Copy	Cut	Delete
Edit	Paste	Pause	Play
Record	Save	SelectAll	Stop
Update	ViewAll		

Audio Palette Properties

The Audio Palette has ten *properties* that you can access or change in the same way that you can access or change properties of any HyperCard objects—that is, by using the HyperTalk commands Get and Set. By setting the Audio Palette's properties, you can change its screen location, make it visible or invisible, adjust the volume of sounds, and make other adjustments in the Audio Palette's appearance and behavior.

To access the Audio Palette's properties, you can execute the Get command using this format:

```
Get property of window AudioPalette
```

In response, HyperCard places the requested property in the variable *It*. For example, you can obtain a point that contains the Audio Palette's current location by executing this statement:

```
Get loc of window AudioPalette
```

Or, you can place the Audio Palette at coordinates 25, 25 by executing this command:

```
Set the loc of window AudioPalette to 25, 25
```

Other Audio Palette properties that you can get or set in the same fashion are listed in Table 5–2.

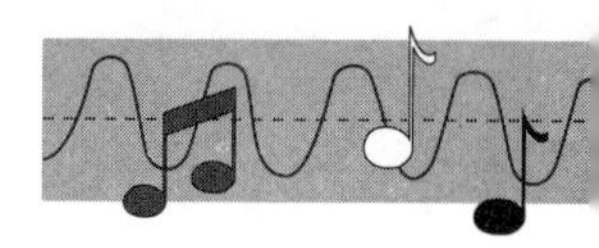

Table 5–2. Audio Palette Properties

Property	Syntax	Function
Visible	`Set the Visible of Window AudioPalette to a` *`Boolean`* `value`	Makes the Audio Palette visible or invisible.
Compression	`Set the compression of Window AudioPalette to` *`compressionSpecifier`*	Sets compression ratio. The *compressionSpecifier* variable is 3to1, 6to1, 1to1, or none. None is the same as 1to1.
Speed	`Set the speed of window AudioPalette to` *`rate`*	Sets sound tempo. The variable *rate* is 11k or 22k.
Volume	`Set the Volume of Window AudioPalette to` *`integer`*	Sets sound volume. The variable *integer* is a number from 0 to 7.
Buffer	`Set the Buffer of Window AudioPalette to` *`myHandle`*	Allocates a buffer for an 'snd 'resource.
Playthrough	`Set the Playthrough of window AudioPalette to` *`condition`*	Can be set to On or Off. When Playthrough is on, sound being recorded plays through your computer's speaker.
AutoRecord	`Set the AutoRecord of window AudioPalette to` *`condition.`*	Automatically sets recording volume. The variable *condition* can be set to On or Off.
Sound	`Set the Sound of Window AudioPalette to` *`resource Name`*	Makes *resourceName* the currently active sound. Works only with Set, not with Get.
SoundName	`Set the soundName of window AudioPalette to` *`resourceName`*	Gets or sets the name of the currently active sound.

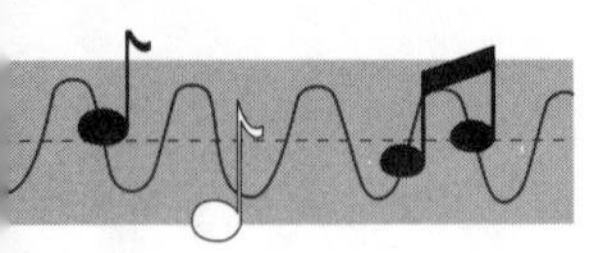

Messages That the Audio Palette Sends

The Audio Palette sends HyperCard messages when certain actions are performed. These messages, listed in Table 5–3, are used internally by the HyperCorder stack.

Table 5–3. Audio Palette Messages

Message	When Message Is Sent
`APSave` *`soundName`*	When the user clicks on the Save button. The parameter *soundName* is the name of the sound resource being saved
`APBeginEdit`	When the Audio Palette receives a Text Edit record containing the name of the current sound
`APEndEdit`	When the Audio Palette releases a Text Edit record containing the name of the current sound
`APClose` *`paletteName`*	When the AudioPalette is being closed or disposed of
`APOpen` *`paletteName`*	When the AudioPalette is being opened

Summary

In this chapter, you learned how to tap the sound power of the Macintosh from HyperCard. The chapter introduced HyperCorder—a powerful sound-processing program written exclusively for this book and included on your bonus disk—and the Audio Palette, created by Apple, which is HyperCorder's sound engine. This chapter explained how you can use HyperCorder and the Audio Palette to record, edit, and play back sound, and to copy sounds from one HyperCard stack to another and between HyperCard stacks and sound files. In a section for HyperCard programmers, this chapter also explained how you can incorporate the Audio Palette sound utility into your own HyperCard stacks.

6 Speech Synthesis

Most of the sounds covered so far in this book are digitized sounds—that is, sounds that have been converted into binary numbers so that they can be stored on computer disks or in a computer's memory. Speech synthesis, the topic of this chapter, is a completely different kind of sound.

When a computer synthesizes speech, it doesn't simply play back sequences of sounds that have been recorded and stored in memory. Instead, a computer generates speech in real time by using tables and mathematical algorithms to mimic the human voice. A speech synthesizer, as its name implies, does its work by generating speechlike sounds.

Since the Macintosh was introduced in 1984, the most popular Macintosh speech synthesizer has been MacinTalk, a utility that can be placed in the System Folder and can then generate sound. To use MacinTalk, you need two things: a copy of the MacinTalk speech generator itself, and an application program or HyperCard stack that has been specifically designed to work with MacinTalk.

Many professional and amateur software designers have written programs that support MacinTalk. Some applications that work with MacinTalk are sold in computer stores, and many more are available from Macintosh user groups and from public and commercial bulletin boards.

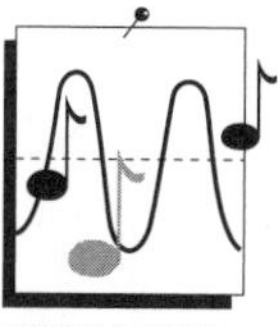

IMPORTANT

Beware of "MacinTalk 2.0"

Macintosh sound buffs received quite a shock not long ago when a speech driver called "MacinTalk 2.0" started showing up on computer bulletin boards. Knowing that Apple had clearly declared its decision not to issue any more MacinTalk revisions, I contacted both Apple and APDA and asked what was happening.

Spokespeople for both Apple and APDA sounded as surprised as I was. They said that Apple had definitely not released any new version of MacinTalk, and still had no plans to revise the product. Apparently, they said, someone has uploaded an unauthorized version of MacinTalk to some bulletin boards and is calling it "MacinTalk 2.0." People who have experimented with "MacinTalk 2.0" say that it is apparently designed to make MacinTalk more compatible with System 7.

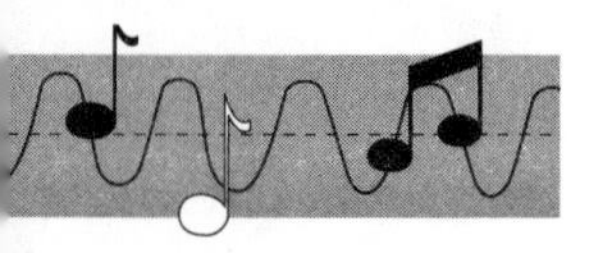

These are the facts about "MacinTalk 2.0": The latest official version is MacinTalk 1.31, a revision of MacinTalk 1.3 dated July 31, 1987. If you run across a version of MacinTalk labeled "MacinTalk 2.0," use it at your own risk. Apple didn't write it, isn't responsible for it, and has no connection with it. So beware. ❍

About MacinTalk

When you buy a program that relies on MacinTalk, you need a copy of MacinTalk to run the program. Therefore, manufacturers of programs that work with MacinTalk usually license the MacinTalk utility from APDA and include a copy of it with their programs.

One popular program that relies on MacinTalk is the Talking Moose from Baseline Publishing. The Talking Moose, shown in Figure 6–1, is an animated cartoon that pops up on your computer screen at various times and says witty things. When you buy the Talking Moose program, you also get a copy of MacinTalk, since the program doesn't work without it.

Figure 6–1. The Talking Moose

Other programs use MacinTalk in other ways. For example, some programs take printed text as input, and—with the help of MacinTalk—read the text out loud. It doesn't matter where the text comes from; MacinTalk can read books, reports, memos—anything that can be typed in ordinary typed characters. And, since MacinTalk does its work in real time, it can even read text while you are typing it on your computer keyboard. That makes programs like MacinTalk valuable for handicapped people, such as people with visual disabilities.

There are also programs that use MacinTalk to read stories, programs that speak random bits of text, and programs that answer typed-in questions out loud.

How MacinTalk Works

Technically, MacinTalk is a software driver that runs under the Macintosh operating system. To use MacinTalk, all you have to do is drag the MacinTalk icon into your System Folder (*not* into your Extensions folder if you're using

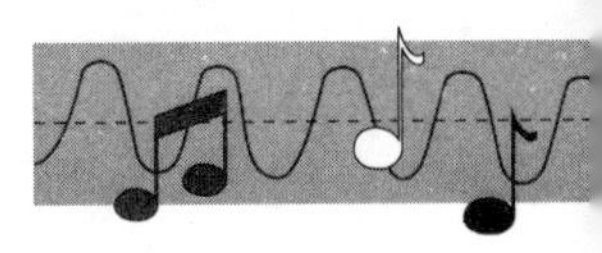

System 7, because MacinTalk is not an extension). When you have installed MacinTalk in your System Folder, you must restart your Macintosh. Then you can launch any application that is designed to be used with MacinTalk.

When you launch a program that uses MacinTalk, what happens next depends on the program. But it's pretty safe to say that all software designed to be used with MacinTalk relies upon MacinTalk's ability to read ordinary text out loud.

In the next section, you'll get a chance to experiment with MacinTalk using the HyperLab program. First, though, it might be helpful to take a brief look at how MacinTalk produces sound.

MacinTalk Pros and Cons

One of MacinTalk's main attributes is that it requires little memory—it consumes only 28K of RAM—so, no matter how small a Macintosh you have, you can almost always run a MacinTalk application.

Paradoxically, one of MacinTalk's main flaws—its comical, cartoon-character voice—can also be rated as an asset in some applications. For instance, MacinTalk's voice sounds perfect in the Talking Moose program. The Talking Moose program relies on MacinTalk's ability to sound like—well, a talking moose. And that feature has sold a lot of Talking Moose programs.

The Future of MacinTalk

As this book was being written, Apple was putting the final touches on a new and improved speech synthesizer called the Speech Manager (see the section "Beyond MacinTalk" later in this chapter). The Speech Manager can generate more realistic-sounding speech than MacinTalk can produce, and it can even imitate real people's voices. The Speech Manager, unlike MacinTalk, can also generate speech in the background, while the Macintosh is performing other functions.

Because MacinTalk has more limited capabilities than those of the new Speech Manager, it's likely that MacinTalk will be gradually phased out once the new Speech Manager becomes available. However, so many programs that rely on MacinTalk are currently on the market that the MacinTalk synthesizer will probably still be around for a while.

Even if MacinTalk winds up being discontinued, it will still be a useful tool for learning how speech synthesizers work. Most speech synthesizers, including both MacinTalk and Apple's Speech Manager, convert ordinary text into phonetic text, and then read the phonetic text that they have

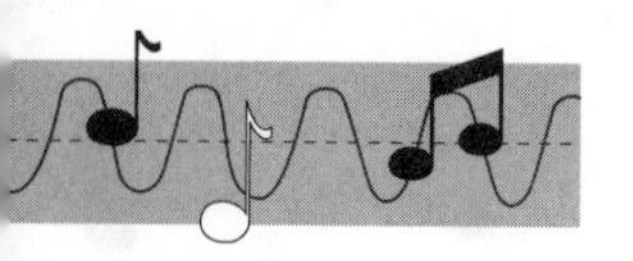

created using some specific set of pronunciation rules. So a good understanding of how MacinTalk works can provide you with a basic understanding of more advanced speech synthesizers.

Also, if you get a kick out of creating and listening to silly voices, MacinTalk can be a lot of fun.

The HyperLab Stack

This chapter demonstrates MacinTalk with HyperLab, a HyperCard-based stack. A copy of HyperLab is provided on your bonus disk, together with a copy of the MacinTalk synthesizer that has been licensed from Apple for distribution with this book.

HyperLab demonstrates MacinTalk's capabilities in an interactive and entertaining way. When you have launched HyperLab, you can type in any text you like, and then listen as MacinTalk reads it back. By selecting buttons and adjusting controls, you can program MacinTalk to read your text at various speeds and pitches, and with various kinds of intonations and pronunciations.

The HyperLab stack has one card, which is shown in Figure 6–2.

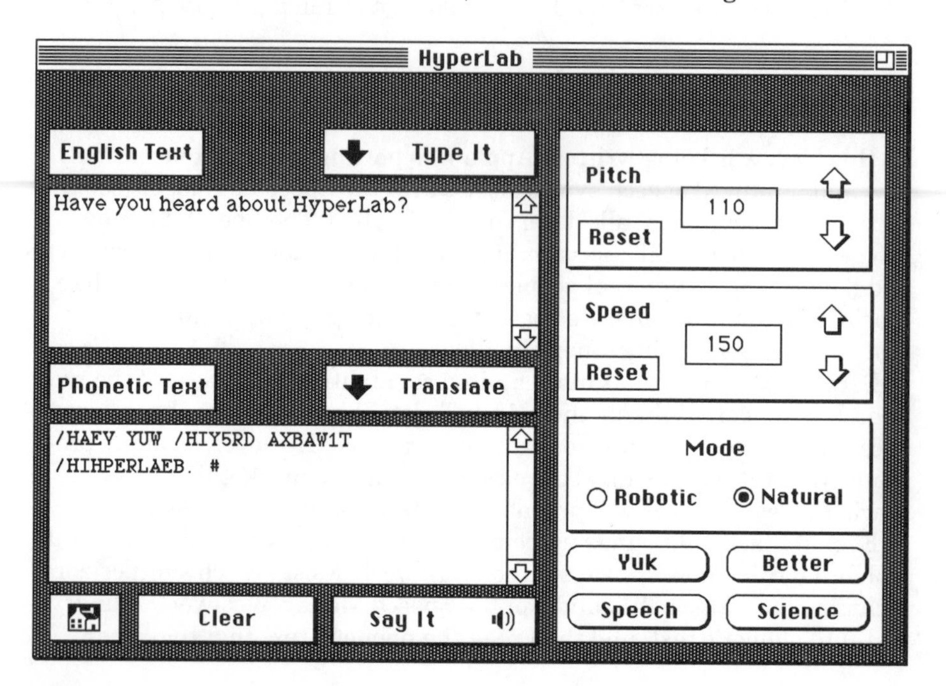

Figure 6–2. HyperLab card

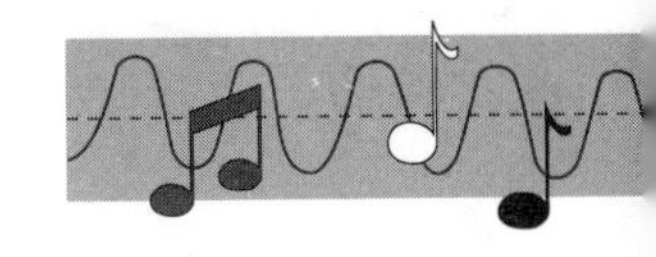

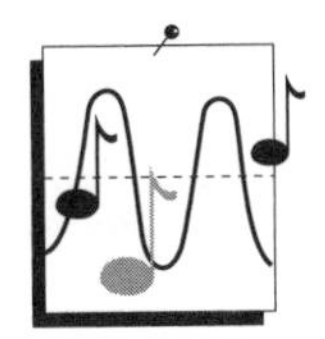

Programming with MacinTalk

MacinTalk works with programs written in any Macintosh-compatible programming language. Therefore, if you're a Macintosh programmer, you can use Macintosh to write your own talking programs.

To write MacinTalk programs, you need a MacinTalk developer's package and a Macintosh compiler such as THINK C, THINK Pascal, or one of the compilers or assemblers that are available for use with MPW (the Macintosh Programmer's Workshop). You can obtain a MacinTalk developer's package from APDA.

The MacinTalk developer's package consists of one 3.5-inch floppy disk and a looseleaf manual. The developer's disk contains a set of interface and library files that support programs written in various languages. The interface and library files on the MacinTalk disk are used just like any other set of interface and library files; the MacinTalk program developer simply places them in an appropriate folder, and then accesses them from whatever compiler or assembler is being used to develop the program.

If you're a HyperCard programmer, you can include MacinTalk routines in your stacks without buying APDA's MacinTalk package. All you need are the XCMDs and XFCNs (X-commands and X-functions) that are in the HyperLab stack. Just copy HyperLab's XCMDs and XFCNs into any stack with ResEdit, and you can execute almost any MacinTalk command directly from HyperCard.

XCMDs and XFCNs are executable code resources that are written in a conventional programming language (such as C, Pascal, or assembly language) and are stored as resources in HyperCard Stacks. When a software designer writes an XCMD or an XFCN and attaches it to a HyperCard stack, the utility created by the XCMD or XFCN becomes a part of the stack in which it is stored. (For more information about resources, see Appendix F.)

For more details about writing MacinTalk programs, see the section "Programming MacinTalk" later in this chapter. ❍

How HyperLab Works

HyperLab is a HyperCard stack that was written exclusively for this book and documented in this chapter. With HyperLab, you can change the pitch of MacinTalk's voice from an unbelievably low bass to a squeaky falsetto, and you can set the synthesizer's reading speed, ranging from the world's slowest drawl to the world's fastest speaker.

With interactive controls that are provided by HyperLab, you can switch MacinTalk's intonation from a lively, natural rhythm to a robotic monotone. You can type a block of original text and watch MacinTalk convert it to phonetic text. Finally, you can edit the phonetic text that MacinTalk produces and listen to the results.

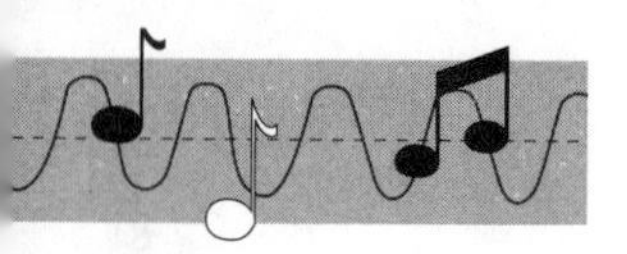

What You Need to Run HyperLab

MacinTalk was designed a long time ago for basic models of the Macintosh, so you don't need much in the way of hardware or memory to use the synthesizer. A Macintosh Plus or better can do the job, and the MacinTalk driver requires only 28K of RAM.

To run the HyperLab stack, however, you need HyperCard 2.0 or later, because that's the version the stack was written for.

Getting Started

If you've extracted the compressed files from your bonus disk, in accordance with the steps outlined in Chapter 1, you're ready to start using MacinTalk and HyperLab. These are the steps to follow:

1. Open the folder labeled 06–Speech Synthesis and find the MacinTalk icon. Drag it into your System Folder. (If you're using System 7, *don't* drag MacinTalk into your Extensions folder. Just drag it into your System Folder, and it will work fine.)
2. Drag the HyperLab stack icon into your HyperCard folder. Then you can double-click on the HyperLab icon to launch HyperCard and open the HyperLab stack.
3. Experiment with all the buttons, and have fun! Try a lot of different pitch and speed combinations, and give MacinTalk a lot of readings, in both the natural and robotic voice modes. You'll have to use the Translate and Say It buttons for some demonstrations, but you won't have to use them for others. You'll learn more about what you're doing later in this chapter, so read on.

Listening to MacinTalk

On the left side of the HyperLab card are two large text fields: one labeled English Text and the other labeled Phonetic Text. These two fields are shown in Figure 6–3.

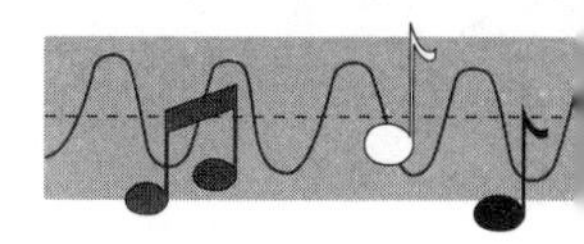

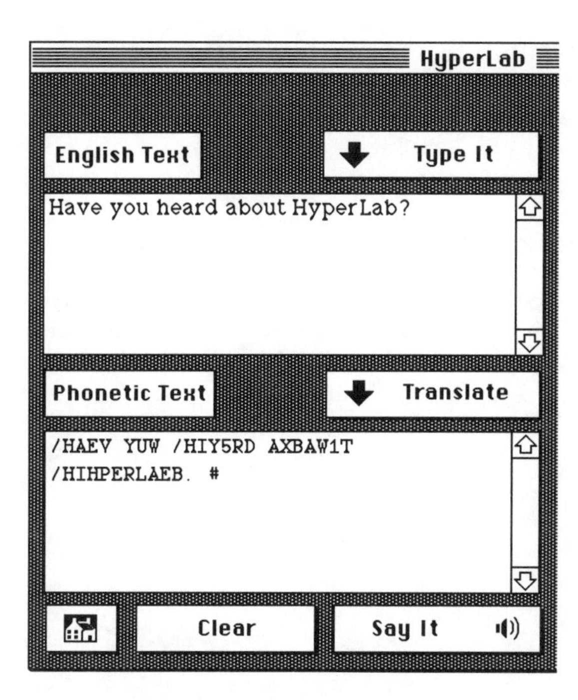

Figure 6–3. English text and phonetic text

To hear MacinTalk read a block of text, these are the steps to follow:

1. Type the text that you want to hear in the large box labeled English Text in the upper left-hand quarter of the HyperLab card.
2. Click on the button labeled Translate. MacinTalk then converts your plain text into phonetic text, and it displays the phonetic text in the large box labeled Phonetic Text in the lower left-hand quarter of the HyperLab card. As you can see, MacinTalk always writes phonetic text in uppercase letters, and when you write phonetic text for MacinTalk to read, you must do the same. If you use lowercase letters in your phonetic text, MacinTalk sits in stony silence, refusing to read what you have written.
3. Click on the button labeled Say It. MacinTalk then reads the phonetic text that it has created.
4. You can usually improve MacinTalk's pronunciation and intonation by editing the text in the Phonetic Text box. For information on editing phonetic text, see the section "MacinTalk Phonetics" later in this chapter.

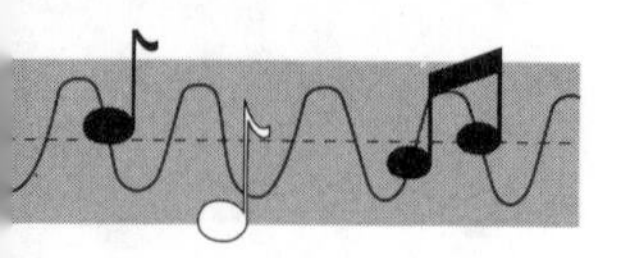

To the left of the Translate button, there's a button labeled Clear. It clears both of the text fields above it so you can enter new information.

The Home button, to the left of the Clear button, takes you to HyperCard's Home card.

The HyperLab Button Panels

On the right-hand side of the HyperLab card, you'll find four button panels. The top three groups of buttons, each enclosed in a rectangle, control the pitch, the speed, and the intonation of MacinTalk's synthesized voice. These three groups of buttons are shown in Figure 6–4.

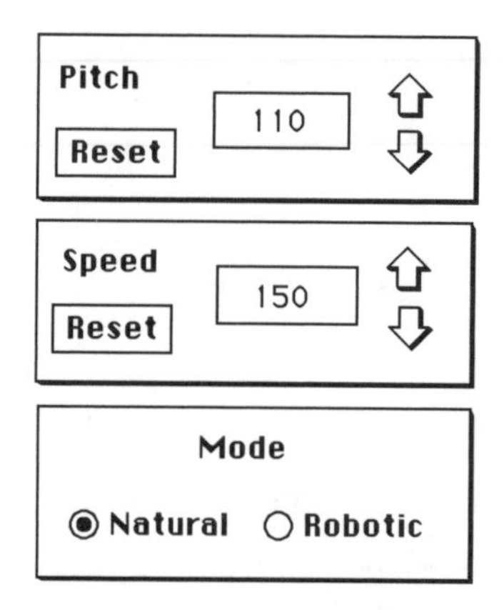

Figure 6–4. The top three button panels

The bottom button panel contains a group of four buttons, shown in Figure 6–5. These buttons display prewritten blocks of text that MacinTalk can read.

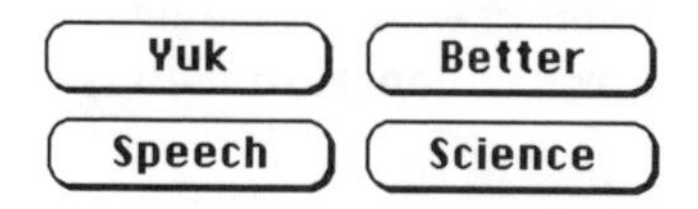

Figure 6–5. The bottom button panel

Pitch

With the controls in the panel labeled Pitch, you can adjust the baseline pitch of the MacinTalk voice. Here's how:

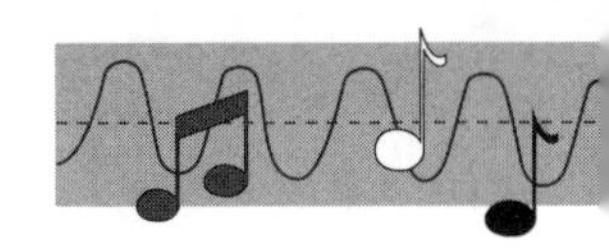

1. In the center of the panel, there is a text box that shows MacinTalk's current pitch, measured in hertz. MacinTalk can speak at a pitch ranging from 65Hz to 500Hz. You can adjust MacinTalk's pitch by clicking on the up and down arrows next to the text box.
2. When you click on the Reset button, the pitch is set to a default value of 110Hz.

Speed

The speed of MacinTalk's speaking voice ranges from 85 to 425 words per minute. To adjust the rate at which MacinTalk speaks, you can use these techniques:

- To set the speed of MacinTalk's voice, click on the up and down arrows in the Speed panel
- With the Reset button, you can set MacinTalk's speed to a default value of 150 words per minute

Intonation

With the radio buttons in the Intonation panel, you can set MacinTalk's intonation to a natural mode (an exaggeration) or to a robotic monotone. Just click on either radio button.

The Bottom Button Panel

With the four buttons in the bottom button panel, you can listen to MacinTalk read samples of prewritten text. When you click on one of the buttons, HyperLab translates the text sample that you have selected into phonetic text. Then you can click on the Say It button to listen to the text. The four buttons work as follows:

- **Yuk**—demonstrates how MacinTalk can butcher the language by mispronouncing words.
- **Better**—shows how you can improve the quality of the MacinTalk voice by editing the synthesizer's phonetic text.
- **Speech**—MacinTalk delivers a speech about how it works. This speech demonstrates one serious shortcoming of MacinTalk: When the synthesizer is running, it takes total control of the Macintosh CPU. So, once this speech starts, the only thing you can do (short of turning off your computer) is listen to the whole thing.

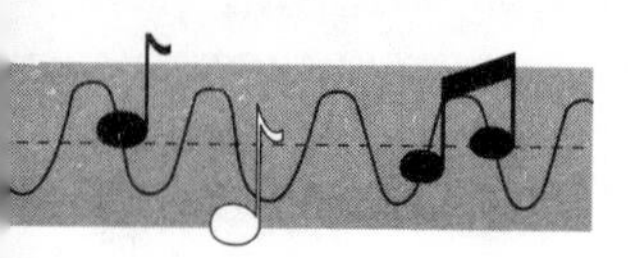

- **Science**—MacinTalk delivers a shorter lecture about smoking and heart disease. This lecture has been extensively edited to improve MacinTalk's pronunciation and intonation. It still doesn't sound great; you probably can't understand every word. But this is about as good as MacinTalk gets. That's the main reason that Apple is scuttling the synthesizer.

MacinTalk Phonetics

If you can't spell, you'll love the MacinTalk phonetic system. To type a word using phonetics, you don't have to know how a word is spelled, just how it sounds.

The phonetics used by MacinTalk are based on a phonetic alphabet called *Arpabet.* Arpabet derives its name from the fact that it was created by the Advanced Research Projects Agency (ARPA). The MacinTalk phonetic alphabet is an expanded version of Arpabet.

The MacinTalk phonetic alphabet attempts to represent every sound in the English language with a one-letter or two-letter symbol. Table 6–1 lists the approximate pronunciations of these symbols, using common words.

Table 6–1. MacinTalk Phoneme Table

Vowels	Phonemes
IY	beet
IH	bit
EH	bet
AE	bat
AA	hot
AH	under
AO	talk
UH	look
ER	bird
OH	border
AX	about
IX	solid

Note: Never use AX and IX in stressed syllables.

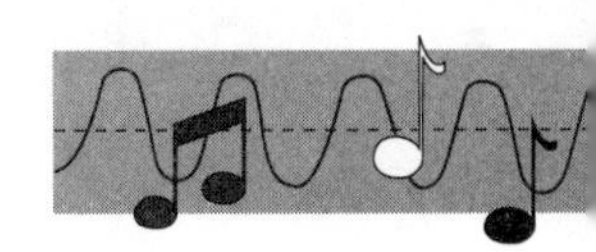

Consonants	Phonemes
R	red
L	yellow
W	away
Y	yellow
M	men
N	men
NX	sing
S	sail
SH	rush
F	fed
TH	thin
Z	has
ZH	pleasure
V	very
DH	then
CH	check
J	judge
/H	hole
/C	loch
B	but
P	put
D	dog
T	toy
G	guest
K	camp

Vowel and Consonant Contractions	
AXL	can be written as UL
IXL	can be written as IL
AXM	can be written as UM
IXM	can be written as IM
AXN	can be written as UN
IXN	can be written as IN

Diphthongs	Phonemes
EY	made
AY	hide
OY	boil
AW	power
OW	low
UW	crew

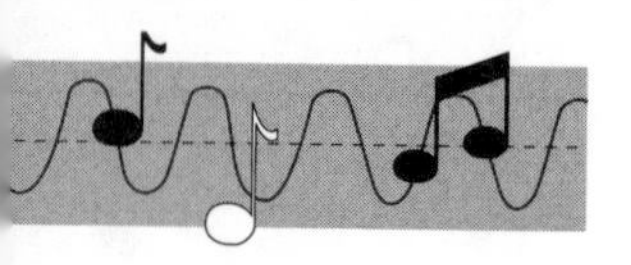

Special Symbols	Phonemes
DX	pity (tongue flap)
Q	kitt_en (glottal stop)
RX	car (postvocalic R)
LX	call (postvocalic L)
QX	sudden (silent vowel)

Stress Marks
The digits 1 – 9

Punctuation	Function
Period (.)	Sentence terminator
Question mark (?)	Sentence terminator
Hyphen (-)	Phrase delimiter
Comma (,)	Clause delimiter
Ellipsis (...)	Noun phrase delimiters

In the MacinTalk phonetic alphabet, there are 12 symbols for vowel sounds, 25 symbols for consonants, and six symbols for vowel/consonant contractions. There are also symbols for diphthongs, special symbols, stress symbols (the digits 1 through 9), and punctuation marks.

Consonant Sounds

The consonant *s* can be voiced or unvoiced. For example, in the word *passes,* the first *s* sound is unvoiced, and the second is voiced. The phonetic symbol for unvoiced *s* is S; for a voiced *s,* the symbol is Z.

Other differences are more subtle. For instance, the symbol for the *s* sound in *pleasure* is represented as ZH.

The combination *th* can also be either voiced or unvoiced. When *th* is voiced, as in *then,* it is represented as DH. When *th* is unvoiced, as in *thought,* the symbol is TH.

Vowel Sounds

When a vowel appears in a short unstressed syllable, you can use the letter *X* after a vowel to shorten the vowel's sound. For example, the *a* in *about* is represented as AX, and the *i* in *solid* is represented by IX. These vowels often occur before the consonants *l, m,* and *n.* To simplify both typing and reading, these contractions are permitted:

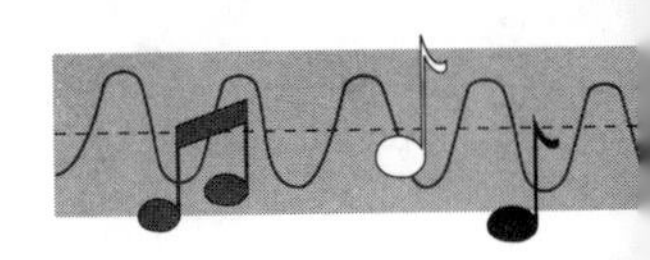

- AXL becomes UL
- IXL becomes IL
- AXM becomes UM
- IXM becomes IM
- AXN becomes UN
- IXN becomes IN

Stress Marks

In the MacinTalk phonetic alphabet, the level of stress applied to a syllable is expressed as a single-digit number in the range 0–9. The higher the number is, the more stress MacinTalk places on the syllable that contains the stress mark. For example, a word used as an exclamation might contain a stress code of 9, while an unstressed preposition or conjunction in a sentence might have a stress code of 0.

A stress mark is optional in a MacinTalk syllable. However, you shouldn't avoid using stress marks simply because they're optional; if you use them too sparingly, MacinTalk reads to you in a boring monotone.

If a syllable does contain a stress mark, the stress mark must appear immediately after a vowel phoneme. If you place it anywhere else, it generates an error. (Usually, an error in writing phonetic text results in nothing but silence; MacinTalk simply does not read the sentence containing the error.)

Stress marks also affect the intonations of syllables, but not in an easily predictable fashion. The inflection that MacinTalk gives a syllable depends not only upon any stress mark that the syllable might contain, but also upon the rising and falling pitches of the syllables around it. In fact, the intonation of a word is affected by the overall pitch contour of the sentence that contains the syllable.

For example, the phonetic equivalent of the term *speech driver,* with a stress mark included in each word, could be written this way:

```
SPIY4CH DRAY5VER
```

If you wanted to write the phonetics for *speech driver* without any stress marks, you could use this spelling:

```
SPIYCH DRAYVER
```

As a first step in learning how to assign stress codes to syllables, it might be helpful to associate the stress values of words with parts of speech, as suggested in Table 6–2. However, this table is only a rough guide to get

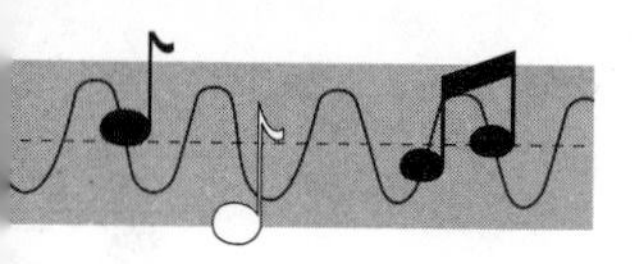

you started; as you become familiar with MacinTalk's stress markers, you'll probably come up with your own values.

Table 6–2. Suggested Stress Markers for Parts of Speech

Parts of Speech	Values
Nouns	5
Pronouns	2
Exclamations	9
Verbs	4
Articles	0
Adjectives	5
Prepositions	0
Adverbs	7
Conjunctions	0
Secondary Stress	1,2

In the MacinTalk's documentation, Apple also suggests that you follow these guidelines:

- **Content words—**always place a stress mark in a *content* word; that is, a word with a meaning. Nouns, adjectives, and verbs are content words. Articles and conjunctions are not content words. The word *is* is not generally a content word. Prepositions are not content words. All of these are called *function* words.
- **Accented syllables—**always place a stress mark on the accented syllable(s) of polysyllabic words, whether content or function. If more than one syllable is stressed, the one that gets the most stress gets the primary stress, and the other stressed syllables get secondary stresses; these should be marked with a value of only 1 or 2. Compound words (like *baseball* or *bandwagon*) should be treated as two separate words for the purposes of placing stress.

Punctuation

The rules of punctuation are simple in MacinTalk's phonetic language. MacinTalk pauses at both commas and dashes, but commas cause a more pronounced pitch rise. So you can use commas to delimit clauses, and dashes to delimit phrases. Remember, though, that you don't have to follow the normal rules of grammar. You can use commas not only where they would appear in normal English, but also in other places where natural pauses occur.

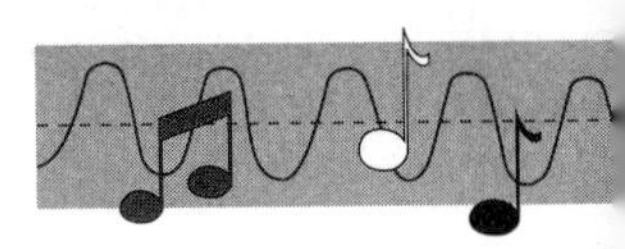

In MacinTalk's phonetic syntax, a sentence ends with either a period or a question mark. But be careful; not every question ends with a question mark. Many questions—such as the digitized sound sequence "How are you today?" that was used as an example in Chapter 5—don't end with rising tones. Therefore, in phonetic text, they don't require question marks.

When you write phonetics for MacinTalk, put question marks only after questions that end with rising tones; usually, questions that require yes/no answers. Other kinds of questions, such as "What did you do in the war, Daddy?" should usually end with a period.

In phonetic text written for MacinTalk, you can place parentheses around certain noun phrases. With parentheses, you can delimit any phrase that contains two or more content words that stand for one object. Thus, a phrase such as *my friend* does not require parentheses, but a phrase like *my girlfriend* does. You can even place parentheses around a phrase such as *the big building over there with the green roof on it*—which is also a noun phrase, although it is a long one.

When you write phonetic text for MacinTalk, the rule is that you should use parentheses liberally—in the right places, of course. Parentheses are a big help to MacinTalk's pronunciation, which (as you probably know by now) needs all the help it can get.

Programming MacinTalk

If you know how to write HyperCard programs, you can copy HyperLab's XFCNs and XCMDs into your own stacks. Then you can program MacinTalk directly from HyperCard. If you don't know how to write HyperCard programs, and you don't care to learn, you can skip this section.

As noted earlier in this chapter, the MacinTalk driver has six commands that can be called from programming languages such as C, Pascal, or assembly language. When you run the HyperCard program, you can execute all six commands from HyperCard.

HyperLab accesses MacinTalk by executing six HyperCard functions and procedures that are implemented as XFCNs and XCMDs. XFCNs and XCMDs, as explained in the box "Programming with MacinTalk" earlier this chapter, are executable code resources that can be called from HyperCard.

For more about how XCMDs and XFCNs are written and used in HyperTalk scripts, see the *HyperCard Script Language Guide,* which is published by Claris and is packaged with the developer's version of HyperCard.

The XFCNs and XCMDs that were written for HyperLab can be copied into any HyperCard stack. When you copy HyperLab's XFCNs and

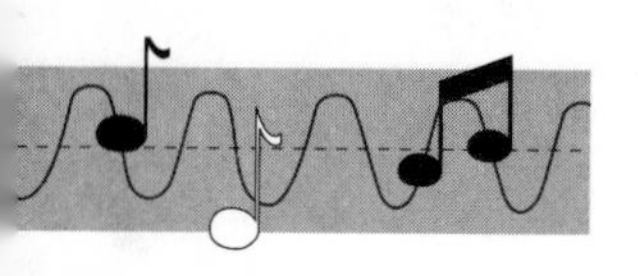

XCMDs into another stack, you can make calls to MacinTalk from that stack by implementing HyperLab's XFCNs and XCMDs.

The easiest way to copy HyperLab's MacinTalk commands to another stack is probably to use ResEdit. Just open both HyperLab and a destination stack in ResEdit, and copy HyperLab's XFCNs and XCMDs into the destination stack. (For more information about ResEdit, see the Addison-Wesley book *ResEdit Complete,* which is listed in the Bibliography.)

If you have ever programmed MacinTalk in a conventional language, such as Pascal or C, you may notice that HyperLab's six XFCNs and XCMDs are similar to—but not identical with—the six calls that are used to program MacinTalk from lower-level languages.

Table 6–3 compares the six commands that are used to program MacinTalk in Pascal with the six XFCNs and XCMDs that you can use to program the synthesizer from HyperLab.

In the remainder of this section, each XFCN and XCMD in the table is described under an individual heading.

Table 6–3. Pascal and HyperLab Calls Compared

HyperLab Commands	XFCN or XCMD	MacinTalk Commands
`SpeechOn` *`exceptionsFile`*	XCMD	`FUNCTION SpeechOn (ExceptionsFile: Str255; VAR` *`theSpeech:`* `SpeechHandle): SpeechErr;`
`SpeechOff`	XCMD	`PROCEDURE SpeechOff (`*`theSpeech:`* `SpeechHandle);`
`MacinTalk` *`phoneticString`*	XCMD	`FUNCTION MacinTalk (`*`theSpeech:`* `SpeechHandle;` *`Phonemes:`* `Handle): SpeechErr;`
`Reader(`*`theEnglishString`*`)`	XFCN	`FUNCTION Reader (`*`theSpeech:`* `SpeechHandle;` *`EnglishPtr:`* `Ptr;` *`InputLength:`* `LONGINT;` *`PhoneticOutput:`* `Handle):`*`SpeechErr;`*
`SpeechPitch` *`pitch, mode`*	XCMD	`PROCEDURE SpeechPitch (`*`theSpeech:`* `SpeechHandle;` *`thePitch:`* `INTEGER;` *`theMode:`* `F0Mode);`
`SpeechRate` *`theRate`*	XCMD	`PROCEDURE SpeechRate (`*`theSpeech:`* `SpeechHandle;` *`theRate:`* `INTEGER);`

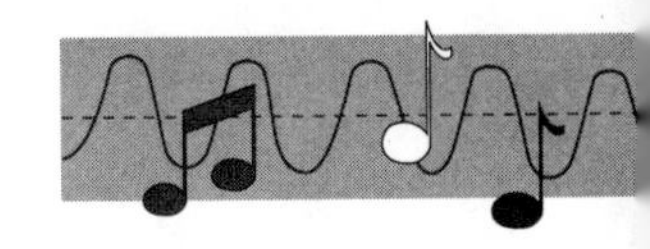

SpeechOn

SpeechOn is an XCMD that initializes the MacinTalk driver. You must execute the SpeechOn command before you can execute other MacinTalk commands. Here is the syntax:

```
SpeechOn exceptionsFile
```

An *exceptions file* is a text file containing special pronunciation rules that MacinTalk must use when it encounters specific letter combinations. You can create exceptions files with the help of a MacinTalk utility called an exceptions editor. The MacinTalk exceptions editor is part of the MacinTalk program developer's package available from APDA.

If you have an exceptions file that you want MacinTalk to use, you can place the path name of the file in the *exceptionsFile* parameter of the SpeechOn command. If you don't have an exceptions file, which is usually the case, you can leave the *exceptionsFile* parameter empty, and MacinTalk will create phonetic text without using any customized pronunciation rules.

When HyperLab executes the SpeechOn command successfully, it returns an empty string in the HyperCard variable *the result*. If an error is encountered, HyperLab returns an error message in *the result*.

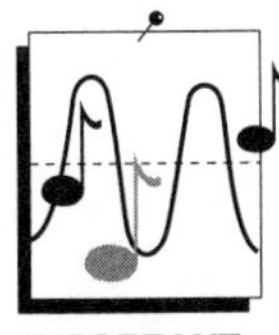

Once Is Enough

When you have activated MacinTalk by executing the SpeechOn command, you shouldn't execute the command again unless you have subsequently turned MacinTalk off. You can turn MacinTalk off by issuing a SpeechOff command.

One way to make sure that SpeechOn and SpeechOff calls are balanced is to call SpeechOn in an OpenStack handler and to call SpeechOff in a CloseStack handler. Another method is to set a global variable to true when speech is turned on and to false when speech is turned off. Use the second method if you want to turn MacinTalk on and off during a single HyperCard session. ❍

SpeechOff

SpeechOff is an XCMD that deactivates MacinTalk. You should call SpeechOff once, and only once, when you have finished using MacinTalk. SpeechOff takes no parameters, so the syntax is

```
SpeechOff
```

If the SpeechOff command is successful, an empty string is returned in the HyperCard variable *theResult*. If the command encounters an error, it returns the error string *Wrong number of parameters*.

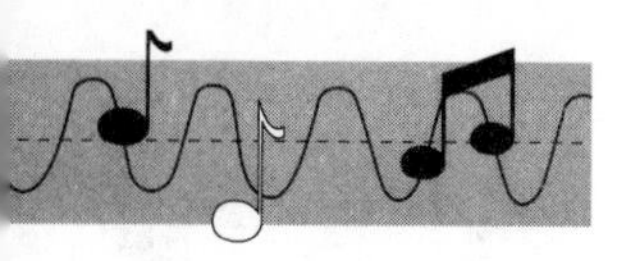

MacinTalk

MacinTalk is an XCMD that takes a phonetic string as an argument, as follows:

```
MacinTalk phoneticString
```

If the MacinTalk command is successful, MacinTalk reads the string and the command returns the empty string in the HyperCard variable *theResult*. If there is an error, an error message is returned.

Reader

Reader is an XFCN that takes one argument: an English-language string to be translated into a phonetic string.

```
Reader (theEnglishString)
```

If the function is successful, it returns a phonetic equivalent of the English string. If an error is encountered, the function returns an error message that begins with a question mark and a space.

Since error messages that are returned by Reader always begin with question marks (and legal MacinTalk phoneme strings never do), you could use the Reader XFCN in this fashion:

```
Put Reader(theEnglishString) into phoneticString
If first char of phoneticString = "?" then
  -- Put an error-handling procedure here
End If
```

SpeechPitch

SpeechPitch is an XCMD that sets both the baseline pitch and the intonation of MacinTalk. The baseline pitch has a default value of 110Hz, but it can be set to any value from 65Hz to 500Hz. This is the syntax of the SpeechPitch command:

```
SpeechPitch pitch, mode
```

The first argument, *pitch,* is a figure that can range from 65 to 500 (the desired baseline pitch measured in hertz). The second argument, *mode,* is optional. If you use a *mode* parameter, it can be one of two constants: the string "natural" or the string "robotic." A natural voice rises and falls, as if it were being spoken by a real person. A robotic voice is spoken in a monotone. You can experiment with varying pitches and modes by using HyperLab's Pitch button panel.

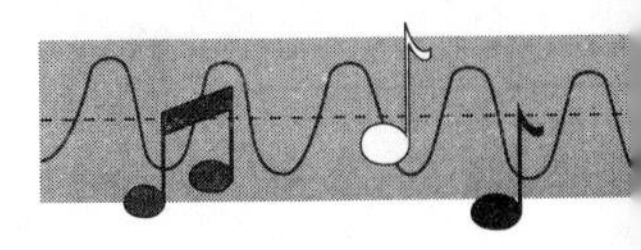

You can change MacinTalk's intonation without changing its pitch by passing a *pitch* parameter of zero to the SpeechPitch command. Similarly, you can change MacinTalk's pitch without changing its intonation by omitting the *mode* parameter.

SpeechRate

SpeechRate is an XCMD that sets the MacinTalk speaking rate. The syntax is:

```
SpeechRate theRate
```

The variable *theRate* is a number ranging from 85 to 425. The variable sets the MacinTalk speaking rate, measured in words per minute.

Beyond MacinTalk

As mentioned earlier in this chapter, in the section "The Future of MacinTalk," Apple has decided to replace the MacinTalk speech synthesizer with a new Toolbox manager called the Speech Manager. Ron Dumont, the head of the team assigned by Apple to develop the Speech Manager, said in an interview that two versions of the product were planned: a version that would require a small amount of memory and would produce a moderately good quality of speech, and a version that would require more memory but would produce very high-quality sound. During the interview, Dumont demonstrated both versions, and both produced remarkably clear and pleasant sound.

There are many differences between MacinTalk and the new Macintosh Speech Manager. For example, the Speech Manager doesn't grab the Macintosh CPU and keep it, as MacinTalk does; instead, it shares the CPU with other computer operations, so they can continue executing while the Speech Manager produces sound.

Another difference is that Apple has created the Speech Manager, owns its source code, and has pledged to support it. Therefore, software designers can be certain that products they develop for the Speech Manager will be compatible with new versions of the Macintosh and will continue to be supported.

Finally, some significant high-tech differences exist between MacinTalk and the Speech Manager. For instance, there is an important difference between the way MacinTalk simulates human speech and the way in which speech is produced by the Speech Manager. The Speech Manager, unlike MacinTalk, can synthesize speech from a real human voice recorded in a studio.

Currently, it takes considerable time and effort to create a voice for the Speech Manager that is based on a real human voice. An engineer creates a table of many sampled sounds, and then uses that table to create a voice for the Speech Manager.

Although this operation is tedious, at least at this stage of development, early demonstrations of the Speech Manager have shown results that were quite impressive. The Speech Manager can speak in various male and female voices, and in various languages. So move over, MacinTalk. You've been a great pal, but your days are numbered.

Voice Recognition

Speech synthesizers—like some people you may know—spend all of their time talking and don't seem to be able to listen. But there are some Macintosh products that can talk and listen. They are known generically as voice recognition systems.

One Macintosh product that can recognize your voice is the Voice Navigator from Articulate Systems, shown in Figure 6–6. Apple is also devoting considerable attention to developing voice recognition systems.

Figure 6–6. Voice Navigator

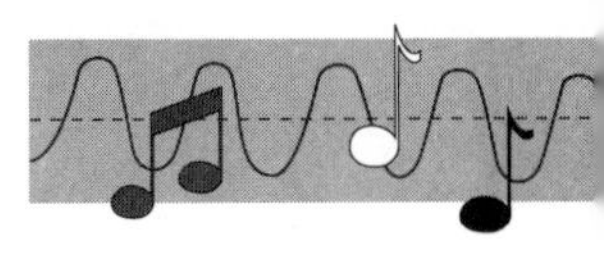

With the Voice Navigator, you can use a microphone instead of a mouse to perform computer operations. Instead of executing a command by selecting a menu item, you can simply tell your computer what to do and how to do it. When the Voice Navigator is connected to your Macintosh, you can select tools, change fonts and point sizes, zoom in and out, click buttons, send voice mail, and perform many other operations, all by voice commands.

The Voice Navigator can't replace all mouse operations—if you're doing word processing, for instance, you must still use the mouse and the keyboard to edit text—but Articulate Systems says that the unit can increase your computer productivity by at least 50 percent, and journalists who have reviewed the product seem to agree.

Before you use the Voice Navigator, you must program it to recognize your voice, and to associate words that you speak with the commands needed to run various applications. Articulate Systems provides programming tools to simplify those operations. Once the Voice Navigator is programmed, you speak commands into the microphone, and the Navigator does the rest.

One of the most interesting features of the Voice Navigator is that you can program it to skip through unnecessary levels of commands. For example, if you wanted to set the next file in a Microsoft Word document to "Chapter 2," you could teach the Voice Navigator to recognize a command such as "Next document, Chapter 2." Then you could perform the operation without having to go through the usual series of menu and dialog commands: "Format, Document, Margin, File Series, Next File, Chapter 2."

Summary

With the help of the MacinTalk speech synthesizer and an interactive HyperCard-based application called HyperLab, this chapter introduced a set of concepts that are universally used in designing, programming, and operating voice synthesizers.

Principles covered included the translation of ordinary text into phonetic text, or phonemes; the setting of pitch, speed, and intonation; and the editing of raw phonetic text into text that sounds appealing and interesting when it is read by a voice synthesizer.

By experimenting with the HyperLab program, you got a chance to listen firsthand to the result of these operations, and to demonstrate for yourself all of the topics covered in the chapter. By demonstrating the principles introduced in this chapter with MacinTalk and HyperLab, you were able to increase your understanding of all speech synthesizers, including more advanced systems such as those that are now under development at Apple.

7 Macintosh Music

There was a time when you didn't have to know how to type unless you were a secretary, a novelist, or a newspaper reporter. Then came the computer, and millions found a new reason to become keyboard-literate.

Today, Macintosh owners are learning to use another kind of keyboard: the kind that was invented for the harpsichord, was later built into the piano, and is now used in all kinds of electronic instruments, such as synthesizers, samplers, and electronic pianos and organs.

Computer keyboards and musical keyboards have a few things in common. To operate a computer, you don't have to type 120 words per minute, but you do have to know where all the keys are and what they do. Similarly, you can do some pretty impressive things with a computer keyboard without being a Vladimir Horowitz or a Stevie Wonder.

When you connect a musical keyboard to a Macintosh, you can lay down musical tracks one at a time, and then play them back all at once. Furthermore, you don't have to play anything in real time to make an electronic recording. You can pick out notes as slowly as you like, correcting your mistakes as you go along. Then, when you're finished, you can play your work back—up to 16 tracks of it—at any tempo. If you know anything at all about composing music, that's sure to impress your friends.

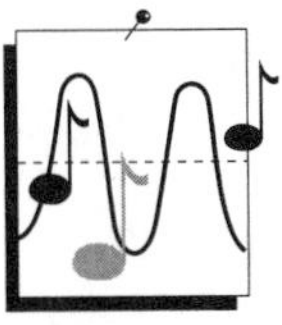

BY THE WAY

Notation Programs and Sequencers

Even though reading music is a tremendous asset for a musician, it isn't an absolute requirement. If you don't know how to read music, you can still compose music on your Macintosh with a program called a ***sequencer.***

A sequencer, like a notation program, can display musical compositions on a computer screen. But a sequencer doesn't usually display a composition in the form of a musical score. Instead, it displays the music in the form of lines that scroll across the screen. A sequencer display is reminiscent—in both looks and effect—of those old-time piano rolls that were used in player pianos.

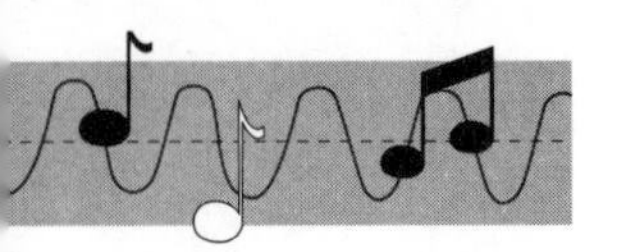

You can play, edit, and record music with a sequencer, just as you can with a musical notation program. In fact, sequencers are more popular than musical notation programs among players of electronic keyboards.

One reason sequencers are so popular is that they are designed to be used with **MIDI instruments** *such as synthesizers, samplers, and drum machines. MIDI, an acronym for Musical Instrument Digital Interface, is a specification that helps electronic instruments and computers communicate. When a musician or an engineer builds a studio around a computer, the instruments that are used in the studio are almost always MIDI instruments. MIDI is such an important factor in the electronic music world that it's the subject of the final chapter of this volume.*

Much more information about the MIDI specification—and instructions for using Songworks with a MIDI system—are presented in Chapter 9. ❍

In this chapter, and in Chapters 8 and 9, you'll learn how to make music on your Macintosh. In this chapter, you'll get a chance to try your hand at composing real sheet music with the help of a new musical notation instruction program called Songworks from Ars Nova software. In Chapter 8, you'll dive a little deeper into the field of music theory with the help of Listen, a music-instruction and ear-training program from Imaja. Finally, in Chapter 9, you'll learn how to connect your Macintosh to various kinds of MIDI devices so you can start building your dream studio, one step at a time.

About Songworks

Songworks is a music entertainment and notation program from Ars Nova, the publisher of the popular music theory and ear-training program Practica Musica. A demonstration version of Songworks, which includes enough features to do the exercises in this chapter, is provided on the bonus disk that comes with this book.

Songworks, according to Ars Nova, "is for everyone, both musicians and nonmusicians. It's a personal entertainer that is also a tool for writing and printing songs." With Songworks, you can compose music, edit music, improvise, learn harmony, and get and try out musical ideas. You can tap out a melody on your computer keyboard or on a musical keyboard displayed on the screen, and you can watch as Songworks creates a musical score from the notes you have played. If you have a MIDI keyboard (MIDI devices are covered in Chapter 9), you can play your music on your MIDI device instead of on your computer speaker or your screen.

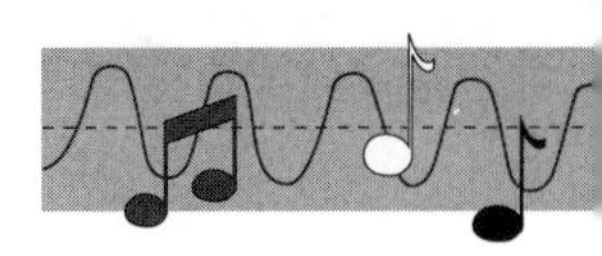

As you compose, you can add chords to your melody—with help from Songworks—and then you can listen to how your tune sounds. (Chords are covered in more detail in Chapter 8.)

Songworks can suggest melody ideas, chord progression ideas, and chords that go with your melody. It can transpose your song into another key, and it can transform your melody in interesting ways.

When you're done, Songworks can print out your composition on a printer, complete with melody, chord symbols, lyrics, and other text.

Some features are disabled in the demo version of Songworks that's on your bonus disk. For instance, you can't save your work with the demonstration version. But there are enough features to show you how the program works, and you can do enough experimenting to learn a lot about music, and to have some fun. For a fully operational copy of Songworks, please see your Macintosh dealer or call Ars Nova for more information.

What You Need to Use Songworks

To use Songworks, all you need is your Macintosh. A hard disk is recommended, but not required.

What you *don't* need is the ability to read music. With Songworks and the information in this chapter, you can easily learn the fundamentals of reading music. With a little practice, you'll be reading more music—and once you're musically literate, you'll be on your way to becoming fluent in the language of musical notation.

Using Songworks

If you have decompressed the programs on your bonus disk, as outlined in the instructions in Chapter 1, you can launch your demonstration version of Songworks by opening the folder labeled 07–Sound and Music, and double-clicking on the Songworks icon. When you have launched Songworks, two windows appear on the screen as shown in Figure 7–1.

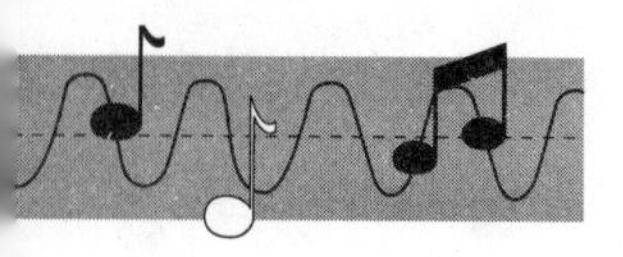

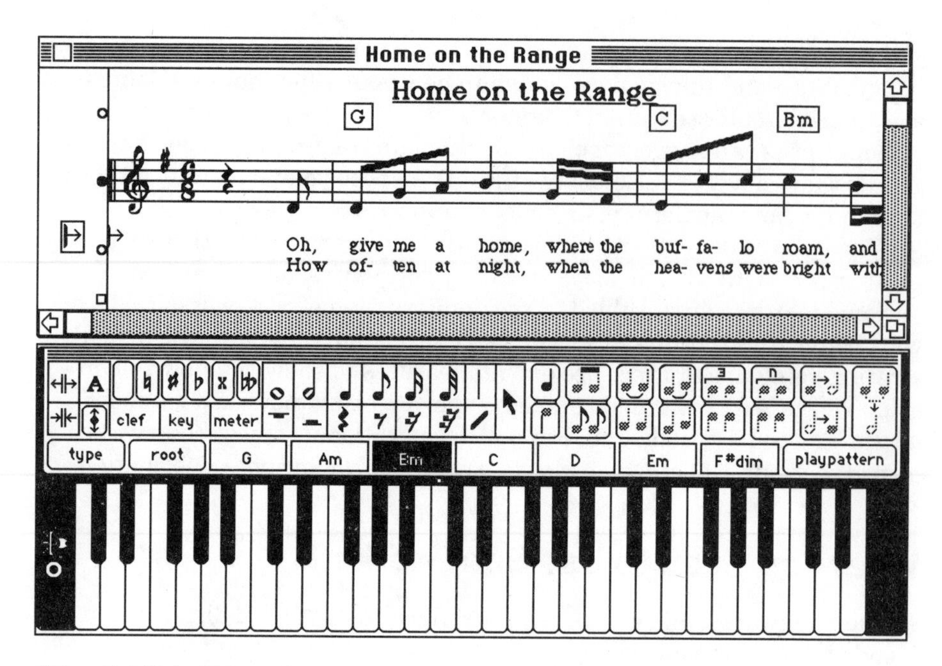

Figure 7–1. Main Songworks screen

The upper window, called the *music window,* contains the sheet music for the song "Home on the Range." The lower window—the keyboard window—contains a musical keyboard and a set of tools for composing and editing songs.

The Music Window

The music window contains a musical staff, a set of accompaniment chords, and a set of lyrics. The chords—which can be played on a guitar, a piano, or any other instrument that can play chords—are the alphabetical symbols in the small boxes above the staff. The lyrics for "Home on the Range" appear below the staff.

At the bottom of the music window, and on its far right, are standard Macintosh scroll bars. With the horizontal scroll bar, you can scroll horizontally through the song, from its beginning to its end.

In the production version of the Songworks program, you can format a musical score for printing by selecting Page Preview from the File menu, and you can then use the vertical scroll bar to scroll up and down through the music. You can't do that in the demonstration version of the program.

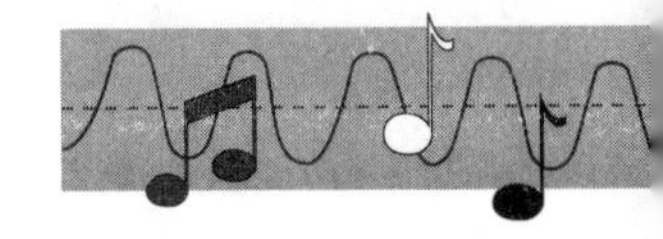

The Keyboard Window

The lower window also contains tools for writing, playing, and editing music. You'll learn to use those tools as you proceed through this chapter.

Playing Music with Songworks

To the left of the keyboard in the keyboard window, there's a speaker icon with a radio button below it. When the speaker button is selected, Songworks plays music when you click on the on-screen keys or type on your computer keyboard. When the speaker button isn't selected, Songworks plays music from a score when you type Command-H, but doesn't make sounds when you click on the on-screen keys or type on your Macintosh keyboard.

To play the on-screen keyboard, make sure the speaker button is on, and then simply click the mouse on the piano keys on your screen. To use your computer keyboard as a musical keyboard, type on your computer's keys. (If you have a MIDI keyboard, you can connect the keyboard to your Macintosh through a MIDI interface. Then you can play music on a real electronic instrument keyboard instead of using your screen keyboard or your computer keyboard. For more about MIDI instruments, see Chapter 9.)

Although you can use Songworks as a musical instrument, its real power lies in its ability to create musical scores, as you'll see later in this chapter.

Playing the Screen Keyboard

To play music on the screen keyboard, all you have to do is click on a key with the mouse. By dragging the mouse up and down the keyboard, you can play slurred scales—with the same effect that you get when you run one finger up and down the keyboard of a piano.

Playing Prewritten Music

Songworks can play music that you have written or music that someone has written for you. The demonstration version of Songworks comes with one sample song—"Home on the Range"—that you can play quite easily. Here's how:

1. Launch Songworks from the Finder by double-clicking on its application icon.

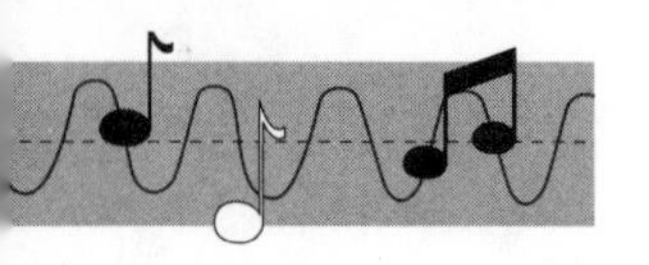

2. In the lower left corner of the music window, just to the left of the lyrics line, there's a small box-shaped control that contains a vertical line and a right-pointing arrow. That control is a *listening point tool.* It controls a *listening point marker.* When you start the Songworks demo, the listening point marker is situated at the beginning of the composition in the music window, as shown in Figure 7–2.

Figure 7–2. Playing the sample song

3. Press Command-H, or select the item labeled Hear (All or Selected) from the File menu. Songworks then plays "Home on the Range," beginning at the location indicated by the listening point marker.

Playing Your Computer Keyboard

If you don't have a MIDI keyboard (or perhaps even if you do), you might want to experiment with playing music on the letter keys of your computer.

With the keys on your Macintosh keyboard, Songworks can create two different kinds of musical keyboards: a *diatonic* keyboard, which includes only the notes of the scale (no sharps or flats), or a *chromatic* keyboard, which includes all of the sharps and flats in its range and can play any melody. Sharps and flats are described later in this chapter, in the section "Fundamentals of Music."

The Diatonic Keyboard

To select a diatonic keyboard, select the Keyboard Options submenu and the Letter Keys: Scale Notes Only item from the Options menu. Songworks then transforms your computer keyboard into a diatonic keyboard. The musical notes that you can then play with your keyboard are shown in Figure 7–3.

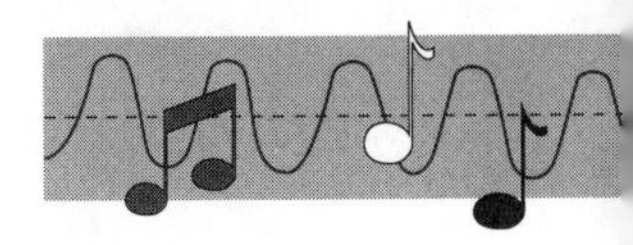

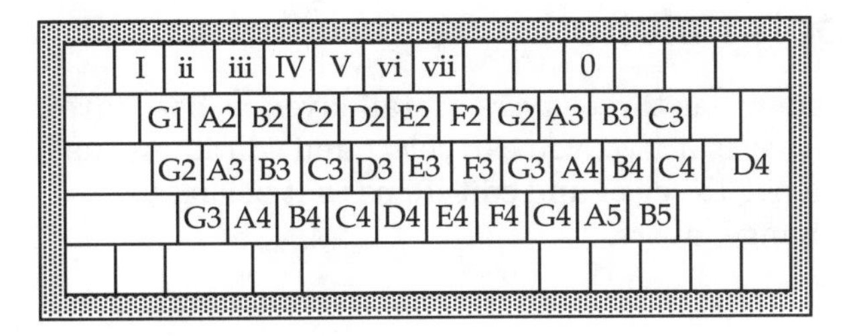

Figure 7–3. Diatonic keyboard

The Chromatic Keyboard

To choose a chromatic keyboard, select the Keyboard Options submenu and the Full 12 Notes item from the Options menu. Songworks then creates a chromatic keyboard, as shown in Figure 7–4.

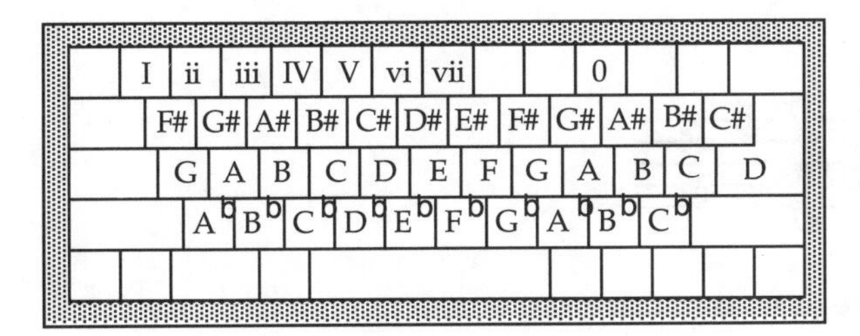

Figure 7–4. Chromatic keyboard

Try out each of the keyboards that Songworks offers, and see which one you like. If you can't yet interpret the notes in the illustrations, don't worry; you'll know your notes by the time you finish this chapter.

Keyboard Techniques

The number keys that are marked with roman numerals in Figures 7–3 and 7–4 produce chords when they are pressed. To stop a chord, press the 0 number key.

With either keyboard arrangement—diatonic or chromatic—you can raise the octave that each key plays by pressing the + key (the Shift key is not needed). Similarly, you can lower each key's pitch one octave by pressing the – key.

When you press a note key and then release it, the note that the key produces sustains (continues to play for a while) when you release the key, as if you had pressed a pedal on a real piano. This makes it easier to play smoothly.

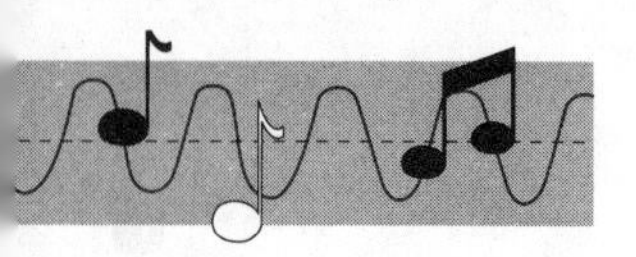

Layers and the Tools Palette

The Songworks music window has three *layers:* a staff layer, a chord layer, and a text layer. When a layer is active, you can select and edit items that are associated with that layer. To select and edit items that belong to another layer, you must change layers.

Changing Layers

You can change layers by clicking on one of the three small round buttons to the left of the music staff in the music window. Those three buttons, called *layer handles,* are shown in Figure 7–5.

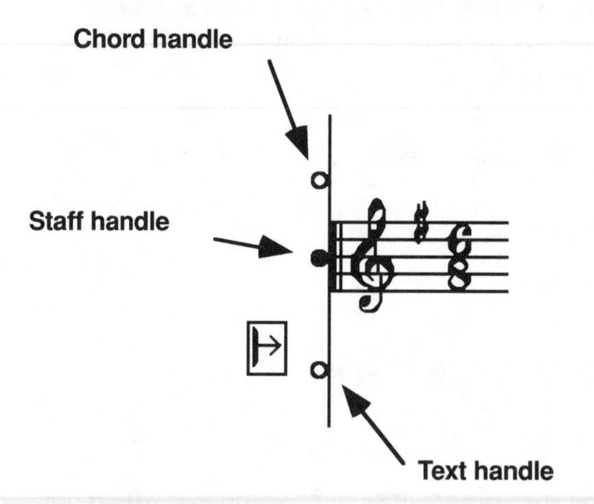

Figure 7–5. Layer handles

You can also change layers by moving the cursor to the keyboard window and selecting buttons from the tools palette: the panel of buttons above the screen keyboard.

Tools and Layers

Each tool in the tools palette is associated with a layer in the music window. When you choose a tool, the appropriate layer is activated, and all other tools in the same layer become active.

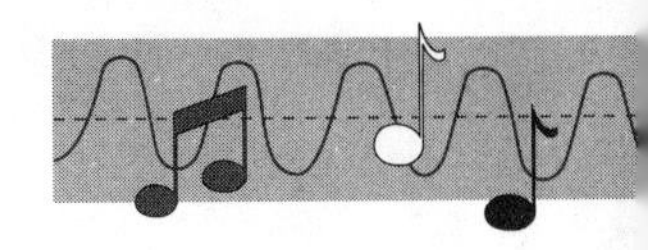

Telling Which Layer Is Active

You can tell which layer of the music window is active by simply looking at it. When the chord layer or the text layer is active, the staff layer is grayed out. When the staff layer is not grayed out, it is the active layer. Also, the handle of the active layer is highlighted.

The top circle, for example, is the chord handle. When the chord handle is highlighted, you can enter and remove chord symbols (for more about chords, see Chapter 8).

The staff handle is the small circle at the left of the staff. When the staff handle is highlighted, you can add notes, edit notes, and delete notes in a song.

The bottom circle is the lyrics or text handle. When it is highlighted, you can write, delete, or edit text.

Songworks Tools

Songworks includes a set of tools that you can use to listen to music, write music, or edit music in various ways. For example:

- You can listen to a composition by selecting the item Hear (All or Selected) from the File menu. If you haven't selected part of a song, Songworks plays the whole song starting at the current listening point. If you have made a selection, Songworks plays the part you have selected. When a song is playing, you can press the spacebar to stop the song.
- You can edit music by selecting tools from the tools palette above the keyboard in the keyboard window.
- To place a note in a composition, select the note that you want to use from the tools palette. Then either click in the staff where you want the note to appear, or play a note on the screen keyboard or an external MIDI keyboard, which you can install by selecting Sound Options from the Options menu (more about MIDI devices is presented in Chapter 9).
- To remove a note, select it and then use the Cut or Clear menu command or press the Delete (Backspace) key. If nothing is selected, the Delete key removes the symbol to the left of the blinking caret, as it would in a word processor.
- You can add a chord accompaniment to a composition by selecting a chord from the chords listed above the piano keys, and then clicking in the musical staff where you want the chord to go. (Chords are examined more closely in Chapter 8.)

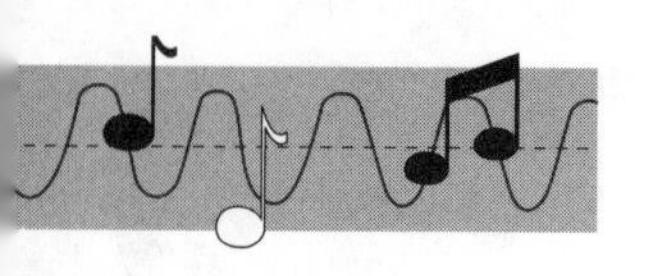

When you select the chord tool, numbered arrows appear. They show every position where a chord could be put. In the demonstration version of Songworks, you are limited to the chords that appear in the chord tool boxes (the rectangles with the names of chords inside them, just above the keys on the screen keyboard).

Other Features

These are some other features of the Songworks demonstration program:

- As noted earlier in this chapter, the *listening point tool* is a small box-shaped control in the lower left corner of the music window, just to the left of the lyrics line. It contains a vertical line and a right-pointing arrow. The listening point tool controls a *listening point marker* that is normally situated at the beginning of the composition shown in the music window. When you execute the Hear command—from the Songworks menu or by typing Command-H—the song in the music window starts playing from the point specified by the listening point marker. To move the marker back to the beginning of a score, just click on the listening point tool again.
- You can transpose music to other keys, or transform it in various other ways, by selecting items from the Transforms menu. You can apply the transformations you select either to the entire composition shown in the music window or to whatever part of the composition is selected. The best way to learn about the Transforms menu is to experiment. (In the demonstration version of Songworks, the items under the Autonotation feature are not available.)
- Songworks has two qualities of built-in sound. Lower-grade sound is automatically selected if you are running a Macintosh Classic, Macintosh Plus, Macintosh SE, or the original Macintosh Portable. You can choose the higher-quality sound in the Sound Options window, but this will cause much slower responses from the computer.

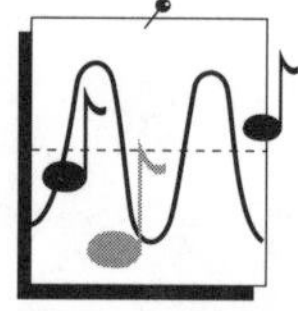

IMPORTANT

Watch out for Incompatibilities

Certain programs may be incompatible with Songworks. These include InterFax and the software for the Wacom Graphics Tablet. Also, remember that Songworks requires either System 6 or System 7. ❍

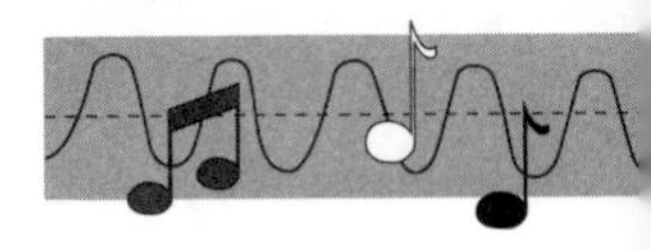

Musical Notation

To get the most out of Songworks—or out of any program that produces musical scores—it's essential to have at least a basic knowledge of musical notation. If you already know how to read music, feel free to skip to the next heading. If you don't know how to read music, please don't go away; you're going to be surprised how easy it is to learn the language of musical notation.

Many people think that musical notation is too difficult and too mysterious to bother learning. Consequently, they remain musically illiterate, and thus miss out on many of the joys of music. It's true, to some extent, that you don't have to know how to read music to play a musical instrument. But if you can't read music, here are some of the other things you can't do:

- You can't learn a new piece of music unless someone plays it for you—usually several times—or until you hear it played on a recording.
- If you compose music, you can't write it down on paper so other people can read it.
- If you want to copyright a piece of music, you have to find somebody who'll write it down for you.
- You can't thumb through music books or sheets of music in search of something that might interest you.

And the list goes on and on.

But there's no need to suffer the inconvenience, embarrassment, and occasional indignity that being unable to read music can subject you to—not when musical literacy is so easy to attain.

With access to a program like Songworks, which can translate music that you play into a musical score, you can learn to read music by just watching the program work! Of course, if you know something about musical notation when you start watching, that can't hurt. So here goes.

Fundamentals of Music

There are two fundamental elements of music: pitch and rhythm. Pitch, which can be expressed as a frequency, refers to how high or low a note sounds. Rhythm is a regulated pattern formed by long or short notes. In music, rhythm regulates the timing of pitches; in a composition, rhythm is made up of patterns of short and long pitches.

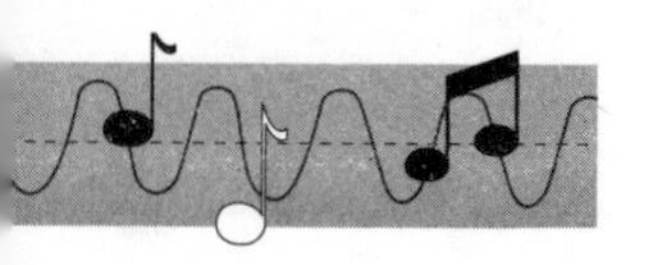

In this section, you'll learn about pitch and rhythm, as well as how to read music.

Pitch

Figure 7–6 is a picture of the Songworks keyboard. Notice the small white dot just above one of the notes near the center of the keyboard. Directly under that dot is a note that is called middle C. Play it, and you'll hear how middle C sounds.

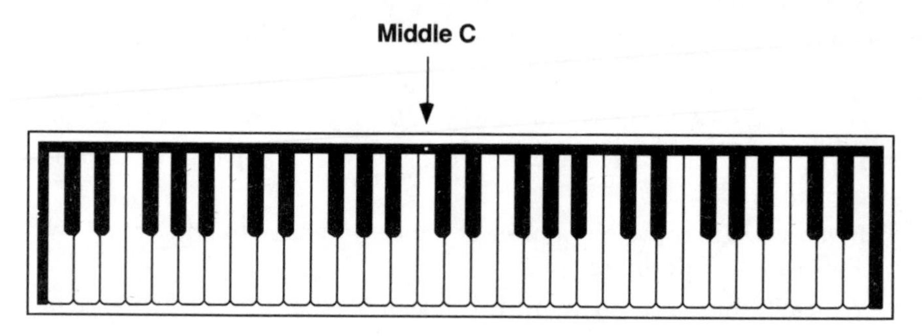

Figure 7–6. Middle C

Now let's examine how a piano keyboard is laid out. Follow these steps:

1. To the right of middle C, there is a pair of black keys with one white key in between. Those keys are, in ascending order, C sharp, D, and D sharp. Find and play middle C, and then play the C sharp, D, and D sharp notes by clicking on them with the mouse.
2. Move to the right of the D sharp key, and you'll find a pair of two adjacent white keys. They are called E and F. Play E, and then play F.
3. To the right of the F key, there's a group of three black keys, each separated by one white key. Those five keys are, in ascending order, F sharp, G, G sharp, A, and A sharp. Play F sharp, G, G sharp, A, and A sharp.
4. To the right of A sharp, there is another pair of adjacent white keys. Their names are B and C. Play B and C.
5. You have now played a *chromatic scale:* a progression of 13 consecutive notes on the piano keyboard. To play the chromatic scale, you've pressed keys arranged in a certain pattern: a white key; a pair of black keys separated by a white key; a pair of adjacent white keys; a set of three black keys, each separated by white key; and two adjacent white keys.

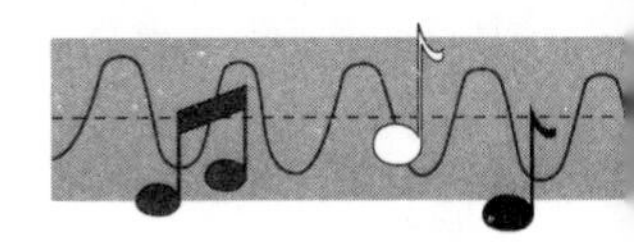

6. If you continued to move up the keyboard, pressing each key, this pattern of black and white keys would repeat itself. It's easy to see the repeating pattern of black and white keys as you look up and down the piano keyboard: there are two adjacent white keys, a pair of black keys separated by a white key, another pair of adjacent white keys, a set of three black keys separated by single white keys, and so on.
7. Now go back to middle C and start moving *down* the keyboard. As you might expect, the pattern repeats itself in that direction, too.

Different Notes That Sound the Same

When you've detected the pattern in the black keys, locate middle C again, and play it. Then move up to the C note that's an octave higher, and play that.

Now play both Cs in succession, and you may be able to tell why they have the same name. One sounds higher than the other, of course. However, except for their *pitch,* they have the same note. You might say that they are the same, but different. This sounds like a paradox, but you can easily prove that it's true:

1. Play middle C, hold the key down, and hum the note while it is still playing.
2. While you are humming middle C, play the C note that's an octave higher. See if this isn't true: Although you're humming one note and playing another, both notes sound the same.
3. Now find a few other C keys on the keyboard, and play those while you hum middle C.
4. You have now proved that every C note sounds the same, no matter what its pitch is. This paradox holds true for all the other notes on the keyboard: All A notes sound the same, all B notes sound the same, and so on.

Scales

Here's another exercise: Play middle C, and then play each ascending *white* key until you reach the C that's an octave higher than middle C. (For now, skip the black keys; you'll return to those later.) If you have listened to enough music and have paid enough attention to it, you may recognize that the sequence of notes that you have just played is a scale. Because the scale you have played starts and ends with the note C, it's known as a *C scale*. The notes in the C scale are C, D, E, F, G, A, B, and C.

You have already seen that the C scale begins and ends on the same note: C. For that reason, it's called the C scale—or, to call it by its full

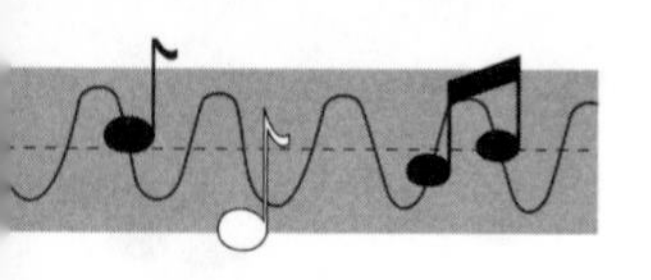

name, the C Major scale (there's also a C minor scale; indeed, there are many other kinds of scales, as you'll learn in Chapter 8).

You've probably heard people play scales many times. You may have also heard someone sing the scale using syllables instead of letters, like this: *Do re mi fa sol la ti do.* If that sounds familiar, it isn't surprising. Singers, as well as players of musical instruments, often practice with scales. You've probably also heard the song that begins "Doe, a deer, a female deer.. ." from *The Sound of Music.*

You can also sing or play a scale by moving downward—playing the notes C, B, A, G, F, E, D, and C, or singing the syllables *Do ti la sol fa mi re do.* The syllables that represent the vocal scale, like the letters that represent the keyboard scale, begin and end on the same note: in the case of vocalized notes, *do.*

The reason musicians pay so much attention to scales is that the scale is almost always the foundation of musical compositions. Many pieces of music can be played using just the notes in the scale. For example, you need only the notes in the scale to play "My Country 'Tis of Thee," "Amazing Grace," and many popular and folk songs. Of course, many other compositions have musical patterns that are much more complicated. To play those, you have to move beyond the scale and use at least some of the black keys—or the sharps and flats—on the piano keyboard. There's more information about sharps and flats later in this section.

Full Steps and Half Steps

You now know there's a pattern in the way the white keys and the black keys are laid out on the keyboard. But what is the reason for the pattern?

Well, for one thing, it makes middle C and the other notes on the keyboard easier to find. But that isn't the real reason. The real reason is related to the concept of steps and half steps between notes in the scale. The best way to illustrate steps and half steps is to listen to them. So here's another exercise:

1. Play middle C. Then press the *white* key to the right of middle C, which is D. Play both notes several times, and notice how far apart they are in pitch; try to get a sense of how much higher in pitch D is than C.
2. Play middle C again, and then play the white key just to the left of it, which is B. Play C and B several times, and pay attention to how far apart *they* are in pitch.
3. Play C and D again, and play B and C again. Do that several times. Do C and D sound like they're farther apart in pitch than B and C? If they do, then you're getting the point. The fact is that there is twice as much difference in pitch between C and D as there is between B

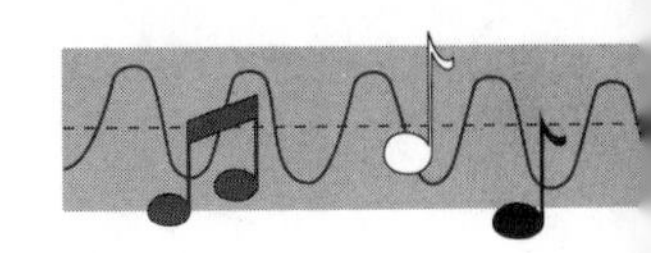

and C. In pitch, B and C are a *half step* apart, and C and D are a *full step* apart. With this in mind, play the two pairs of notes again and see if you can hear the difference.

4. If you can't, then try something else: Play middle C again, and press the first *black* key to the right of middle C, which is called C sharp (it's a little higher, or *sharper,* than C). Then play B and C. The distance in pitch between those two pairs of notes should sound the same, because B and C are a half step apart, while C and C sharp (or C#) are a half step apart also. (Incidentally, you can also refer to C sharp as D flat, which is a half step lower, or *flatter,* than D.)
5. If you need more listening practice, keep playing the notes B, C, C#, and D, and listening to pitch differences between them. B and C are a half step apart, as are C and C#. The notes B and C# are a full step apart, as are C and D.
6. Now look at the two white keys to the right of D. If you count upward from middle C, you can calculate that the names of these two notes are E and F.

   Notice that E and F, like B and C, are adjacent white keys; there is no black key between them. If the rules about pitch that you have discovered thus far are correct, that must mean E and F are just a half step apart.
7. If you have now trained your ear to detect the difference between a half step and a full step, you can play E and F and hear that they are indeed a half step apart. (If you need to compare it with a full-step difference between some other two notes, go ahead.)

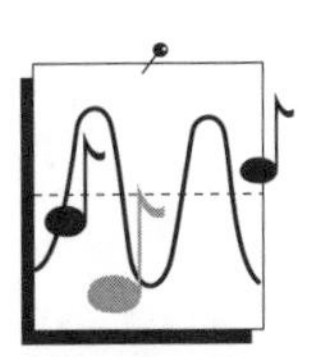
BY THE WAY

Ups and Downs

Is a black key a sharp or a flat? It can be either, depending upon the way it is used in a musical composition.

For example, if you raise the pitch of middle C by pressing the black key just to the right of middle C, then you can call the black key C sharp. But if you lower the pitch of the note D by pressing the black key just to the left of the D key, then you can call the same black key D flat.

Long ago, when medieval music was all the rage, there were subtle but audible differences between notes that were played as sharps and notes that were played as flats. In fact, up until the classical period began in the mid-1700s, Bach and his contemporaries were still using "in-between" notes that had not yet been incorporated into the piano keyboard.

Today, skilled musicians still use sharps and flats differently from time to time to lend subtle flavors to their music. In Chapter 8, which covers musical intervals, you'll get a chance to listen to some antique scales that make distinctions between sharps and flats.

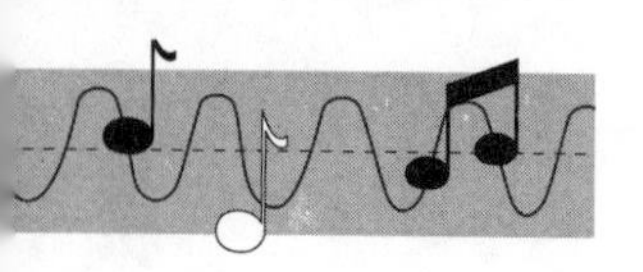

For modern listeners, though, the subtle differences between the sounds of raised notes and lowered notes are little more than historical curiosities. For the most part, the tuning of modern instruments eliminates the subtle distinctions between sharps and flats, and sharp notes and flat notes are generally treated identically. ❍

Now let's review what you've learned so far, and let's try to put it all together:

- The scale is the foundation of most musical composition.
- The C scale, which has no sharps or flats, extends from any C to the next C on the keyboard, in either direction.
- Between each adjacent note in the C scale, there is a measurable difference in pitch.
- Between the notes B and C, and between the notes E and F, there is a half step of difference in pitch. Between all other adjacent notes on the keyboard, there is a full step of difference in pitch. Visually, you can detect this difference by looking at the piano keyboard; there are no black keys between B and C, or between E and F, so they must be a half step apart. You can also detect this difference by listening to the various notes on the keyboard and paying attention to the differences in pitch between them.

Facts and Speculation

By now, you may be wondering about something that every student of music eventually puzzles over: What is the reason for this? Why are there full steps between some notes, and half steps between others?

The reason is partly scientific and partly cultural—but it's mostly cultural. Largely because of the kinds of music that we have become accustomed to hearing in Western countries, a musical scale with a half step of pitch difference between its third and fourth tones and another half step between its seventh and eighth tones just seems to sound right; it's something we're used to. Try to put half steps in other places, and the scale just doesn't sound like the scales that we've been hearing all our lives. So, to our ears, music based upon other kinds of scales—sometimes called *modes*—can sound wrong.

That doesn't mean, however, that the scale you've been examining (the diatonic scale) is the only scale that musicians use. If you move up the scale in full steps from one C to the next C, pressing black keys when needed, what you have is a seven-note *whole-tone scale*—and many composers, such as Claude Debussy, have used whole-tone scales in music very effectively. By moving up the keyboard from one C to the next C a half step at a time, playing all the white *and* black keys, what you wind up with is a *chromatic* scale, which can also be used effectively in music.

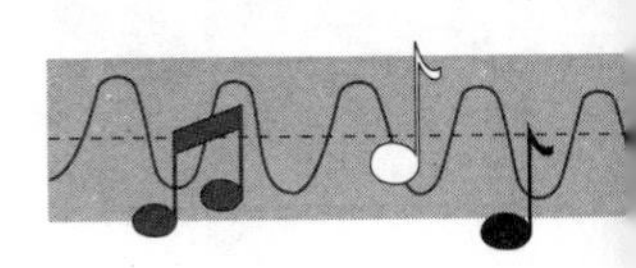

Another kind of scale—one that most music listeners are quite familiar with—is the minor scale. The minor scale is one of several scales, or *modes,* that date back to medieval times. Other early modes included the Dorian mode, which started on D; the Phrygian mode, which started on E; and the Lydian mode, which started on G. Interestingly, the Dorian mode and the Lydian mode are still sometimes heard in modern music, mostly in blues and rock music.

In a minor scale, there is a half step of pitch difference between the second and third notes in the scale, and another half step of pitch difference between the fifth and sixth notes.

In Western culture, the musical scales that we hear most are the major and minor scales. To many people's ears, music composed using major scales sounds happier and more straightforward than that based on minor scales. Music composed using minor scales tends to sound more exotic, more mysterious, or even sad. Happy, lilting music is usually based on major scales, and funeral marches and compositions that are supposed to sound foreign or exotic are often based on minor scales.

You can play one minor scale on the keyboard using only the white keys —that is, using no sharps and flats. That's the scale in A minor. To play an A minor scale, press the lower (left-hand) A key shown in Figure 7–7. Then play, in succession, each white key up to and including the higher (right-hand) A key shown in the illustration. When you have done that, you have played an A minor scale.

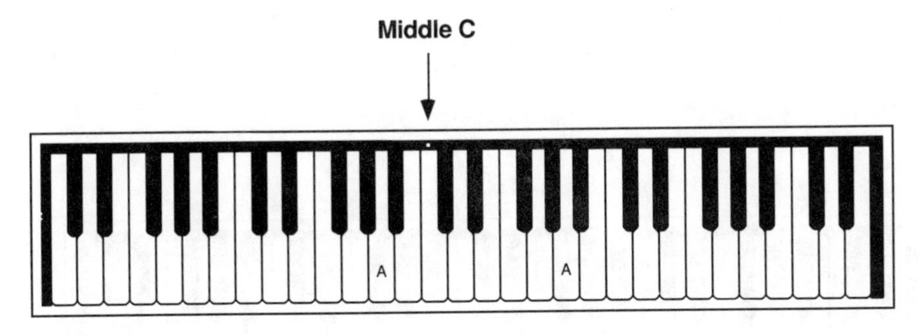

Figure 7–7. The A minor scale

If you play the A minor scale several times, and it still doesn't seem to have a coherent sound, then simply hold the mouse down while you drag the cursor up and down the scale, in the same way that you would drag one finger up and down the keys of a piano keyboard. That should give you an idea of how a minor scale sounds.

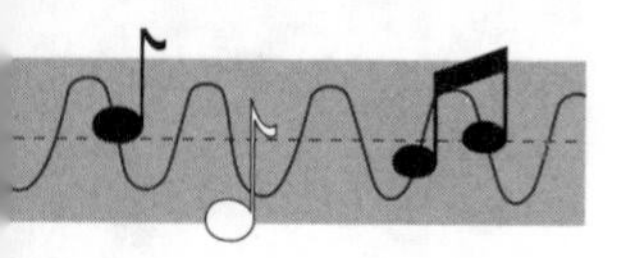

Playing in Different Keys

The C Major and A minor scales are the keys that music students usually learn first, since students can play many simple tunes in C Major and A minor using only the white keys on the piano keyboard. The keys of C Major and A minor have no sharps or flats, and tunes that have no sharps do not require the use of black keys.

However, not all music is based on the C Major scale or the A minor scale. In fact, although A minor is a relatively popular key signature, musicians don't write much music in C Major. Most composers prefer to create music that is based on other scales—that is, music that is written in other *keys*.

In music, the *key signature* of a composition is the name of the scale on which the composition is based. For example, a melody that is based on the C Major scale is said to be written in the key of C Major. Similarly, a composition that is based on the A minor scale is said to be written in the key of A minor.

"Home on the Range," the sample tune that comes with the Songworks demonstration program, is an example of a song that is not written in C Major or A minor. It happens to be written in the key of G. To find out what that means, read on.

Playing a G Scale

Here's an experiment with the G scale. Play a scale that ascends from one G key to another, making sure that you press only the white keys. Figure 7–8 shows the starting and ending G notes that you should use for this exercise.

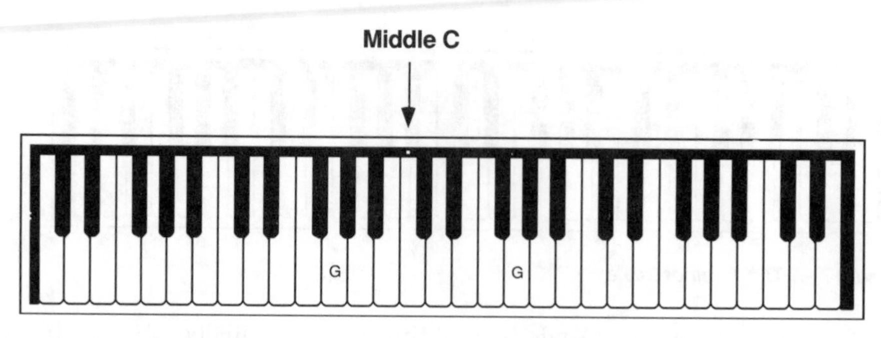

Figure 7–8. The G scale

When you play your G scale, listen carefully to each note you play. The intervals between the notes in this scale should sound exactly the same as the intervals that you heard when you played a C scale—with two exceptions.

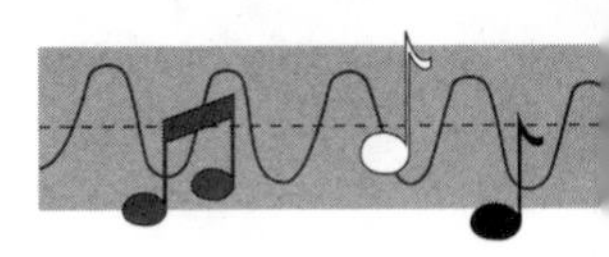

The two intervals that sound different are those that come before and after the seventh (next-to-last) note in the scale. By carefully comparing the intervals in the C scale and the G scale that you have played, you can find out why.

As you may recall from the analysis of the C scale that was presented earlier in this section, each ascending note in the C major scale is one step higher than the note that precedes it—except for the third and fourth notes and the seventh and eighth notes, which are each just a half step apart. Now let's see if the intervals in the C Major scale, which you know are correct, match those in the G scale that you just played. To check that, follow these steps:

1. Locate the G note where your scale started. Then, starting with that G, move up the keyboard slowly, examining the interval between each pair of notes that you played.
2. The first three notes that you played were G, A, and B. These notes, like the first three notes in the C Major scale, ascend in full steps.
3. The third and fourth notes in your G scale were B and C. The notes B and C, like the third and fourth notes in the C Major scale, are a half step apart. So it isn't surprising that the half-step interval between B and C sounds correct.
4. The next two notes in the G scale were D and E. The notes D and E, like the fifth and sixth notes in the C major scale, are one step apart. So, as you might expect, they also sound fine.
5. Now you come to the sixth and seventh notes in the G scale that you played—the only notes in the scale that sounded different from their counterparts when you played the C scale. Recall that in the C Major scale, the sixth and seventh notes are A and B, which are a full step apart. But when you play a G scale on just the white keys, the sixth and seventh notes are E and F, which are only a half step apart.
6. Another difference arises when you move on to the seventh and eighth notes in the G scale. When you played the C Major scale, the seventh and eighth notes were B and C, which are a half step apart. But in the G scale that you hear when you play only white notes, the seventh and eighth notes are F and G, which are a full step apart.

And that's why a G scale played only on white keys sounds different from the C scale.

Now that you know why the C Major scale sounds different from a G scale played only on white keys, you can use just one black note on the keyboard to make the intervals between the notes in the two scales sound the same. To make the two scales sound more similar, do this:

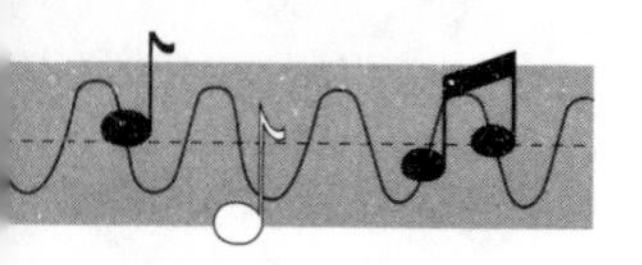

1. Play the G scale again—but this time, when you reach the seventh note in the scale, don't play an F. Instead, press the *black* key to the right of the F key. That key, which is a half step higher than F, is called F sharp.
2. When you've played F sharp, play the last note in the scale, which is G.
3. You have now played a scale that has one sharp, and starts and ends on the note G. In other words, you have played a G Major scale.

Now that you know how to play a G Major scale, you have completed your first lesson in the use of sharps. From now on, each time you play a G scale, you press the F sharp key instead of the F. That way, every time you play a scale that starts and ends on G, you'll get a G Major scale.

You have now learned another important musical concept: By using both the white keys and the black keys on a musical keyboard, you can play scales (and melodies) in any key. To play a G Major scale, as you have seen, you must use one black key: F sharp. That black key raises the seventh note of the G scale by half a step—and that half-step boost is needed to make the G major scale sound right.

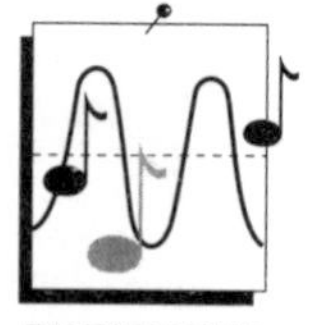

BY THE WAY

Why Composers Write Music in Different Keys

Since it's so easy to play in the key of C Major—which has no sharps or flats—why would anyone want to write a composition in other keys (such as G) that require the player to use the black keys on the keyboard?

One reason is that people's voices have different ranges. You might be able to sing "Home on the Range" in G, but you might not be able to reach all the notes if the piece were played in C.

Also, until the mid-1750s or so, the half steps that made up the scales in different keys were not the same, and musical instruments sounded different when they played different scales. Organs, especially, were tuned unequally, so that different keys had different sound qualities. For example, the key of B Major had a different quality than the key of E Major.

Because of these subtle differences in the sounds of different keys, post-medieval composers noticed that different key signatures had subtly different characteristics that affected the character of musical compositions. The key of C Major, for example, was considered to be open and clear, while the key of B flat was thought to be strong and regal, and the key of F sharp was considered dark, even sinister.

In today's music—and in today's musical instruments—the half-step intervals between notes in the scale have been rounded off and evened out, so you can now play a scale in any key on any piano keyboard, and no major scale will have a different quality from any other major scale. Thus, the differences in the characteristics of key signatures have become more academic than real. But tradition dies hard. ❍

Playing Other Scales

In the same way that you made a G scale sound right by adding one sharp, you can play other scales by starting on a given note and then adding

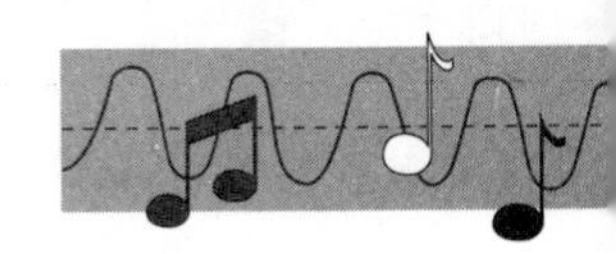

sharps and flats in the right places. For example, just as the G Major scale has one sharp, the F Major scale has one flat. To play an F Major scale, you can play the tones from one F to another using only one black key: When you get to the note B, you must skip it and play the black key to its left, which is B flat. That *lowers* the pitch of the note B by half a step—to B flat —and corrects the one interval that must be corrected in an F Major scale.

By using the appropriate black keys to raise and lower tones, you can play a major scale that starts in any note on the piano keyboard. For example, the key of D Major has two sharps (F sharp and C sharp), the key of A Major has three sharps (C sharp, F sharp, and G sharp), and the key of B flat Major has two flats (B flat and E flat).

There are mathematical formulas that you can use to calculate how many sharps and flats you must use to play in any key. The simplest technique is simply to figure out where you need to place sharps and flats in order to create half-step intervals between the third and fourth notes in the scale, and between the seventh and eighth notes in the scale.

In practice, most musicians simply memorize which black keys they must use to play in various keys. This is probably the best technique, because it's the only one that allows playing on the black keys to become second nature—as it must if you ever want to perform before a live audience in real time.

The Software Solution

BY THE WAY

To find out how many sharps and flats are used in various keys, you can consult the Songworks program. First, make sure that the keyboard window is open. Then find the tool labeled Key; it's on the left side of the window, two rows above the keyboard.

When you've found the button labeled Key, select it with the mouse and hold the mouse button down. Songworks then displays a chart listing all major and minor keys, and showing the number of sharps and flats that you must use to play each one.

If you know how to read music, the chart shows you not only the number of sharps and flats in each key, but also the notes that the sharps and flats raise and lower. If you don't know how to read music—well, that's the topic of the next section. ❍

Reading Music

Now that you know how musicians play in different keys, it's time to tackle the subject of learning to read music. Then you can tell just by looking at a piece of music what key it's in.

Armed with the information that you've covered so far in this chapter, there's no reason to fear reading music. You know the principles; now all you need to learn is how to interpret the symbols on a sheet of music—or, easier still, on a computer screen.

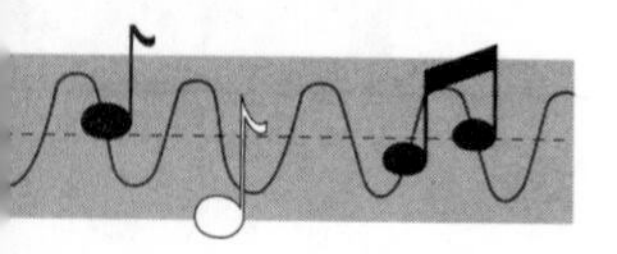

The Musical Staff

For almost a thousand years, composers have written music on a musical *staff* and have used a *clef sign* to show which notes are on which staff. The melody of a song is usually written on the *treble clef,* and a bass accompaniment is generally written on the *bass clef.* There are also several other kinds of clefs, but the bass and treble clefs are used most often.

Figure 7–9 shows a treble clef and a bass clef, combined to form what is sometimes referred to as the *grand staff.* On the grand staff, the upper clef is the treble clef and the bottom clef is the bass clef.

Figure 7–9. The grand staff

You can tell the difference between the two clefs on the grand staff not only by their respective positions on the staff, but also by the fact that each clef starts with a distinctive symbol, or *clef sign.* The treble clef has an elegantly curved sign, and the bass clef has a sign that looks something like a seashell followed by two dots. The treble clef sign evolved from the letter G, and the bass clef sign evolved from the letter F. The swirl near the bottom of the treble clef encircles the note G, and the two dots in the bass clef sign surround the note F. You also start on the F note when you draw a bass clef.

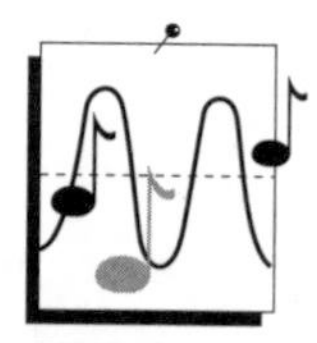

BY THE WAY

Things Not to Ask about Right Now

Figure 7–9 includes a couple of features that aren't going to be covered right now, but are covered later in this section. One feature is the **time signature**—*a pair of numbers that follows the clef sign in each clef. The time signature describes the rhythm that is used to play a piece of music.*

The other feature that will be explored later is the shape of the note on the line between the staffs. The note is hollow and has no stem because it's a whole note. More information about whole notes—and other kinds of notes—is provided later in this section. ❍

As you can see, each clef on the grand staff is made up of five lines and four spaces. You can write notes on any space in either clef, and on any line. If that is still not enough room to hold all the notes that you want to

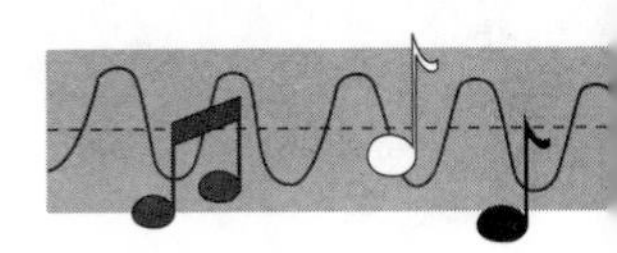

write, you can add extra lines above and below both staffs. For example, in Figure 7–9, a line has been added below the treble clef, and a note has been written on the line. That note is placed on an extension line because it lies between the treble and bass clefs. And it's an old friend of yours: middle C.

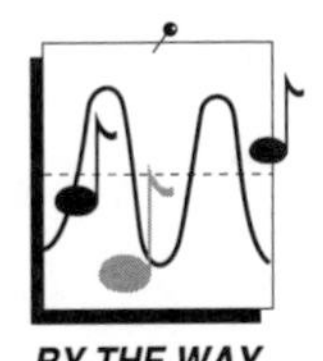

BY THE WAY

The Staff That Wasn't There

Although most pieces of sheet music contain both a treble clef and a bass clef (and some even have an extra treble clef for a vocal part), the Songworks program displays one staff of music that can have any clef sign. Accompaniment is noted with chord names instead of being written on additional staves. This is a practice often used in song books and in musicians' "lead sheets." ❍

A Musical Score: The C Scale

Figure 7–10 is the C scale written as a musical score in the treble clef. The bass clef is not needed for this exercise, and it is not shown.

Figure 7–10. The C scale

The scale starts with middle C and proceeds up the white keys on the keyboard, ending with the C note that is one octave above middle C.

When you play the C scale shown in Figure 7–10, the notes on the musical staff exactly match the notes on the piano keyboard, but there is an important difference in the way the notes are represented: On the musical staff, there is no distinction between notes that are a full step apart and notes that are a half step apart. In that respect, the keyboard shows a truer picture of the relationships between the notes than the musical staff does.

Learning the Notes on the Staff

The best way to become familiar with the notes on the treble (or the bass) clef is to memorize them (keeping in mind the notes that the treble and bass clefs "point to," as noted earlier in this section). You already know that if you draw an extension line below the treble clef and then put a note on it, that note is middle C. As you master the skill of reading music, you will soon learn that the space just below the bottom line on the staff is D, the bottom line itself is E, the first space above the bottom line is F, and so on.

You can use some tricks to learn where all the notes are. Over the years, music teachers have come up with some silly-sounding acronyms to

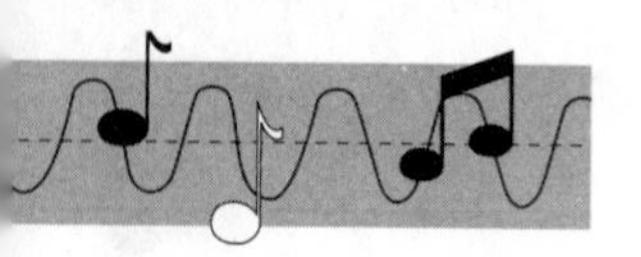

help students learn note positions. For example, if you start with the first space above the bottom line of the staff (which is the note F) the notes that fall on the *spaces* in ascending order spell FACE. Also, if you start with the first line at the bottom of the staff and move upward, the notes on the *lines* are E, G, B, D, and F—an acronym that once meant "Every Good Boy Does Fine," but these days is more often taught as "Every Girl (and) Boy Does Fine." You can also use the sentence "Every Good Bird Does Fly." Do what works; no one will ever know.

Key Signatures

You've already seen how sharps and flats are used in musical compositions, so it won't be difficult for you to understand how sharps and flats are expressed in written music. Figure 7–11 shows the symbols that are used for sharps and flats in musical scores. The illustration also shows the symbol for a *natural*—a note that doesn't have a sharp or a flat. Composers sometimes use the symbol for a natural to cancel out a sharp or a flat that occurs in a key signature or pops up somewhere else in a composition.

Sharp ♯

Flat ♭

Natural ♮

Figure 7–11. Sharps, flats, and naturals

Take another look at the song "Home on the Range" that's provided with the Songworks demonstration program, and you'll see a composition that's written in a key that contains one sharp—specifically, the key of G.

Figure 7–12 shows the first line of "Home on the Range." Notice that the score begins with one sharp symbol. That sharp, called a *key signature,* appears on a line that represents the F note one octave above middle C. It means that every F note in the song that follows—no matter what octave the F is in—is to be played as an F sharp, not an F. In other words, it means that the melody that follows is in the key of G.

Figure 7–12. The key of G

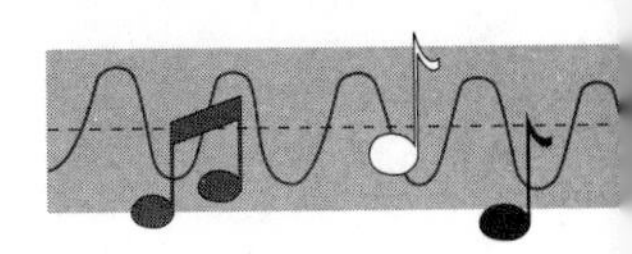

As mentioned earlier in this chapter, Songworks can provide you with a quick screen view of all the most common key signatures. All you have to do is open the keyboard window and select the button labeled Key. Songworks then displays a key signature chart like the one in Figure 7–13. The first entry in the chart shows that a one-sharp key signature does raise the note F a half step, and does result in a key signature of G. The chart also shows that one minor key also has one sharp. That is the key of E minor.

G	D	A	E	B	F#	C#
e min	b min	F#min	C#min	G#min	D#min	A#min
F	Bb	Eb	Ab	Db	Gb	Cb
d min	g min	c min	f min	bb min	eb min	ab min

Figure 7–13. Key signatures

If this section has made sense so far, you now know everything you need to know about how pitch is expressed in musical compositions. When you learn one more set of rules—the rules about rhythm—you will have mastered the art of reading music.

Accidentals

Sometimes a sharp or a flat that is not declared in a key signature pops up in the middle of a song. A sharp or a flat that suddenly appears in this fashion is called an *accidental.*

Despite their name, accidentals don't occur accidentally—they're placed in music on purpose. But it's easy to miss one accidentally when you read a piece of music, and maybe that's how they got their name.

Accidentals occur in music quite often; sometimes, for reasons that are beyond the scope of this chapter, they are needed to make a musical phrase sound right. For now, all you need to know is that accidentals occur in music, and that an accidental raises (if it's a sharp) or lowers (if it's a flat) the pitch of the note that follows it.

To be more accurate, an accidental doesn't raise or lower the pitch of just one note; actually, the effect of an accidental lasts for the rest of the measure that contains it (*measures* are the units of music that are separated

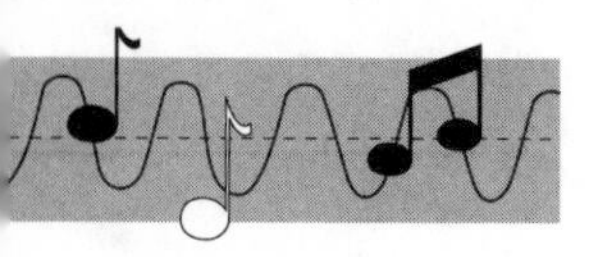

by vertical lines in a score; there's more about measures later in this section). If you need to use an accidental in a subsequent measure, you must create a new one.

In the Songworks example tune "Home on the Range," an accidental sharp occurs at the beginning of the chorus, as shown in Figure 7–14. When you play the song, locate where the accidental is, and listen carefully to that section. The effect of the accidental is quite dramatic: It raises the pitch of a note half a step, and it gives the music a kind of sparkle where it appears.

Figure 7–14. An accidental

If you like, you can remove the sharp from "Home on the Range" and listen to the difference that the change makes. Just follow these steps:

1. Scroll the music window to the beginning of the chorus of "Home on the Range," as shown in Figure 7–14.
2. Make sure that the listening point marker (the small box-shaped control with the arrow in it that was shown earlier in Figure 7–2) is placed at the beginning of the song. Then type Command-H to play "Home on the Range." When the song plays, listen carefully to the sharped note.
3. Move the listening point marker to the beginning of the chorus—that is, to a point just before the word *Oh* shown in Figure 7–14.
4. Type Command-H to play the chorus of "Home on the Range."
5. Click on the pointer in the tools palette, and then with the mouse, select the note that contains the sharp.
6. Click on the Natural tool in the tools palette—that is, the button with the natural sign on it. The tool is in the upper left-hand corner of the keyboard window (to the right of the blank key).
7. Click anywhere in the music window to deselect the note.
8. Type Command-H to hear the effect of your change.

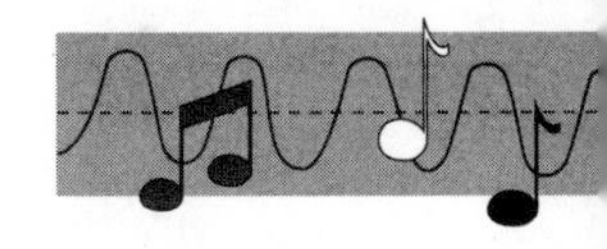

Rhythm

The two basic elements of music are pitch and rhythm. You've already learned about the element of pitch. Now it's time to introduce the element of rhythm.

Beats and Measures

In every musical composition, a *meter,* or *beat,* recurs over and over. A short composition, such as a song, usually has only one meter. Longer compositions, such as symphonies or concertos, can have many meters. But each meter usually repeats itself for some significant time.

One easy meter to follow is the meter of a military march. Usually, a march follows the rhythm of marching feet, and thus has a beat you can follow clearly by saying, "Left, right; left, right," or "One, two; one, two."

In a musical composition, the meter that underlies the beat is divided into units called *measures.* Since a military march is usually based upon the rhythm of a pair of feet (or many pairs of feet) marching, it is usually divided into measures of two beats each. In contrast, a waltz usually has a beat that can be expressed as "One, two three; one, two three," and is therefore divided into measures of three beats each.

Although many marches and waltzes have been written over the years, the most commonly used meter in folk music and popular music is a meter that was once known as the foxtrot: a meter that follows a beat of four beats to the measure.

Figure 7–15 shows the first two measures of "Frère Jacques," a well-known French folk song that has a meter of four beats to the measure.

Figure 7–15. Frère Jacques

Two measures of "Frère Jacques" are shown, and each measure contains four beats. The two measures are separated by a vertical line—the convention for expressing the division between measures in musical scores.

Although a complete song doesn't appear in Figure 7–15, the portion of "Frère Jacques" that is shown in the illustration ends with two vertical bars—a symbol traditionally used to represent the end of a composition.

Sometimes you'll come across a section of a song that begins with a pair of vertical lines followed by two dots, and ends with a pair of vertical lines preceded by two dots. That convention means the portion of the composi-

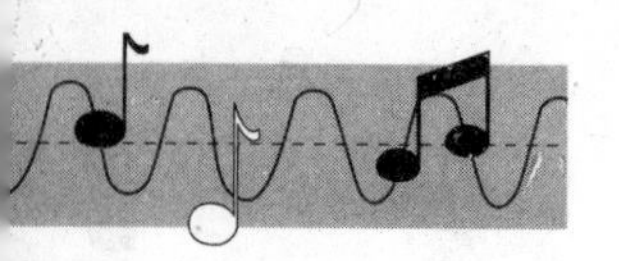

tion that lies between the two pairs of vertical lines is to be repeated. The sample Songworks tune "Home on the Range" contains one such section.

Time Signatures

The two digits at the beginning of the "Frère Jacques" score—the stacked pair of 4s—define the meter of the song. Together, they are referred to as the song's *time signature.*

A time signature is usually made up of two numbers, one on top of the other. The top number tells how many beats are in each measure, and the bottom number tells what kind of note lasts for one beat.

In the "Frère Jacques" time signature, the two 4s mean that there are four beats in each measure, and that a kind of note called a *quarter note* gets one beat. A musician would say that the song is in *4-4 time,* or *common time.* Four-four time is sometimes referred to as common time because it is the most commonly encountered time signature.

Kinds of Notes

Figure 7–16 shows the kinds of notes that are used in musical scores. The quarter note, which gets one beat in "Frère Jacques," is the third note down from the top. In the remainder of this section, each kind of note in the illustration is described.

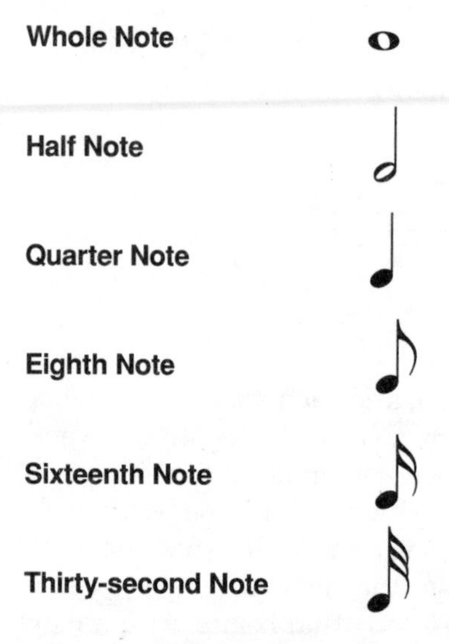

Figure 7–16. Varieties of musical notes

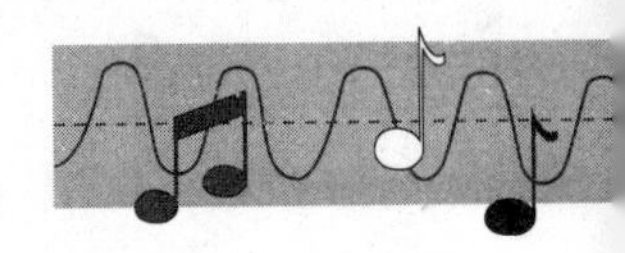

The note in Figure 7–17 is a *whole note*. It is hollow and has no stem. In a composition written in 4-4 time, a whole note is held for four beats, or a complete measure.

Figure 7–17. Whole note

Figure 7–18 shows a *half note*. It is hollow and has a stem. In a composition written in 4-4 time, a half note is held for two beats, or for half a measure.

Figure 7–18. Half note

A *quarter note* is shown in Figure 7–19. It is filled in and has a stem. In a composition written in 4-4 time, a quarter note is held for one beat, or for a quarter of a measure.

Figure 7–19. Quarter note

By putting flags on the stem of a quarter note, you can turn it into an eighth note (one flag), a sixteenth note (two flags), or a thirty-second note (three flags). An eighth note is held for one eighth of a measure, a sixteenth note is held for one sixteenth of a measure, and a thirty-second note is held for one thirty-second of a measure.

An eighth note, a sixteenth note, and a thirty-second note are shown in Figure 7–20.

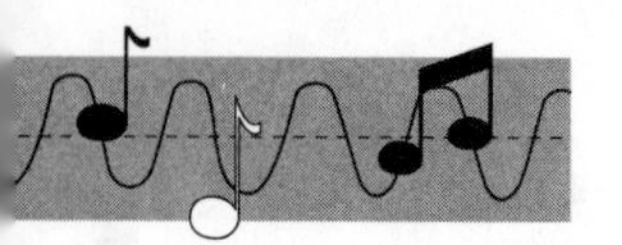

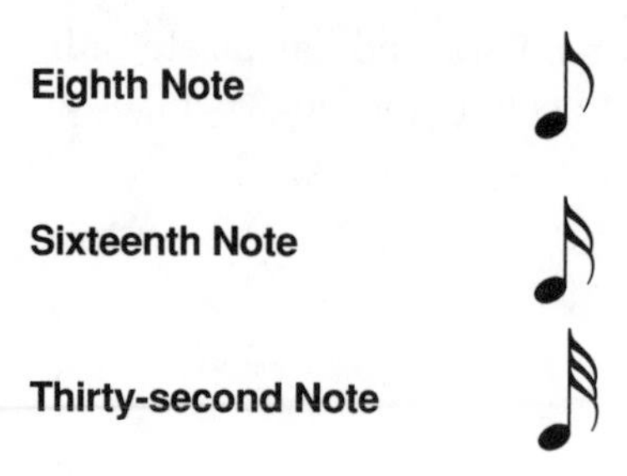

Figure 7–20. Flagged notes

Rests

When you write music, you can't leave part of a measure blank. If a note doesn't fill up a measure and leaves a period of silence, you must fill the silence with an object called a *rest.* Rests are silent; they merely fill space, but you have to use them so that every beat in a measure is somehow accounted for.

Rests are named just as notes are; their names tell how many beats they are held for.

Figure 7–21 shows the rests used in music and the note that each rest corresponds to. The illustration is taken from the tools palette in the Songworks keyboard window. By selecting one of the notes from the palette, you can place the note in any song that is shown in the music window. In the same way, you can select a rest from the palette and paste it into a song.

Notes

Rests

Figure 7–21. Rests

You can find several examples of how rests are used by examining the sample song "Home on the Range."

Dotted Notes and Rests

When you place a dot after a note or a rest, the note or rest is held for one and one-half times its normal length. That extra length must come from somewhere; by convention, it is subtracted from the length of the note or rest that follows the dotted note or rest. You can find several dotted notes and rests in "Home on the Range." If you listen carefully to the measures

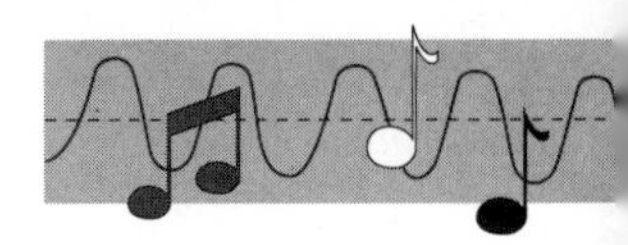

that contain dotted notes and rests, and you count the beats of the measures, you can get a good idea of how dotted notes and dotted rests are used in musical compositions.

Writing Music

Now that you know how notes and rests are used in music, you're ready to try your hand at writing a musical score with the Songworks program. These are the steps to follow:

1. Launch Songworks and make sure that the example song "Home on the Range" is visible in the music window.
2. Activate the chord layer of the Songworks music window by clicking on the upper dot in the line of three dots at the beginning of "Home on the Range." (The chord handle was shown earlier in Figure 7–5.)
3. Either type Command-A or choose the Select All command from the Edit menu. That selects all the chords in "Home on the Range." Then type Command-X or Delete to remove all the chord symbols from the song.
4. Activate the staff layer of the Songworks music window by clicking on the staff handle (the dot to the immediate left of the staff.)
5. Either type Command-A or choose the Select All command from the Edit menu. That selects all the notes and rests in "Home on the Range." Then type Command-X or Delete to remove all the notes and rests from the song.
6. Select the time signature and the key signature by dragging the mouse. Then type Command-A or choose the Select All command from the Edit menu to delete the time signature and the key signature.
7. Activate the text layer by clicking on the text handle (the lower dot).
8. Again, either type Command-A or choose the Select All command from the Edit menu. That selects all the text in "Home on the Range." Then type Command-X or Delete to remove all the text from the song.
9. You now have a blank score in the music window to work with. Using the mouse, hold down the button labeled Meter. Then, from the hierarchical menu that Songworks displays, select the C with a vertical line through it—a time signature that looks like the one used in Figure 7–22. It's the signature for *cut time*—a shorthand way of referring to 2-2 time—in which there are two beats to a measure and a half note gets one beat. Click on the staff to insert the time signature.

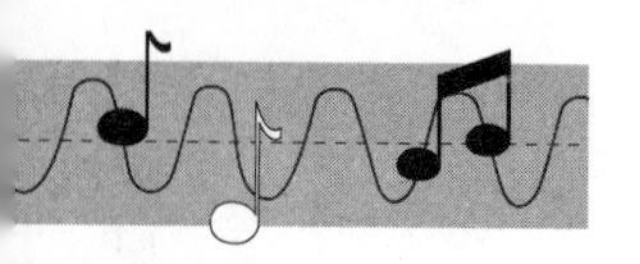

Figure 7–22. Writing music

10. By selecting notes from the tools palette and placing them in the score, enter into the music window the composition shown in Figure 7–22. Then play the piece by typing Command-H.

    Congratulations! You have just scored your first musical composition!

Other Notation Software

Songworks isn't the only notation program on the market. It's a great program for writing a song with chords, or for writing a single instrumental part. But if you want to write piano music or band or orchestra arrangements, you'll need a program that deals with more than one staff of music at a time.

Several software companies market programs that contain music notation features. For example, ConcertWare+ and ConcertWare+ MIDI, both published by Great Wave Software, come with notation modules that you can use to score musical compositions. Super Studio Session from Bogas Productions also has a notation feature that lets you experiment with writing music. Among professional and semiprofessional composers, however, four musical notation applications dominate the market:

- Finale, a $749 notation program from Coda Music Software
- Music Prose, also from Coda, which has many of Finale's features but sells for considerably less: $249
- Encore, a $595 program from Passport Designs
- Professional Composer from Mark of the Unicorn, which retails for $495

In this section, you'll learn about these four programs, as well as the musical notation features of the Great Wave and Bogas products.

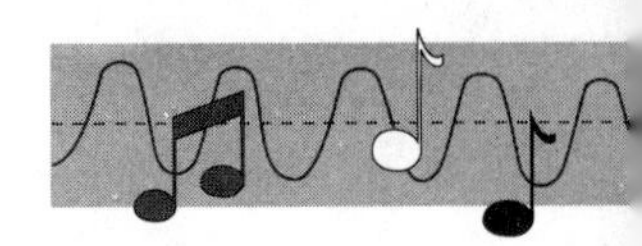

Finale

Finale stands at the pinnacle of musical notation programs. It produces musical scores so professional-looking that they can be printed as sheet music. Indeed, music publishers do print sheet music using both Finale and Encore—which is Finale's major competitor.

The Finale screen display, shown in Figure 7–23, has tools that can place virtually every kind of note, rest, and musical symbol into a musical score. (Although the illustration shows a Finale score on a large-screen Macintosh, you don't need a big-screen Mac to use Finale. The program works fine with nine-inch Mac screens.)

Figure 7–23. Finale

You can display your score in either a page view or a scrolling view, and Finale can add anything you like, from guitar chords to harp diagrams to slurs. It can even change the shapes of the notes in the score.

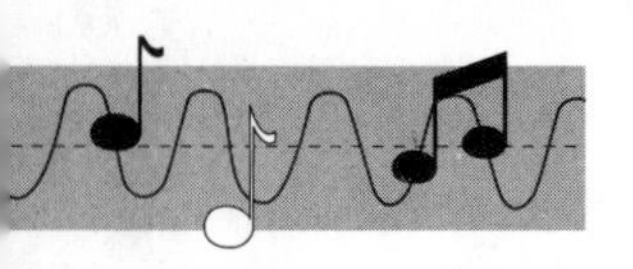

Finale is especially useful for incorporating lyrics or any other kind of text into a composition. The program accepts lyrics that you have created with a word processor or a text editor. It loads the words you have written and then automatically places them—complete with the appropriate hyphens between notes—exactly where they belong. Finale also features an option that can quickly and efficiently extract instrumental parts from a score, and then print each part as an individual document.

The Finale program is compatible with the MIDI electronic instrument standard, described in Chapter 9, so you can write and play Finale scores with electronic instruments such as synthesizers and samplers.

With Finale, as with most musical notation programs, you can enter a score directly from a MIDI keyboard, by simply playing it; or you can write your music by hand, using both a keyboard and a mouse. Also, Finale has a special quick-keys feature that makes it especially easy to enter music from the Macintosh keyboard.

Music Prose

If you like Finale but can't justify its high cost, you can find many of Finale's most often-used features in a less expensive package from Coda called Music Prose. With Music Prose, you can create lead sheets, scores with piano and vocal parts, and even music for small ensembles. Music Prose is much easier to learn than Finale, but it still has plenty of features. It offers excellent flexibility in working with lyrics and chords, and it features multiple layers of music with multiple voices in each layer.

Encore

Encore is a superb musical notation program from Passport Designs, one of the top designers and publishers of music software. Whether you like Encore or Finale better depends on your personal taste; many professional musicians prefer Encore because it's user-friendly and extremely well designed, and because it's a perfect match for another popular Passport Designs product: a top-rated sequencer called Master Tracks Pro. The newest version of Master Tracks Pro, named Master Tracks Pro 5, is described in Chapter 9.

Figure 7–24 shows the Encore screen display.

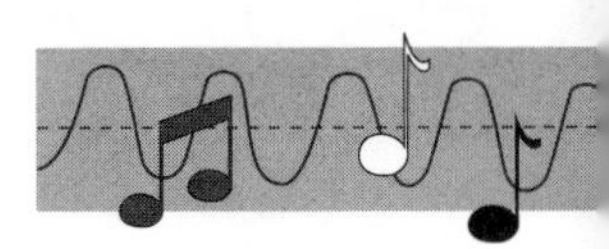

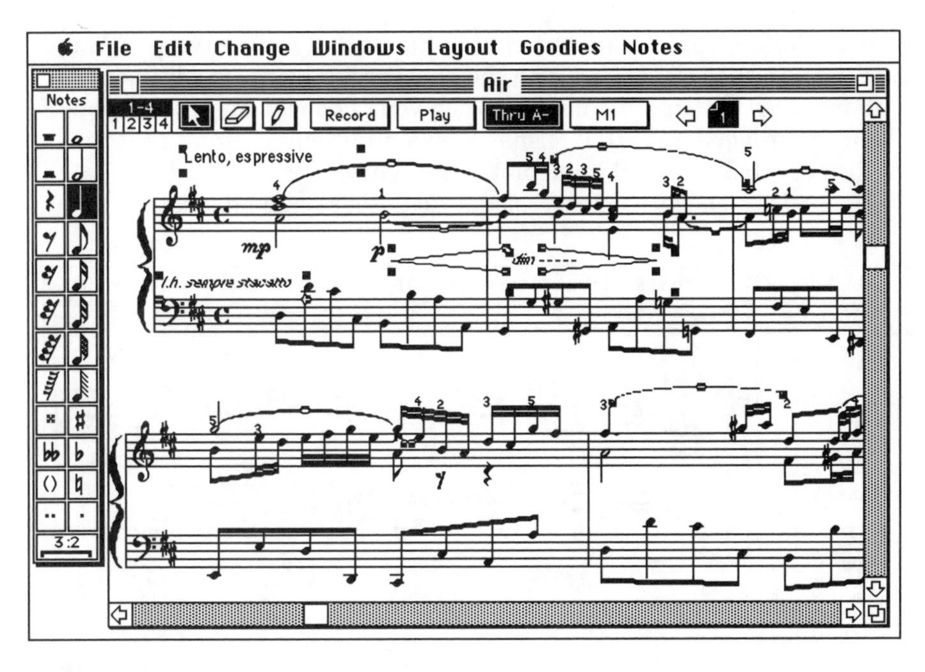

Figure 7–24. Encore

With Encore, as with Finale, you can compose a score either by playing it on a MIDI instrument or entering its notes with a mouse. Encore can piece together a score from multiple files, and it can handle very large scores. And you can see what your score will look like when it's printed, thanks to Encore's page-oriented display.

Professional Composer

Professional Composer is a notation program from another leading MIDI software publisher, Mark of the Unicorn. Professional Composer has a twin product, a sequencer called Performer, which is also published by Mark of the Unicorn. Both Performer and Professional Composer have an excellent reputation among performers. Many musicians write compositions with Professional Composer and then edit and record them with Performer.

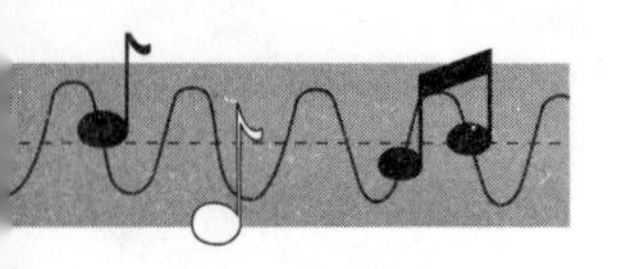

With Professional Composer, as with Finale and Encore, you can compose music either by playing it on the keyboard or by using editing tools with the keyboard and the mouse. When you're done, you can save your file in either a general MIDI format or in a proprietary format that the Performer sequencer will immediately recognize.

Figure 7–25 shows the Professional Composer screen display.

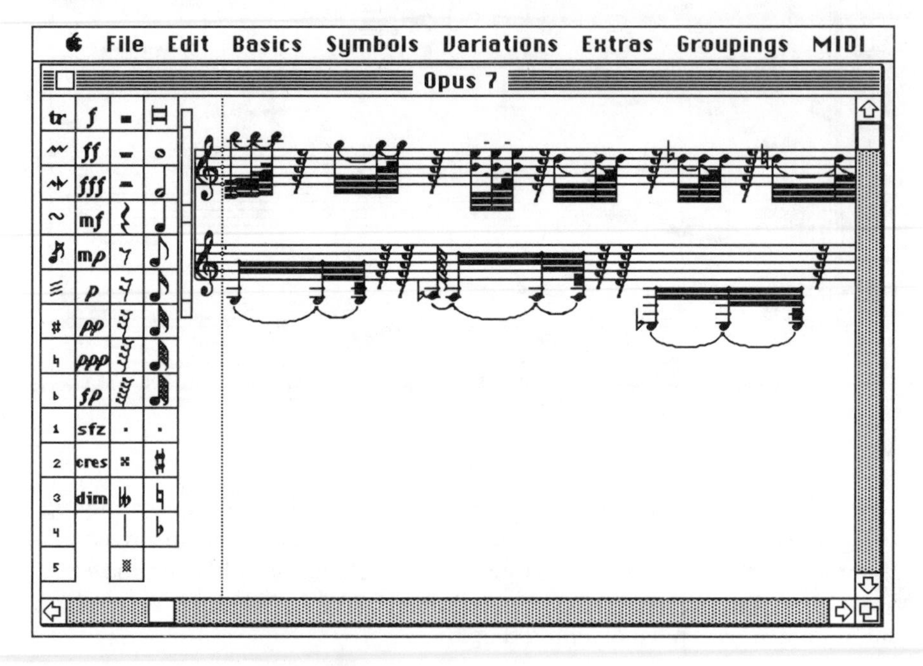

Figure 7–25. Professional Composer

ConcertWare+

For the music composer on a budget, Great Wave Music Software offers ConcertWare+: a program that includes not only a notation module, but also a module that plays the music and a module that creates musical sounds. The program supports eight musical staves, as well as lyrics and text, and lets you enter chords along with the music.

ConcertWare+ uses the Macintosh Sound Manager and the Macintosh speaker to produce sound, but a higher-end version—ConcertWare+ MIDI—supports the MIDI electronic instrument standard and can be used as part of a MIDI system. ConcertWare+ retails for $69.95. The suggested retail price of ConcertWare+ MIDI is $189.95.

Figure 7–26 shows the ConcertWare+ screen display.

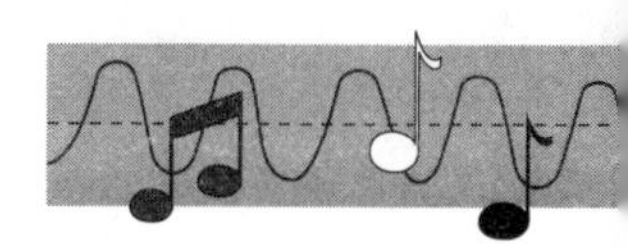

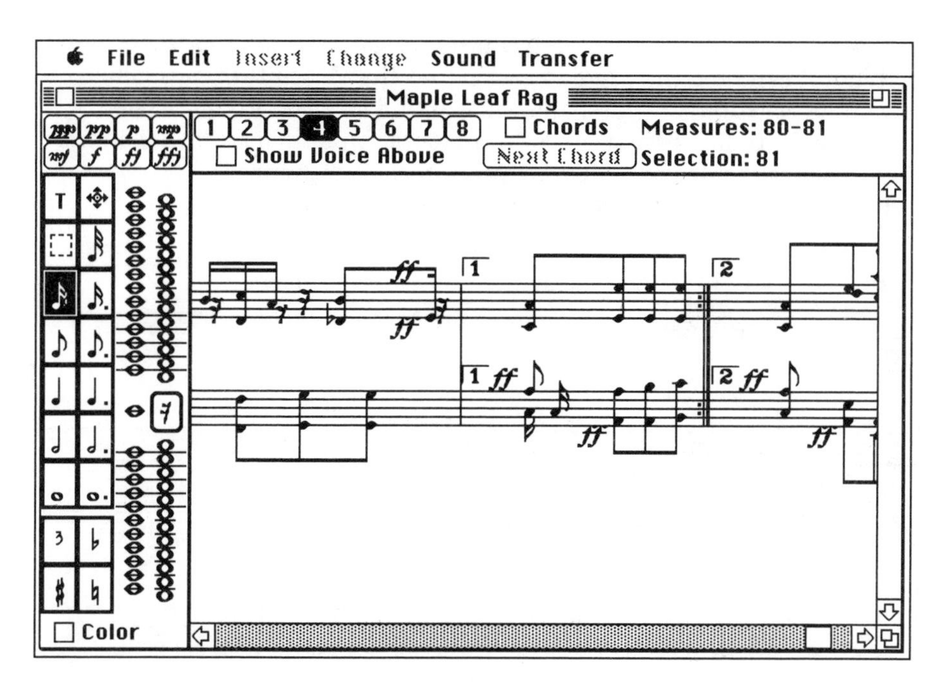

Figure 7–26. ConcertWare+

Super Studio Session

Super Studio Session, from Bogas Productions, is the newest version of the venerable Studio Session music program. With Studio Session or Super Studio Session, you can write music and then play it, using the built-in sound capabilities of your Macintosh. If you have a MIDI system, you can use it with Studio Session and Super Studio Session, but a MIDI system is not required.

When you use Super Studio Session without MIDI, the program can make your Macintosh create sounds that you never dreamed were possible. It can emulate practically any instrument with astounding results, and it can play up to eight tracks of music simultaneously—using only the sound hardware that's built into your Macintosh! What's more, Super Studio Session is a musical notation program. You can write a score, edit it, and print it out, just as you can with more expensive musical notation programs.

Super Studio Session plays songs using sampled instrumental sounds that you can create yourself. Studio Session songs use memory and disk space efficiently, because they're not stored as waveforms; instead, they're stored as sequences of instrument sounds, along with pitch and tempo data, so that a series of instrument sounds can be played back as a song.

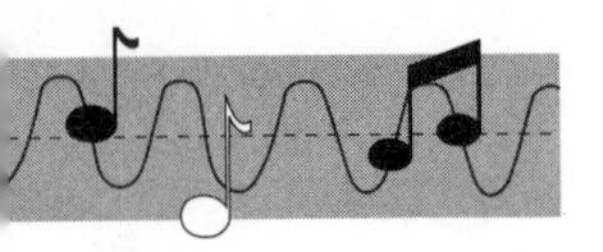

The Super Studio Session program stores sounds in a proprietary format, but it can read the Studio Session files that Macintosh musicians have been creating for years, and you can find loads of Studio Session sounds and Studio Session songs on computer bulletin boards and on freeware disks that are available from Macintosh user groups.

Figure 7–27 shows the Super Studio Session screen display.

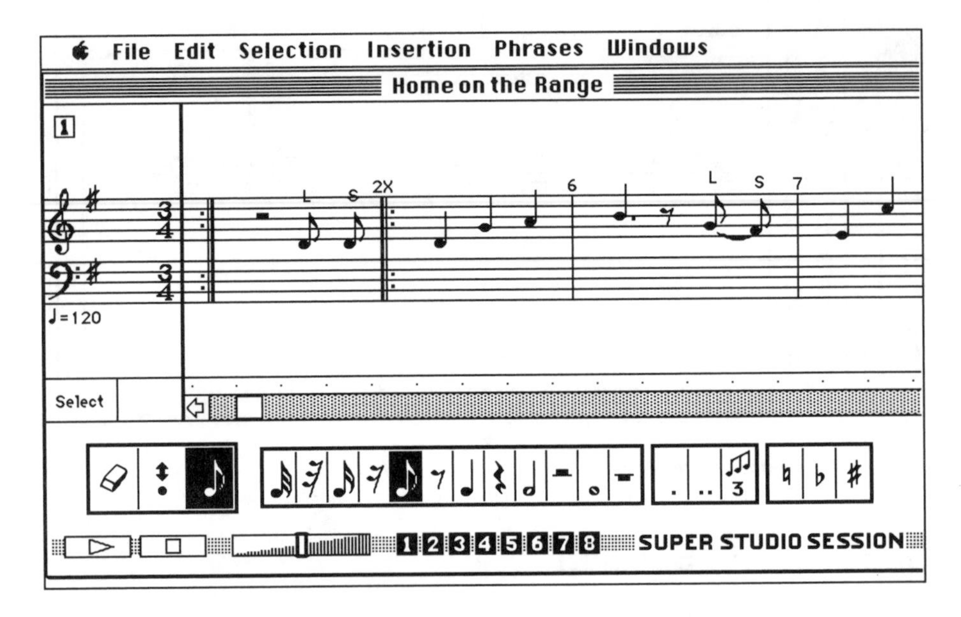

Figure 7–27. Super Studio Session

Summary

If you understand everything in this chapter, you have completed the first step in your journey to start reading music. Now, to become fluent in the written language of music, you'll need to do just three things: practice, practice, and practice. To become expert at reading or writing music, the first thing you must be able to do is look at a note on a staff and tell, at a glance, what note it is. That's called sight-reading, and it is an essential part of becoming musically literate.

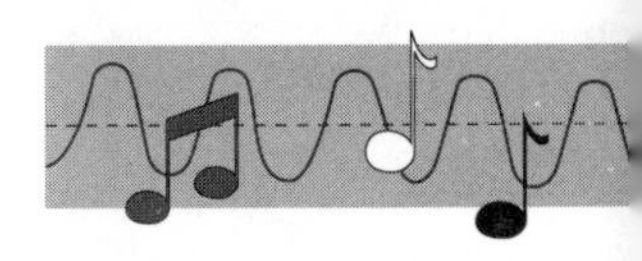

In Chapter 8, you'll get a chance to improve your sight-reading ability with a demonstration version of Listen, a music-learning program from Imaja. You'll also have a chance in Chapter 8 to conduct another interesting experiment with the Songworks program.

If you didn't know how to read music before you started this chapter, you're probably not yet ready to go out and start writing symphonies. Many important subjects were touched upon only briefly in this chapter, and many others were not mentioned at all. Therefore, if you want to become an expert at reading and writing music, you'll have to supplement what was covered in this chapter with information from other sources. The documentation that comes with some music programs may help, but you should also thumb through some of the many books that have been written on musical notation, some of which are listed in the Bibliography.

8 Melody and Harmony

The two basic principles of music are rhythm and pitch. But music wouldn't be very interesting without melody and harmony.

When you play two or more notes in succession, that's melody. When you play two or more notes simultaneously, that's harmony—if you know what you're doing. If you don't, it's disharmony, which can sound pretty awful.

In this chapter, you'll learn some basic concepts about melody, harmony, and disharmony—and about dissonance, which is sometimes mistaken for disharmony, but is actually something quite different. This chapter may not make you a great composer overnight, but it can give you a better understanding of some subtle but important musical concepts.

The Listen Program

To help you learn more about melody and harmony, this chapter uses a music-learning program called Listen. A demonstration version of Listen—a program published by Imaja—is included on the bonus disk that comes with this book.

What You Need to Use Listen

To use Listen, you need a Macintosh Plus or better, and System 6.0.2 or later. A hard disk drive is not required, but it is suggested.

Launching Listen

If you have decompressed the files on your bonus disk, as outlined in Chapter 1, you can find the Listen program in the folder titled 08–Melody and Harmony. To launch Listen, just double-click on Listen's application icon.

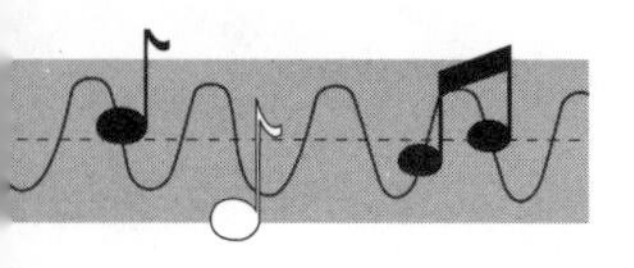

When you launch Listen, it opens three windows like those shown in Figure 8–1. They are (from the top) a piano window, a progress window, and a guitar window.

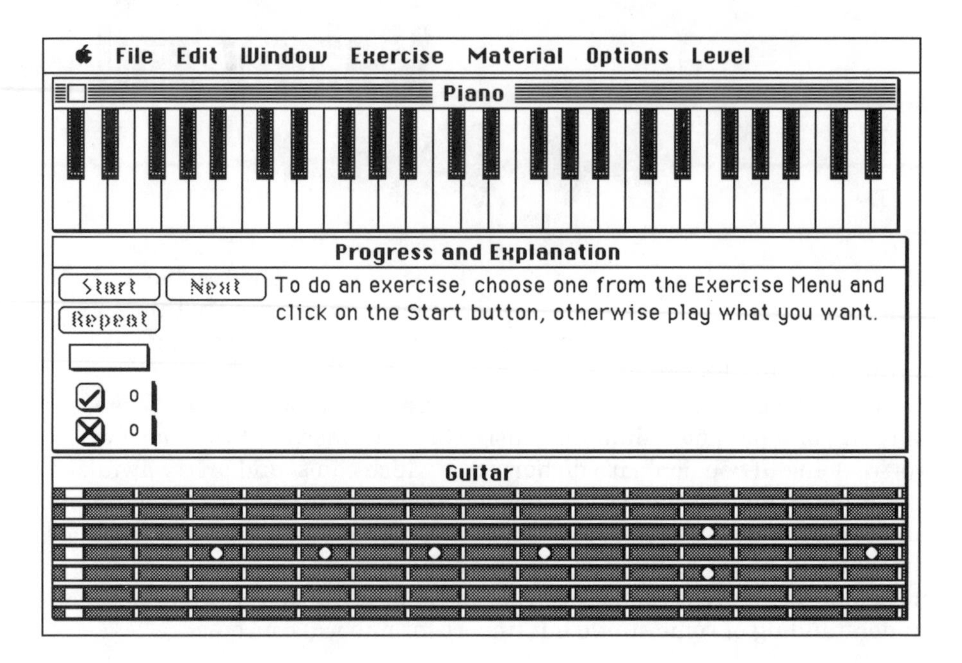

Figure 8–1. Listen

Selecting Sounds

One welcome feature of Listen is that you can vary the sound that you hear when you do the exercises. The version of Listen that's on your bonus disk comes with only a few interesting sounds. But the commercial version of the program comes with a much larger selection of sounds. To pick the sound you want, just select the Open Sound item from the File menu. Listen then displays a dialog that you can use to select a sound.

If you have a MIDI instrument connected to your Macintosh, you can use it as an input device, an output device, or both. Otherwise, you can play music on your computer keyboard or on a screen keyboard, and your Macintosh will produce your music through its built-in speaker. For more information about MIDI devices, see Chapter 9.

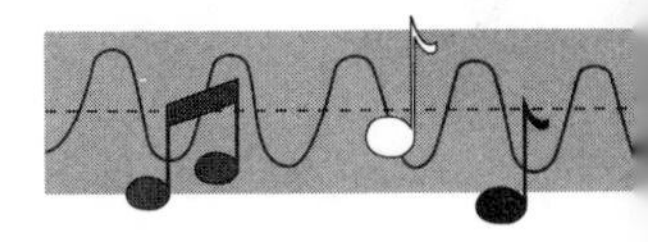

The Exercise Menu

To use Listen, you must select a musical exercise from an Exercise menu like the one in Figure 8–2. Listen then guides you through the exercise you have chosen.

Exercise
✓No Exercise ⌘N
Single Note
Two-Note Melody
Growing Melody
Melody
Interval
Triads
7th Chords
9th Chords
11th Chords
13th Chords
Random Atonal Chords
Tuning
Interval Naming
Triad Chord Quality
7th Chord Quality
Triad Inversion Naming
7th Chord Inversion Naming

Figure 8–2. Exercise menu

You can play the answers to the exercises on either the piano keyboard in the piano window or on the guitar fretboard in the guitar window. The progress window shows you the name of the exercise you have selected, describes it briefly, and provides controls that you can use to do the exercise and check your progress.

With the demonstration version of Listen, you can perform only the three exercises that are enabled in Figure 8–2. They are designed to test your ability to recognize and repeat melodies, triads (three-note chords that meet special criteria), and musical intervals, or harmony.

The No Exercise option simply lets you play tunes and listen to them. With the production version of the program, you can do any exercise on the Exercise menu, including those that are grayed out in Figure 8–2.

Another limitation of the demonstration version is that you can use Listen for only seven minutes at a sitting. With the production version of the program, you can play as many exercises as you like for as long as you like.

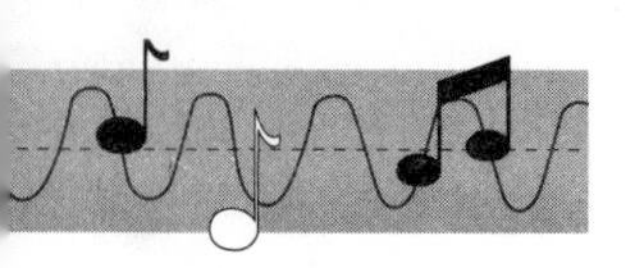

The Melody Exercise

You don't have to know much about music to do the melody exercise. Just follow these steps:

1. Select the Melody item from the Exercise menu. In the progress window, Listen displays a brief list of instructions for the exercise you've selected.
2. Click on the Start button in the progress window. Listen now plays a series of notes.
3. Repeat the notes you've heard by playing them on either the piano keyboard in the keyboard window or the guitar fretboard in the guitar window.

   Each time you play the melody correctly, Listen displays a smiling face, puts three check marks in the three question-mark windows, and tallies your score by updating the two numbers in the lower right-hand corner of the progress window. If you make a mistake, Listen responds with an "Oops" face and gives you a chance to try again.
4. If you'd like to hear a melody again, you can instruct Listen to repeat it by clicking on the Repeat button.

Other Exercises

Listen's triad and interval exercises work much like the melody exercise. The main difference involves what's required from you.

To follow and repeat a melody, the primary requirements are a good memory, a knowledge of the piano keyboard (or the guitar fretboard), and a keen ear. To score well in Listen's interval and triad exercises, you need something more: a basic understanding of how the intervals between the notes in the scale are used to create melody and harmony.

Intervals

The difference in pitch between two notes is known as an *interval.* If the notes are played in succession, the interval between them is a *melodic interval.* If they are played at the same time, the interval between them is a *harmonic interval.*

You can determine the interval between two notes by comparing their positions on the piano keyboard. You can also determine the interval between two notes by comparing their positions on the musical staff.

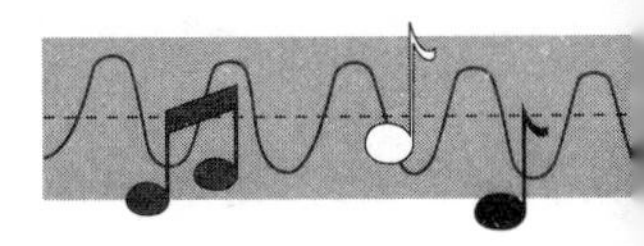

Learning Intervals with Listen

The Listen program can help you learn about intervals. Just follow these steps:

1. Choose the Interval Naming item under the Exercise menu. Listen then displays a dialog box like the one in Figure 8–3.

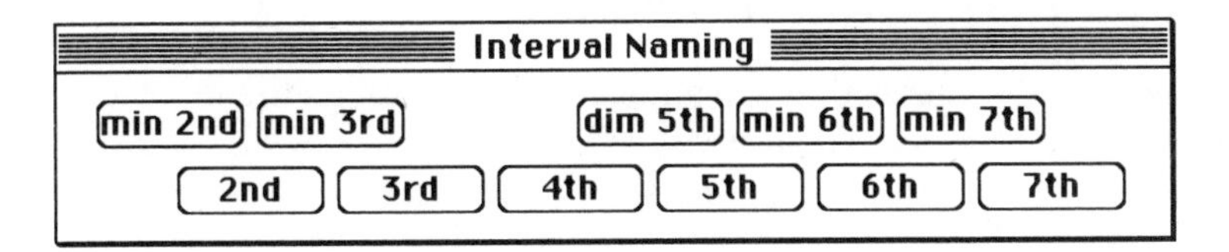

Figure 8–3. Interval naming

2. Pick the kind of interval that you want to learn about by clicking on the appropriate button.
3. When you have chosen an interval, click on the Start button in the progress window. Listen then plays two notes simultaneously.
4. Identify the kind of interval that Listen has played by clicking on the appropriate button in the Interval Naming window.
5. If you answer correctly, the cursor becomes a smiling face. If your answer is incorrect, Listen displays an "Oops" face.

When a group of three or more notes is played at the same time, the result is a *chord*. Music is full of chords that accompany melodies, and the sound of a chord depends upon the intervals between the notes in the chord.

When musicians talk about chords, they use all kinds of terms that sound mysterious to the musical novice—terms like major, minor, diminished, augmented, and so on. In this section, all of those terms are explained.

The Tonic

When you start examining the intervals between notes, a logical place to start is with the first note of the scale. For several reasons, the first note in the scale is also the most important. One hint of its importance is that it occurs twice in the scale—once at the beginning and once at the end—while each of the other notes in the scale appears just one time.

More significantly, perhaps, when you play a melody that's based on a certain scale, the note that ends the tune usually happens to be the first (or last) note in the scale on which the tune is based. A melody that ends on any other note—whether it's in a major key or a minor key—somehow

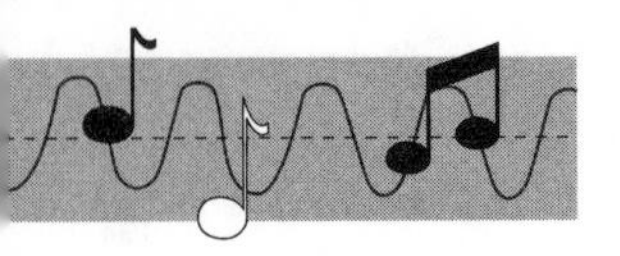

sounds incomplete. The reason is primarily cultural; in the West, we've been taught that this is the way music should sound.

Because of its special qualities, the note that starts and ends a scale has a special name. It's called the *tonic.*

The Dominant and Subdominant

Every scale has two other notes that are almost as important as the tonic. One of these is called the *dominant.* The other is called the *subdominant.* Figure 8–4 shows the tonic, dominant, and subdominant notes in the key of C.

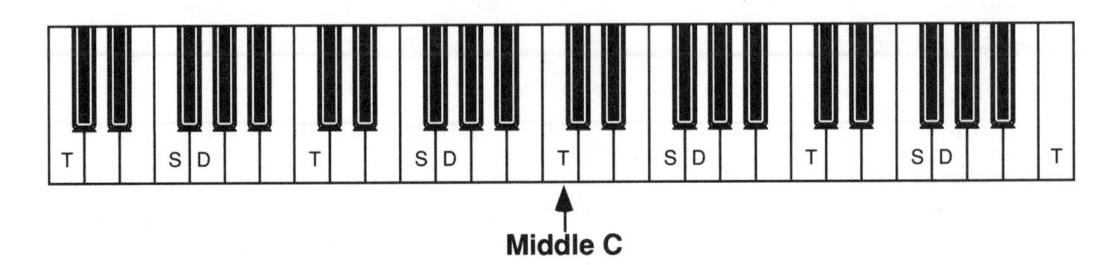

Figure 8–4. Tonic, dominant, and subdominant notes in C

For reasons that are rooted in the science of acoustics as well as in our musical culture and traditions, the tonic, dominant, and subdominant notes are very important in musical compositions written in the West.

From an acoustic point of view, the dominant tone has a close acoustic relationship to the tonic. In respect to their distances from the tonic, the dominant and the subdominant notes are mirror images of each other. The dominant is exactly the same number of half steps *above* the tonic as the subdominant is *below* the tonic.

The reasons that these relationships are so important are beyond the scope of this chapter. But there are many books on music theory that cover this topic in detail, and some of those books are listed in the Bibliography.

Musical Math

The intervals between notes have specific names, but you'll have to learn a new kind of math to understand them. The mathematics of music, probably because of its medieval origins, has some odd rules that take some getting used to.

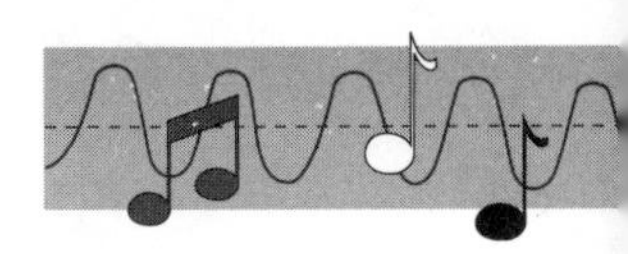

For an example of how this works, look back at Figure 8–1 and count the keys from middle C to the subdominant note above it (which is F). The number you'll probably arrive at is 3.

Musical math is different. In music, you don't *count* notes; instead, you consider the *positions* that notes occupy in the musical scale. Therefore, when you count the distances between keys on the piano keyboard, you always include the first key in your calculation. So, if a musician counted the distance between middle C and the F above it, the result would be 4, not 3.

Similarly, when you use musical math to count upward from middle C to the dominant note above it—which is G—the number you wind up with is 5, not 4.

Therefore, the dominant note in a scale is considered to be the fifth *scale step* upward from the tonic. Similarly, the subdominant is considered to be the fifth *scale step* downward from the tonic.

Interval names are based on the degrees of a scale. When counting up to find an interval number, you count scale steps based on a major scale from the lower note. If you count chromatic half steps, the interval is in semitones.

Names of Intervals

As you might expect, the intervals between musical notes are named in accordance with the rules of musical math. Thus, the interval between middle C and the F just above it is referred to as a *fourth*, and the interval between C and the G just above it (the dominant) is called a *fifth*.

Octaves and Unisons

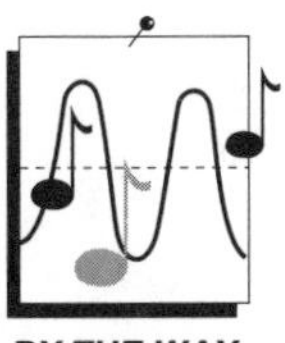

BY THE WAY

An eighth interval—which refers to two notes that are an octave apart on the keyboard—is usually referred to (logically enough) as an octave. *Two instances of the same note playing at the same time are called a* **unison.**

You can't play a one-note unison on a piano, of course, because you can't play two notes on one key at the same time. However, when several instruments are playing simultaneously—in a band or an orchestra, for example—it's quite common to have several instruments playing the same note in unison. ❍

When you become accustomed to referring to intervals by their numbers, you will have come a long way toward understanding the language of music. Musicians often speak of intervals in terms of thirds, fifths, sixths, sevenths, and so on. When you hear such terms, the important thing to remember is that they refer to the intervals between pairs of notes, *always including the first note in the calculation.*

To see how the names of musical intervals work, examine Figure 8–5.

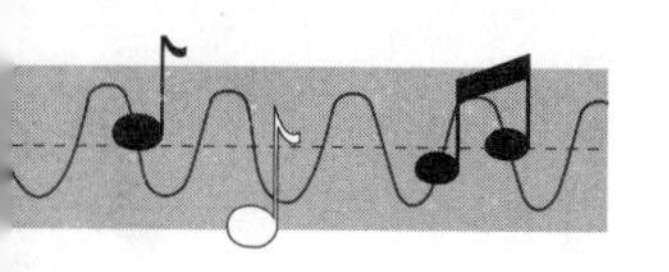

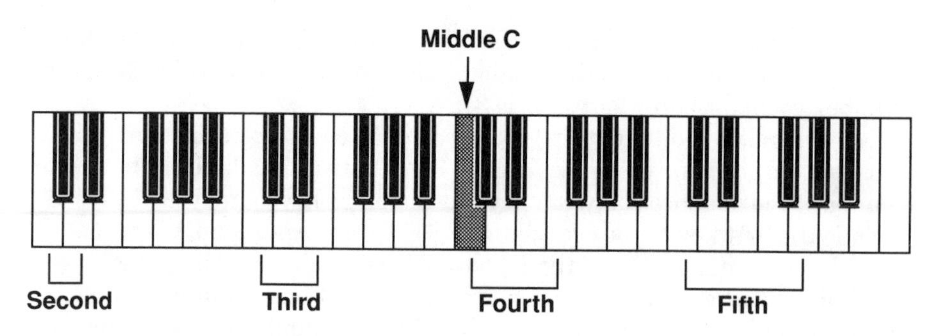

Figure 8–5. Intervals

When you refer to a musical interval by its number, you consider only the notes that are present in the scale on which the interval is based; any other half steps that may be present in the interval are disregarded. You can see this by examining the intervals shown in Figure 8–5. Some of the intervals include half steps, and some don't.

Look carefully, and you'll see that the second interval at the far left of the keyboard spans a full step: the step between C and D. If you moved the start of the interval two white keys to the right, the interval would extend from E and F, which are only a half step apart. But it would still be called a second.

Similarly, the third interval in Figure 8–5—which extends from a C to an E—includes two full steps. If you moved the start of the interval one white key to the right, it would extend from D to F—a distance of only a step and half. But it would still be called a third.

Major and Minor Intervals

To eliminate any confusion that might result from calling intervals of different sizes by the same names, musicians say that intervals have certain *qualities*. The qualities that an interval can have are *major, minor, augmented, diminished,* and *perfect.*

You can determine whether an interval is major or minor by counting the half steps that it contains. For example, Figure 8–6 shows a major third and a minor third. The major third contains four half steps, while the minor third contains only three.

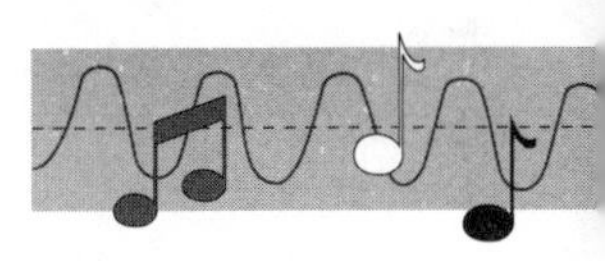

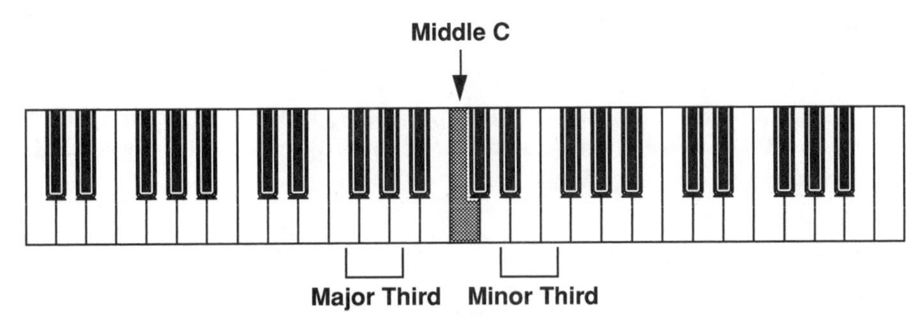

Figure 8–6. Major and minor intervals

Augmented and Diminished Intervals

An interval can be larger than major or smaller than minor. If an interval is half a step larger than major, it's said to be *augmented*. You can create a diminished interval by simply making a minor interval half a step smaller.

The symbol + is often used to identify an augmented interval, and the symbol ° is often used to identify a diminished interval. Diminished and augmented intervals are widely used in popular music, jazz music, and modern symphonic music.

Figure 8–7 shows an augmented third and a diminished third on a musical staff. In the lower half of the illustration, the same two notes are shown on a piano keyboard.

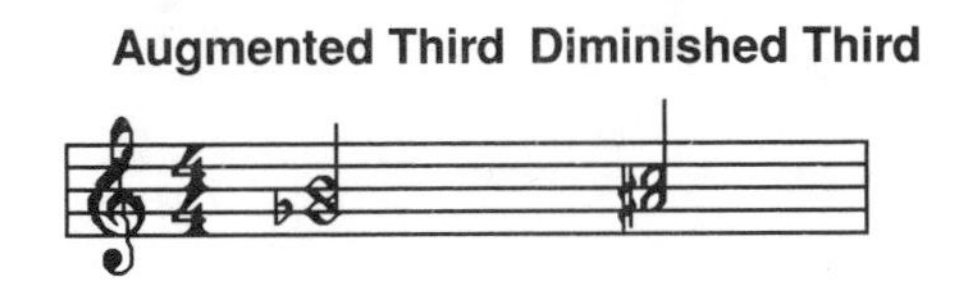

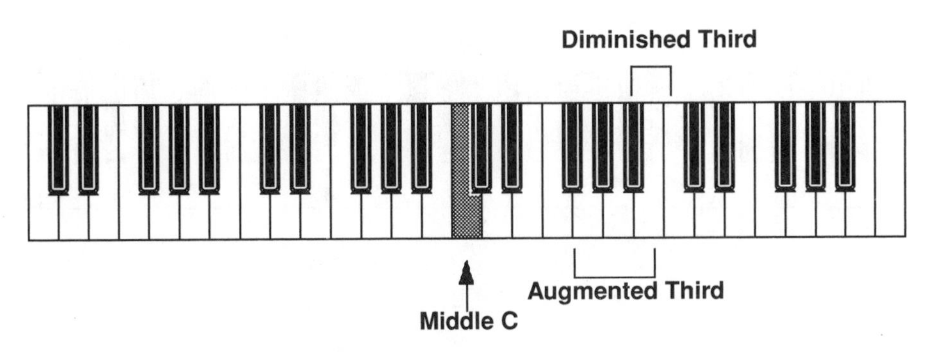

Figure 8–7. Augmented and diminished intervals

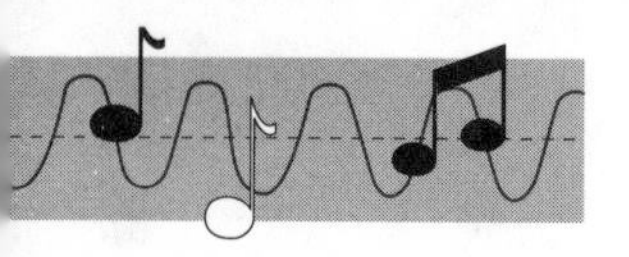

Augmented Intervals

To see how augmented intervals work, examine the augmented third that's shown on the musical staff. If it were a major third, it would extend from G to B. However, the first note in the interval has been lowered to G flat, so it's an *augmented third.*

Diminished Intervals

If an interval is half a step smaller than minor, it's said to be *diminished.* You can create a diminished interval by simply making a minor interval half a step smaller. In Figure 8–7, the interval that starts on A sharp (or B flat) is a *diminished third.* If it were a minor third, it would extend from A to C. However, the first note in the interval has been raised to A sharp, so it's a *diminished third.*

Perfect Intervals

Unisons, fourths, fifths, and octaves can never be major or minor. Therefore, they are called *perfect intervals.* A perfect fourth always has five half steps, a perfect fifth has seven half steps, and an octave always has twelve half steps. Figure 8–8 shows a perfect fourth, a perfect fifth, and an octave on both a musical staff and a piano keyboard.

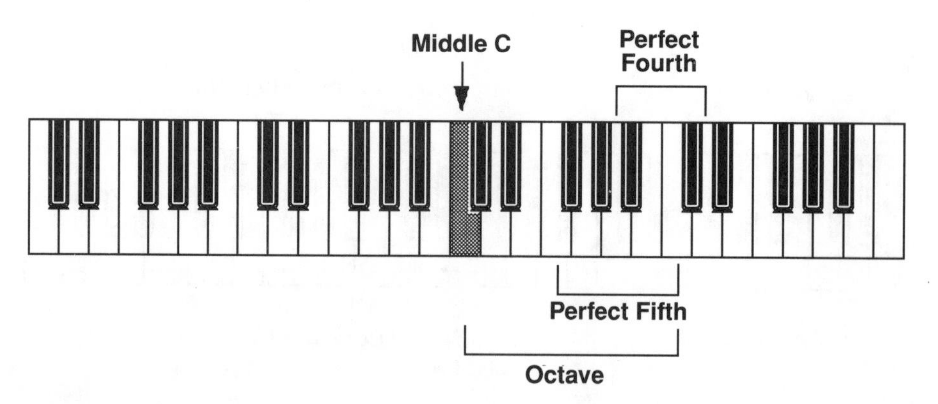

Figure 8–8. Perfect intervals

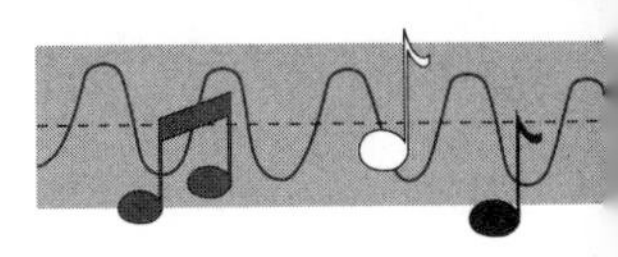

A unison obviously can't be major or minor, since it has only one note. An octave can't be major or minor, because it always extends from one note on the staff to the next note of the same name.

You can prove that a fourth can't be major or minor by conducting an experiment on a musical keyboard. Examine a fourth on a piano keyboard carefully, and you'll see that it includes one, and only one, pair of white keys that are a half step apart. No matter where you start the fourth, this rule holds true. Try it by counting out the notes in a fourth on the keyboard shown in Figure 8–8.

Every fifth also includes one, and only one, pair of white keys that are a half step apart. So a fifth can't be major or minor, either. You can confirm that, too, with the fifth shown in Figure 8–8.

Although a fourth is never major or minor, you can turn a fourth into a diminished interval by either raising its lower note or lowering its higher note. For example, you can change the fourth in Figure 8–8 into a diminished fourth by raising its lower note to B flat or lowering its higher note to D flat. You can augment the fourth by either lowering its lower note to A flat or raising it higher note to D sharp.

You can diminish the fifth shown in Figure 8–8 by either lowering its higher note to C flat (B) or by raising its lower note to F sharp. You can augment the fifth by raising its higher note to C sharp or by lowering its lower note to F flat (E).

You can diminish the octave in Figure 8–8 by either lowering its higher note to C flat (B) or by raising its lower note to C sharp. You can augment the octave by raising its higher note to C sharp or by lowering its lower note to C flat (B).

You can augment a unison, and you can also diminish it. For example, the unison shown in Figure 8–8 consists of one note: middle C. You can augment that unison by turning it into two notes: C and C sharp. When you expand the unison in this way, it is still a unison, because C and C sharp have the same base name. But when one instance of the unison is raised, this covers a half a step, so you can say it's augmented.

Similarly, you can diminish a unison by dropping one of its instances by a half step. For example, the unison C and C flat (B) is a diminished unison.

Consonant and Dissonant Intervals

An interval can be *consonant* or *dissonant.* Consonant intervals contribute a sense of stability and resolution to a musical composition. Dissonant intervals —used wisely—can contribute a feeling of suspense, tension, and drama.

As you'll see in the next section, the chords that are used to accompany music can also be described as consonant or dissonant. Whether a chord is

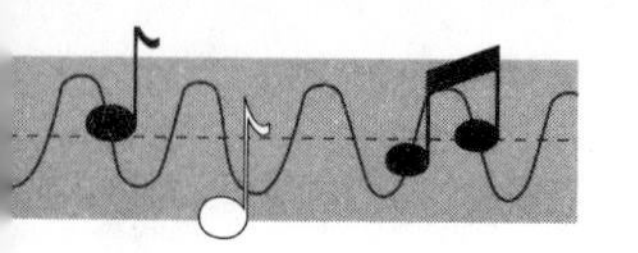

consonant or dissonant depends upon the consonance or dissonance of the intervals that the chord contains.

Consonant Intervals

With a little practice, it's easy to spot a consonant interval, because there are only five kinds: the unison, the third, the fifth, the sixth, and the octave.

Figure 8–9 shows a musical staff that contains the five kinds of consonant intervals in the keys of C Major and C minor that are measured from the tonic note C. The labels below the notes are abbreviations for the kinds of intervals shown. P means perfect, U means unison, M means major, m means minor, and O means octave.

Figure 8–9. The consonant intervals

The first five intervals (from left) are the consonant intervals in the key of C Major: a perfect unison, a major third, a perfect fifth, a major sixth, and a perfect eighth, or octave.

The last two intervals in the picture are a minor third and a minor sixth. The interval from C to E flat is the consonant third that naturally appears in the key of C minor. The interval from C to A flat is the consonant sixth that naturally appears in the key of C minor.

Dissonant Intervals

All intervals measured from C that are not shown in Figure 8–9—except for a perfect fourth, which is a special case—are dissonant intervals. Dissonant intervals are sometimes called unstable intervals. (The reason that a perfect fourth is a special case involves issues of harmony, counterpoint, and music history that are beyond the scope of this chapter. For more information on this topic, see a good book on music theory; several such books are listed in the Bibliography.)

Dissonant intervals include seconds and sevenths, and all augmented and diminished intervals—especially the augmented fourth and the diminished fifth.

Figure 8–10 shows dissonant intervals in the key of C. The labels below the notes are abbreviations for the intervals shown. The intervals are, left

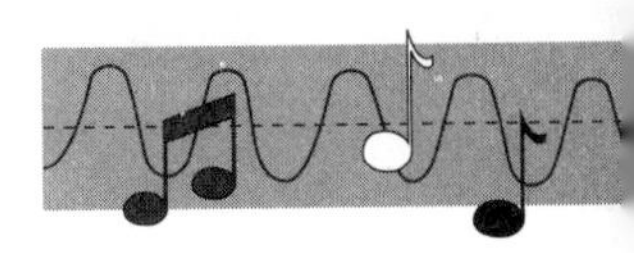

to right: a minor second, a major second, an augmented fourth, a diminished fifth, a minor seventh, and a major seventh.

Figure 8–10. Dissonant intervals

As Figure 8–10 shows, the symbol for an augmented interval is +, and the symbol for a diminished interval is °. The letters M and m represent major and minor chords, respectively.

Chords

When three or more notes are played at the same time, they are called a *chord.* The chords used in a musical composition can be consonant or dissonant, depending upon the intervals that they contain. Also, notes with various intervals can be added together to form more complex chords.

Consonant Chords

The chords that sound the most stable in a composition—and therefore contribute most to its melodic foundation—are consonant chords. Usually, as a composition progresses, dissonant chords appear and keep resolving into consonant chords. Since consonant chords sound complete, stable, resolved, and finished, melodies usually end on consonant chords.

An example of a song that ends on a consonant chord is the sample song "Home on the Range," which was examined in Chapter 7. The song is scored in the key of G, and it ends on a consonant G Major chord.

Dissonant Chords

Some people confuse dissonance with discord, and believe that dissonant chords sound "unpleasant" or "bad." Actually, dissonance in music is like the element of suspense in a play or a movie: When it is used by a skilled composer, it adds a sense of excitement and movement to a composition. Dissonance can make the listener feel uneasy, or even temporarily uncomfortable—but when everything gets resolved in the end, there's a sense of peace and satisfaction. In music, dissonance is not something to be completely avoided; it's practically mandatory. Without dissonant chords, music would be boring.

Triads

A *triad* is a group of three notes with pitches that are separated by thirds—for example, C, E, and G. Triads occur naturally in music when you try to make several different musical parts consonant with each other. When you play three notes, and all three are consonant with each other, what you have is a triad.

In its simplest form, a triad looks like one of the two chords shown in Figure 8–11. In a musical score, such major triads such as those in Figure 8–11 are easy to spot, because their notes fall either on three consecutive lines of the staff, or on three consecutive spaces.

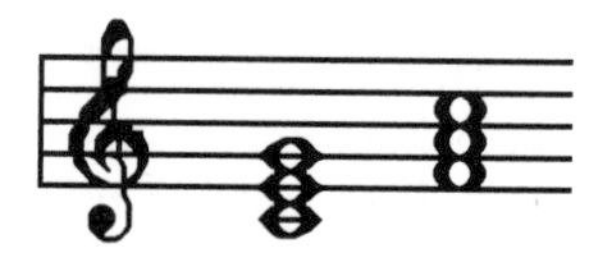

Figure 8–11. Triads

Triads are important in *tonal harmony,* the kind of harmony that our ears are accustomed to in the West. Tonal harmony depends upon an interplay between consonance and dissonance, with dissonance being repeatedly resolved into consonance, and this kind of interplay depends mainly upon the use of triads.

Learning Triads with Listen

Because of the importance of triads, Listen has a whole section of exercises devoted to triads. You can do the triad exercises by following these steps:

1. Choose Triads from the Exercise menu.
2. Select the kinds of triads that you want to work with by choosing the Included Triads item from the Material menu.
3. When you select Included Triads, Listen displays a dialog box that lets you select the kinds of triads you want included in the Listen exercises.
4. To preview chords as you choose them, you can click on the Play Chord check box.

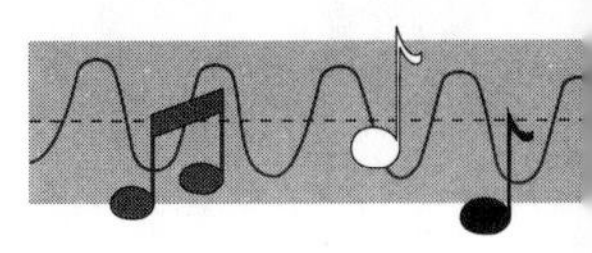

Triadic Harmony

A consonant triad includes a major third and a minor third, which add up to a perfect fifth (there's that musical math again!). If the major third is in the lower position, the triad is a *major triad.* If the minor third is in the lower position, the triad is a *minor triad.*

The lowest note in a triad is the note that the triad is built on. Therefore, it is called the *root.*

The middle note of a triad is always a third above the root. Therefore, the middle note of a triad is called the triad's *third.*

The highest note of a triad is always a fifth above the root. Therefore, the highest note of a triad is called the triad's *fifth.*

Major and Minor Triads

Figure 8–12 shows three major triads. Their roots are, respectively, C, F, and G. Therefore, the three major triads could be called the C, F, and G major triads.

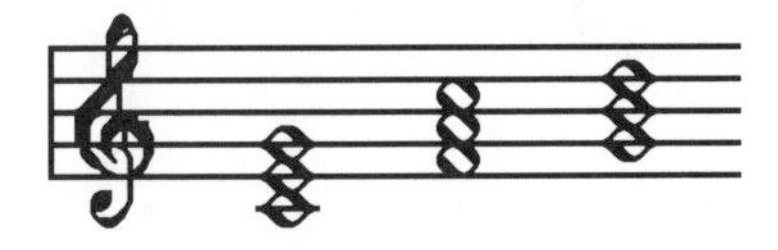

Figure 8–12. Major triads

Figure 8–13 shows three minor triads. Their roots are, respectively, D, E, and C. These three minor triads could be called the D minor, E minor, and C minor triads.

Figure 8–13. Minor triads

Natural Triads

You can make only seven triads out of the notes of a single major or natural minor scale. These seven triads, called the *natural triads,* define the harmonic world for the key that the scale is written in.

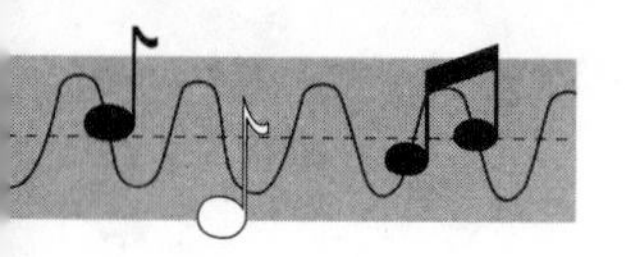

Each triad in a set of natural triads has a label that is a roman numeral. If a triad in a set of natural triads is a major triad, its label is an uppercase roman numeral. For example, the triad that is built on the first note of a major scale is a major triad, so it has the label I. The triad that is built on the fifth note is also a major triad, so it has the label V.

If a triad in a given key is a minor triad, its label is a lowercase roman numeral. For instance, the chord based on the third note of a major scale is labeled iii, and the chord based on the sixth note of a major scale is labeled vi.

Figure 8–14 shows the natural triads in the C Major scale. Notice that the vii triad, written vii°, is a diminished triad. In popular and folk music, the vii° triad is not often used except in its first inversion (inversions are described in the section "Features of Listen," later in this chapter). When a seventh triad is needed in a musical selection—and that is quite often—accompanists usually use a more natural-sounding (but still dissonant) kind of triad called a *dominant seventh.* The dominant seventh chord is described in more detail later in this section.

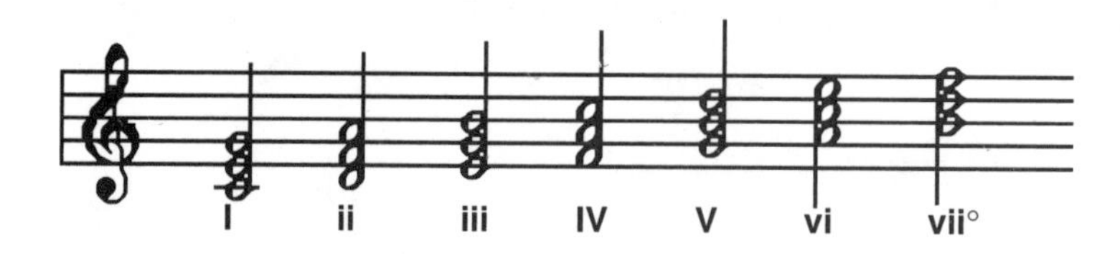

Figure 8–14. Natural triads

Primary Triads

In any set of natural triads, only three triads are major. These are the triads labeled I, IV, and V. Collectively, the I, IV, and V triads are called the *primary triads.* Individually, they are called the *tonic* triad, the *subdominant* triad, and the *dominant* triad respectively, as shown in Figure 8–15.

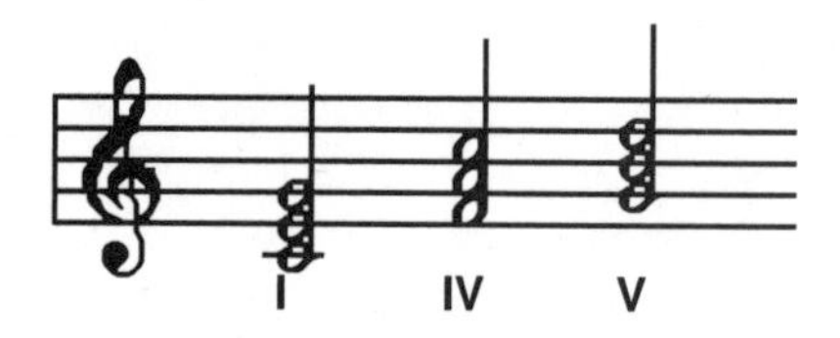

Figure 8–15. Primary triads

Guitarists and pianists often accompany songs with chords that are based on tonic, dominant, and subdominant triads. For example, the

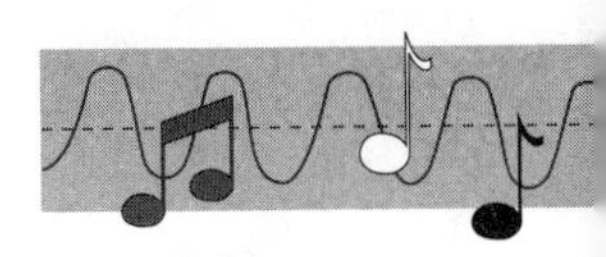

Songworks program—which was examined in Chapter 7—plays the sample song "Home on the Range" with a chord accompaniment that is based on the chords G, C, and D. (Actually, the D chord is a dominant seventh chord, and some C minor chords are also used to add flavor; those enhancements, and others that can add still more complexity to the song, are described later in this chapter.)

Many popular and folk songs, like "Home on the Range," can be played with three-chord or four-chord accompaniments that are based on their tonic, dominant, and subdominant triads. When you've learned to accompany enough melodies with tonic, subdominant, and dominant chords, you often develop an almost instinctive ability to sense where the right chords go, and to improvise appropriate accompaniments by ear.

The Dominant Seventh Chord

From a technical point of view, a dominant triad (the V triad) is made up of two third intervals. Accompanists often find that they can make a dominant triad sound more interesting by adding an extra third to the stack of two thirds that it already contains.

When a musician applies this treatment to a dominant triad (or chord), the chord that results is called a *dominant seventh* chord. In the accompaniment to a song that contains dominant triads, dominant chords, and dominant seventh chords can be used almost interchangeably. Of course, when accompanists have a choice, they usually play the dominant seventh chord.

When a composer or an accompanist turns a dominant chord into a dominant seventh, the change makes the dominant chord more dissonant, but it's a colorful and not unpleasant kind of dissonance. What happens is that the dominant seventh chord almost cries out to be resolved; that is, to be followed by the consonant triad that provides the melodic foundation of the song.

Another way to describe this process is by focusing on the lead voice of a melody. In terms of voice leading, the seventh in a dominant seventh chord resolves down to the third in the I (tonic major triad), and the third in a dominant seventh chord resolves up to the root of the I (tonic major triad).

Technically, the instability of the dominant seventh chord is caused by the fact that a dominant seventh chord contains not only a dissonant seventh, but also a dissonant diminished fifth. Musicians usually use a dominant seventh chord just before a tonic triad or just before a vi-type triad, because either a tonic triad or a vi triad can resolve the dominant seventh's instability.

Figure 8–16 shows how dominant seventh chords are constructed in several keys. The chords in the illustration are labeled the same way

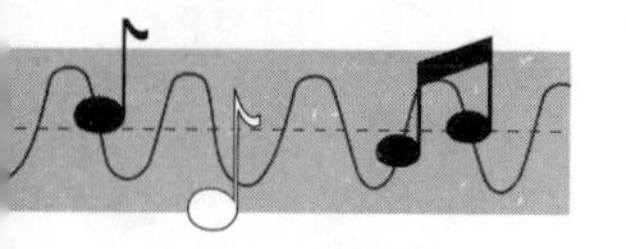

they're usually labeled in sheet music; the C dominant seventh is labeled C7, and so on.

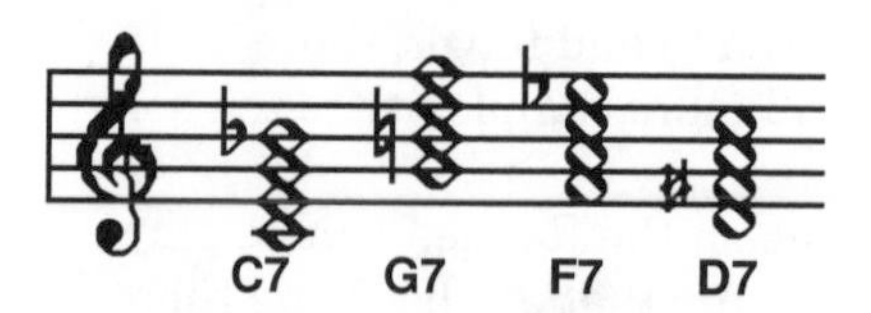

Figure 8–16. Dominant seventh chords

Secondary Triads

Although the tonic, dominant, and subdominant chords are the ones most often used in popular and folk music, *secondary triads* are sometimes used in music to add variety, complexity, and color to musical compositions. In any set of natural triads, the secondary triads are the ii, iii, vi, and vii° triads. Secondary minor chords, in particular, can make a melody sound more exotic and interesting.

The sample song "Home on the Range," which was introduced in Chapter 7, is a simple song that uses secondary triads—as well as the tonic, dominant, and subdominant chords—in an interesting way. However, there are other ways to arrange the song's accompaniment, as you can see by doing the following exercise.

Adding Secondary Triads to a Song

In this exercise, you'll alter the accompaniment that the designers of Songworks wrote for the song "Home on the Range." Try the exercises and see if you like the changes. These are the steps to follow:

1. Launch the Songworks program by clicking on its icon.
2. Play "Home on the Range" by pressing Command-H or selecting the Hear (All or Selected) item from the File menu. As the song plays, watch the chord symbols displayed above the staff and listen carefully to the chords being played. You might want to play the song several times to get a good feel for how the accompaniment sounds.
3. Find the part of the song, not far from the beginning, that's shown in Figure 8–17. In that section of the song, you won't see the A minor chord that's shown in the illustration above the word *antelope.* In the next step, you'll add that chord to the song's accompaniment.

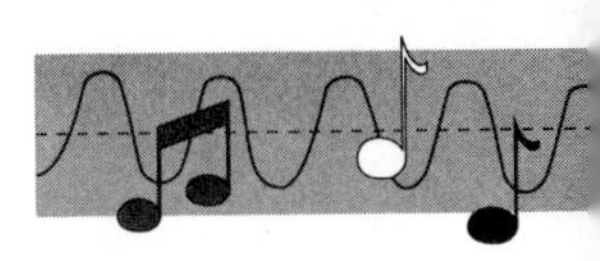

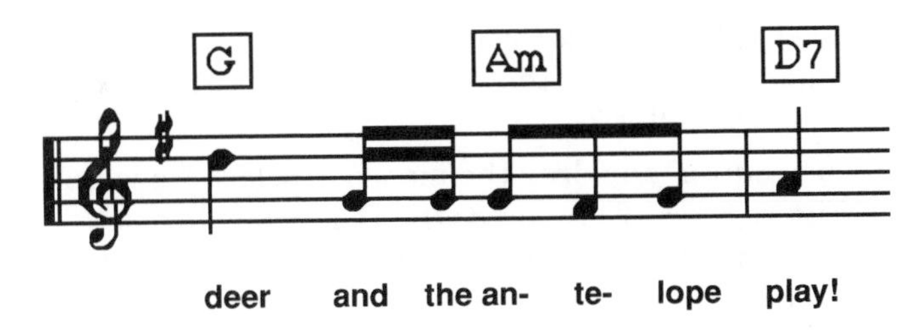

Figure 8–17. Adding a secondary chord

4. Activate the chord layer of the Songworks program by clicking on the chord handle (the top dot just to the left of the score of "Home on the Range"). Or, if you prefer, activate the chord layer by clicking on one of the chord names just above the keyboard in the keyboard window.
5. Select the button labeled Am just above the keyboard in the keyboard window. The Am button is between the button labeled G and the button labeled Bm.
6. Move the cursor to the spot in the song window that matches the section shown in Figure 8–17. Then click on the grayed-out down arrow just above the word *antelope*. Songworks responds by placing an A minor chord symbol in the location you have selected.
7. Activate the staff layer, play "Home on the Range," and listen to the chord you have added.
8. With the arrow cursor, select the chord you have added and type Delete or Command-X to delete it. Then listen to the song without the extra chord.
9. Scroll "Home on the Range" to the place where the Chorus begins: the spot shown in Figure 8–18.

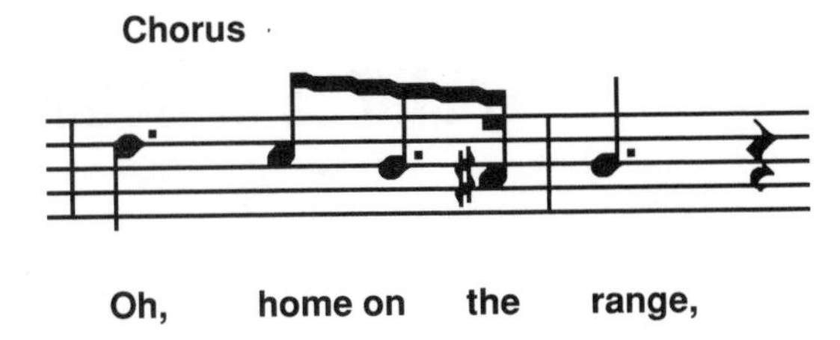

Figure 8–18. Chorus of the sample song

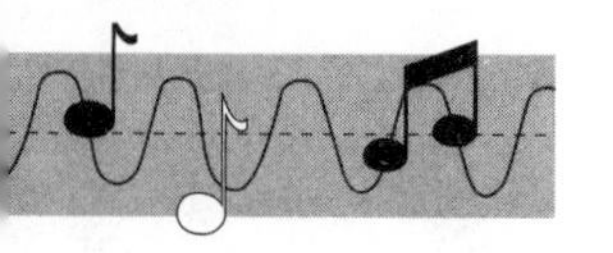

10. Activate the text layer of Songworks by clicking on the text handle (the bottom button just to the left of the staff). Then select the text tool (for its location, see Chapter 7).
11. Hold down the mouse button and drag the mouse to select the word *Chorus* shown in Figure 8–18. Then, press the Delete key to delete the word *Chorus* from the score. (You'll need the space occupied by the word *Chorus* to add a chord.)
12. Click on the chord handle to activate the chord layer.
13. Select chord tools from the keyboard window and add them to the sample song's accompaniment line until the accompaniment above the beginning of the chorus looks like the accompaniment shown in Figure 8–19.

Figure 8–19. More secondary chords

What the Exercise Shows

When you do the above exercise, you see that there's more than one way—indeed, there are countless ways—to arrange the accompaniment of a song. The Songworks version of "Home on the Range" sounds quite different from the version that the exercise creates—and if more chords were made available in the demonstration version of Songworks, you could try other arrangements. The point is that if you know your chords, you can do a lot of things with a song.

Features of Listen

In this chapter, you've had an opportunity to use several features of the demonstration version of Listen that's on your bonus disk. But there are many other features you haven't yet used. This chapter describes more things you can do with the program.

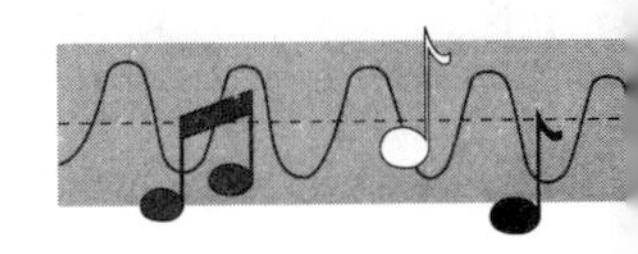

Modes and Alternate Scales

In modern popular and classical music, the two kinds of scales that are used most often are the major scale and the minor scale. However, music can also be based on other kinds of scales.

In medieval times, musical keyboards had only white keys, but you could play scales in different *modes* by starting the scales on different notes. For example, there was a *Dorian* mode that started on D, a *Phrygian* mode that started on E, and a *Lydian* mode that started on G. You can hear what each of these three modes sounds like by playing a scale in D, a scale in E, and a scale in G, using only the white keys.

Since today's musical keyboards have both white keys and black keys, you can now use the black keys as well as the white keys to play scales in different modes, as long as you make sure that you use the correct intervals. In fact, both the Dorian mode and the Lydian mode are used today in blues and rock tunes that are written in many keys.

With Listen, you can experiment with these three modes, and with several more modes and alternate kinds of scales. To choose a mode or alternate scale, select Pitch Set from the Material menu. Listen then displays a dialog like the one in Figure 8–20.

Starting Pitch (Tonic)
◉ C
○ F ○ G
○ Bb ○ D
○ Eb ○ A
○ Ab ○ E
○ Db ○ B
○ F#
☐ Play Scale
OK

Scales
◉ Ionian (Major)
○ Dorian
○ Phrygian
○ Lydian
○ Mixolydian
○ Aeolian (Natural Minor)
○ Locrian
○ Melodic Minor (Ascending)
○ Harmonic Minor
○ Whole Tone ○ Pentatonic
○ Diminished ○ Chromatic
○ Jazz Altered

Included Pitches
☒ B ☐ A#/Bb
☒ A ☐ G#/Ab
☒ G ☐ F#/Gb
☒ F
☒ E ☐ D#/Eb
☒ D ☐ C#/Db
☒ C
Cancel

Figure 8–20 Pitch Set dialog

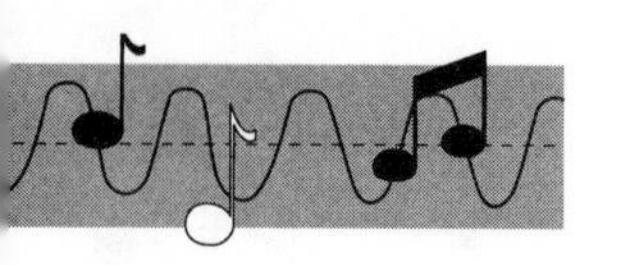

The Pitch Set dialog box has three columns. The first column lets you select the starting note of a pitch, the second column lets you select a kind of scale, and the third column lets you select the pitches that you want included in the scale. With the third column, you can make alterations in the scales named in the middle column.

You can use these three columns to create a scale or mode automatically instead of setting included pitches by hand. For example, to create melodic material in the Dorian mode but with a tonic pitch of F, you can choose Dorian in the Scale column and F in the Tonic column. That way, you don't have to check F, G, Ab, Bb, C, D, and Eb in the Included Pitches column.

By clicking on the buttons in the Pitch Set dialog box, you can set Listen to play not only in various medieval modes, but also in several alternate kinds of scales, such as the chromatic, whole-tone, and pentatonic scales (the pentatonic scale contains only five notes, with the octave being reached at the sixth position, or *degree).*

When the Pitch Set dialog is displayed, you can change the keys that Listen uses to play its melodic and interval examples. Simply click on the Play Scale check box in the lower left-hand corner of the dialog box, and then choose from the various pitches, scales, and included pitches in the dialog window. Then click on the OK button, do some exercises, and listen to the results.

Setting Limits

You can specify high and low limits for the notes that Listen uses to play its examples. Here's how:

1. Choose the Range item from the Material menu. Listen responds by displaying a dialog like the one in Figure 8–21.

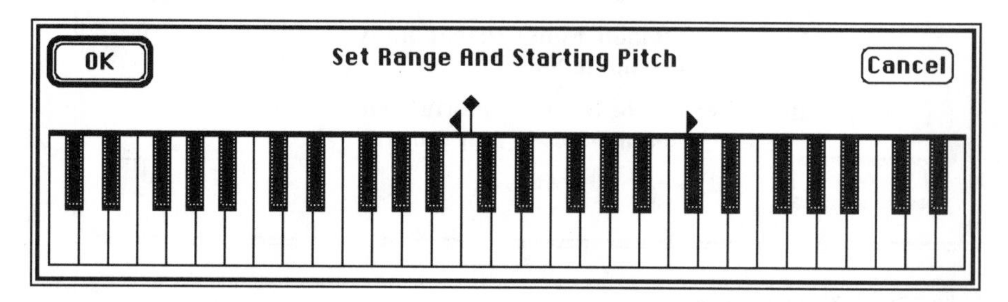

Figure 8–21. Range dialog box

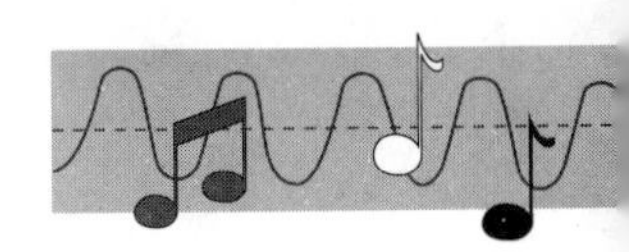

2. To set the pitch at which each exercise starts, drag the center marker to the position above the desired note.
3. To set the lower limit that you want, drag the triangular marker on the left of the keyboard to the position above the desired note.
4. To set an upper range limit, drag the triangular marker on the right of the keyboard to the position above the desired note.
5. Click on OK to close the dialog and activate the range that you have specified.

Inversions

When you change the lowest note of a chord from its root to another note in the chord, the chord that results is called an *inversion.* For example, a C major triad—which includes the notes C, E, and G—is ordinarily played with C in the bottom position, as shown in Figure 8–22. In this configuration, the position of the note C—on which the chord is based—is in the lowest position on the staff. This position is known as the note's *root position.*

Figure 8–22. C major triad in root position

If you move the C note in Figure 8–22 up an octave, the result is a C major triad in what is known as a *first inversion.* This chord, shown in Figure 8–23, sounds a little different than a C major triad with C in its root position.

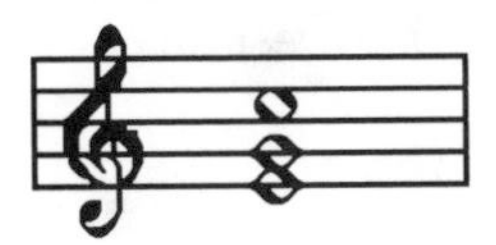

Figure 8–23. C major triad in first inversion

If you raise the E note in Figure 8–23 one octave, you have a *second inversion* of a C major triad, which sounds different still. Figure 8–24 shows the second inversion of a C major triad.

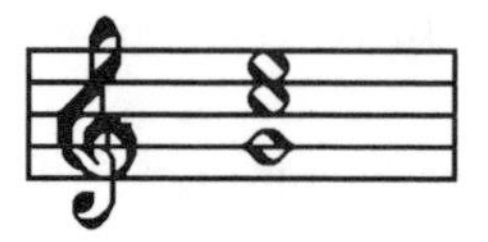

Figure 8–24. C major triad in second inversion

Listen can play chords in various inversions. Just choose the Included Inversions item from the Material menu, and Listen responds by displaying a dialog that lets you choose a set of inversions.

There are only two inversions of triads, but there are three inversions of seventh chords. For example, the third inversion of the seventh chord D-F-A-C is C-D-F-A.

There's more information about inversions in the documentation that comes with Listen, Practica Musica, and other music-learning programs.

Chord Options

Listen offers several options that affect its chord and interval exercises. To see what kinds of chord and interval options are available, choose the Chord Options item from the Options menu. Listen then displays a dialog box that lets you specify how you'd like chords and intervals to sound and appear in the exercises.

Floating and Locked Chords

When the Chord Options dialog window is displayed, you can specify whether you want Listen to play intervals and chords in a floating mode, or whether you want them locked. Floating intervals and chords are played within the currently specified range (which is set using the Range dialog box, described earlier in this section). Locked intervals and chords use the current starting pitch (which you also select with the Range dialog box) as their lowest tone.

Choosing Highlighted Notes

When Listen plays chord examples, it can highlight one note in the chord to give you a clue to where the chord might be. The bottom or top note of the chord may be highlighted. In answering the chord examples, you still have to play the chord one note at a time from the lowest to the highest tone. With the bottom three radio buttons in the Chord Options dialog, you can specify whether you want chord notes highlighted, and if so, how.

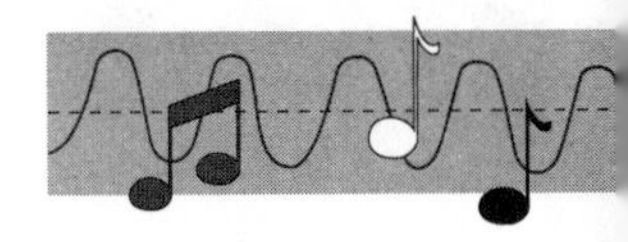

Choosing Included Chords

You specify various kinds of chords that you want Listen to generate in its chord, inversion, and chord quality examples. To customize the kinds of chords that Listen plays, you can choose the Included Triads item from the Material menu, or one of the four Included *n*th Chord items that follow it.

Each of these five menu items opens a dialog box, and each dialog box works the same way, presenting various permutations of each chord type. For example, to choose the kinds of chords that Listen plays in all of its triad exercises, you can choose the Included Triads command. Listen then opens a dialog showing four types of triads that the triad exercises use. When the dialog box is displayed, you can choose the kinds of triads that you want Listen to generate. The Included Triads dialog is shown in Figure 8–25.

OK | Cancel | ☐ Play Chord

Included Triads

☒ Major Triad (Major 3, Perfect 5)
☒ Minor Triad (Minor 3, Perfect 5)
☐ Diminished Triad (Minor 3, Diminished 5)
☐ Augmented Triad (Major 3, Augmented 5)

Figure 8–25. Included Triads dialog

Other Music-Learning Programs

Listen is one of the leading music-learning programs on the market, but it isn't the only one. Listen has several excellent competitors, and three of them are described in this section.

Each music-education program has its own personality. For example, Listen stresses ear training. Another popular program in the genre—Practica Musica, from Ars Nova Software—is also interactive but takes a more academic approach. Harmony Grid, from Hip Software, has an unusual interface that features timed exercises. And MiBAC Music Lessons, from MiBAC Music Software, is great for beginners.

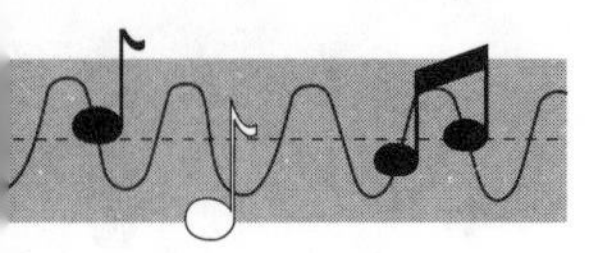

Practica Musica

Practica Musica is published by Ars Nova Software—the same company that makes Songworks, which was featured in Chapter 7. Practica Musica is a classic in the field of music-training programs, and as soon as you try it, you'll see why. It's highly interactive. You play a chord—either by clicking a mouse on a screen keyboard or by pressing the keys on a MIDI keyboard—and Practica Musica immediately tells you what kind of chord you've played. Figure 8–26 shows the Practica Musica screen display.

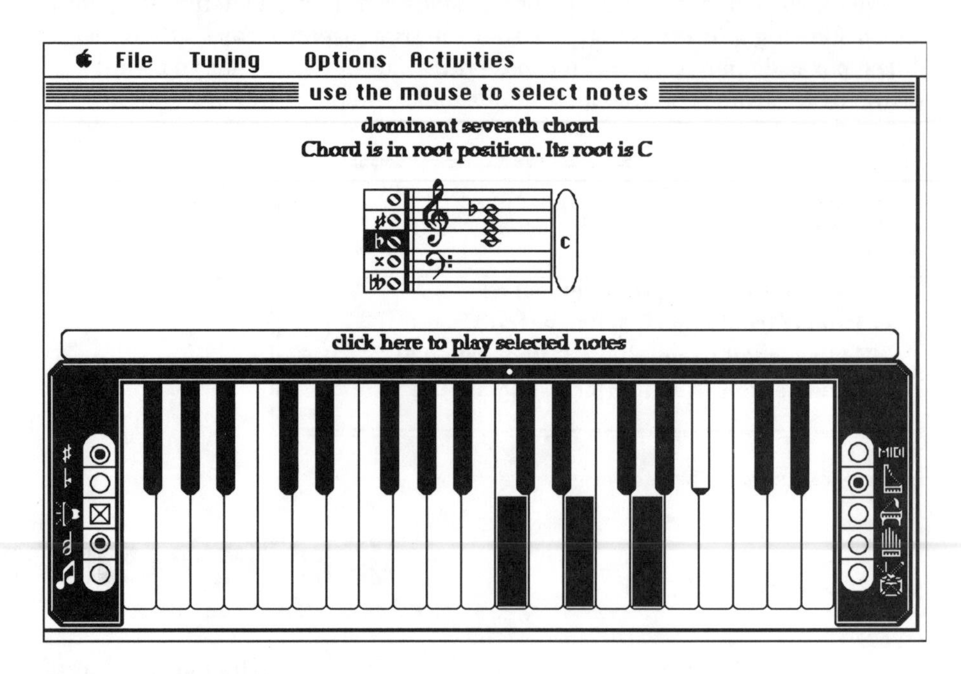

Figure 8–26. Practica Musica

With this kind of interaction, you can learn a lot without even opening the instruction manual—but you should, because the program's documentation alone is worth the price of the whole package. Together, the Practica Musica program and manual are a complete course in music theory.

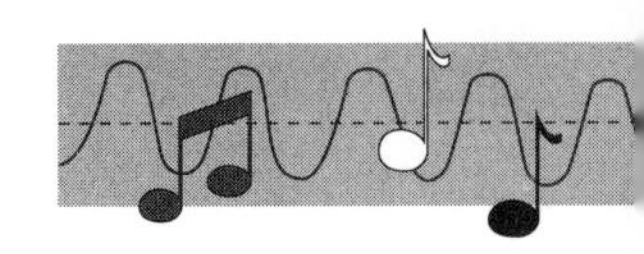

Practica Musica organizes its lessons into eleven activities, ranging from simple note reading to scales, modes, interval recognition, chord spelling, and ear training. Each activity is then broken into four levels of difficulty.

As you work your way through Practica Musica's lessons, you earn points for correct answers and lose points for mistakes. As you master each level, you get a round of applause and a grade, just as if you were in a real class. You can even have classmates; as many as four people can do the program's exercises simultaneously, and Practica Musica can keep progress reports on file for each person doing the exercises.

Harmony Grid

Harmony Grid, as its name implies, breaks musical harmony down into grids, arranged so that scales can be viewed as repeating patterns.

Using Harmony Grid is something like playing musical tic-tac-toe. The program sets up a grid on which horizontal movements equate to musical whole steps and vertical movements are seen as half steps. That means that you can play an ascending major scale in any key by moving in the same pattern: three dots right, one dot up, three dots right, and one dot up.

One result of this approach is that you can easily see the whole- and half-step relationships in a scale, without having to learn the keyboard fundamentals that are explained in this chapter (although a graphic keyboard is included at the bottom of the screen). That is both an advantage and a disadvantage. You can learn scales easily, but while you're at it, why not also learn the keyboard? I haven't run across a musical instrument yet that arranges music in a harmony grid.

MiBAC Music Lessons

The MiBAC Music Lessons program takes a more traditional approach to music teaching; it gives you scales, drills, and ear training, and it uses a carefully graded learning curve to move the student gently from beginning lessons to intermediate and advanced exercises. For a beginner, it's an excellent choice. Figure 8–27 shows the MiBAC Music Lessons screen display.

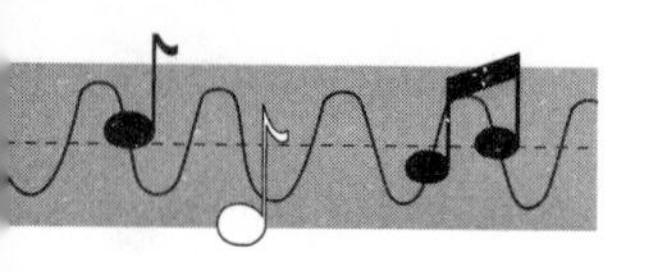

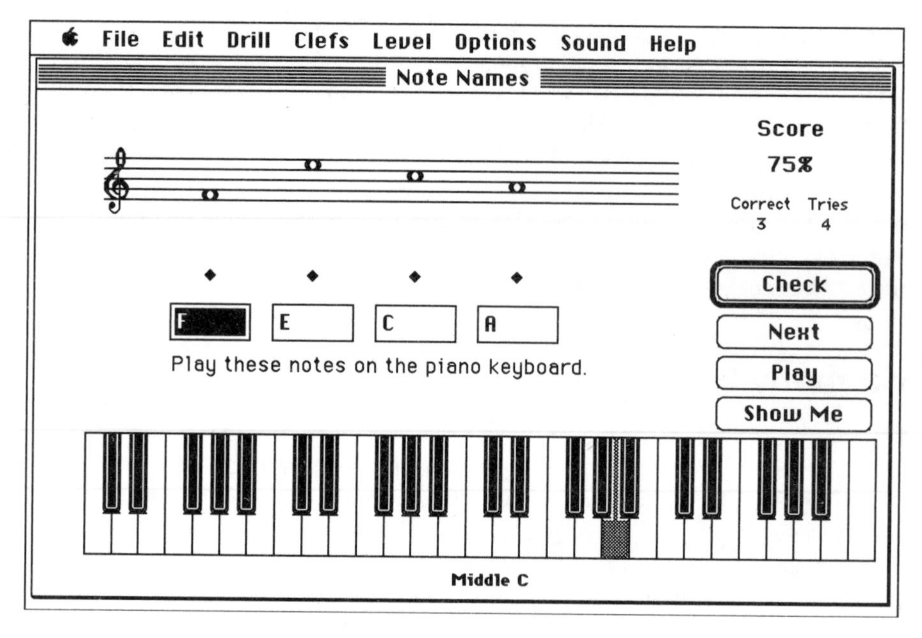

Figure 8–27. MiBAC Music Lessons

The MiBAC lessons come with a small manual divided into three sections: "Getting Started," "Using Music Lessons," and "Menu Reference." "Getting Started" tells how to set up your Macintosh—and, optionally, a MIDI instrument. The "Using Music Lessons" section explains a few fundamentals of music and leads the student through a set of drills, starting with simple exercises and progressing to more advanced levels. Finally, the "Menu Reference" section provides help with menu commands.

MiBAC's documentation is skimpy, but its teaching approach is well thought-out. If there's a young person in your house who wants to learn to play music from the ground up—or if you fall into that category yourself—MiBAC's lessons are a good buy. But be sure to supplement the program's documentation with a good text on basic music theory.

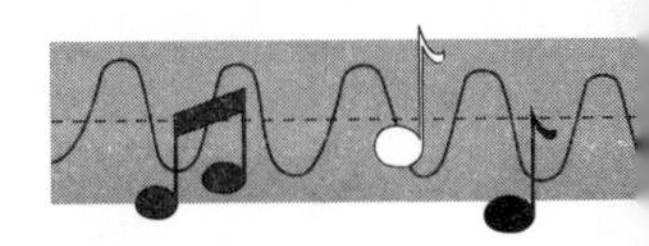

Summary

In this chapter, you learned some basic—and not so basic—principles of music and harmony. You learned the architecture of chords, intervals, and triads. You saw—and heard—how simple melodies depend on tonic, dominant, subdominant, and dominant seventh chords. You even learned about major and minor harmonies; consonance and dissonance; and diminished and augmented chords.

To let you hear what you were learning, and to help you practice what you'd learned, this chapter introduced you to Listen, a music-instruction and ear-training program. You got a chance to do some hands-on exercises using a demonstration version of the program and you also learned about some other fine music-learning programs.

If you understand everything you've read in Chapters 7 and 8, you're now pretty familiar with the principles of music theory. That means you're ready to move on to Chapter 9, which will introduce you to the world of MIDI and tell you how to turn your Macintosh into one mean MIDI music machine.

9 MIDI and the Mac

MIDI is the new frontier of computer music. Hitch your Macintosh to a MIDI interface, and you can blast off into a whole new universe of Macintosh sound.

MIDI, which stands for Musical Instrument Digital Interface, is a specification that lets electronic musical instruments speak to each other. Before the MIDI standard was defined, keyboard synthesizers and other electronic instruments could make music individually but couldn't be connected and centrally controlled. With MIDI, you can now connect a whole studio full of instruments together and play them all simultaneously from a central control panel, such as a personal computer.

In more technical terms, MIDI is both an electronic language and a communications protocol. The MIDI language is made up of a collection of electronic messages that all MIDI instruments can understand. The MIDI protocol describes how devices—such as keyboard synthesizers, keyboard samplers, and other electronic instruments—can communicate with each other through a central control panel, such as your Macintosh.

The MIDI Specification

Besides being an electronic language and a communications protocol, the MIDI standard is a hardware specification. It mandates the kinds of inputs and outputs that MIDI devices must have, the speed at which messages between MIDI devices must travel, and the kinds of cables that connect MIDI devices to one another. Musicians and engineers use MIDI instruments and other MIDI devices both in recording studios and in live performances.

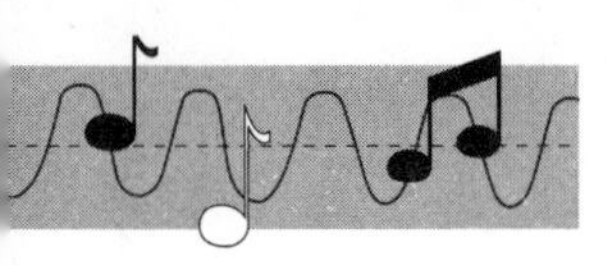

Making MIDI Music

Many performers have discovered that by combining sequenced sound with a live performance, one musician can sound like a one-person band, and a small ensemble can sound like a symphony orchestra. With a MIDI system, a musician can control several instruments and other MIDI devices at the same time; for example, one or two synthesizers, a sampler, a drum machine, and an electric guitar. And performers can switch from one set of MIDI sounds to another—without changing instruments—at the touch of a button.

The MIDI specification does have some limitations, as you'll see later in this section. Nevertheless, it has managed to redefine popular music. If you doubt that, just listen for the synth sounds on almost any pop recording—and the world of classical music is just waiting for a MIDI genius to come along.

What a modern-day Mozart or Beethoven could do with MIDI is anybody's guess; it's clear that MIDI synthesizers have the potential for reshaping classical music, too.

About This Chapter

This chapter tells what kinds of hardware and software you'll need if you want to make your Macintosh the centerpiece of a MIDI system. If you decide to add MIDI capabilities to your Macintosh—or if you already have a MIDI setup—you can configure two programs on your bonus disk for use with your MIDI system.

One of the MIDI-compatible programs is the Songworks musical notation system introduced in Chapter 7. The other program is the Listen music-learning program documented in Chapter 8. For instructions on using Songworks and Listen as MIDI programs, see the section "MIDI Software" later in this chapter.

MIDI Technology

Until 1983, synthesizers from different manufacturers couldn't communicate with each other because they didn't speak the same language. In that year, Sequential Circuits introduced a synthesizer called the Prophet 600, and MIDI first became commercially available.

Before MIDI came along, a musician who wanted rapid access to the different kinds of sounds that different synthesizers, samplers, and other electronic instruments could produce had to have a whole collection of

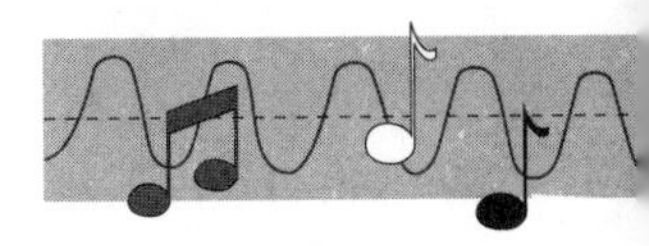

instruments that could be played one at a time. So rock performers filled concert stages with huge banks of instruments, which pulled audiences in because they gave a stage a look of raw power. Stagehands were less impressed; they knew that this was an expensive, inconvenient, and unwieldy way of doing things.

When MIDI made its debut, a standard was so badly needed that the MIDI standard caught on rapidly. Today, all popular keyboard synthesizers speak and understand the MIDI language, and so do many other kinds of electronic instruments, such as samplers, drum machines, and guitars. Many of those all-purpose electronic keyboard instruments sold in mass-market electronics stores are also MIDI-compatible.

Thanks to the MIDI specification, a musician or an audio engineer can link many kinds of electronic instruments and other devices, including keyboard synthesizers, samplers, drum machines, mixers, tape recorders, VCRs, and timers. When a MIDI system includes more than one MIDI device, one of the devices in the system is generally used as a control device that dispatches MIDI messages to all of the other MIDI devices in the system.

MIDI Messages

MIDI devices communicate with each other by sending and receiving instructions called *MIDI messages*. It's important to understand that a MIDI message is not an audio waveform and does not describe an actual sampled sound. In comparison with an audio waveform, a MIDI message contains only a few essential facts about a sound.

When you play a note on a keyboard instrument that's part of a MIDI system, the instrument transmits a MIDI message that tells when the note starts, when it stops, what its pitch is, and how much pressure was applied to the key that produced the note. A MIDI message also contains other information (which will be described later in this chapter), but it does not contain any information at all about the timbre, or tonal characteristics, of a sound.

The lack of timbre information in a MIDI message can be considered an asset as well as a liability, because it makes the MIDI specification versatile. Since a MIDI message doesn't contain any specific tonal information about the sound that it describes, the same MIDI message can be sent to different MIDI instruments that can then play it in different ways.

For example, if you send a MIDI message to an instrument that's programmed to sound like a trumpet, the note will sound as if it's being played on a trumpet. But if you send the same MIDI message to an instrument that's programmed to sound like a guitar, the note will sound as if it's being played on a guitar.

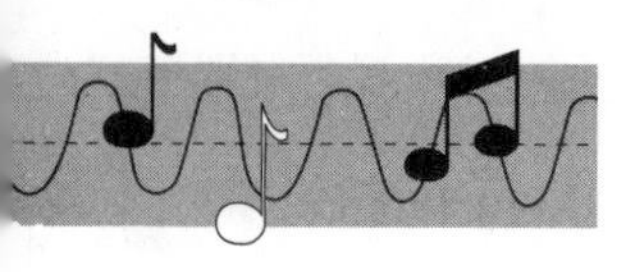

A MIDI message can even be played in different ways by the same MIDI instruments. Most modern synthesizers and samplers can be programmed to sound like many different kinds of instruments. Therefore, by changing a few settings on the front panel of a MIDI instrument, you can make the same MIDI message produce many different kinds of sounds, even on the same sampler or synthesizer.

In short, a MIDI message never tells you what kind of instrument a sound was recorded on, or what the sound's tonal characteristics should be when the sound is played back. But with the data contained in a MIDI message, a MIDI instrument can *re-create* the sound.

MIDI Systems

MIDI devices transmit and receive MIDI messages through *MIDI ports* like those that are labeled In, Thru, and Out in Figure 9–1. Many MIDI instruments can also produce audio signals, which are transmitted to sound-producing devices through standard RCA ports called *audio ports.* The audio ports in Figure 9–1 are the ports labeled Audio Left and Audio Right.

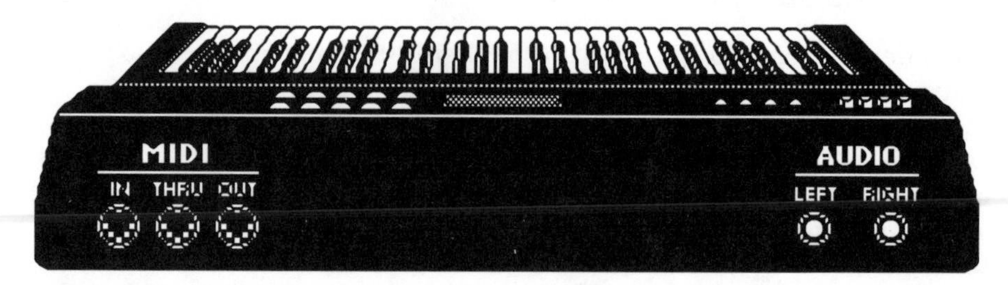

Figure 9–1. MIDI and audio ports
From *The Book of MIDI,* published by Opcode Systems; used by permission

Figure 9–2 shows how a MIDI instrument can be connected to a sound source through an audio port. When you connect a MIDI instrument to a sound source using this configuration, you can play a melody on the instrument and send the instrument's audio output directly to an audio amplifier and a pair of speakers, which then convert the audio signal into sound.

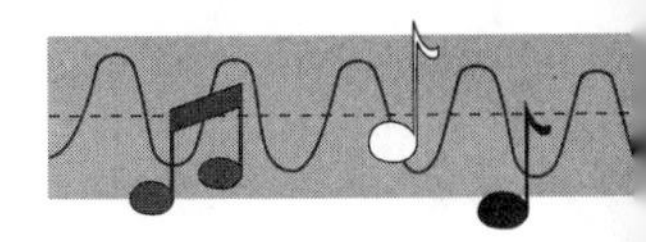

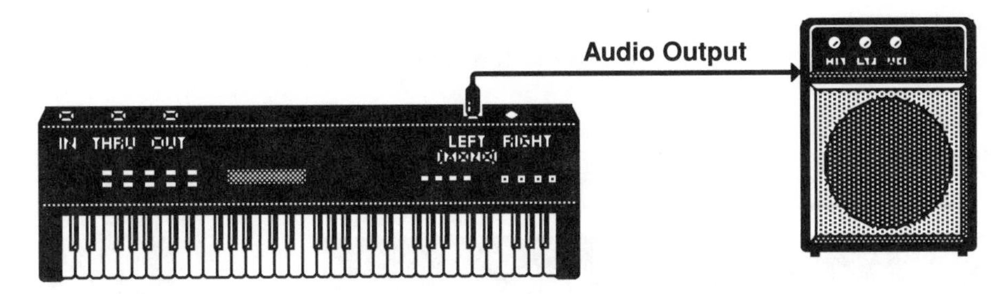

Figure 9–2. MIDI instrument and sound source
From *The Book of MIDI,* published by Opcode Systems; used by permission

The MIDI system shown in Figure 9–2 is a monophonic system; if you wanted to play the instrument shown in the picture through a stereo sound system, you could connect its left and right audio outputs to the left and right inputs of a stereo amplifier or receiver.

MIDI Channels

One important fact about the MIDI specification is that it allows MIDI messages to be sent over sixteen channels simultaneously. That means that you can use a separate MIDI channel for each kind of musical voice that you want to record. For example, you can use one track for a piano sound, one track for a drum sound, one or more tracks for strings, and so on.

There is one significant restriction on the use of MIDI channels. On each MIDI channel, messages can flow in only one direction at any given time. Therefore, a MIDI instrument usually has two MIDI ports on its back panel: one labeled In and the other labeled Out. Most MIDI devices also have a third MIDI port labeled Thru.

Going My Way

Although a MIDI cable can carry a message in only one direction, the modem and serial ports of the Macintosh—which connect the computer to a MIDI interface—can carry signals in both directions, as shown later in this chapter in Figure 9–8. ❍

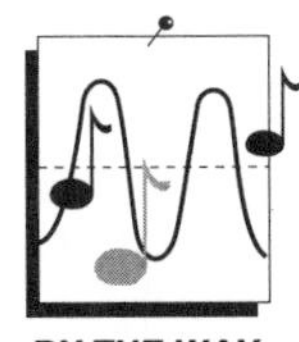

BY THE WAY

By using the In and Out ports on the back panel of a MIDI device, you can configure the device to send a MIDI message to another device that actually generates the sound. Alternatively, you can program the second MIDI device to send MIDI messages to the first MIDI device so that the first MIDI device generates the sound. In this way, you can connect two MIDI instruments that produce different kinds of sounds so that they

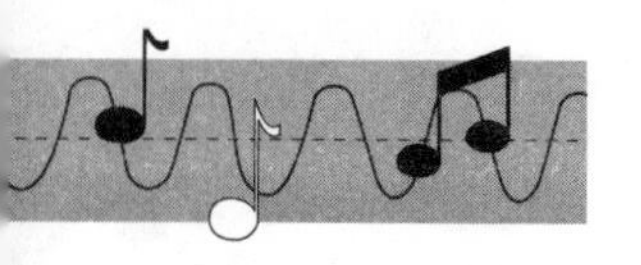

work together as if they were one instrument. You can control either instrument from the other instrument, as shown in Figure 9–3.

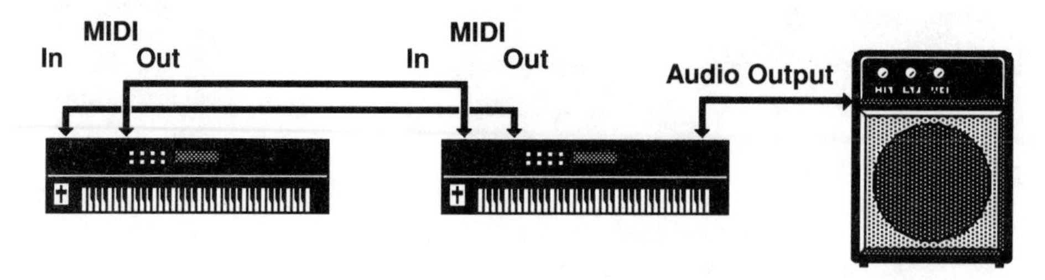

Figure 9–3. MIDI In and MIDI Out
From *The Book of MIDI,* published by Opcode Systems; used by permission

Using Sound Modules

Unless you have two pairs of hands or you like to play keyboard duets, there is some obvious redundancy in the system shown in Figure 9–3. It's a kind of redundancy you often see in rock concerts, when a performer stands behind a bank of two or more MIDI keyboard devices.

You can eliminate that kind of redundancy by substituting *sound modules* for keyboard-style MIDI devices. A sound module is a MIDI instrument that lacks an input device such as a keyboard. A sound module can send and receive MIDI messages, but it does not accept direct input from a performer—for example, a musician playing a keyboard. To play a sound module, you simply send it MIDI messages. Sound modules are often designed to be mounted in 18-inch racks such as those used in sound studios.

By setting up a MIDI system using a single keyboard device and one or more sound modules, you can play any instrument in the system through the one keyboard in the system. That's an efficient and space-saving arrangement that cuts down on cost, too.

Figure 9–4 is a MIDI system that contains a keyboard instrument, a sound module, and an amplifier and speaker system.

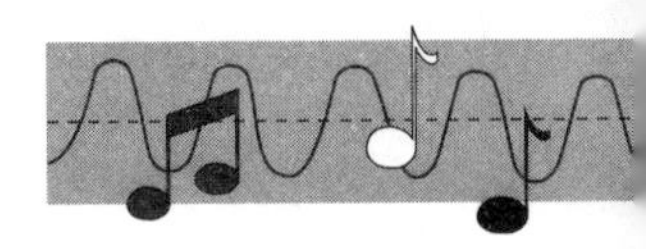

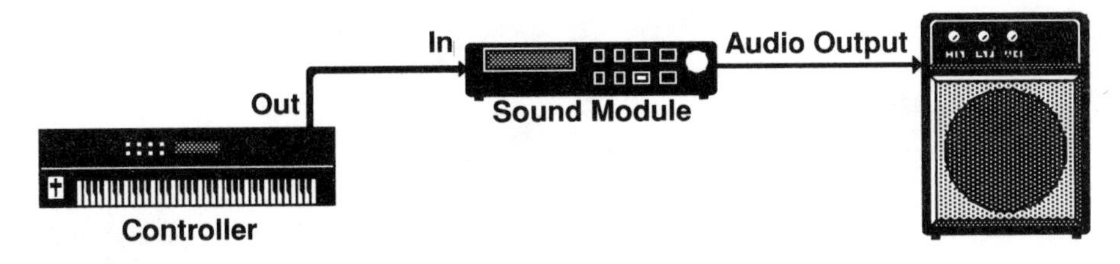

Figure 9–4. MIDI system with one keyboard
From *The Book of MIDI,* published by Opcode Systems; used by permission

Signal Processors

Besides a MIDI keyboard and one or more additional MIDI instruments, a MIDI system usually includes some kind of *signal processor.* A signal processor is a device that receives MIDI messages from the instruments in a MIDI system and blends them into audio signals that can be either recorded on tape or played through an amplifier and speaker system. Signal processors include mixers, sequencers, and computers running, mixing, or sequencing software.

Almost every MIDI system includes some kind of *mixer*—a dedicated mixer, a mixer console, or a software-based mixer that you can display on a computer screen. A mixer is an important part of a MIDI system because it can control the signal levels of all the instruments in a MIDI system so that they produce an audio signal with a pleasing mix of sounds.

A *sequencer* is a device that you can use to edit MIDI signals. With a sequencer, you can switch from one signal source to another, adjust the tempo and pitch of the tracks in a composition, and even add special effects to MIDI sounds.

Some sequencers are hardware devices, and others are software programs that can be run on computers such as the Macintosh. Software-based sequencers are steadily becoming more popular because they are easier to use, more versatile, and less expensive than hardware sequencers. For more about software sequencers, see the section "MIDI Software" later in this chapter.

Figure 9–5 is a diagram of a MIDI system that includes a signal processor.

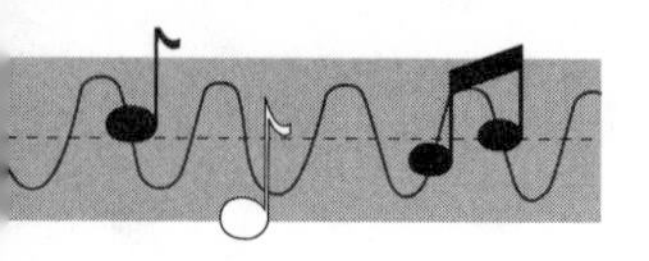

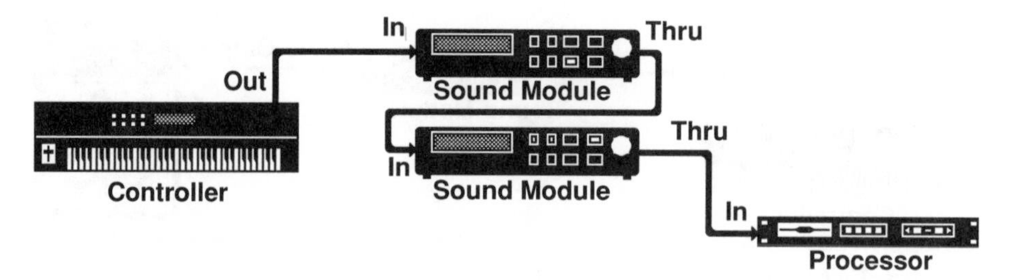

Figure 9–5. MIDI system with signal processor
From *The Book of MIDI,* published by Opcode Systems; used by permission

MIDI In and MIDI Out

As noted earlier in this section, a MIDI channel can carry a signal in only one direction. To make two-way communication possible, you must use two MIDI channels, and you must use a separate MIDI cable for each channel.

To connect two MIDI devices, you must connect one device's MIDI Out port to the other device's MIDI In port. You must then use another cable to connect the first device's unused MIDI In port to the second device's unused MIDI Out port.

MIDI Thru

In addition to their MIDI In and MIDI Out ports, most MIDI instruments are equipped with a third port labeled MIDI Thru. In a multidevice MIDI system, the MIDI Thru port is very important, typically used more than MIDI In or MIDI Out.

A MIDI Thru port is an output port. When a device has a MIDI Thru port, the signal that is transmitted by the MIDI Thru port is an exact copy of the signal that is received by the instrument's MIDI In port. If the device with the MIDI Thru port generates MIDI messages of its own, however, they are not sent to the MIDI Thru port; they are sent only to the MIDI Out port.

When a MIDI device receives a signal from a MIDI In port, the device can easily route the signal to a MIDI Thru port unchanged because—as you may recall—up to sixteen different MIDI messages can be transmitted simultaneously over sixteen different channels. That means signals don't have to interfere with each other, whether they are sent and received via MIDI In, MIDI Out, or MIDI Thru channels.

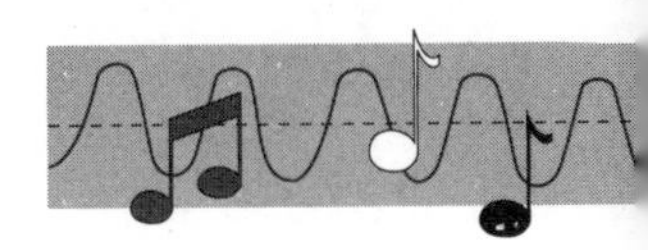

Figure 9–5, earlier in this section, shows how the MIDI In, Out, and Thru ports can be used in a MIDI system.

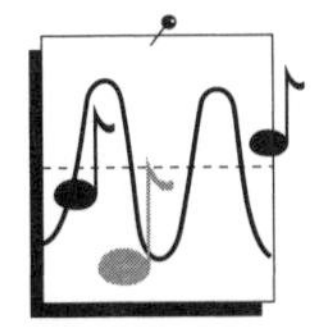
BY THE WAY

What You See Is More Than What You Get

The MIDI standard uses a number to define every note in the musical spectrum, and the MIDI standard supports many more MIDI notes than the number of keys that you can fit on the keyboard of a MIDI synthesizer. MIDI note numbers cover more than ten octaves, from 1 (the lowest note) to 127, the highest. But the keyboards of most synthesizers are much too short to show you all of those notes at the same time. In contrast, a piano has 88 keys, but you can see all of them.

Although most synthesizer keyboards are too small to make every MIDI note usable at the same time, you can program a synthesizer keyboard in such a way that its lowest note goes down to Note No. 1, or in such a way that its highest note extends all the way up to Note No. 127. Middle C is MIDI Note No. 60. (There is also a Note No. 0, but it's a **note off** *message in the MIDI language, not a note that can be played.)*

On most synthesizers, you can "split" the keyboard into two or more parts by setting certain adjustments on the front panel. Then you can program each part of the keyboard to make a different kind of sound. For example, you could program the high end of a keyboard to sound like a piano, while the low end sounds like a string bass. In a more complex split, you could divide the keyboard into four parts and program them to sound like strings, a trumpet, a bass, and a set of drums. ❍

MIDI Controllers

A MIDI device that controls other MIDI devices is known, logically enough, as a MIDI controller. MIDI devices that are controlled by other MIDI devices are often called *sound modules* or *slave devices.*

A controller is a MIDI device that is programmed to send control messages to other devices. For example, a keyboard synthesizer is often used as a MIDI controller.

A controller sends MIDI messages to other MIDI devices through a MIDI Out port. The devices that receive the messages can then generate the sounds that the MIDI messages from the controller module describe.

When a MIDI instrument is used as a controller, it can do two jobs at once: While it transmits MIDI messages to other MIDI instruments, it can generate audio sound signals through its audio ports. A MIDI instrument can thus be used as controller and as a sound module at the same time.

Figure 9–6 shows the structure of a MIDI system that uses a keyboard instrument as both a controller and a sound module.

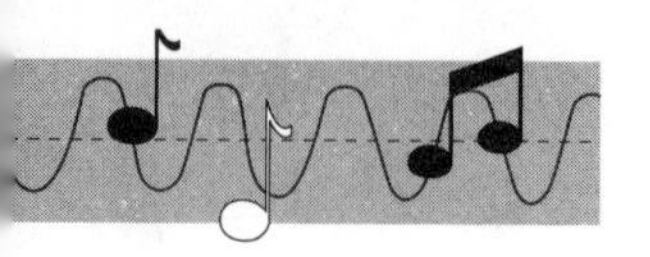

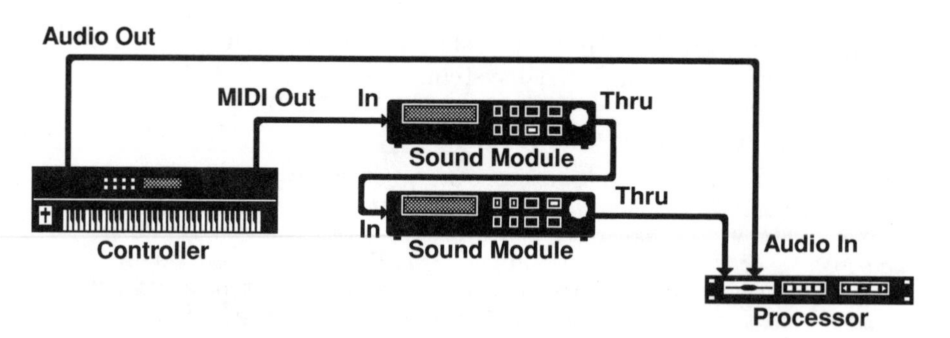

Figure 9–6. Keyboard controller
From *The Book of MIDI,* published by Opcode Systems; used by permission

Using a Computer as a Controller

Although a computer usually functions as a signal processor in a MIDI system, in some situations a computer functions as a controller. For example, musical notation programs such as Songworks, Encore, or Finale can play musical scores by sending MIDI signals to a MIDI device—such as a synthesizer—that generates the actual sound. When you use a musical notation program in this way, your Macintosh functions as a MIDI controller, and the MIDI instrument that's connected to your computer functions as a sound module.

You can also configure Songworks and some other musical notation programs to accept MIDI signals from a MIDI device and to generate music through your computer's sound-producing circuitry. You can then play music on the MIDI device that's connected to your computer, and the notation program you're using can display the music that you're playing as a musical score on your computer screen. When you use a musical notation program in this way, the MIDI instrument that's connected to your Macintosh becomes your system's controller, and your computer functions only as a display device, not as a controller.

Controllers That Aren't Sound Modules

Some MIDI keyboards are designed to be used strictly as controllers; they can't be used as sound modules because they don't contain any sound-producing circuitry at all. With a keyboard that's designed to be used solely as a controller, you can send MIDI messages to sound modules. Some people prefer that method of synthesizing sound; it's convenient and efficient, and it can be considerably less expensive.

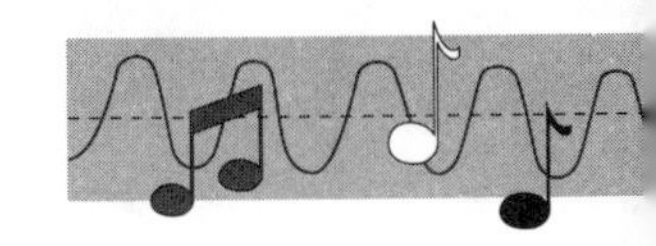

One popular controller that contains no sound module is the Roland PC-200, shown in Figure 9–7. The PC-200 sells for a suggested $350—a much lower price than you'd have to pay for a synthesizer—and it's small and convenient, too. It has a 49-note velocity-sensitive keyboard, and it's ideal for a computer-controlled MIDI system equipped with sound modules.

Figure 9–7. Roland PC-200

Setting Up a MIDI System

In Chapters 7 and 8, you learned how to create musical scores with programs such as Songworks, and you discovered you can develop your ear for music with music-training programs such as Listen. Both programs are MIDI-compatible, so now it's time to examine a feature of both programs that you can't take advantage of unless you own a MIDI system.

If your Macintosh is part of a MIDI system, both Songworks and Listen can be programmed to play music that is produced by a MIDI keyboard. You can therefore play your music on a real electronic keyboard instead of having to click your mouse on a screen keyboard or type out tunes on your computer keyboard.

If your MIDI system includes a keyboard that can produce sound as well as send MIDI messages, you can also improve the quality of the sound produced by Songworks and Listen. And of course you can use your keyboard with other MIDI software programs, such as sequencing and sound-editing programs.

To connect your Macintosh to a MIDI system, you need both hardware and software: a MIDI interface and a MIDI Manager.

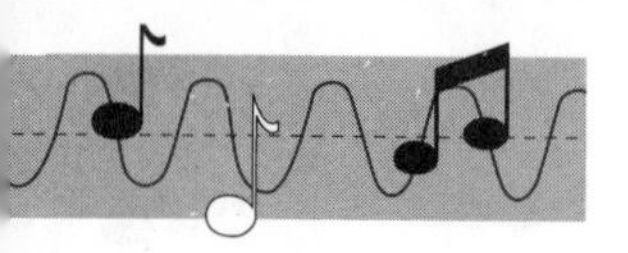

Using a MIDI Interface

A *MIDI interface* is a connection box that you can connect to your computer's modem or printer port. Then you can connect the MIDI devices in your system to your MIDI interface.

There are many ways to set up a MIDI system that includes a Macintosh computer and a MIDI interface. Figure 9–8 shows one configuration for a simple Mac-and-MIDI system. For more information on MIDI interfaces, see the section "The MIDI Connection."

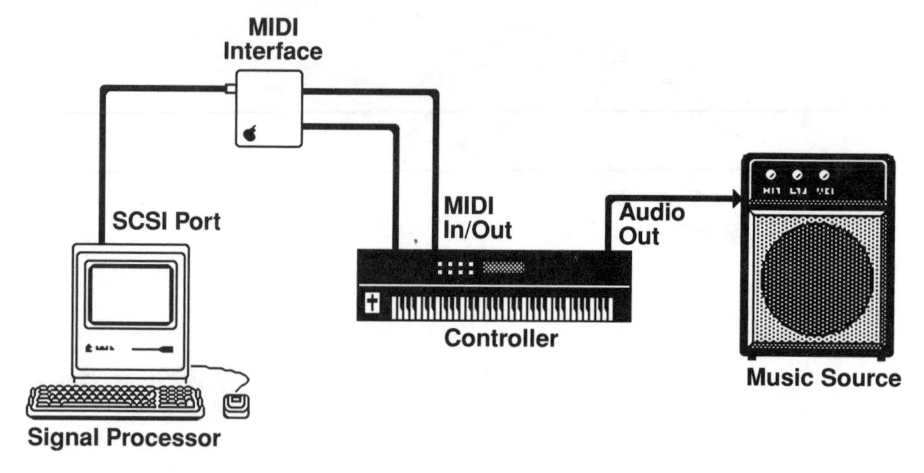

Figure 9–8. MIDI system with interface
From *The Book of MIDI,* published by Opcode Systems; used by permission

MIDI Managers

To connect a Macintosh to a MIDI system, you need a software interface called a MIDI Manager. Apple manufactures a MIDI Manager for the Macintosh, and many software publishers distribute the Apple MIDI Manager with their products. Other software companies have designed proprietary MIDI Managers and include them with their programs.

The Apple MIDI Manager is a software toolkit that Apple markets to software developers through APDA. With the Apple MIDI Manager, software designers can create programs that link the Macintosh to MIDI devices through its modem and printer ports. Other companies also manufacture MIDI Managers that perform similar functions.

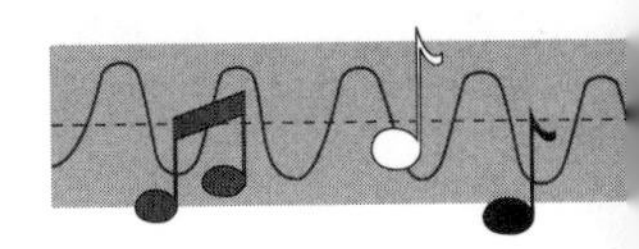

Some MIDI programs—including both the Songworks program introduced in Chapter 7 and the Listen program documented in Chapter 8—can be used without separate MIDI Managers. However, to use most name-brand sequencers and most other kinds of studio-quality MIDI software, you must have some kind of MIDI Manager installed in your System Folder.

The use of the MIDI Managers is beyond the scope of this chapter, but most software packages that include a MIDI Manager contain all necessary instructions for using it.

MIDI Software

When you have set up a MIDI system that includes a Macintosh, you can run many kinds of MIDI software. Musical notation programs such as Songworks and music-training programs such as Listen work better and sound better when they are used with professional-quality MIDI instruments. With music-editing programs such as Alchemy from Passport Designs, you can combine MIDI music with 16-bit sampled audio. And with sequencer applications—the most popular programs available for MIDI owners—you can create, edit, and record MIDI sound.

With a sequencer program, you can use your Macintosh to edit the musical signals produced by the MIDI devices in your system. You can mix your MIDI channels down into two-track or four-track recordings, and you can then store your MIDI files on a hard disk, in much the same way that an audio engineer records music on a multitrack tape recorder. Sequencer programs are described in more detail under the heading "Sequencing Software," later in this section.

The Songworks Program

You can configure Songworks to work with your MIDI system by selecting Sound and MIDI Settings from the Sound Options menu. Songworks then displays a window like the one in Figure 9–9.

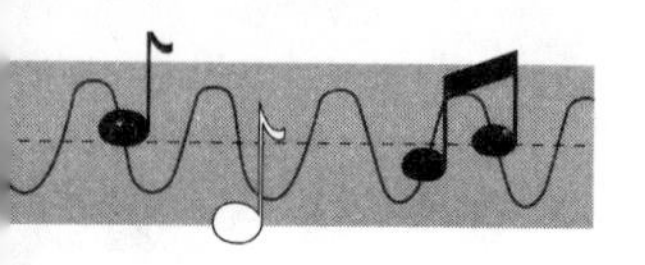

For Mac sound we recommend headphones (big ones) or external speakers. The small speaker inside the Macintosh may not always produce the best results.

If you own a MIDI instrument ("MIDI" = Musical Instrument Digital Interface) you could use that instead of Macintosh sound. You could use it for input as well.

Songworks can run either its own MIDI or Apple Computer's MIDI Manager for MIDI input and output. Songworks' own MIDI will be used unless you check the MIDI Manager box below.

Music output:
- (•) Macintosh sound: piano
- ( ) MIDI

Music input:
- (•) Letter keys or mouse
- ( ) Letter keys or mouse or MIDI

Type of MIDI:
- ( ) MIDI Manager
- (•) Songworks' own

	MIDI Channel:	MIDI Volume:
Melody	1	
Chords	2	
Metronome	3	

Cancel

OK

MIDI Through: ☐

Figure 9–9. Songworks Sound and MIDI Settings window

By selecting controls in the Sound and MIDI Settings window, you can set Songworks so that it works with a MIDI input and a MIDI output. You can also select the following:

- The MIDI channels that Songworks uses to play melodies, chords, and time (metronome) signals. When you select the channels that Songworks uses, you should make sure that they match the channels that you have selected for melodies, chords, and time signals on the MIDI instruments in your system. (For instructions on setting up the instruments in your system, see the documentation that comes with your MIDI devices.)
- The volume that Songworks uses to play melodies, chords, and metronome signals.
- The MIDI Manager that you want to use (the Apple MIDI Manager or the one that comes with Songworks).

The MIDI Through box, in the lower right-hand corner of the Sound and MIDI Settings window, is designed to be used with a certain kind of MIDI system. Specifically, if you have a MIDI keyboard that doesn't produce sound and you want to connect a separate sound module, you can connect both devices to the same MIDI interface. Then you can play your keyboard and produce sound with the Songworks program by checking the MIDI Through box.

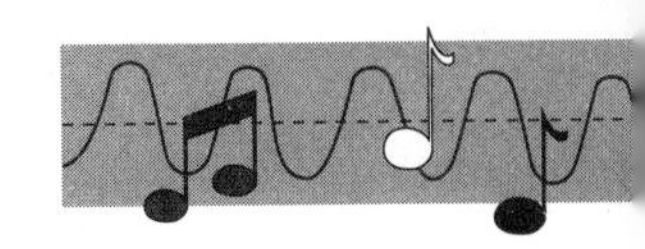

The Listen Program

You can configure the Listen program to work with a MIDI system by selecting the Setup MIDI item under the Options menu. Listen then opens a dialog like the one shown in Figure 9–10.

MIDI Interface Clock Rate:
- ○ 500 KHz
- ◉ 1 MHz
- ○ 2 MHz

Macintosh Port:
- ◉ Modem
- ○ Printer

MIDI Channel:
◉ 1 ○ 2 ○ 3 ○ 4 ○ 5 ○ 6 ○ 7 ○ 8 ○ 9 ○ 10 ○ 11 ○ 12 ○ 13 ○ 14 ○ 15 ○ 16

☐ Patch Through

Use MIDI | Cancel

Figure 9–10. Listen Setup MIDI dialog

With the controls in the Listen Setup MIDI dialog, you can choose a MIDI channel, a MIDI port (the port you have used to connect your MIDI interface), and a MIDI interface clock rate (for details, see the documentation that comes with your MIDI interface; 1MHz is the most common setting).

The check box labeled Patch Through works like the MIDI Through checkbox in the Songworks Sound and MIDI Settings window. If you have a MIDI keyboard that doesn't produce sound and you want to generate sound with a separate sound module, you can connect your keyboard and your sound module to the same MIDI interface. Then you can play your keyboard and produce sound with the Listen program by checking the Patch Through box.

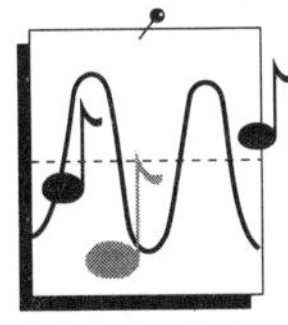

TECH TALK

Patches

Every synthesizer contains a collection of built-in synthesized sounds called **patches.** *These patches are stored in blocks of memory called* **banks.** *The patches that are built into the synthesizer can make the synthesizer sound like many other kinds of instruments, both acoustic and electronic.*

Most synthesizers contain several banks of patches to choose from. Synthesizers with banks of patches have front-panel controls that can switch quickly from bank to bank and from patch to patch as you record a composition or play a composition in a live performance. Most synthesizers also have plug-in cards or other media on which additional patches can be stored.

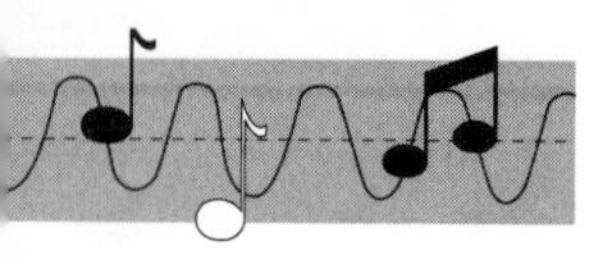

Patches derive their name from the pre-MIDI, pre-Macintosh days when a synthesizer could play only one musical voice at a time. In those days, it took a lot of time and effort to change the way a synthesizer sounded, so banks of synthesizers were preset with the voices they would play and were then connected with patch cords. The sound that each synthesizer generated was called a patch. Today, the cords are gone, but the word **patch** *remains.* ❍

Listen also has a dialog window that lets you start or repeat musical exercises by pressing certain keys on a MIDI instrument. You can choose this option by selecting the MIDI Instrument Control command from the Options menu. Listen then opens a dialog like the one shown in Figure 9–11. You can use the MIDI Instrument Control dialog to assign instrument keys to the Start, Repeat, and Next buttons that Listen displays in its Exercise menu.

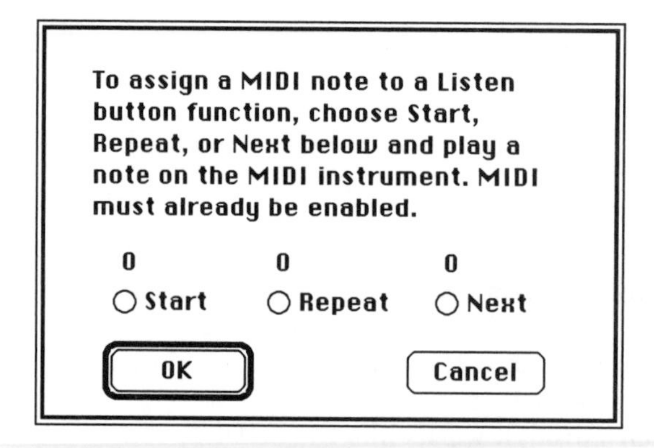

Figure 9–11. Listen MIDI Instrument Control dialog

Sequencing Software

When the MIDI standard made its debut in 1983, studio engineers monitored MIDI traffic with electronic control panels called *sequencers.*

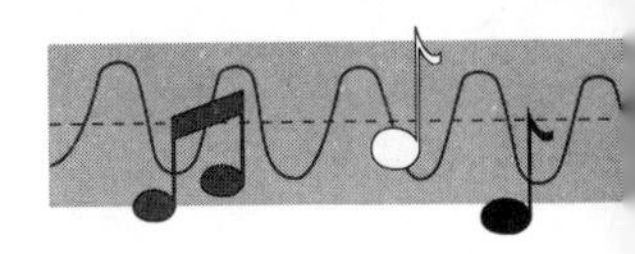

Sequencers derived their name from the fact that they could program and record sequences of events. They could memorize notes played on a keyboard and play them back, with perfectly duplicated tempo, dynamics, and phrasing.

In those days, sequencers had lots of knobs and dials and LED displays, and were notoriously user-unfriendly. But at about the same time MIDI made its debut, the world was discovering the personal computer. And it didn't take software designers long to move the control panel on the front of an equalizer to a computer screen.

When software sequencers made their debut, it was obvious that they had several advantages over their hardware ancestors. They were easier to use, they had more features, and they were even less expensive. There was an immediate demand for software sequencers, and software developers quickly met the challenge.

Macintosh Sequencers

Because of its powerful computer hardware and its easy-to-use graphic interface, a Macintosh makes an excellent platform for sequencing programs. Instead of the small LCD panel that early sequencers offer, the Macintosh now displays a full screen of text and graphics.

Furthermore, instead of forcing you to do your editing with a small set of cryptic controls, software sequencers let you edit music with a versatile typewriter-style keyboard and a mouse. Add to that the printing and networking capabilities of the Macintosh—along with convenient disk-storage capabilities—and you have a system that almost seems to have been designed from the ground up with MIDI sequencing in mind.

Today, four companies manufacture most of the sequencing software available for the Macintosh: Opcode Systems, Passport Designs, Mark of the Unicorn, and Dr. T's Music Software.

One modern sequencer—Beyond, from Dr. T's Musical Software—is shown in Figure 9–12. Beyond, like most software sequencers, can display several kinds of windows, depending on what kinds of operations are being performed. Only three of Beyond's windows are shown in the illustration.

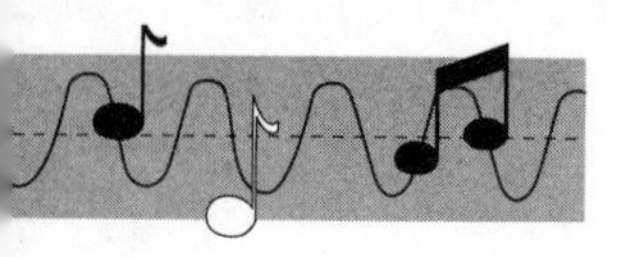

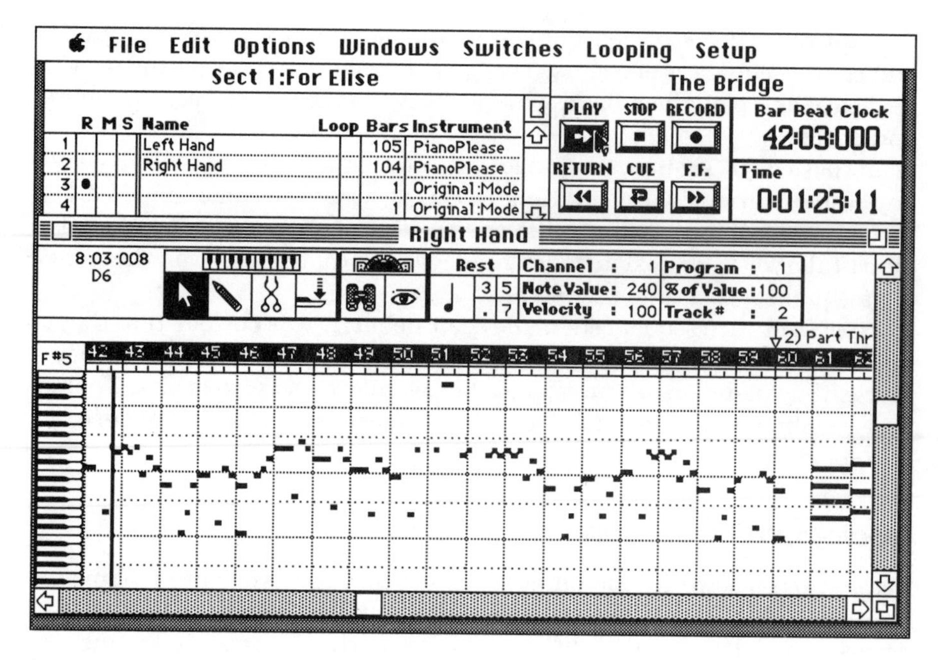

Figure 9–12. Beyond sequencer

On-screen Sequencing

Although several companies manufacture sequencing software, most sequencing programs have screen displays that are remarkably similar. A typical sequencer displays the tracks of a musical composition in the form of lines that scroll horizontally across the screen. This format reminds many people of an old-time piano roll playing on a player piano.

With a sequencer, however, you can edit the lines on the display in much the same way that you can edit text on a word processor. You can extend or shorten notes by extending or shortening the lines that represent them, and you can change the pitch of a note by moving it up or down. You can cut and copy notes, and move them from one place to another—either within the same MIDI file, or from one MIDI file to another. Best of all, from the point of view of performers who aren't musically literate, you don't have to know how to read music to edit a score on a sequencing screen.

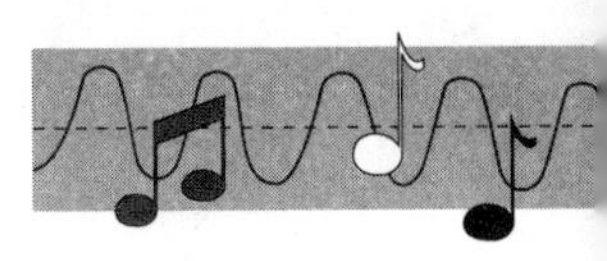

Another difference between a musical notation program and a sequencer is that a sequencer usually gives you more control over a MIDI system than a notation program does. A sequencer can be programmed to recognize many kinds of MIDI devices, and to send the correct kinds of MIDI messages to the many kinds of devices that can be included in a MIDI system.

Besides their piano-roll displays, most sequencers also have on-screen controls that are designed to resemble the controls on a multitrack tape deck. Most sequencers have on-screen controls that look and work much like the Play, Stop, Fast Forward, Rewind, and Record buttons on a tape recorder.

When you click on a sequencer's Record button, the sequencer starts recording. You can then start playing music. When you click on the Stop button, recording stops. When you click on the Play button, your Macintosh transmits the MIDI data back to the instrument that produced the data. Your MIDI system can then play back your composition.

How Sequencers Work

Besides the controls you find on tape recorders, most sequencers offer specialized features such as:

- Controls that turn a metronome on and off
- Sophisticated tempo controls
- Auto-rewind features, and features that can start playing or recording at a predetermined point in a song
- Automatic "punch-in": a feature that can play a song up to a certain point and start a recording at that exact spot
- Loop functions that can play a given track or section of a track repeatedly; some sequencers, such as Performer from Mark of the Unicorn, even allow you to create nested loops at any point in any track

Using a Sequencer

There are two ways to use a sequencer: Sequencers can play musical signals that have been stored or on disk, or create new compositions in real time.

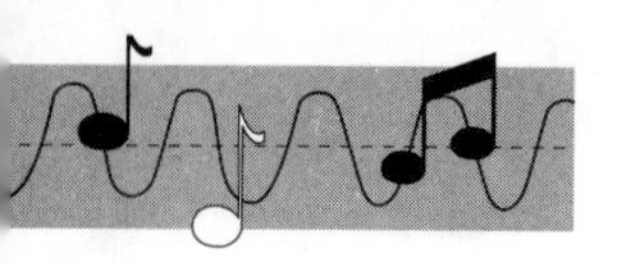

When you create a composition with a sequencer, you can assign different synthesizer voices, or patches, to each of the MIDI channels that are available. While you are working on the composition, you can play each MIDI channel to make sure that it sounds exactly the way you want it. Then, when you finish your composition, you can save it on a disk.

When you have saved a sequenced composition on a disk, you can play back your composition by transmitting the MIDI signals that it contains to the instruments that originally created the sounds.

Alternatively, you can record the entire performance on an analog or digital tape. Then you can listen to the performance by simply playing your tape, or by transferring the tape to some other medium and playing that.

When you save a MIDI performance on a disk, it's important to remember that *you can't re-create a MIDI performance unless you either record the performance or have access to the instruments on which the music was created.* That's because MIDI messages don't contain audio waveforms—they contain only instructions that MIDI instruments can use to recreate their original sounds.

The Art of Sequencing

Editing a musical composition with a sequencer is known as *sequencing.* There are two ways to sequence a musical composition: by loading a composition recorded on a disk into your computer's memory, or by playing a composition in real time.

When you play a MIDI instrument that you have connected to your Mac, the instrument sends out MIDI messages describing the start time, pitch, duration, volume, and other parameters of the notes you play. As your Macintosh receives MIDI messages, your sequencer graphically displays the contents of those messages on the screen. As you monitor the messages, you can edit them (or sequence them) with your mouse and your keyboard. When you have finished recording your sequence, you can store it on a disk.

As noted earlier in this section, most sequencers display the notes in a composition as lines that scroll across the screen, in a format that is reminiscent (in both looks and effect) of an old-time player-piano roll. Figure 9–13 shows the Trax sequencer, from Passport Designs, playing a musical composition.

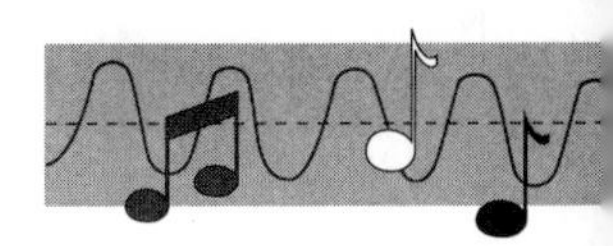

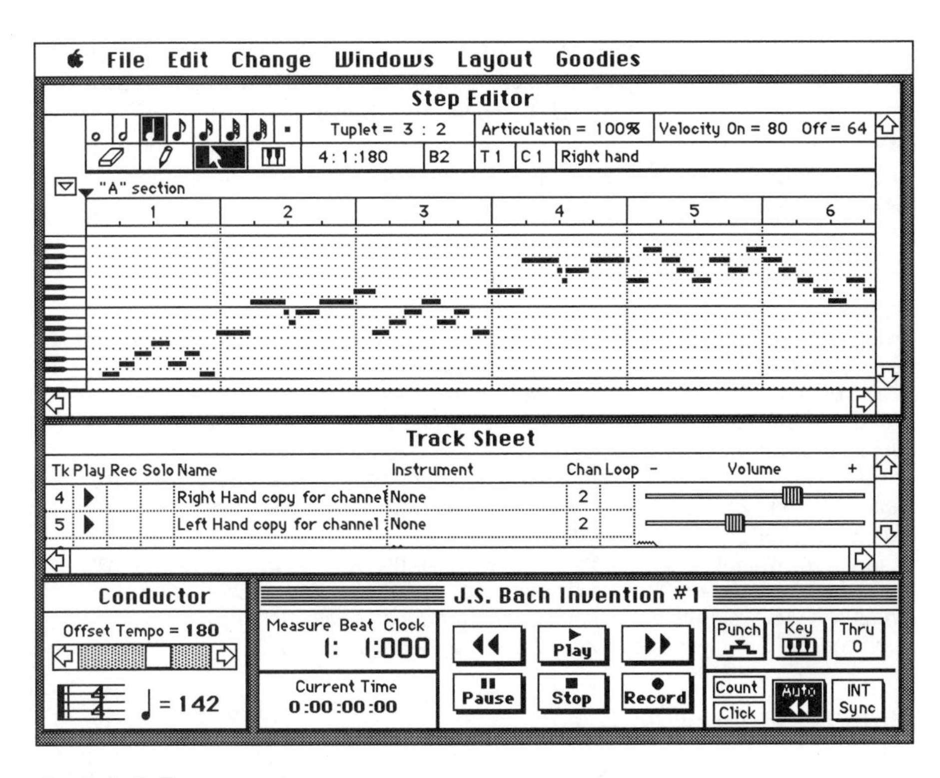

Figure 9–13. Trax sequencer

Editing and Recording with a Sequencer

When you sequence MIDI music, you can edit it in many ways: You can edit out wrong notes, transpose the key, change the tempo, *quantize* (correct the timing of) some or all of the song, and many more. All of these processes are known collectively as *sequencing.*

When you record music with a sequencer, you can slow the tempo during parts of a performance that give you trouble, and then speed your recording up to normal speed when you play it back. You can also record in *step time;* that is, you can tell the sequencer in advance how fast you're going to play. You can then play notes one at a time, at your own pace. When you decide you want to change your speed again, you simply adjust the duration control and continue.

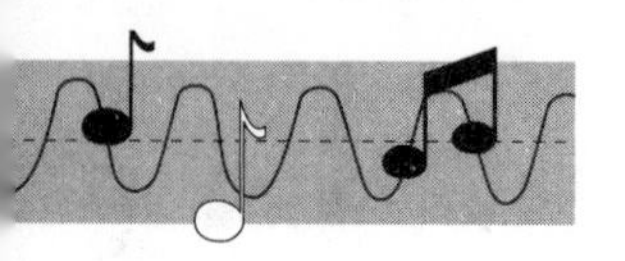

All popular sequencers let you cut, copy, and paste single notes, tracks, groups of tracks, or entire songs; transpose, invert, or reverse notes or phrases; and send different MIDI tracks to different instruments. The controls and menu items that execute these commands vary from sequencer to sequencer, but most operations require just a few keyboard operations or mouse moves.

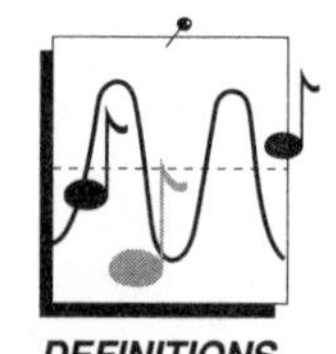

DEFINITIONS

Quantizing and Humanizing

One important feature of sequencers is that they let you **quantize** *recorded notes; that is, they let you edit or move notes around so they start or end on the nearest beat, even if the timing of the original performance was sloppy.*

But quantization can sometimes make music too precise. When music is overquantized, it sounds robotic, as if it were written by a computer (which, of course, it sometimes is).

To reverse the effects of overquantization, many sequencers have a humanize *feature that lets you introduce a bit of sloppiness into a mechanical-sounding performance to make it sound more natural.*

Ironically, when you instruct your sequencer to humanize a performance, it carries out your instruction by applying computer algorithms. Some humanizing algorithms can even recreate human musicians' tendencies with techniques such as "robbing time" from weak beats to make strong beats stronger. ❍

Multitrack Recording

A sequencer, like a multitrack tape recorder, can record a musical performance one track at a time. That provides you with a separate MIDI channel for each kind of musical voice you want to record. For example, you can use one track for a piano sound, one track for vocals, and other tracks for drums, bass accompaniment, and so on.

While you're sequencing a composition, you can play each MIDI channel separately. Alternatively, you can play the channels either in various combinations or all at the same time. Finally, when your composition sounds just the way you like, you can store it as MIDI data on a disk.

As you lay down one track after another, you can monitor tracks, edit tracks, and change tracks as you go along. When you have finished recording a track, you can monitor it while you record another track. You can keep doing this until you have made a complete multitrack recording.

Saving MIDI Sound

There are two ways to record the music that you create with a sequencer. One way is simply to play the music and record it on an analog or digital

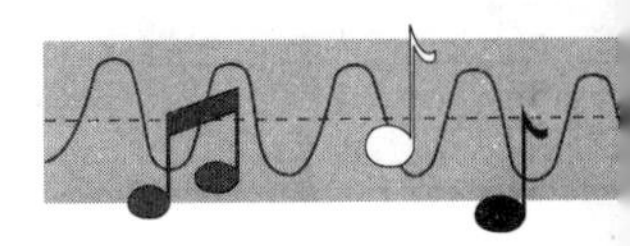

tape recorder, in real time. The other way is to store your MIDI data on a hard disk, in the same way that you would store any other kind of data file.

Some MIDI studios are equipped with fancy sixteen-channel mixing consoles and sixteen-track digital tape recorders. If you are fortunate enough to have access to such a studio, you can record MIDI music on sixteen-track digital tapes. You can then mix the music down for transfer to two-track or four-track analog tapes, or for transfer to a CD recording. Alternatively, you can mix the music down to two or four tracks and transfer it directly to audiotape.

You can also save a piece of MIDI music as an ordinary data file on an ordinary hard disk. It's important to remember, however, that the data stored in a MIDI file is different from the sound data stored in a sampled sound file. As noted earlier in this chapter, a MIDI file does not contain an audio waveform, but simply contains a selection of essential information about a sound. Therefore, a MIDI file contains much less information than a sampled sound file.

MIDI Files and Sampled Sound Files

Specifically, what a MIDI file lacks is information about the timbre, or tonal characteristics, of a sound. Therefore, when you save a MIDI sound file and then play it back, you must play the file back *on the same MIDI instrument that produced it* if you want the file to sound exactly the same way when it is played back as it sounded when it was recorded.

Furthermore, when you play the file back on the instrument that produced it, the settings on the instrument must all be identical to what they were when the sound was recorded. If they aren't, the file you're playing back won't sound exactly as it did when it was recorded.

Since a MIDI file contains much less information than a sampled sound file, a MIDI file requires less disk space—*much* less disk space—than a file of sampled sound. Even a file of sound data recorded by a simple 8-bit digitizer, such as a MacRecorder, contains much more sound information than a MIDI file contains.

Sequencer Files

When you create a MIDI file with one of the more popular sequencers—for example, Vision from Opcode Systems, Master Tracks Pro from Passport Designs, Beyond from Dr. T's, or Performer from Mark of the Unicorn—you can have your fidelity and store it, too. That's because these sequencers

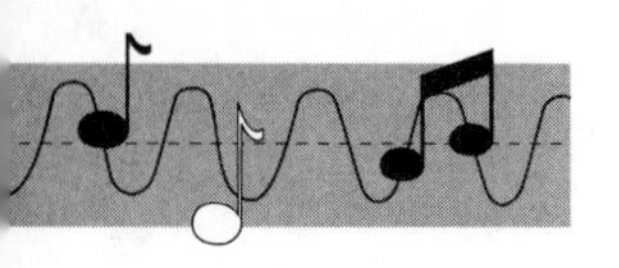

(and most other Macintosh sequencers) are designed to store MIDI information not in standard MIDI files, but in proprietary files that contain more information than ordinary MIDI files contain.

When you create a file with a sequencer and then save it, your sequencer usually saves the file in a proprietary format that includes not only the usual MIDI information, but also information about the instrument that was used to create the file, and about the instrument settings that were in effect when the sound file was recorded.

Unfortunately, sequencers manufactured by different software companies use different formats to save their MIDI-plus files. So you can't create a proprietary-style file with a sequencer made by one company and then play it back with a sequencer made by another company. However, all sequencers can store MIDI information in the standard MIDI format, and they can also play back standard MIDI files. So, if you stick with the bare-bones MIDI format and stay away from proprietary MIDI formats, all MIDI sequencers are compatible (sort of).

Program Numbering Systems

One of the most important functions of a sequencer is to keep track of the MIDI messages being transmitted over different MIDI channels. This is an important job because manufacturers of synthesizers use different *program numbering systems* to identify the musical voices that they build into their instruments.

The MIDI standard specifies 128 *programs,* or musical voices, numbered 000 to 127. Musicians often refer to these programs as patches. Therefore, program numbering systems are really systems for identifying the musical voices, or patches, that are built into a synthesizer.

Manufacturers of different synthesizers use different program numbering systems. For example, the Yamaha TX81Z stores programs in four banks of thirty-two voices each (numbered 1–32), while the Roland D550 stores sixty-four programs in each of two banks, with each bank organized in eight rows of eight voices each (numbered 1–1, 1–2, 1–3, and so on). The D550's other sixty-four programs are stored in a similar way on an external card.

Because of this difference in program numbering systems, the Yamaha TX81Z refers to MIDI Channel 36 as B4, while the Roland D550 refers to MIDI Channel 36 as Int 5–4. Figure 9–14 illustrates this difference. The specific numbers shown in Figure 9–14 aren't important unless you own a Yamaha TX81Z or a Roland D550. The important point to remember about all of this is simply that synthesizers from different manufacturers use different program numbering systems.

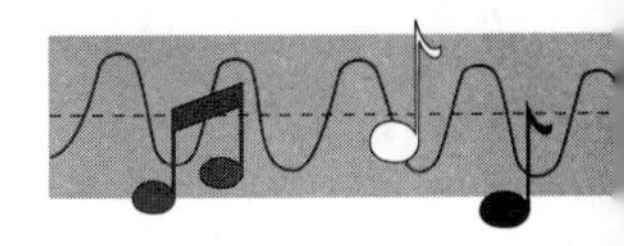

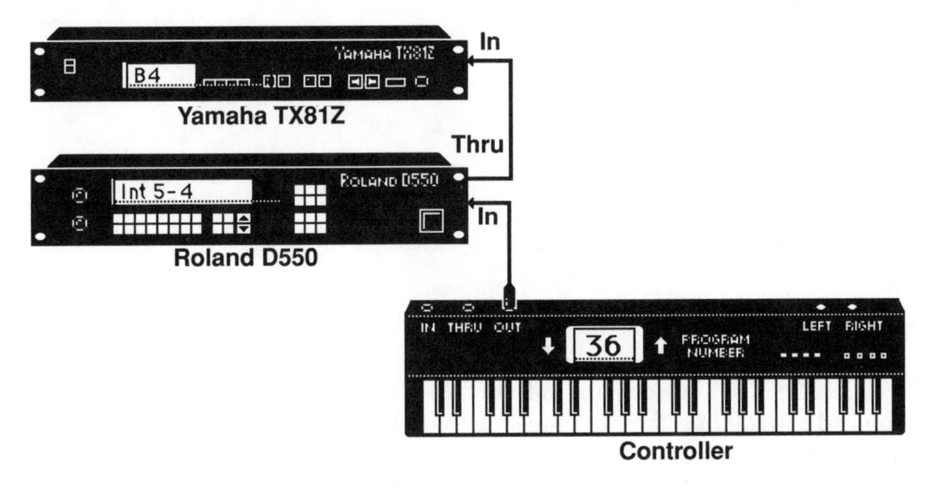

Figure 9–14. Program numbering systems

From *The Book of MIDI,* published by Opcode Systems; used by permission

Patches

Every synthesizer contains a collection of built-in synthesized sounds, or musical voices, called patches, stored in blocks of memory called *banks.*

Different makes and models of synthesizers have different-sounding patches, and that's why one musician often uses several different synthesizers in a studio or in a stage performance. Manufacturers of sequencers know what kinds of patches are built into the most popular synthesizers, and most sequencers can translate the patch-and-bank scheme of almost any popular synthesizer into English and can display the names of the synthesizer's voices on your computer's screen.

If your sequencer has this translation feature, you don't have to switch your synthesizer from patch to patch manually, using its tiny LED panel and its push-button controls. Instead, you can simply click on a patch name that's displayed on your screen, and your sequencer can automatically activate the patch that you choose.

The MIDI Connection

The MIDI standard describes one piece of hardware that doesn't look very impressive: an ordinary DIN plug with five pins, only three of which are used. The MIDI specification uses Pins 4 and 5 for the transmission of music data, and it uses Pin 2 as a ground. Pins 1 and 3 aren't currently used, but are reserved for future applications.

Figure 9–15 shows a side view of a MIDI connector.

Figure 9–15. MIDI connector
From *The Book of MIDI,* published by Opcode Systems; used by permission

MIDI Interfaces

To connect a MIDI device (or a collection of MIDI devices) to your Macintosh, you need a *MIDI interface:* a connection box with a serial cable attached, and with MIDI ports built in. To use a MIDI interface, you simply plug its serial connector into your computer's modem or printer port. Then you can connect MIDI devices to as many In and Out ports as your MIDI interface has.

A MIDI interface can be as simple or as elaborate as you like (and can afford). MIDI connectors range from simple but perfectly serviceable boxes that cost less than $100 or so to professional-quality instruments in the $500 price range. Manufacturers of inexpensive MIDI interfaces include Altec Systems and Opcode Systems. High-end interfaces include the $495 MIDI Time Piece (MTP) from Mark of the Unicorn, shown in Figure 9–16, and the $379 Studio 3 from Opcode Systems. The MTP and the Studio 3 are high-end MIDI interfaces with similar specifications. They go well beyond the needs of the average Macintosh owner who just wants to set up a one- or two-instrument MIDI system.

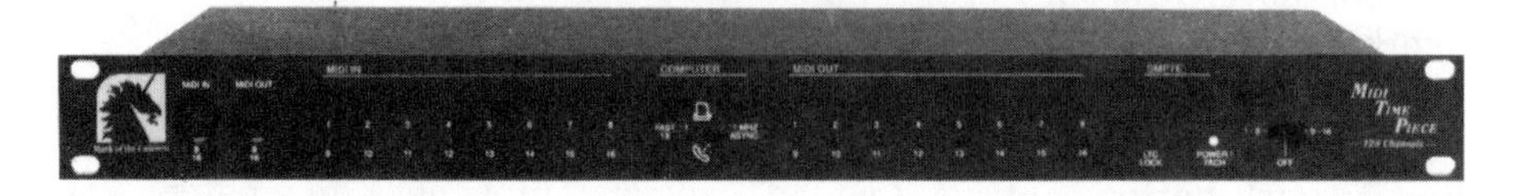

Figure 9–16. Midi Time Piece

Both the MTP and the Studio 3 have several In and Out ports, and both contain circuitry that can synchronize MIDI music with audiotape recorders or VCRs.

The MTP has eight In ports and eight Out ports. In case that's not enough, you can daisy-chain up to four MTP interfaces together, for a total of sixty four In and Out ports and 512 MIDI channels. A special feature of the MTP that has become especially useful with new models of the Macintosh is a fast mode that boosts performance when it is used with 68020- and 68030-equipped machines.

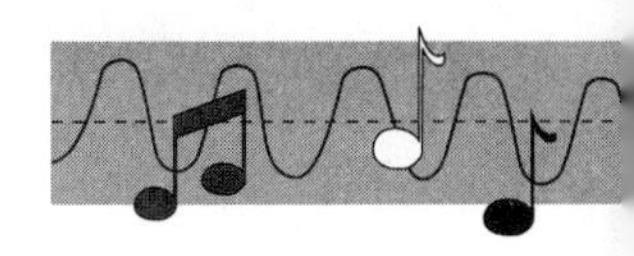

The Studio 3 has two MIDI In channels and six MIDI Out channels. It can handle up to three foot switches and has an internal power supply.

Figure 9–8, earlier in this chapter, shows a typical Macintosh system with MIDI interface. Figure 9–17 shows a much more complex MIDI system connected to a Macintosh through two different MIDI interfaces.

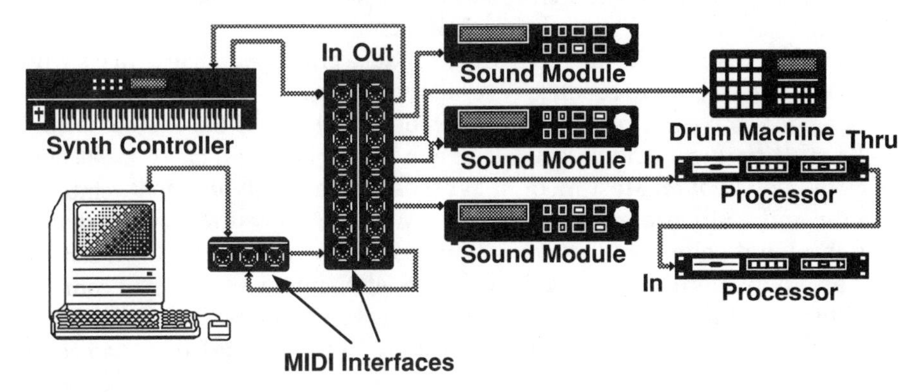

Figure 9–17. MIDI interfaces

From *The Book of MIDI,* published by Opcode Systems; used by permission

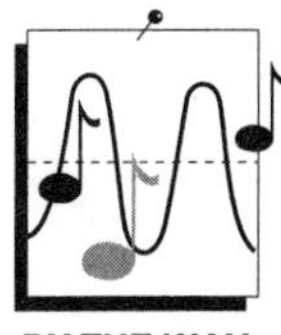

Consolidating Control

Notice that there is only one keyboard in Figure 9–17. Before the MIDI era, a musician had to have several keyboard synthesizers to obtain fast access to different sounds with different qualities. But the MIDI standard gives a performer so much control over the instruments in a MIDI system that it is now simpler (and less expensive) to connect just one master keyboard to a collection of sound modules (sometimes called slave devices*). Sound modules are MIDI instruments without keyboards. They require less space, cost less, and sound just as good.* ❍

The MIDI Message Format

As Figure 9–17 shows, data within a single MIDI line can travel in only one direction: from a single source to a single destination. In other words, a MIDI message is transmitted in a single direction through a single MIDI cable.

A MIDI message is a series of bytes. There are only two kinds of bytes in a MIDI message: a *status byte* and a *data byte.* The status byte serves as a message header; it tells what channel a MIDI message is addressed to, and it tells what kind of MIDI message is being sent.

The MIDI message format is described in more detail in Appendix G.

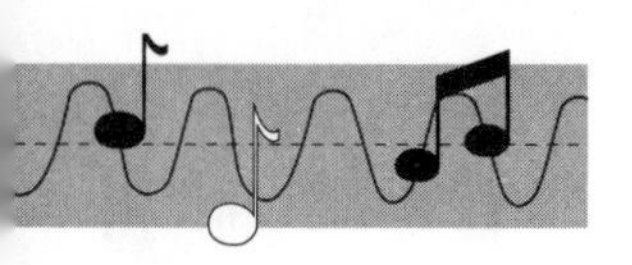

The Poly and Omni Switches

The MIDI standard defines a set of guidelines, called *reception modes,* that enable a MIDI instrument to transmit or respond to MIDI messages in several ways. For example, one instrument might be programmed to respond to all sixteen MIDI channels at the same time, while another might be set to respond to only one MIDI channel.

Also, one instrument might be set to produce only one musical voice, while another might be set to produce several music voices at the same time.

A device that can produce more than one voice at the same time is said to be *multitimbral.* And a device that can play more than one note at once is called *polyphonic.* Most modern synthesizers are polyphonic instruments, and many are multitimbral, too. When an instrument is both multitimbral and polyphonic, it can play more than one note at a time, and it can also play more than one musical voice at a time.

When you have a polyphonic synthesizer, you can usually set its reception mode with a pair of front-panel switches (or a pair of front-panel LCD displays) labeled *Poly* and *Omni.*

When an instrument is in *poly mode,* it can receive messages over more than one MIDI channel, and it can respond polyphonically to each MIDI channel; that is, it can produce more than one note at a time.

When the instrument is not in poly mode, it can respond only monophonically to each channel; that is, it can produce only one note at a time. This mode is called *mono mode.*

When an instrument has an Omni switch, the switch's settings are on and off. When an instrument's Omni switch is on, the instrument can respond to MIDI messages that are transmitted on all MIDI channels. When its Omni switch is off, it can respond only to a single MIDI channel or to a set of specified channels.

Since an Omni switch has two settings, and a Poly switch also has two settings, an instrument's Omni and Poly switches can be configured in four possible combinations:

- Omni on/Poly on: The instrument can receive performance data on any MIDI channel and can play more than one note at a time.
- Omni on/Mono on: The instrument can receive performance data on any MIDI channel but can play only one note at a time. This mode is rarely used.
- Omni off/Poly on: The instrument can receive performance data on several assigned MIDI channels and can play more than one note at a time.

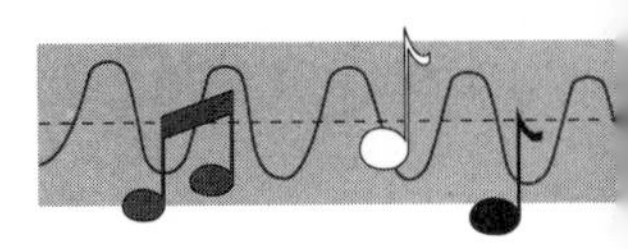

- Omni off/Mono on: The instrument can receive and play one note per channel. This combination is often used with MIDI devices such as MIDI electric guitars, since one channel can be used for each string.

The Omni and Poly settings are used by different MIDI instruments in different ways. For more detailed information on specific MIDI instruments, refer to the instruments' documentation.

Since most polyphonic synthesizers are also multitimbral, a synthesizer that can play more than one note at a time can usually play in different musical voices, too. That makes the Omni and Poly switches an extraordinarily powerful pair of controls.

MIDI Hardware

When you control a MIDI studio from a Macintosh, your Mac works much like one of those giant mixer consoles that are used in recording studios. But a Mac is much less expensive than a studio-quality mixing console, and it can do some things even better than a big console can.

For example, your computer's floppy and hard disks can hold MIDI data, and software programs can change that data in many ways. You can edit it, transpose it, store it as specific performances, print it, and so on.

MIDI devices that you can connect to your Macintosh through a MIDI interface include controllers, synthesizers, samplers, drum machines, and other kinds of devices that are described under the headings that follow.

Synthesizers

You know what a synthesizer is: an instrument that creates, or synthesizes, digital sounds from scratch. Some synthesizers are equipped with keyboards, and some aren't, but all synthesizers can create sounds from scratch, and that's how they got their name.

There are many synthesizer manufacturers—Roland, Kawai, Yamaha, Korg, Ensoniq, E-mu, and many more. You can choose from so many fine synthesizers that it's almost unfair to single out one and publish a picture of it, but the new Kawai KC-10 (shown in Figure 9–18) is such a beautiful 16-bit digital synthesizer that a picture of it is worth at least a thousand words.

Figure 9–18. Kawai KC-10 synthesizer

The KC-10 features a 61–note keyboard, multitimbral performance, a drum section, an automatic arpeggio creator, wheel modulation and pitch bend controllers, a carrying case, and a design so slim and light that you can sling the whole thing over your shoulder.

In the early days of synthesized sound, a synthesizer could produce only one kind of sound at a time. To synthesize a different kind of sound, you had to stop playing, reset the synthesizer's controls, and then start playing again.

Today, most synthesizers are *multitimbral;* that is, they can play multiple voices simultaneously. That means you can now record multiple voices over multiple MIDI channels at the same time.

You can switch a synthesizer from one instrumental sound to another by making what is known as a *program change.* With most sequencers, you can automate program changes by labeling each track of a composition with the name of the instrument sound you assign to it.

Samplers

A *sampler* is a device that can convert an audible sound into a digital sound and then play it back. Musicians often use samplers in their MIDI setups because a sampler can reproduce the sound of a live instrument more accurately than a synthesizer can.

A sampled sound, as noted in earlier chapters, is an analog sound that has been recorded and converted into a digital sound. This process is sometimes called *digitization.*

In previous chapters, you saw how small digitizers, such as the MacRecorder, can sample live sounds that a computer can then play back. MIDI samplers also sample sounds, but they can record and reproduce sound

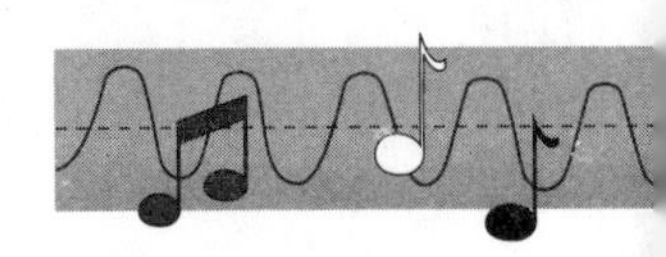

with much higher fidelity than a MacRecorder can. Also, they can change the pitch, the tempo, and many other characteristics of sampled sounds.

There aren't as many samplers on the market as there are synthesizers, probably because samplers are more expensive than synthesizers and aren't designed to produce as many kinds of fancy sounds. Also, many modern synthesizers produce sounds that originated as sampled music, and therefore sound as realistic as many sounds produced by samplers. But if you want a sampler and you shop around, you can still find quite a few excellent samplers in high-end music stores.

One highly regarded sampler is the Ensoniq EPS 16-plus Digital Sampling Workstation—actually a combination sampler and synthesizer—shown in Figure 9–19. Along with the sampling functions that you'd expect in a sampler, the EPS 16-plus offers twenty-voice polyphony (the ability to generate twenty voices at once); multiple filters and sound contours; and special effects such as reverb, chorusing, flanging, phasing distortion, and delay.

Figure 9–19. Ensoniq EPS-16 sampler

The EPS 16-plus also offers on-board digital effects processing, and it offers 16-bit linear oversampling with sampling rates of up to 44.64kHz. Other features include auto-looping, volume smoothing, and many kinds of cross-fading to give you control over its sampled sounds.

Sound Modules

A *sound module,* as previously noted, is a name for a MIDI instrument that lacks a keyboard. Sound modules are often mounted in studio-style racks. One popular sound module is the E-mu Proteus, a sample playback

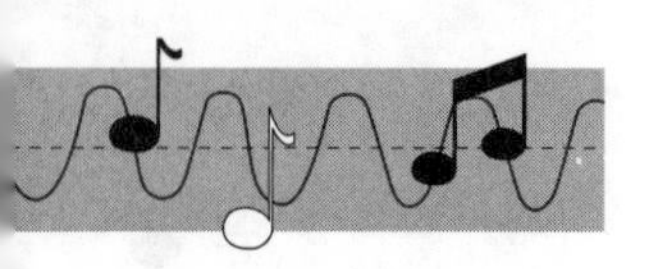

synthesizer with 4-Mb (upgradable to 8Mb) of 16-bit sample ROM. Features of the Proteus include panning, chorusing, delay, reversed sample playback, and cross-fade, plus extensive control over on-board sound.

Drum Machines

A drum machine is much more than a set of electronic drums. Drum machines come with built-in rhythm patterns that can provide you with some impressive background rhythms even if you aren't a drummer. But a drum machine can't make you a professional drummer overnight, any more than a great-sounding synthesizer can instantly turn you into a professional keyboardist. To use a drum machine most effectively, it still helps to be a drummer who understands rhythm, can handle a pair of drumsticks, and listens and thinks like drummers do.

Workstations

A workstation is an instrument that combines a synthesizer or sampler, a hardware sequencer, a drum machine, and effects in one package. The Korg M1 was the first true dedicated workstation. The Fairlight and Synclavier are also workstations of a sort, but they don't come all in one package. Today, any Macintosh with a MIDI interface and appropriate MIDI software can be used as a workstation.

Effects

Effects, or audio processors, are devices that modify preexisting sounds. Effects include reverbs, delays, equalizers, and compressors.

Effects can be analog or digital. For example, analog processors use electronic circuits to alter input signals. Digital processors, in contrast, perform mathematical calculations to change sounds. A digital processor usually contains an ADC (analog-to-digital converter), which can convert analog sounds to digital signals, and a DAC (digital-to-analog converter), which does the same job in reverse.

Other MIDI Devices

You can add many other kinds of devices to a MIDI system: MIDI foot pedals that can change the quality of sounds, sophisticated MIDI interface

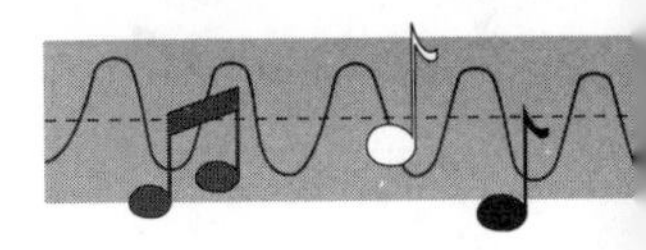

and timing devices, and pitch-to-MIDI converters that can accept analog input (such as from a microphone) and convert it into MIDI data.

There are also MIDI devices that respond to body movements, MIDI mixers that contain time-synchronized audiotape recorders, and even lighting controllers that respond to MIDI signals.

Another MIDI device, a MIDI patch bay, helps you configure and control the data that flows to and from the individual MIDI devices in a MIDI system without having to plug and unplug cords manually. To use a patch bay, you connect the MIDI In and MIDI Out ports of each MIDI device in your system to a pair of In and Out ports built into the patch bay. Then you can connect a MIDI control device to the front panel of the patch bay, and you can plug other MIDI devices into the patch bay, too. Some patch bays are programmable; they remember particular master-slave configurations that can be easily recalled by sending the patch bay a MIDI program change message.

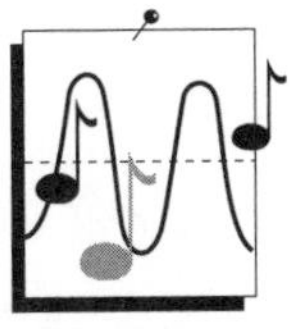

TECH TALK

Patch Bays

With the proper software, your Macintosh can perform the functions of a patch bay. For example, a patch bay is built into the MIDI Manager utility from APDA. (For more about the MIDI Manager, see the section "Setting Up a MIDI System" earlier in this chapter.)

The MIDI Manager actually provides two patch bays: an application and a desk accessory. With the desk accessory patch bay, you can patch devices together—that is, connect them with each other—by simply drawing a line on the screen with a mouse.

Figure 9–20 shows the MIDI Manager's PatchBay DA. The icon in the upper left-hand corner of the PatchBay window is the MIDI Manager driver, provided to software developers by Apple as part of the MIDI Manager package. The icon in the lower left-hand corner represents the Performer sequencer from Mark of the Unicorn. The lines that join the two icons show that the MIDI Manager driver is currently driving the Performer sequencer and synchronizing its timing. The icon in the upper right-hand corner of the PatchBay window represents the OMS (Opcode MIDI System) driver from Opcode Systems. If a sequencer from Opcode (such as Vision) were running, it would probably be connected to the OMS driver, since all Opcode software products are designed to be compatible with each other. ❍

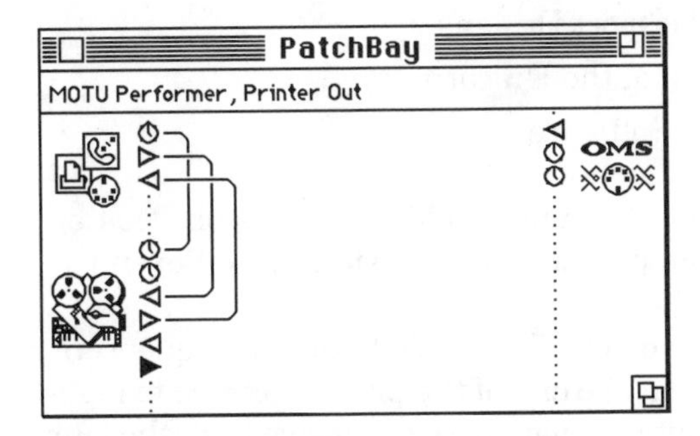

Figure 9–20. MIDI Manager PatchBay window

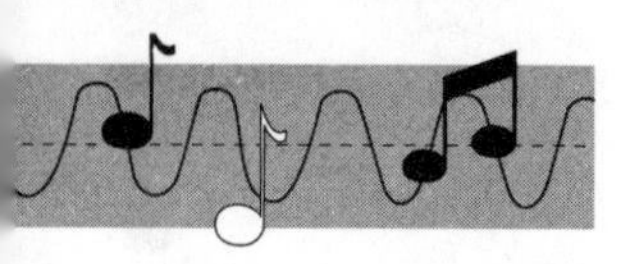

The MIDI Software Buyer's Guide

When you walk into the music department of a software store—or the software department of a music store—you may feel overwhelmed by the vast numbers of MIDI-related products available: sequencers, notation programs, MIDI interfaces, editors, librarians, music-learning programs, entertainment programs, and programs of many more varieties.

This situation is complicated even more by the fact that the major publishers of MIDI software almost seem to have entered into a conspiracy of silence regarding package labeling. Although Passport Designs has recently started listing some facts on the boxes that a few of its products come in, most MIDI software manufacturers have traditionally provided hardly any consumer information on their packaging.

Most MIDI-related software packages cryptically mention the name of the product and the name of the manufacturer, and that's about all. Furthermore, since most software salespeople aren't musicians (and since most musicians aren't software salespeople), you usually can't get much help from the clerks who work in computer and music stores.

This section was written to demystify MIDI software. It describes some of the leading MIDI products, tells who their manufacturers are, and even provides some prices (at this writing) and a few tips on shopping for MIDI software.

Shopping for a Sequencer

Several software companies publish sequencer programs for the Macintosh, but four sequencers dominate the professional market:

- Vision, published by Opcode Systems
- Master Tracks Pro 5, from Passport Designs
- Performer, published by Mark of the Unicorn
- Beyond, from Dr. T's Musical Software

These are professional sequencers with pro-scale prices. Vision, Master Tracks Pro, and Performer are each priced at a suggested $495. Beyond has a suggested retail price of $319.

Besides the top four sequencers, you can find special-purpose sequencers, ranging from basic no-frills models on one end of the price spectrum to high-end, professional-style packages that are even more expensive than the four

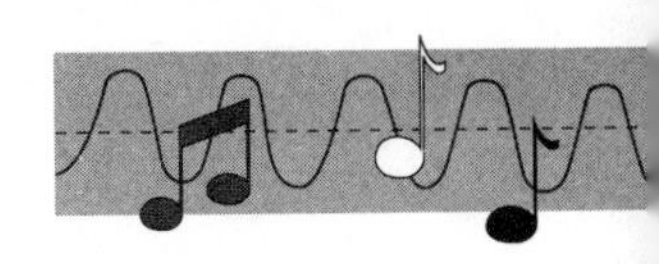

listed above on the other end. These alternative sequencers include the following:

- EZ Vision, published by Opcode Systems, a no-frills version of Vision priced at $149
- Trax, published by Passport Designs, a simplified version Master Tracks Pro with a suggested retail price of $99
- Audio Trax, also from Passport Designs, a $249 sequencer that synchronizes 8-bit digital audio (from the Macintosh speaker or an external, non-MIDI stereo system) with multiple tracks of MIDI data
- Studio Vision, a $995 program that can generate super-high-fidelity music but must be used with a digital sound board such as the $3,495 Sound Tools II board from Digidesign or the $995 Digidesign Audiomedia II board (for more information on Digidesign's line of digital hardware for the Macintosh, see the section "MIDI Sound and Digital Audio" later in this chapter)
- Digital Performer, a high-end sequencer from Mark of the Unicorn. Digital Performer is similar to Mark of the Unicorn's Performer Sequencer, and is designed for use with digital sound boards.

Early in the MIDI era, you could find significant differences between the major brands of software sequencers. But today's sequencers are like today's automobiles: They look and work pretty much alike, and choosing one is often a matter of personal preference—largely a matter of taste and feel.

Companies that manufacture MIDI-related products also have their own personalities. For example, Opcode Systems offers a wide range of software products that are known for their diversity, their superb quality—and their complexity. Opcode Systems makes products designed for professionals, and you can't go wrong buying them—but be prepared for a steep learning curve, and possibly some calls to the company's technical-support line, before you get all the features of this company's products figured out.

Products from Opcode Systems

The flagship product in the Opcode Systems line is Vision, a superb sequencer that's a top seller among MIDI professionals. Vision has more features than any other sequencer, including the ability to play multiple sequences with different time signatures and tempos simultaneously. Vision also has advanced instrument-layering and channel-setting features that make the most of a multi-instrument MIDI system. The main window of the newest version of the Vision sequencer is shown in Figure 9–21.

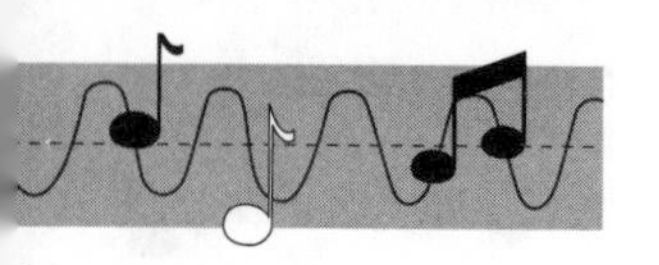

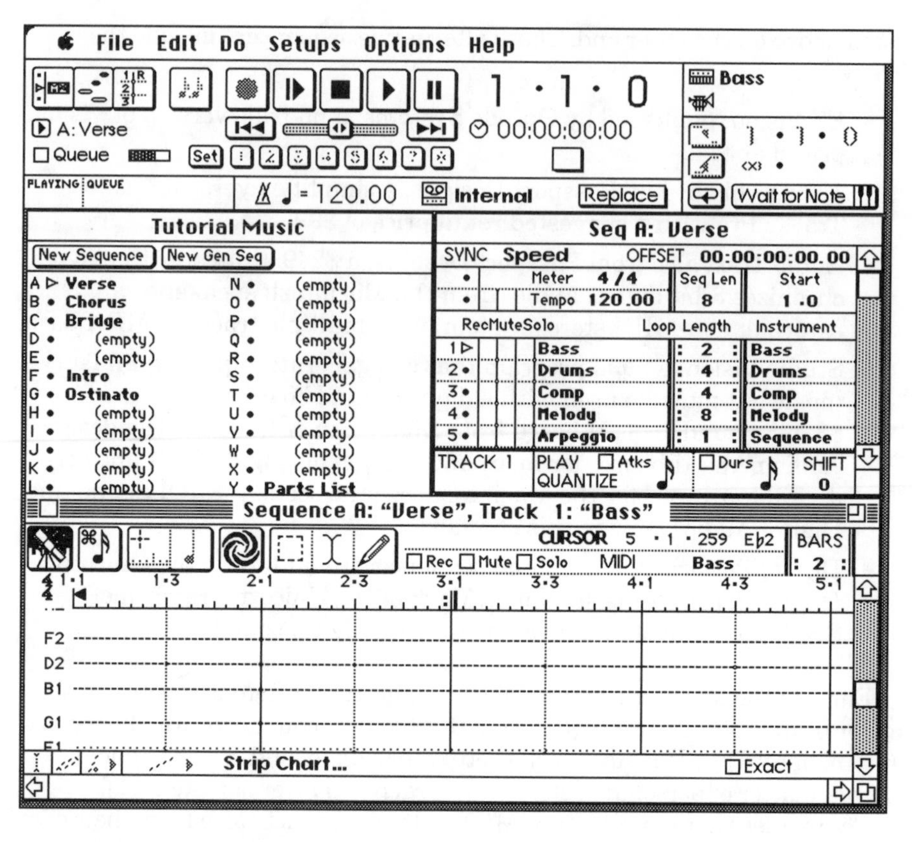

Figure 9–21. Vision sequencer

Another member of the Vision sequencer family is Opcode Systems' Studio Vision, which must be used with plug-in digital boards that produce 16-bit, CD-quality sound. Studio Vision is described in the section "MIDI Sound and Digital Audio."

Passport Designs

Passport Designs manufactures a line of full-featured, top-quality products designed mainly for professionals. Over the past couple of years, however, Passport Designs has been introducing products that are simpler, lower-priced, easier to learn, and aimed more at the home market. For example, the Passport Designs line includes a no-frills sequencer called Trax that's a great buy at $99, and a higher-priced sequencer called Audio Trax that lets you combine MIDI music with 8-bit, MacRecorder-style sampled sound.

With Audio Trax, you can combine 8-bit digitized music files with MIDI files that have been created with a MIDI music system. Audio Trax is

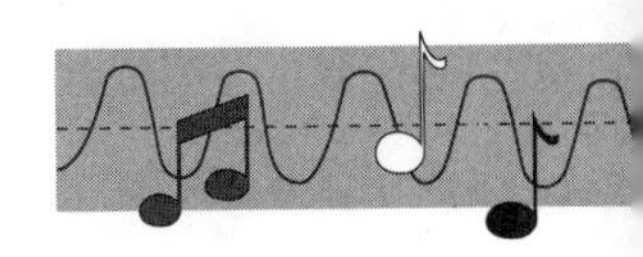

really two programs in one: It combines a mid-priced, sixty-four–track MIDI sequencer with a two-track analog sound module similar to the SoundWave program introduced in Chapter 4.

Audio Trax is not designed for professional musicians who want to make CD-quality recordings. It doesn't have the power to do that because of the 11kHz upper frequency limit of its sound-processing module. But it's a fun product for home music studios, and it can add terrific sound effects to multimedia presentations. The Audio Trax screen display is shown in Figure 9–22.

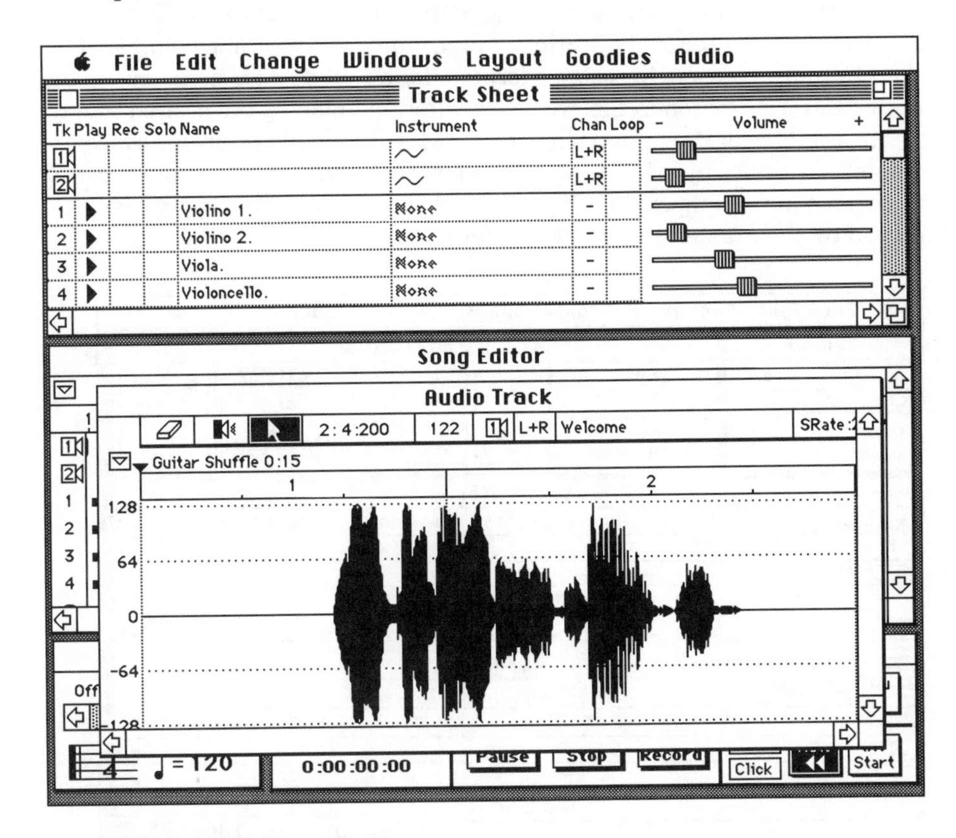

Figure 9–22. Audio Trax sequencer

The flagship product from Passport Designs is not Audio Trax but Master Tracks Pro 5, a top-rated sequencer with an enviable reputation among MIDI professionals.

Master Tracks Pro has all the features that you'd expect in a $495 sequencer, and it is outstanding in the area of graphical editing. The product has always been known for its intuitive interface, and the latest version has an even more improved design. With the new interface, for example, it's easier to change note velocity either on a note-by-note basis or for a block of notes at a time.

Master Tracks Pro 5 also features faders that link an automated mixer directly to a track sheet. This automated mixing capability lets the user record volume changes for any of the program's sixty-four channels of MIDI playback information without having to manage each one in real time.

Still another improvement is that Master Tracks Pro now supports the SMPTE (Society of Motion Picture and Television Engineers) time code, which synchronizes synthesized sound with audiotape recorders. This improvement facilitates the scoring of film, video, and multimedia presentations by allowing users to assign a location for a sound effect or cue by typing in the SMPTE location in the event list editor and playing the desired sound.

Master Tracks Pro adheres more closely to Apple's Human Interface Guidelines than any other leading sequencer, making it easier to learn than most of its competitors. Figure 9–23 shows several windows displayed by the Master Tracks Pro 5 sequencer.

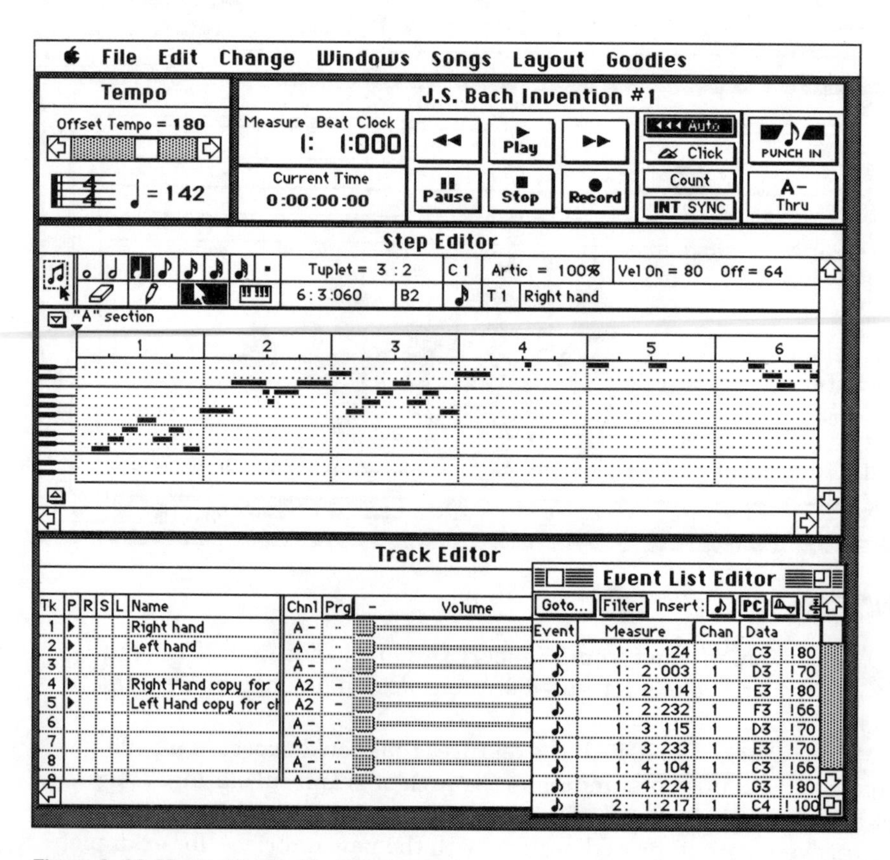

Figure 9–23. Master Tracks Pro 5 sequencer

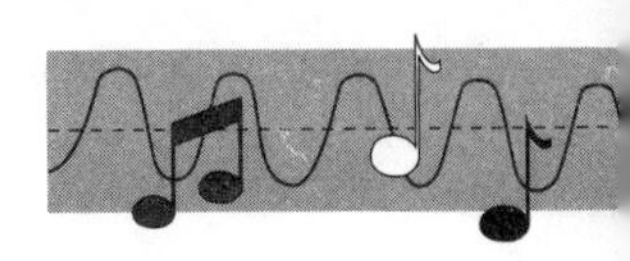

Besides its sequencers, Passport Designs offers several other MIDI-related products. One of the company's newest products is Media Music, a library of original production music that can help Macintosh users add professional-quality sound tracks to multimedia presentations.

The Media Music library contains many styles of music stored in 8-bit and 16-bit sound files, as well as in the MIDI format. Producers of multimedia presentations can use the music without having to pay licensing fees—and Passport Designs even markets a MIDI Jukebox application that can play the selections. Figure 9–24 shows the display that you see when you launch the MIDI Jukebox program.

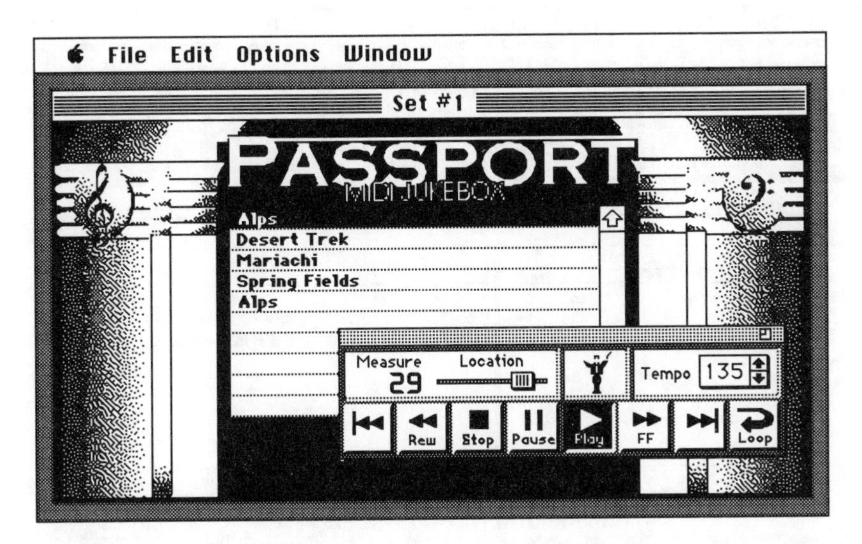

Figure 9–24. MIDI Jukebox

Another popular program from Passport Designs is the Encore musical notation program, which was mentioned in Chapter 7.

Mark of the Unicorn

Mark of the Unicorn manufactures a sequencer (Performer) and a musical notation program (Professional Composer) that have become a real dynamic duo in the world of MIDI—they're the all-out favorites of many professional musicians. Performer and Professional Composer are often used together because they work together beautifully. Their storage files for MIDI data are compatible, so a musician who can both read and play music can create and then publish music while sticking with the Mark of the Unicorn brand.

Professional Composer features a new guitar-chord symbol font, a full set of command-key equivalents, many notation options, and support for the Adobe Sonata font, the best-known type font for musical notation.

The Performer sequencer, shown in Figure 9–25, interprets Apple's Human Interface Guidelines in an interesting way. Apple's officially blessed controls—scroll bars, title bars, and the rest—are all there. But the program designers at Mark of the Unicorn (lovingly dubbed MOTU by its fans) have changed the looks of many of the controls to fit the company's own tastes. You may like it or you may not, but the look is different—that you have to admit.

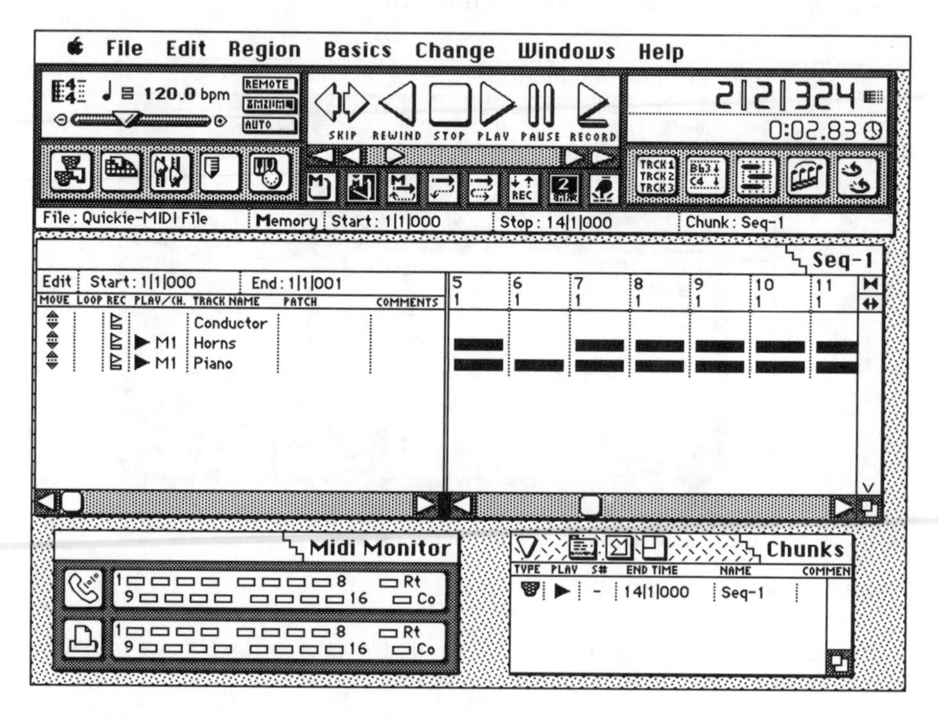

Figure 9–25. Performer

Performer also has many interesting features that are more substantive. For instance, you can change the tempo of a melody at your own speed—instantly, quickly, or slowly—and that means you can squeeze or stretch a passage to fit a predetermined length of tape or film.

A nested looping feature eliminates the need to copy and paste looped passages repeatedly. And there's a handy single-step Snip and Splice feature that lets you remove a section of music without leaving a gap or paste a section in without covering up what was already there.

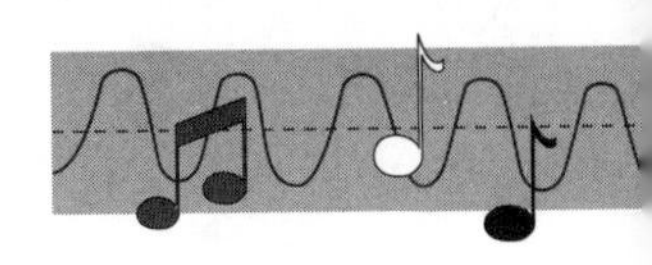

Also, Performer (like Master Tracks Pro) has been updated to recognize the growing importance of the SMPTE time code. The sequencer's counter now ticks off movie frames, as well as elapsed time and measures.

In the area of documentation, Performer outranks most of its competitors. The program's manual is a perfect-bound book that is not only informative and well written, but even looks good enough to place in a bookshelf alongside volumes that are not computer manuals.

Dr. T's Musical Software

Dr. T's Musical Software, as you might guess from its name, is a company known for doing things a little differently. For example, Dr. T's MIDI sequencer, Beyond, is priced lower than its leading competitors, but it has a host of features that are quite advanced.

Dr. T's major product for Macintosh owners is Beyond, illustrated earlier in this chapter in Figure 9–12.

Beyond hasn't been around as long as its three main competitors, but it has gained a large following, and it isn't hard to see why. One of the program's advantages is its price—it costs $319, compared with a $495 retail price that's charged by each of its competitors.

But price is not Beyond's only claim to fame; it has some leading-edge features, too. For example, Beyond actually helps you write music. It has a function called Chromatic and Intelligent Harmonies that can add harmonies to a melodic line from six different modes. Beyond provides graphic editing, track looping, and record filtering of controller information and offers the user the ability to overdub and punch in parts.

Also included are most of the same features offered by Beyond's higher-priced competitors: SMPTE synchronization, programmable software faders, track harmonization, and a multiple-take loop style that assigns each recorded take to its own track and then mutes it. Multiple-take loops are particularly useful if you want to record different solos over the same basic track and then cut and paste bits of each solo to create the perfect track while maintaining a live feel.

Beyond features a design that lets you assemble a composition section by section. You can record up to thirty-two sections of music, each with up to ninety-nine parallel tracks of data. A flexible cue-looping and loop-recording feature lets you audition successive takes as you record them.

Still other features include a pop-up list of subsections on each track and a multitrack view in a track list window that graphically represents the current section. Dr. T's sequencer conforms well to Apple's Human Interface Guidelines, and the product comes with excellent documentation.

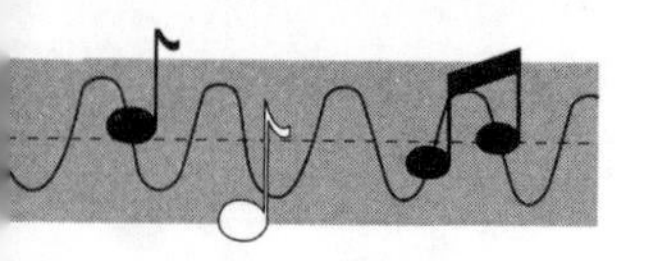

The Compatibility Question

All MIDI sequencers can record and save MIDI data, but that doesn't mean all MIDI sequencers are completely compatible. Every leading manufacturer of sequencers has its own format for storing MIDI data and uses that format in all of its products. But the compatibility that exists within each manufacturer's product line never extends beyond that line, so when you create a musical composition using a sequencer manufactured by one company, you can't simply play it using a sequencer made by another company—unless you first perform some kind of file conversion.

Fortunately, it isn't usually difficult to perform this conversion, because there is one kind of file—a General MIDI (GM) file—that all sequencers can read. As its name implies, a GM file is a file of data that complies with MIDI specifications.

To create a composition on one company's sequencer and then play it on another company's sequencer, you must explicitly save the composition as a GM file. You can usually do that by selecting a special save command—such as such as Export or Save As—from the File menu. Once you have saved a composition as a plain MIDI file, you can import the file into some other company's sequencer.

This technique can come in handy when you do a lot of work with MIDI music, because different manufacturers produce different kinds of products, and sometimes you might want to create a composition with a product manufactured by one company, and then edit or play it using a product made by another company.

For example, you might want to write a composition using the Encore notation program manufactured by Passport Designs, and then edit it using the Vision sequencer published by Opcode Systems. That could be a problem, since products made by Passport Designs save compositions as Master Tracks Pro files, while products made by Opcode Systems save files in the Vision sequencer format.

Fortunately, the solution to this problem is simple: You just save the composition as a plain MIDI file instead of as a Passport Master Tracks Pro file. Then you import your MIDI file into Vision.

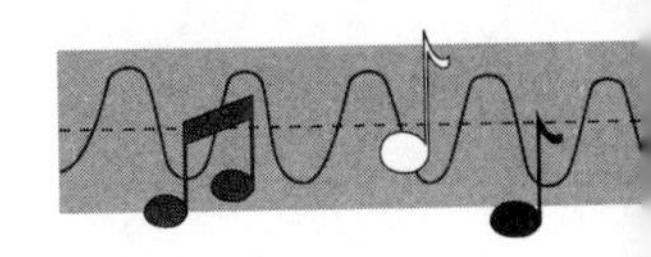

There is one drawback to this system. When you save a music file in the MIDI format instead of in a proprietary file format, you lose some data—usually the data that identifies the kind of MIDI devices that you created your composition on. But since most leading sequencers are equipped with built-in tables that recognize most makes and models of MIDI instruments, that kind of data usually isn't difficult to restore after you've moved your MIDI file from one application to another. Also, programs called *editors and librarians* can help you in these kinds of endeavors.

Editors and Librarians

When you've recorded a few dozen compositions, with combinations of MIDI patches or even combinations of different devices, you'll begin to feel a need for a program that can help you organize the work you've done. Since you must recreate a complete musical environment in order to recreate a composition exactly, you'll begin to wonder if there isn't a way to save a snapshot of a musical environment automatically, so that you can recreate it at the touch of a button.

If that becomes a problem—and eventually, if you're a MIDI fan, it will—then your solution is to buy an editor-librarian program. An editor-librarian can help you create patches, and it can also help you organize them.

The unquestioned leader in editor-librarian programs is Opcode Systems: Opcode's multidisk Galaxy Plus package is the best known editor-librarian program, and it has become a *de facto* industry standard.

One interesting feature of Galaxy Plus is a window that contains a small picture of a keyboard. The keys are called MouseKeys because you can play them with a mouse. By playing the MouseKeys, you can audition patches to make sure they're what you want before you use them in compositions or load them into memory.

Figure 9–26 shows the Galaxy Plus screen display.

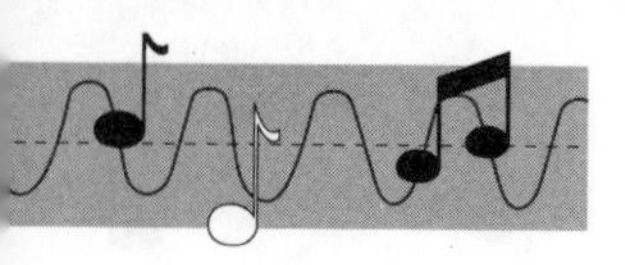

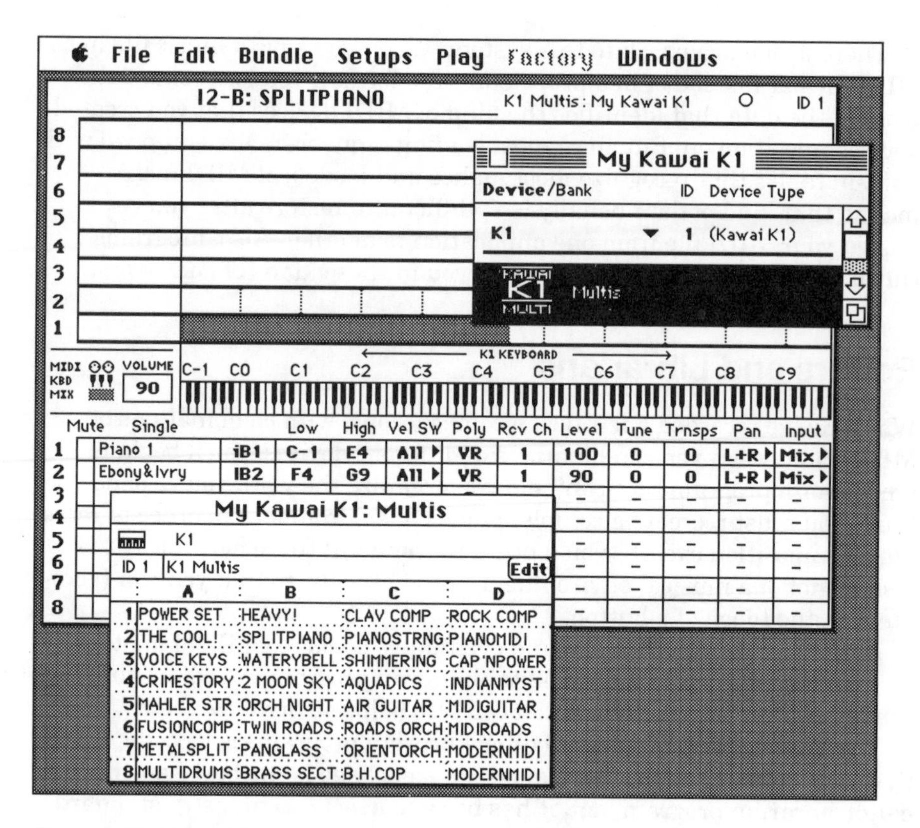

Figure 9–26. Galaxy Plus

A newer entry in the field, and one that's coming up fast, is the X-oR package from Dr. T's Musical Software, which is billed as "the complete MIDI system organizer and patch management system for the Apple Macintosh computer." X-oR supports patch interchange between different brands of personal computers (IBM, Amiga, Atari, and Macintosh); automatic patch creation utilities; and a Compare feature that can automatically shows you the differences between two patches.

The X-oR screen display is shown in Figure 9–27.

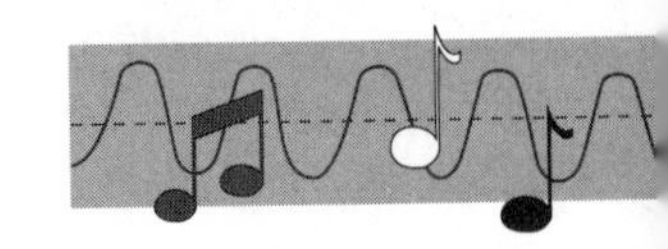

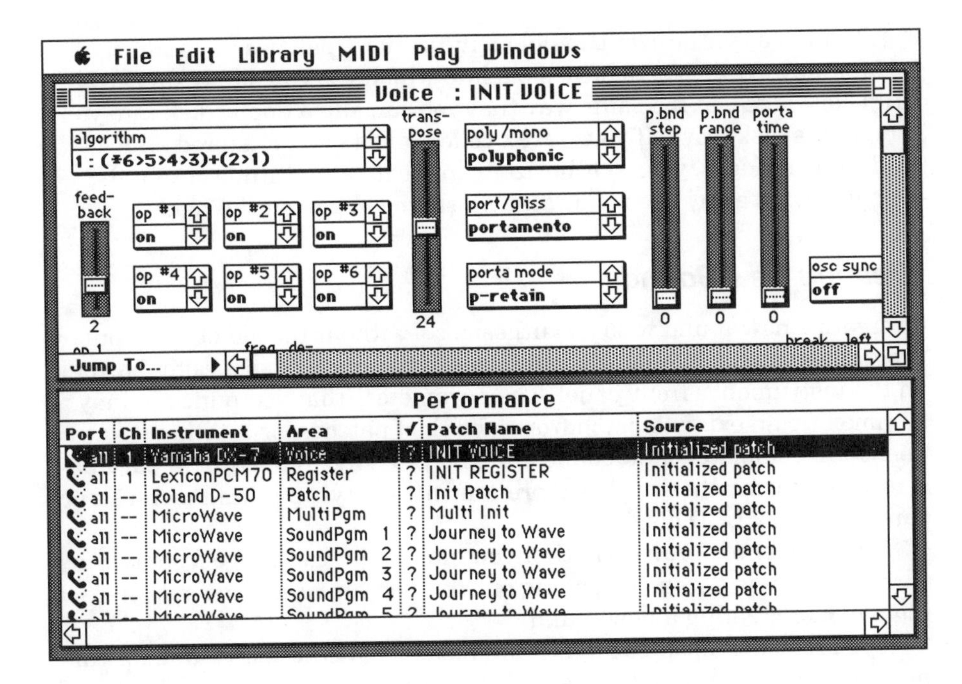

Figure 9–27. X-oR

Downloading and Uploading Patches

Most synthesizers have small memories in which they can store patches as banks of instrumental sounds. Every make and model of synthesizer has a different collection of patches stored in its RAM. And every synthesizer has a front panel that you can use to retrieve or edit those sounds.

Most synthesizers have memories that can hold only a few dozen patches at the same time. But you can download whole banks of patches from your synthesizer into your Macintosh, and you can then store them on hard disks or floppy disks for safekeeping. When you have done that, you can transfer collections of patches from your Macintosh back into your synthesizer. The patches that you load back into your synthesizer can be patches that you created yourself, or patches that you obtained from other sources. You can buy collections of patches from music stores, or you can download free patches from computer services such as America Online and from public bulletin boards.

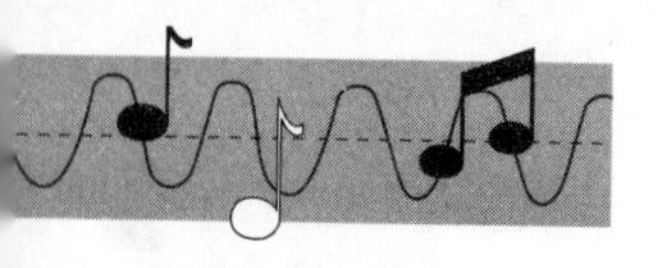

Although a synthesizer can hold only so many patches in its internal RAM, many synthesizers have slots into which you can slip RAM cards or RAM cartridges, in the same way that you can slip a floppy disk into your computer's disk drive. If you start a collection of patches stored on RAM cards or cartridges, your synthesizer can create a multitude of sounds, even when it's away from your Macintosh and you're on the road.

Creating New Sounds

To create a new sound with a synthesizer—without the aid of a computer program—you have to punch in a series of parameters on a set of buttons on the instrument's front panel. The parameters that you punch in may summon up an existing patch from a bank of patches, or they may describe a completely new sound. To help you enter the required parameters, a typical synthesizer has a pre-Macintosh-style pyramid menu structure and a tiny LCD display.

The number of parameters that you must enter can range from two or three to a couple dozen, depending on whether you're seeking out an existing patch or creating a new sound.

If you're using a popular make and model of synthesizer—and, for this purpose, several hundred models of synthesizers are considered "popular"—your sequencer can usually simplify the job of selecting a given patch. That's because your sequencer can usually supply a data table that contains the names of your synthesizer's patches. Once it finds that table, it can simply display the names of your synthesizer's patches on the screen, and you can click on the mouse to select the patch you're looking for.

A problem can arise, however, when you edit various patches to change their sounds, and then put together a musical arrangement of edited and unedited patches. Then what you wind up with is an assortment of original and customized patches that describe a complex mosaic pattern on a multitrack recording. That's fine for one performance, but what happens a couple of months later when you want to play the same arrangement again?

How Editors and Librarians Work

That's where editor and librarian programs come in. Editors and librarians work so closely together that they're usually sold in a single package that has been dubbed, not too creatively, as an editor-librarian program. With the editor part of such a program, you can edit synthesizer patches, altering them to suit specific needs. Then, with the librarian part, you can store your patches (both edited and unedited) in an organized fashion that makes it possible to retrieve them easily.

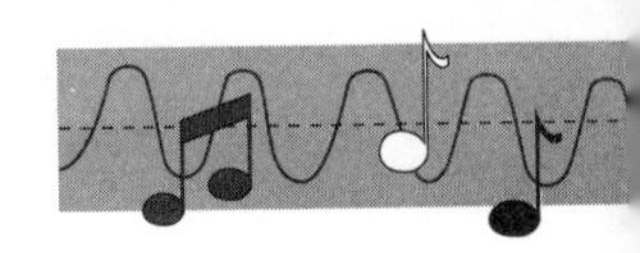

A library program can hold thousands of patches and can organize them in various ways: by kind (guitar sounds, horn, new-age sounds) or by project ("My Performance at Carnegie Hall"), for example. You can cut, copy, and paste patches from one library category to another or from one synthesizer bank to another, or back and forth between libraries and synthesizers. Within categories, libraries are arranged alphabetically.

With the help of an editor-librarian, you can send patch data back and forth between your Macintosh and your synthesizer using a set of MIDI commands technically referred to as *system exclusives*. System exclusives make patch editing and patch storage your computer's job, not yours. If your synthesizer has an unmanageable user interface (and it seems they all do), you can ignore it and use your Mac's friendly user interface instead.

MIDI Sound and Digital Audio

The transition to digital recording, which lasted from the mid-1970s to the late 1980s, was the most significant advance in the history of recorded sound. Until the advent of digital audio, all records were made using the analog technique invented by Thomas Edison. When a sound was recorded, a stylus inscribed the sound's waveform on a revolving surface. When the sound was played back, a needle tracked the recorded waveform, producing sound.

Today, virtually all recordings are made using digital techniques. Before a sound is recorded, its waveform is converted into a stream of binary numbers. Those numbers can then be stored on a digital tape or on a digital compact disc. When the sound is played back, it is converted back into an analog signal that can be used to produce sound.

Varieties of Digital Sound

The development of digital audio was a giant leap forward in recording technology. When music is recorded on an analog disc, the needle that tracks the record picks up imperfections in the disc's surface and reproduces those imperfections—along with the sound—in the form of annoying record scratches.

When an analog tape is used as a recording medium, a similar problem is encountered. When you record sound on an analog tape, the sound's waveform is converted into a magnetic signal that is stored in a metallic oxide coating on the surface of the tape. When the tape is played back, background hiss on the tape's magnetic surface is picked up along with the sound—and, together with the sound, is amplified. Although sophisti-

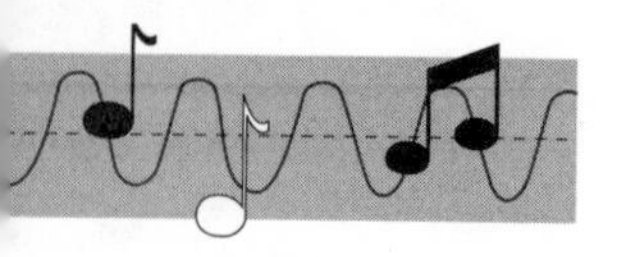

cated electronic devices can reduce tape hiss, they can never entirely remove the problem.

When music is recorded on a digital tape or on a digital compact disc, however, record scratches and tape hiss are completely eliminated. In a digital recording, the sound signal is hard-coded as a stream of binary numbers, and the surface quality of a recording medium can never change the characteristics of the numbers that make up the signal.

No matter how uneven a recording surface may be, a binary 0 is always a binary 0, and a binary 1 is always a 1. If the recording medium that you're using can store numbers accurately, that is all that is required. Thus, no matter how the signals that make up a digital recording are stored, the quality of the recording is never plagued with the noise of record scratches and never descends into a blanket of tape hiss. The sound of a digital recording always emerges from a background of total silence.

Mixing MIDI Signals with Digital Audio

As you learned in Chapter 1, Macintosh users can record digital sound with 8-bit sound digitizers. Some models of the Macintosh have plug-in recording microphones and built-in digitizers, and others can be wired for recording with plug-in digitizers such as the MacRecorder recording module from Macromedia.

Sound that is recorded with a small 8-bit module such as the MacRecorder or a built-in Macintosh digitizer is often called sampled sound, or digitized sound.

Eight-Bit and 16-Bit Sound

As noted earlier in this chapter, some Macintosh programs—such as the Audio Trax sequencer from Passport Designs—can combine 8-bit sound recorded on the Macintosh with 16-bit audio signals generated by MIDI instruments. With programs such as Audio Trax, you can mix live sound—such as vocals, live speech, or the sounds of acoustic instruments—with digital tracks produced with MIDI instruments. In this way, you can create recordings similar to those made by live performers in concerts and recording studios.

However, when you mix an 8-bit sound track recorded on a small Macintosh digitizer with the 16-bit audio signals that professional-style MIDI instruments can produce through their audio outputs, the result is not a professional-quality recording. No matter how you record a half-digitized, half-MIDI performance, the sound quality of the digitized por-

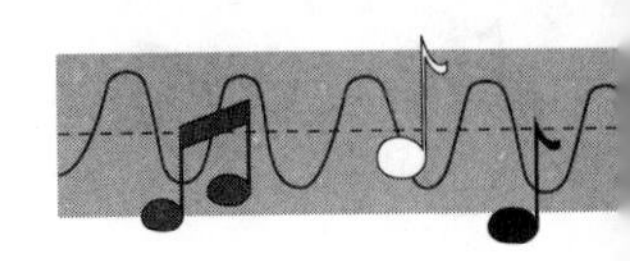

tion is limited both by its 8-bit word length (for more details on word length, see Chapter 2) and by the inexpensive sound circuitry that is built into small digitizers such as MacRecorder.

In contrast, when you record the MIDI portion of your performance through the audio outputs of the same instruments that created it, the result is full-fidelity, CD-quality sound.

When you mix the two tracks together, the sound quality of the MIDI part of the recording far outshines the quality of the digitized portion, and the overall sound quality of the recording is quite uneven.

If digital recording systems for the Macintosh do have limitations, the limits are financial; it costs several thousand dollars to turn a Macintosh into a 16-bit digital recorder. However, compared with what it costs to set up a digital recording system *without* a Macintosh, that's a bargain. When you consider the prices of other kinds of digital hardware—such as digital mixing consoles and studio-quality digital tape recorders—the price of a Macintosh with a plug-in sound board doesn't sound so unreasonable.

Improving the Mix

Fortunately, there is a way to record 16-bit, CD-quality sound on the Macintosh. You can now get plug-in sound boards for the Macintosh that contain all of the hardware you need to generate true studio-quality digital sound. By simply plugging a sound board into your Macintosh, you can equip your Mac to make CD-quality sampled sound recordings.

In the same way the Audio Trax sequencer can mix MIDI sound tracks with 8-bit sampled sound, some sequencers are specifically designed to mix MIDI tracks with the 16-bit audio signals produced by a plug-in Macintosh sound board. And that's a significant improvement in the Audio Trax technique of mixing MIDI tracks with 8-bit sampled sound.

Two sequencers that can mix 16-bit sampled sound with tracks produced by MIDI instruments are Studio Vision from Opcode Systems and Digital Performer from Mark of the Unicorn.

Studio Vision, which retails for $995, is designed to be used with digital sound boards such as the $3,495 Sound Tools II board from Digidesign or the $995 Digidesign Audiomedia II board. The main screen of the newest version of Studio Vision is shown in Figure 9–28.

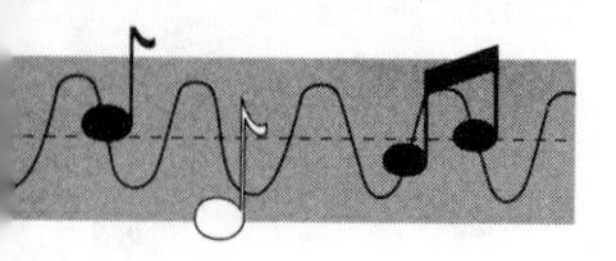

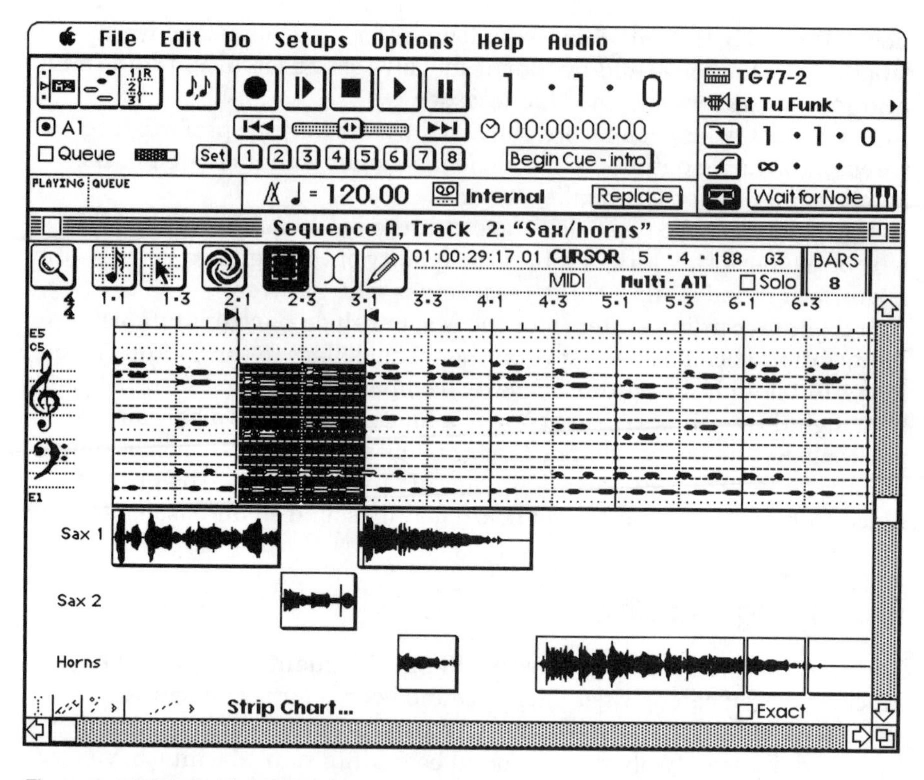

Figure 9–28. Studio Vision display

Also, some companies publish CD-ROMs that contain libraries of sounds in two formats: both in MIDI files and in files that are stored as digital sounds.

Building Your Dream Machine

The industry leader in digital audio for the Macintosh is Digidesign, a small company in Menlo Park, California. Digidesign manufactures the Sound Tools system for the Macintosh, the most widely used computer-based recording and editing system in the music industry. The newest version of the Sound Tools package, Sound Tools II, includes a recording software package called Sound Designer II; an audio interface; and a custom-designed NuBus card called the Sound Accelerator II.

Sound Tools II, designed for professional audio applications, retails for $3,495. Users of the Sound Tools package include CD-mastering houses, record producers, dance and music studios, film sound-effects specialists, multimedia producers, and audio studios.

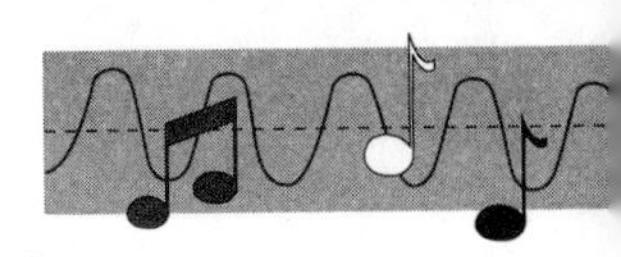

For audio enthusiasts with more modest budgets, Digidesign offers a junior version of the Sound Tools II kit called Audiomedia II. The Audiomedia II package, which sells for a relatively modest $995, offers sound fidelity nearly as good as that of Sound Tools II and is ideally suited for multimedia applications.

Sound Tools II comes in a single-rack space unit that combines four balanced analog inputs and outputs with two digital inputs and outputs. It supports several software packages that combine MIDI sequencing and digital audio recording, such as Digidesign's own Deck digital multitrack software; the Studio Vision sequencer from Opcode Systems; the Digital Performer sequencer from Mark of the Unicorn; and Alchemy from Passport Designs, an editing package for 16-bit sampled audio.

Other products from Digidesign include the following:

- Pro Tools, an ultra-high-end multitrack recording system designed for use in professional studios. Pro Tools is available in several configurations. Systems with four channels are priced at $5,995; an eight-channel system costs $14,495; a twelve-channel configuration is $19,495; and a sixteen-channel system is $24,495.
- SampleCell, a $1,995 board that doesn't record but can play back sampled sound. SampleCell can reduce the cost of high-quality sampling by harnessing the power of the Macintosh CPU. SampleCell offers a less expensive alternative to a sampling instrument by relying on the Macintosh to do the sound processing. SampleCell provides software tools for editing and modifying prerecorded sound samples, and a selection of sampled sound is provided on a CD-ROM that comes with the SampleCell package. You can also use two other Digidesign products—Sound Tools II and Audiomedia II—to supply the SampleCell board with sounds.

Summary

This brings you to the end of an adventure: a journey across the largely uncharted universe of Macintosh sound. Your sound trek started at the Sound Control Panel, where you began to discover your computer's audio capabilities. Chapter 2 introduced the Sound-Trecker program and explored the basic principles of the science of sound. In Chapter 3, with the help of the SoundApp program, you learned the secrets behind the three sound synthesizers that are built into every Macintosh.

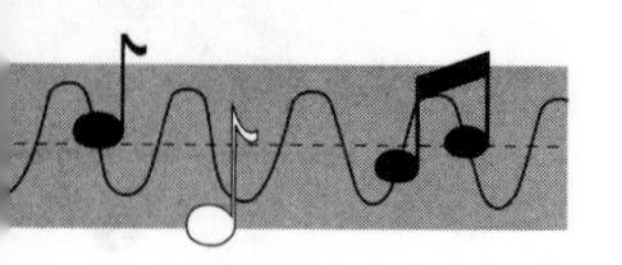

In Chapter 4, you were introduced to SoundWave, the top-rated sound-processing program created by Authorware and packaged with the Voice Impact Pro recording system. In Chapter 5, you learned about the Audio Palette and the HyperCorder program, and Chapter 6 introduced voice-synthesis programs.

You learned about musical notation in Chapter 7, melody and harmony in Chapter 8, and the world of MIDI in this chapter. And the programs on your bonus disk gave you a guided tour of the topics covered in each chapter.

So now you know how your computer's sound system works. How you use that system is up to you. If you're a Macintosh programmer, you now know how to access the Sound Manager. If you're a HyperCard programmer, you've learned how to add sound to your HyperCard stacks. If you're a composer or a performer, you now know how to a make your Mac the centerpiece of a MIDI system. And if you're a Macintosh user like the rest of us, you can just sit back and enjoy.

Happy listening!

Appendix A

The Sound Input Device

This appendix is an almost verbatim[1] copy of "SID™+ Hardware," a document written by the SID Trio and distributed free over computer bulletin boards and through Macintosh user groups. The document provides instructions for building the Sound Input Device (SID), an 8-bit sound digitizer introduced in Chapter 1 of this book.

If you decide to build the SID digitizer, you do so at your own risk; neither I nor Addison-Wesley guarantee the SID module or make any claims about its effectiveness, its usefulness, or the safety of using it with your equipment.

Section 1 tells how to build SID using a ceramic resonator. Ceramic resonators are inexpensive but can be difficult to obtain in small quantities. Sections 2 through 4 explain how SID can be built using alternatives to ceramic resonators.

1. SID+ Hardware Description

Eric Gould, Jeffrey Siegel, and Dave Fleck
(Reprinted by permission of the SID Trio)

The Sound Input Device (SID) is an audio digitizer designed for the Macintosh computer. It produces a continuous stream of digitized samples at 22kHz and is software-compatible with other existing audio digitizer software. A schematic for the SID digitizer is presented in Figures A–1.a through A–1.d. The pin numbers for the Mac 8-pin mini-DIN are shown with the 9-pin D connector pin numbers following in parentheses. The SID can be constructed by normal construction techniques. The first few units built were wire-wrapped. You should use some care in parts placement and ground distribution to avoid coupling noise into the more sensitive analog input sections, especially from the digital signals.

[1]Verbatim except for headings, cross-references, and minor grammatical corrections.

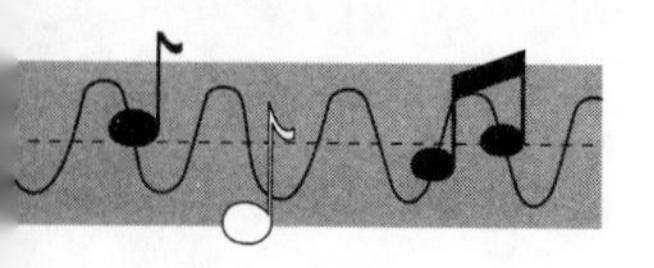

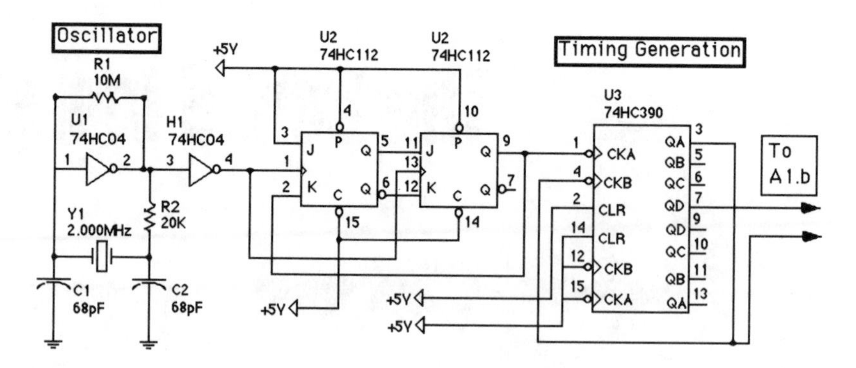

Figure A–1.a. SID+ schematic—1

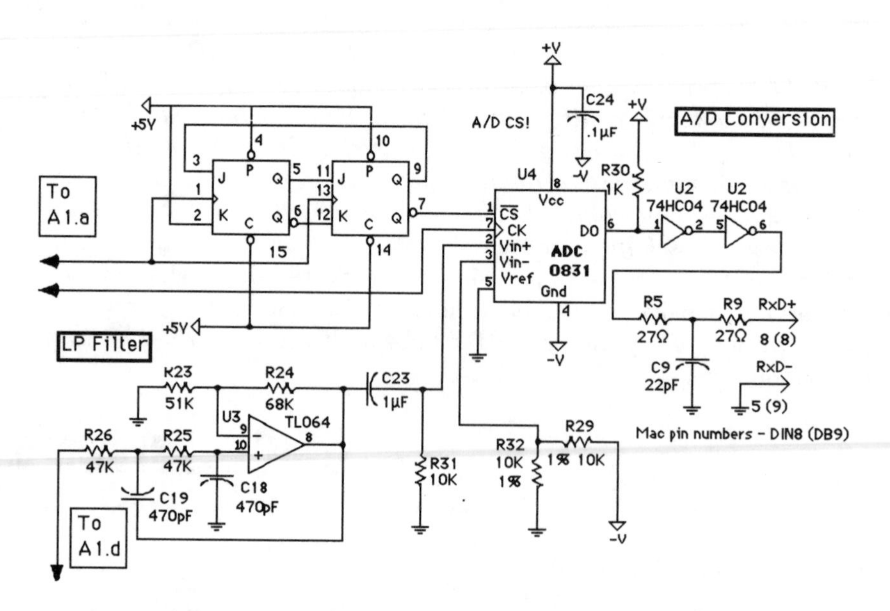

Figure A–1.b. SID+ schematic—2

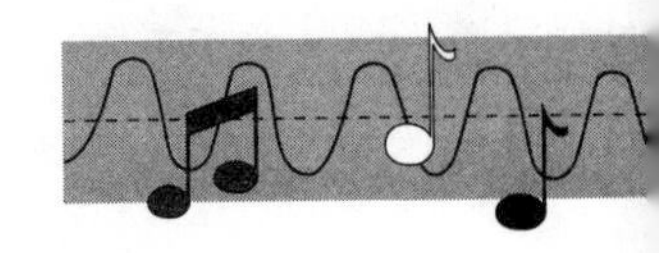

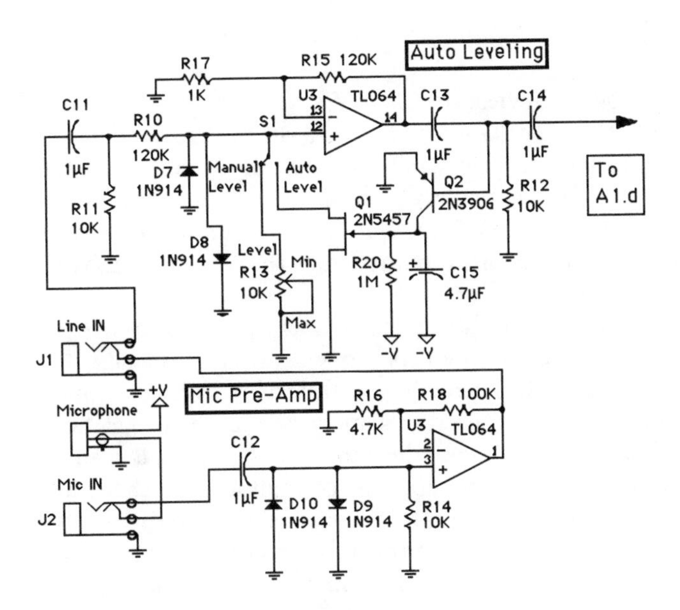

Figure A–1.c. SID+ schematic—3

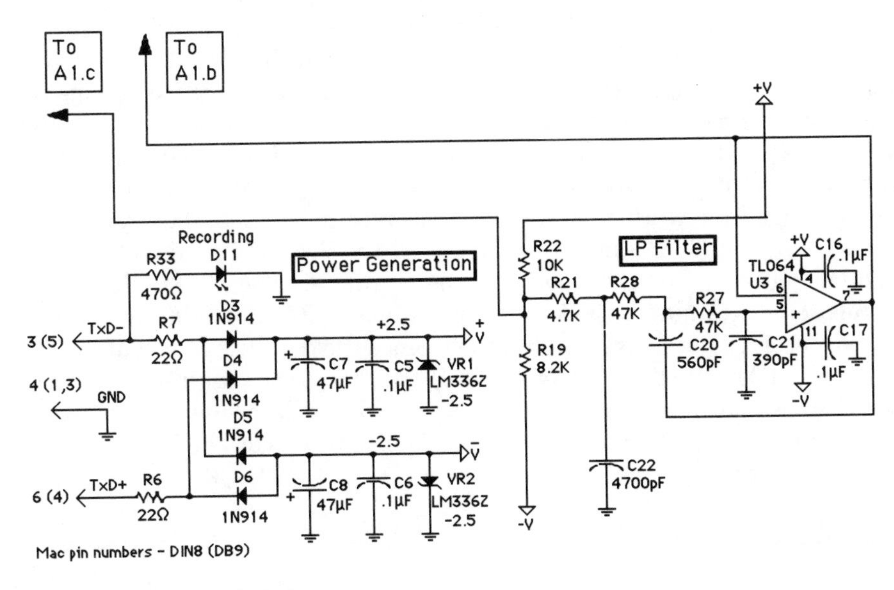

Figure A–1.d. SID+ schematic—4

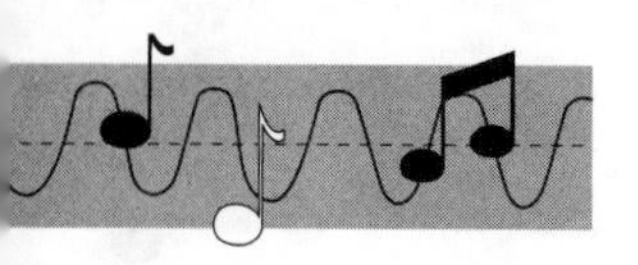

Power Generation

SID is a *parasitically powered* device; that is, it draws its power from the signal lines coming from the Mac. This is similar to serial mouse devices in the PC world. They draw power from up to three of the signal output lines from the PC. The SID draws its power from the two serial transmit data lines (TxD– and TxD+) from the Mac. The short-circuit drive capability of each of these lines is up to 150mA, many times the few milliamps of current required by the SID.

In addition to low current availability, a parasitically powered device must overcome two other problems. One is polarity reversal of the signal during data transmission, the other is dealing with the low voltage available. The polarity reversal can be ignored in some cases, as the program collecting the digitized data does not send data to the SID. There is also the possibility, however, of future digitizers receiving commands for other purposes. The problem is solved by directing the positive voltage to the positive supply with diodes D3 and D4 (see schematic), and directing the negative voltage to the negative supply with D5 and D6. Since the transmit signals from the Mac are differential, one of the transmit lines is always positive and one is always negative, so both voltages are always available.

The positive voltage available is typically three to four volts (V). This is less than the 5V normally used for powering digital circuitry. The negative voltage is also typically three to four volts negative. The positive voltage is regulated to 2.5V by VR1 and the negative voltage is regulated to –2.5V by VR2. This provides a ± 2.5V split supply for the analog circuitry and a 5V supply differential (+2.5V to –2.5V) for the digital circuitry. For the analog-to-digital (A/D) converter, oscillator, and timing generation, the –2.5V supply acts as ground and the +2.5V supply acts as Vcc (+5V). This solves another problem. The Mac requires a signal that goes positive and negative in relation to ground for the handshake input (HSKI) and a differential signal for received data (RxD+ and RxD–). Since the digital signals output from the SID swing from +2.5V to –2.5V, they meet the requirements for the HSKI signal, and by tying RxD– to ground, the data signal out of the SID presents a ±2.5V differential to the receive inputs on the Mac.

Oscillator

A 1.558MHz master clock is provided by a ceramic resonator and two sections of a hex inverter. The oscillator circuit is taken from the muRata Erie application notes. For high-volume production (1000 or more), ceramic resonators are ideal due to their low cost. If you are building a smaller number of SIDs, alternatives are listed in sections 2 to 4 of this appendix.

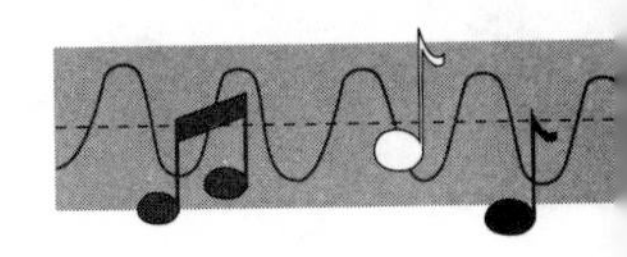

Timing Generation

Two timing signals are needed by the A/D converter. One is a clock, which determines the output bit rate and maximum conversion rate. The other is a chip select (CS), which determines when data is sent, and therefore the conversion rate. The conversion rate must be 22254.5454Hz, the rate at which the Mac will resynthesize the data. Programs that offer slower sample rates accomplish this by discarding every other sample (for 11127.2727Hz sample rate) or three of every four (for 5563.6363Hz). Note that these odd numbers are referred to as 22kHz, 11kHz, and 5kHz sample rates. Additionally, Apple provides MACE through APDA, which performs some real-time audio compression and expansion in software.

The master clock is divided by 5 using part of U1, 74HC390, a dual-decade counter. This 311.6kHz data clock signal becomes the A/D clock signal. Bits will output from the A/D converter at half this rate. This signal is also output to the Mac as the HSKI signal. Two sections of the hex inverter U2 act as drivers for the HSKI signal. The serial port on the Mac is initialized to use an external clock at a times-one rate, the external clock being the HSKI signal. It is also set for asynchronous, no parity, with 1 or 2 stop bits. Figure A–2 shows the relationship between the master clock, data clock (HSKI), and data signals.

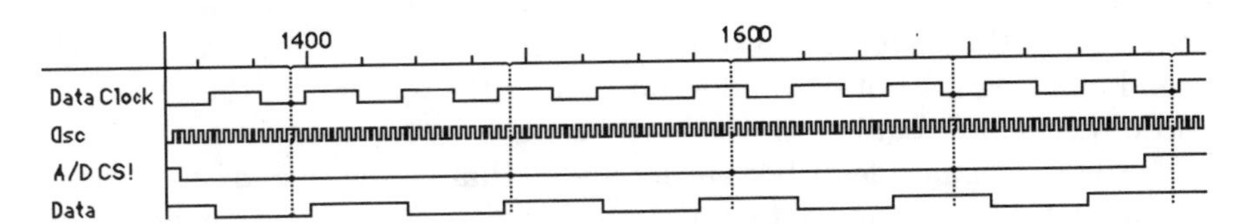

Figure A–2. Fine timing

The data clock is further divided by 14 by the remaining sections of U1 to provide the A/D CS signal. The rate of this signal is 22257.142Hz, the required data rate. The divide by 14 is really a divide by 20 that is cut short by a reset generated by D1, D2, and R1 acting as an AND gate. The A/D CS signal is low for 10 counts and high for 4 (at which point the reset occurs). The 10 low counts is the time period when the A/D converter outputs 10 bits of serial data (1 start bit, 8 data bits, and 1 stop bit). The time the output is disabled can be considered as a second stop bit plus a 3-bit gap between bytes, or as a 4-bit gap. See both Figure A–2 and Figure A–3.

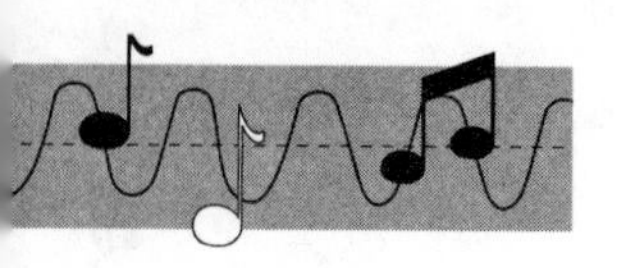

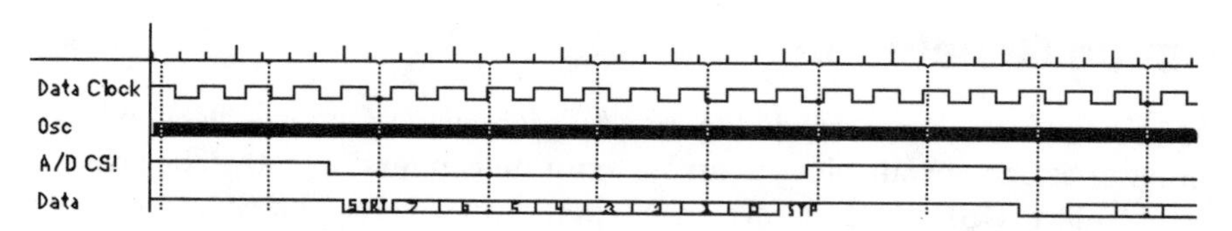

Figure A–3. Coarse timing

A/D Conversion

A/D conversion is performed by a National Semiconductor ADC0831CCN 8-bit serial A/D converter. It has several features that make it ideal for use in the SID:

- Serial output
- Single +5 supply required
- Low power consumption
- Zero is output on the first clock, which becomes the serial start bit

The A/D converter uses a successive approximation method. This is essentially a half-interval search. The output is the result of the current interval test. Therefore, the converter outputs the most significant bit first (the result of the "is it greater or less than halfway" test), followed by the second most significant bit, and so on. This is the opposite of the serial data protocol and requires the software to reverse the data.

The digital signals described earlier are all that are needed to cause the A/D converter to generate data at the proper rate. The data output signal is pulled up by R30 (the output is open drain) and driven by two of the sections of the hex inverter U2. This signal is the receive input to the Mac, and a trick similar to one used by RS-232 serial devices is used to provide the differential input required (ground RxD– and drive RxD+ with a bipolar signal).

The software is expecting an A/D output value of 128 to represent no signal input. Zero represents maximum negative swing, and 255 represents maximum positive swing. Since the operational amplifiers (OP Amps) in the analog portion are not capable of handling signals that reach the positive supply voltage, a swing of less than 5V total must represent the full digital output range. By connecting the A/D converter's Vref pin to ground, a swing of 2.5V (the difference between Vref and the A/D converter's ground) becomes the full range swing. Vin– is tied to a voltage divider (R29 and R32), which provides 1.25V. This is subtracted from Vin+ inside the A/D converter. Vin+ is referenced to ground by R31.

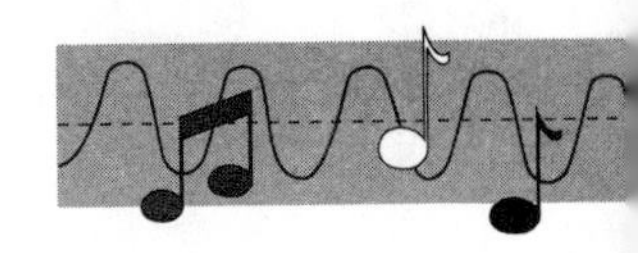

With no signal (0V) input Vin+ is at ground, which is at 2.5V above A/D ground. This input has 1.25V subtracted by Vin–, leaving 1.25V. This is one half of Vref, one half the total range, and therefore 128 counts. Similarly, a maximum input signal of 1.25V above ground, which is 3.75V above A/D ground at Vin+, has 1.25V subtracted by Vin–, leaving 2.5V. This is equal to Vref, which is maximum, which is 255 counts. An input signal of –1.25V referenced to ground is 1.25 above A/D ground. The 1.25V is then subtracted by Vin– leaving 0, which outputs a zero. To summarize, the 2.5V on Vref restricts the range and the 1.25V on Vin– converts the ± swing in relation to ground in the analog circuitry to the different ground reference used by the A/D and other digital circuitry.

Microphone Preamp

One section of the quad OP Amp U3 is used to boost microphone-level signals to line-level signals. A built-in microphone can be used and is automatically switched out when an external microphone is connected. Diodes D9 and D10 prevent damage in the event too strong a signal is connected.

Auto-Leveling

Another section of OP Amp U3 is used to bring line levels up to a higher amplitude (± 1V). Again, D7 and D8 provide protection from strong signals. The Mic Pre-Amp is switched out when a line input is connected. When switched to manual-leveling mode, the stage is a simple amplifier. In auto-leveling mode, Q1 acts as a variable resistor, the resistance being proportional to Q1's gate voltage. R20 discharges C15, pulling the gate of Q1 lower, increasing the gain. As the output of the stage increases, Q2 turns on, pulling C15 toward ground and lowering the gain. An equilibrium is established at around 1.4V peak-to-peak output. The gain is always reduced immediately as C15 is charged through Q2. The gain increases slowly, as determined by the discharge rate of C15 through R20. To get a slower gain increase rate, you might want to increase the size of C15.

LP Filter

With a 22kHz sample rate, the *highest* signal that can theoretically be produced is an 11kHz signal. Signals above 11kHz produce unwanted frequencies at less than 11kHz. The low pass (LP) filter attenuates signals above 11kHz to avoid undesirable results. The filter was actually computed to attenuate signals above 7kHz. This number was arrived at as a compro-

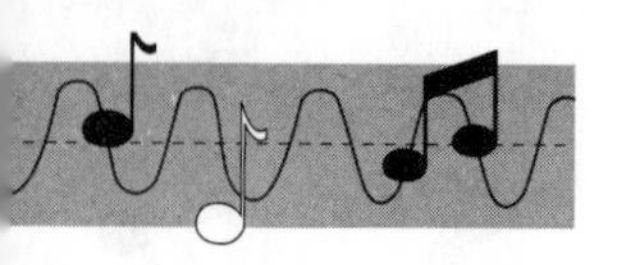

mise of the desire to have the widest unattenuated range and the need to attenuate signals above 11kHz so that they produce *no* signal (less than 1 bit of signal strength). The more filter "poles," the closer the filter frequency can be to 11kHz. SID uses a five-pole filter. The first three poles are implemented with one section of the Op Amp U3, the last two sections with another section of the Op Amp. The last two poles also provide a slight amount of gain, boosting the signal from a 2V swing to the 2.5V swing required by the A/D converter.

Construction

Table A–1 is a list of parts to construct the SID. The part numbers listed are for Digi-Key Corporation unless otherwise noted. Many more parts are available at Radio Shack than shown in the parts list but at a higher price. Since Digi-Key is a source for the more difficult to find A/D converter, you may as well purchase the less expensive parts from them along with the A/D. Active also has many of the parts available and several convenient showrooms.

Table A-1 Parts to Construct the SID

Each	Description	Part No.	Cost	In Fig. A–1
2	22 Ohm ¼W Resistor	22Q	.25/5	R6, R7
4	27 Ohm ¼W Resistor	27Q	.25/5	R4, R5, R8, R9
1	470 Ohm ¼W Resistor	470Q	.25/5	R33
3	1K ¼W Resistor	1.0KQ	.25/5	R2, R17, R30
2	4.7K ¼W Resistor	4.7KQ	.25/5	R16,R21
1	8.2K ¼W Resistor	8.2KQ	.25/5	R19
2	10K 1% ¼W Resistor	10.0KX	.50/5	R29, R32
5	10K ¼W Resistor	10KQ	.25/5	R1, R11, R14, R22, R31
4	47K ¼W Resistor	47KQ	.25/5	R25, R26, R27, R28
1	51K ¼W Resistor	51KQ	.25/5	R23
1	68K ¼W Resistor	68KQ	.25/5	R24
1	100K ¼W Resistor	100KQ	.25/5	R18
2	120K ¼W Resistor	120KQ	.25/5	R10, R15
1	1M ¼W Resistor	1.0MQ	.25/5	R3
2	22pF ceramic capacitor	P4016	.56/10	C9,C10

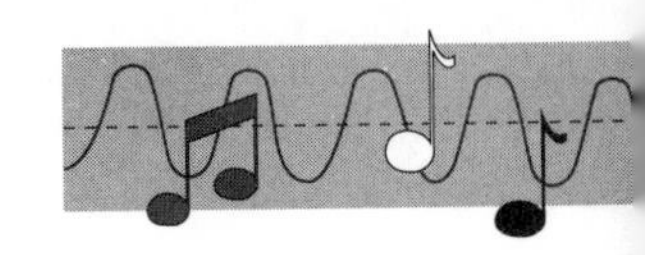

Table A-1 (cont.) Parts to Construct the SID

Each	Description	Part No.	Cost	In Fig. A–1
2	100pF ceramic capacitor	P4024	.56/10	C2,C3
1	390pF ceramic capacitor	P4031	.79/10	C21
2	470pF ceramic capacitor	P4032	.79/10	C18,C19
1	560pF ceramic capacitor	P4033	1.05/10	C20
1	4700pF ceramic capacitor	P4193	1.09/10	C22
7	0.1uF ceramic capacitor	P4164	1.13/10	C1, C4, C5, C6, C16, C17, C24
4	1uF ceramic capacitor	P4537	.76	C11, C12, C14, C23
2	47uF electrolytic capacitor	P6608	.21	C7,C8
1	TL064 quad Op Amp I/C	Active 54041	.84	U3
1	ADC0831CCN A/D conv. I/C	ADC0831CCN*	3.13*	U4
1	74HC390 dual-decade cntr I/C	MM74HC390N	.70	U1
1	74HC04 hex inverter I/C	MM74HC04N	.28	U2
10	1N914 signal diodes	1N4148	.60/10	D1–D10
1	Low-power LED	HLMP–1700QT	.52	D11
2	LM336Z–2.5 2.5V Ref.**	LM336Z–2.5	1.20	VR1, VR2
1	1.558Mhz Cer. Res., muRata Erie	CSA1.558MK040	1.00***	Y1
2	⅛" closed-circuit jack	Radio Shack 274–248	1.69/2	J1, J2
1	Electret Microphone	Radio Shack 270–092	2.99	
1	10K Potentiometer	Radio Shack 271–218	.69	R13
1	Enclosure	Radio Shack 270–233	2.19	
1	8-Pin mini-DIN conn.	Jameco Elect. 8MDJ	1.49	J3
1	Mac serial cable****	Jameco Elect. APC3	4.95	

*The latest Digi-Key catalog shows the price at $15.90, which is quite an unusual price increase. (As an alternative, see sections 2 to 4 of this appendix.)

**Leave the adjust pin disconnected. LM385Z–2.5 works also (Active 54151)

***In quantity 1000. Small quantities are not generally available. See text.

****Note that this is a Mac-to-Mac serial cable. Transmit and receive lines are interchanged, as are handshake in and handshake out. All part numbers are Digi-Key part numbers unless specified otherwise.

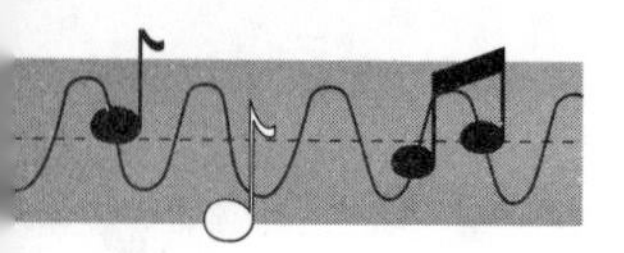

Troubleshooting

Before attempting to fix the unit, make sure there really is a problem. Make sure everything is connected and that the proper ports are selected in the software. *Also note:* Since the unit draws power from the transmit lines, *the transmitter in the Mac must be enabled.* The SID software as well as existing commercial sound-input software enable the transmitter lines properly.

If SID is not operating properly, test the following:

- Check for +2.5V and –2.5V supplies. If not present, make sure the transmitter is enabled, then check for shorts.
- Check for the presence of the Osc master oscillator signal.
- Check for the A/D converter's clock (CK) and chip select (CS) signals.
- Check for A/D converter data out (DO).
- Check the analog sections for signals that are nominally at ground level.
- Check the analog sections using a signal generator to ensure that the signal is not being distorted.

How to Order

Telephone numbers of the suppliers are as follows:

Digi-Key	800–344–4539
Active	800–677–8899 (also local stores)
Jameco Electronics	415–592–8097
muRata Erie	404–436–1300
Radio Shack	Check White Pages

2. SID Crystal Update

The original reason for designing SID with a ceramic resonator was because the resonators are much less expensive than crystals, which can also be used. We didn't realize just how difficult it is to get these custom parts in small quantities (less than 1000). This document should solve this problem by giving the changes necessary to use a crystal instead.

We have not found a good source for the ceramic resonator that will sell them in reasonable quantities (meaning one). As an alternative, a crystal can be used with the following additional circuit changes, as shown in Figure A–4:

- Remove R2 (1K resistor) and replace with a short
- Change C2 & C3 from 100pF to 33pF (DigiKey Part No. P4018)

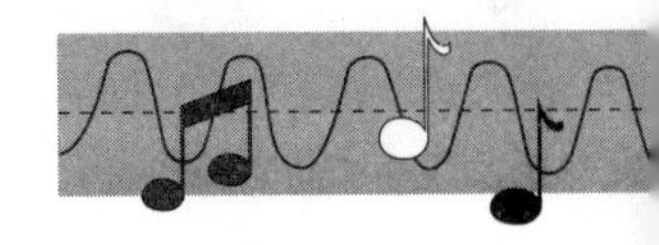

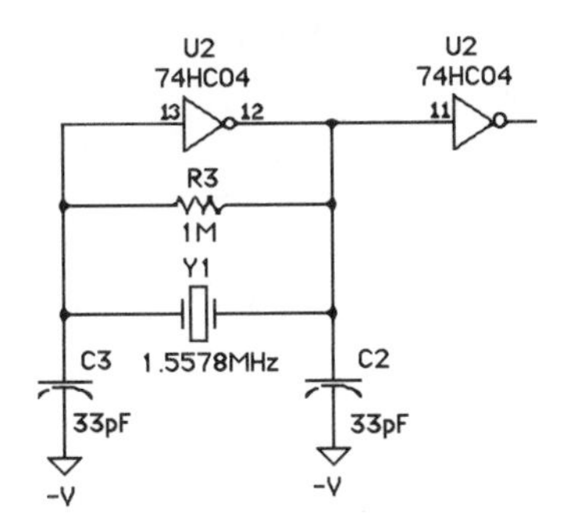

Figure A–4. SID crystal update

A source for crystals in a quantity of one with relatively quick turn-around is JAN Crystals, 813–936–2397. The number of the JAN crystal is 1.5578MHz, HC33U case, parallel resonant, 20pF load capacitor 0.005%. The JAN crystals cost around $10 and take two to three weeks for delivery.

Another crystal source is Fox, 813–693–0099. The number of the Fox crystal is 1.5578MHz, HC49U case (a smaller case), parallel resonant, 20pF load capacitor, 30/50/20/20 (standard tolerance numbers that Fox understands). Fox crystals cost $24.38 each and can take as much as 12 weeks for delivery.

With this information, you should find it easier to produce your own SID. We've heard of many being made already—keep up the great work! If you develop interesting software, please send us a copy or let us know what you've done. The SID Trio can be reached at Evergreen Technologies, 19751 Frederick Rd., Suite 401, Germantown, MD 20874.

3. Ceramic Resonator Alternative

By Bruce F. Field, 1402 Grandin Avenue, Rockville, MD 20851

This section describes an alternative to the ceramic resonator.

An LC tank circuit can be used in place of the ceramic resonator with only a minor (imperceptible) degradation in performance. Since the exact values of the circuit components depend on the wiring layout of the circuit and some experimentation may be necessary, *this modification should only be considered by experienced builders* who have access to an oscilloscope and/or a frequency counter. Figure A–5 is a schematic for the modification. As a start, the changes to be made to the original circuit are as follows:

- Remove R2 (1K resistor) and replace with a short.
- Change C3 from 100pF to 33pF (DigiKey Part No. P4018).

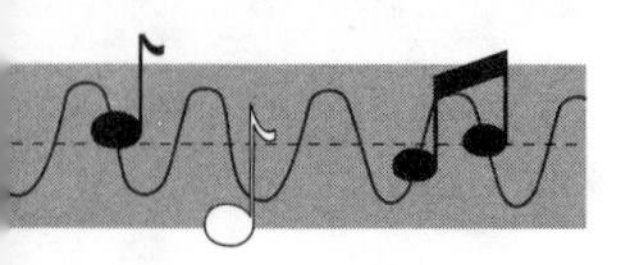

- Replace R3 with a 100µH Inductor (DigiKey Part No. M8037).
- Change C2 from 100pF Ceramic disc to a 100pF Mica (DigiKey Part No. SE104) and connect as shown in Figure A–5. (The original ceramic disc capacitor can be used, but the stability will be better with a mica capacitor.)
- Substitute a 74C04 for U2 in place of the 74HC02.

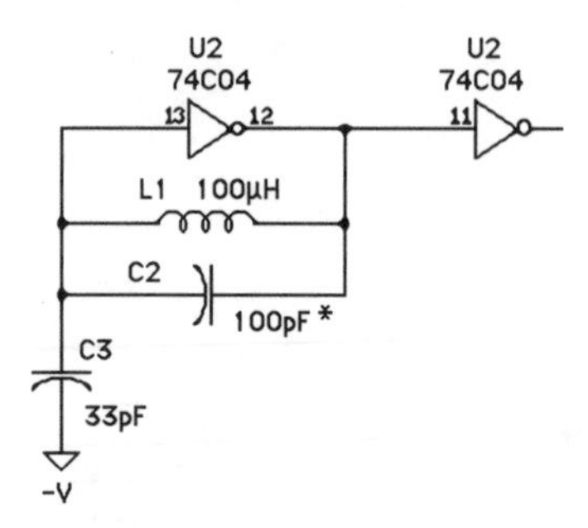

Figure A–5. Resonator alternative

The exact value required for C2 will depend on the stray capacitance in your circuit and thus will depend on exactly how you wire the circuit. Follow good wiring practice for high frequencies and keep the leads short. After assembly, check the frequency with a frequency counter and change C2 (if necessary) to produce the proper 1.558MHz frequency output. To make adjustment of the frequency relatively easy, capacitor C2 shown in Figure A–5 can be replaced with two capacitors in parallel: an 82pF fixed-value mica capacitor and a 7 to 25pF variable capacitor. These capacitors are not available from DigiKey, however. Substituting the 74C04 for the 74HC02 is necessary, as the reduced bandwidth of the 74C04 prevents "ringing" in the circuit that occurs with the 74HC02 and subsequently produces extra unwanted pulses.

R29 and R32 determine the output value of the A/D converter when no input is applied to the converter. As shown in the original schematic, R29 = R30 = 10K. I found that this produced an output code value of 112 for most converters rather than the desired 128. This slightly reduces the dynamic range of the SID, as the signal to the A/D can only go negative by 1.09V (1.25 * 112/128) rather than the one designed for 1.25V. To increase the output code to nearer 128 (with no input), an 8.2K resistor can be used for R29 in place of the original 10K.

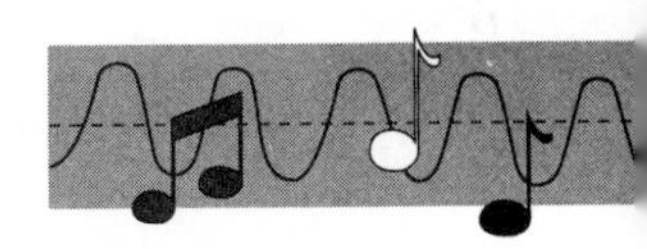

4. The 2MHz Crystal Solution

Joseph Palmer provided the following:

I have found a lower-cost method of replacing the ceramic resonator in the SID with a standard-frequency crystal. When I first examined the circuit, I was disheartened to discover the single piece of "Nonobtainium," more commonly called a special-order ceramic resonator. I spent a couple of hours working through catalogs trying to locate either the resonator or a crystal that could be divided down to create the resonator frequency. No luck.

Further analysis determined the important parameter was only the sample start rate, which was 44.935µS/Sample, which is only 0.00145% different from 45µS. Because the clock is also provided by the Macintosh, the actual bit rate was not that critical.

Examining the specifications for the resonator showed that the absolute frequency accuracy of the resonator is only 0.05%. Table A–2 shows that a 1MHz 0.002% crystal divided by 45 (÷3,÷5,÷3) would actually be guaranteed to be closer to the Macintosh Sample rate than the resonator would. While the center frequency of the crystal would be off by 0.00145%, the maximum and minimum errors for the crystal would still be less than those for the resonator! *(Note: More precise resonators are available at additional cost. — Dave.)*

Table A–2 Resonator specifications

Resonator	Specifications	Base Frequency	Min-Max Frequency	Divided Frequency	Frequency Error (Hz)	Percent Error
Ceramic	+0.05%	1558000	1565790	22368.4285	113.8831	0.00509%
	+0.00%	1558000	1558000	22257.1428	2.597457	0.00012%
		1558000	1550210	22145.8571	–108.6882	–0.00491%
Crystal	+0.002%	1000000	1000200	22226.6666	–27.87873	–0.00125%
	+0.000%	1000000	1000000	22222.2222	–32.32317	–0.00145%
	–0.002%	1000000	999980	22221.7777	–32.76762	–0.00147%

For my SID, I elected to use a 2MHz crystal and divide once more to get a square wave at the clock input to the A/D convertor, to guarantee the duty cycle requirements. The schematic is shown in Figure A–6.

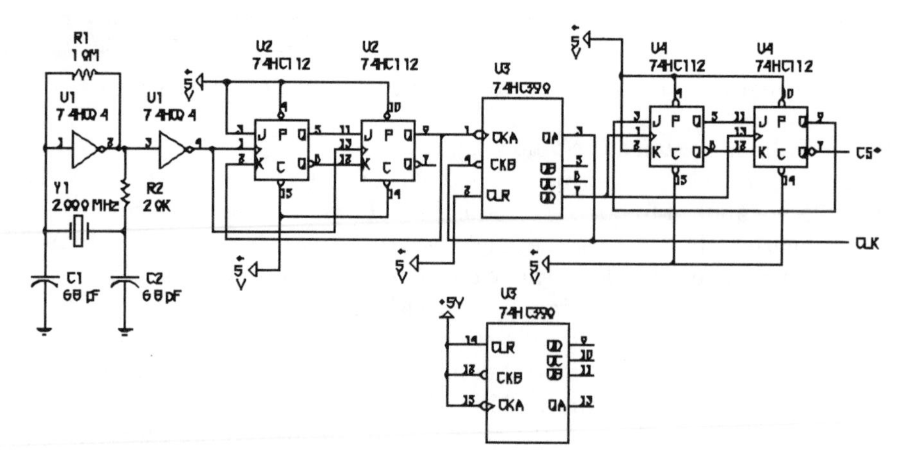

Figure A–6. 2-MHz crystal schematic

The timing circuit is an oscillator (from the National Semiconductor Data book) followed by a ÷3 made from J-K flip flops (U2). The first section (CKA) of the '390 is a ÷2 to create the clock to the D/A convertor. The second (÷5) section of the '390 drives another ÷3 (U4) to create the CS* signal for the D/A.

Note that there is an extra section of '390 that can be put inline so that a 4MHz crystal could be used. For reasons unknown to me. crystals less than 4MHz are far more expensive than those 4MHz and above. For example, a new 4MHZ crystal can be found in commercial quantities for $0.50, vs. $4.00 for the 2MHz. (I haven't calculated how much extra power this will use, though.)

(Maybe with a few diodes and a resistor, the unused portion of the '390 could be used as a divide by 6—replacing U2 with the first divide by 3, eliminating a chip, and allowing for a 4Mhz crystal. – Dave.)

DAs and Sample & Holds

On another subject, the ADC0831 can be replaced by a Micro Linear component, the ML2280BCP (±½ LSB Error), or ML2280CCP (±1 LSB Error). The Micro Linear part has a built-in Sample & Hold, should be pin-compatible, and is about the same price!

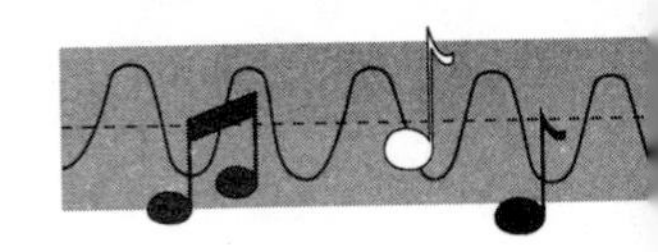

Anti-Aliasing Filters

I ran a SPICE simulation of the input sample filter and found that the rolloff was 30dB/octave, with a 3dB point of about 7kHz. To get < ½ LSB of alias with a 30dB/octave filter for an 8-bit sample, the 3dB point would have to be 1.6 octaves below the Nyquist frequency:

```
(8 Bits = 48dB) ÷ (30dB/octave [on the filter]) = 1.6
octaves
```

With Nyquist at 11000Hz, one octave down would be 5500Hz, and 1.6 octaves down would be about 3437Hz.

The SID filter can provide only about 23dB Signal / Alias at Nyquist.

(Commercial recording devices cheat horribly at getting zero counts at the Nyquist. I didn't want the commercial vendors claiming higher bandwidth than SID, so I also cheated. In a proper design, the 5-pole filter will provide wider bandwidth than the 4-pole filters used by commercial devices. — Dave.)

Appendix B

The Macintosh Sound Enthusiast's Buying Guide

This appendix lists the names, addresses, telephone numbers, and fax numbers (if available) for manufacturers of sound-related hardware and software for the Macintosh. The list is not complete—no such list could be—but it does include the names of most major manufacturers in the Macintosh sound industry. The listing also includes telecommunications companies that have sound-related software available on line, as well as BMUG, the largest and best-known Macintosh user group.

Altech Systems
MIDI Interfaces and MIDI software
122 Faris Industrial Park Drive
Shreveport, LA 71106
318–868–8036
Fax: 318–868–7402

America Online
Telecommunications service; sound software available on line
8619 Westwood Center Drive
Vienna, VA 22182
800–827–6364

Apple Computer, Inc.
Computers and peripherals; sound and music hardware and software
20525 Mariani Avenue
Cupertino, CA 95014–6299
408–996–1010

APDA
Sound and music hardware and software for program developers
Apple Computer, Inc.
20525 Mariani Avenue
Mail Stop 33–G
Cupertino, CA 95014
800–282–2732
Fax: 408–562–3971

Ars Nova Software
Music and MIDI software
Box 637
Kirkland, WA 98083–0637
206–889–0927

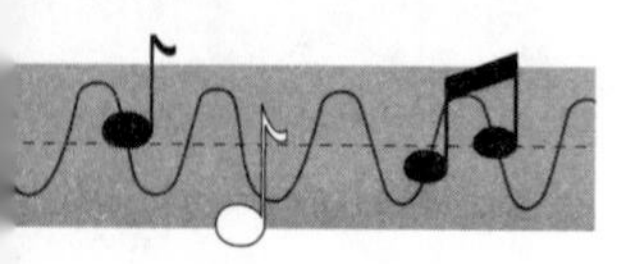

Articulate Systems
Sound-recording and speech-recognition products
600 W. Cummings Park, Suite 4500
Woburn, MA 01801
800–443–7077; 617–935–5656
Fax: 617–935–0490
Tech support: 800–835–0440

Baseline Publishers
Speech synthesis software
5100 Poplar Avenue, Suite 527
Memphis, TN 38137
901–682–9676

BMUG, Inc.
Macintosh user group; sound freeware and shareware available on line and on disk
1442A Walnut Street #62
Berkeley, CA 94709–1496
Business office: 510–549–BMUG
Helpline: 510–540–1742
Bulletin board: 510–849–BMUG
Fax: 510–849–9026

Bogas Productions
Music and MIDI software (Super Studio Session)
520 Heather Way
San Rafael, CA 94903

Sales information: Bill Collins/ Bogas Productions
P.O. Box 6699
Terra Linda, CA 94903–0699
415–332–6427
(415–ED-BOGAS)

Brøderbund Software
Games and software with high-tech sound
P.O. Box 6130
Novato, CA 94948–6130
415–382–4400
Fax: 415–382–4382

Casio
Synthesizers and other electronic musical instruments
15 Gardner Road
Fairfield, NJ 07006
201–361–5400

CD Technology
CD-ROM players, CD-ROM software, and sound software distribution
766 San Aleso Avenue
Sunnyvale, CA 94086
408–752–8500
Fax: 408–752–8501

Claris Corporation
Sound- and music-related software; HyperCard, the Audio Palette
5201 Patrick Henry Drive, Box 58168
Santa Clara, CA 95052–8168
408–987–7000
Tech support: 408–727–9054

Coda Music Software
Musical notation software
1401 East 79th Street
Bloomington, MN 55425–1126
800–843–2066; 612–854–1288
Fax: 612–854–4631

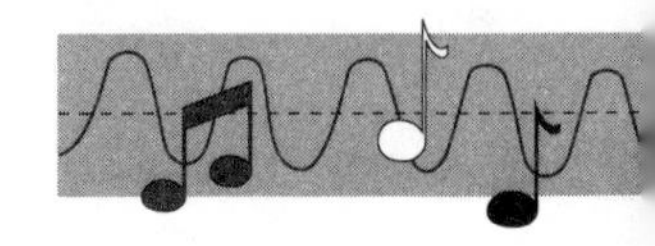

CompuServe
Telecommunications service; software and freeware on line
5000 Arlington Centre Boulevard.
P.O. Box 20212
Columbus, OH 43220
Customer support: 800–848–8990; 614–457–8650

Digidesign, Inc.
Digital sound hardware and software
1360 Willow Road, Suite 101
Menlo Park, CA 94025
800–333–2137; 415–327–8811
Fax: 415–327–0777

Dr. T's Music Software, Inc.
MIDI software
124 Crescent Road, Suite 3
Needham, MA 02194
800–989–6434; 617–455–1454
Fax: 617–455–1460
Tech support: 617–455–1458

Educorp Computer Services
Sound and multimedia software and hardware
7434 Trade Street
San Diego, CA 92121–2410
Orders: 800–843–9497
Information: 619–536–9999
Fax: 619–536–2345

Electronic Arts
Music and MIDI software
1450 Fashion Island Boulevard
Music and MIDI software
San Mateo, CA 94404
800–245–4525; 415–571–7171
Fax: 415–571–7995
Tech support: 415–572–2787

E-mu Systems, Inc.
Synthesizers, samplers, and other MIDI instruments
1600 Green Hills Road
Scotts Valley, CA 05066
408–438–1921

Ensoniq
Synthesizers, samplers, and other electronic musical instruments
155 Great Valley Parkway
Malvern, PA 19355
215–647–3930

First Byte
Talking Moose (speech-synthesis program)
19840 Pioneer Avenue
Torrance, CA 90503
800–545–7677; 310–793–0600
Tech support: 800–524–2983

Freq Sound
Music and MIDI software
5451 Watercress Place
Columbia, MD 21045
410–964–3548

Great Wave Software
Music and MIDI software; games with high-tech sound
5353 Scotts Valley Drive
Scotts Valley, CA 95066
408–438–1990
Fax: 408–438–7171

HyperGlot Software Company, Inc.
Language-learning software
P.O. Box 10746
Knoxville, TN 37939–0746
615–558–8270
Fax: 615–588–6569

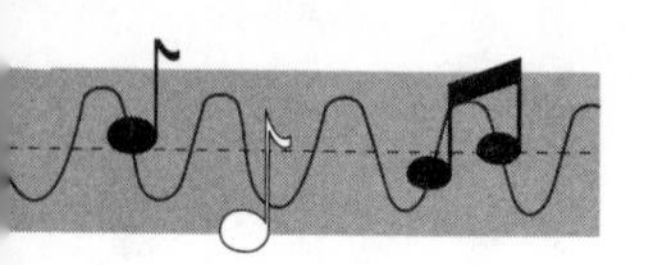

Imaja
Music-instruction software
P.O. Box 6386
Albany, CA 94706
415–526–4621

Kawai America Corporation
Synthesizers and other electronic musical instruments
P.O. Box 9045
Compton, CA 90224
310–631–1771

Korg USA
Synthesizers and other electronic musical instruments
89 Frost Street
Westbury, NY 11590
516–333–9100

Kurzweil Music Systems
Synthesizers and other electronic musical instruments
13336 Alondra Boulevard
Cerritos, CA 90701
213–926–3200

Macromedia, Inc.
Sound-recording and multimedia software and hardware; speech synthesis products
600 Townsend Street, Suite 310W
San Francisco, CA 94103
800–248–4477; 415–442–0200
Fax: 415–442–0190

Mark of the Unicorn, Inc.
MIDI software and hardware
222 Third Street
Cambridge, MA 02142
617–576–2760
Fax: 617–576–3609

MiBAC Music Software, Inc.
Music and instruction software
P.O. Box 468
Northfield, MN 55057
507–645–5851
Fax: 507–645–9291

OpCode Systems, Inc.
MIDI software and hardware
3950 Fabian Way, Suite 100
Palo Alto, CA 94303
415–369–8131
Fax: 415–369–1747
Tech support: 415–369–1676

Passport Designs, Inc.
MIDI software and hardware
100 Stone Pine Road
Half Moon Bay, CA 94019
415–726–0280
Fax: 415–726–2254

Personal Composer
Musical notation software
3213 W. Wheeler Street, Suite 140
Seattle, WA 98199
800–446–8088; 206–236–0105
Fax: 206–284–3898

Praxitel, Inc.
Recording and voice-synthesis software
P.O. Box 452
Pleasanton, CA 94566
510–846–9380
Fax: 510–846–2681

Primera
MIDI Software
650 Cragmont Avenue
Berkeley, CA 94708
415–525–3000

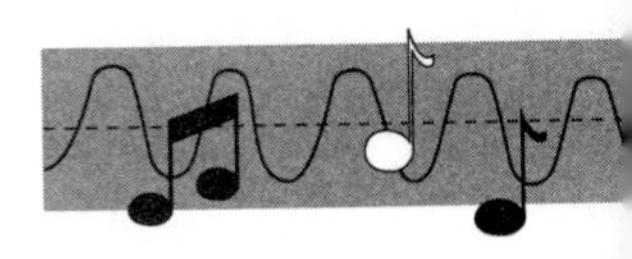

Roland Digital Group
MIDI hardware and software
1961 McGaw Avenue
Irvine, CA 92714
714–975–0560
Fax: 714–975–0569

Sierra On-Line, Inc.
Games and software with high-tech and MIDI sound
P.O. Box 485
Coarsegold, CA 93614-9850
209–683–4468

Sound Source Unlimited, Inc.
Sound software
2985 E. Hillcrest Drive, Suite A
Westlake Village, CA 91360
805–494–9996

The Voyager Company
Software with high-tech music and sound
1351 Pacific Coast Highway
Santa Monica, CA 90401
800–446–2001; 800–443–2001 (CA); 310–451–1383
Fax: 310–394–2156

Warner New Media
Sound software
3500 W. Olive Avenue
Burbank, CA 91505
818–955–9999

Yamaha Corporation of America
Synthesizers and other MIDI and electronic musical instruments
6600 Orangethorpe Avenue
Buena Park, CA 90620
714–522–9011

Appendix C

Freeware and Shareware

This appendix lists and describes freeware and shareware programs that are available from commercial and public bulletin boards, from Macintosh user groups, or from the creators of the programs.

Freeware is just what its name implies: it's free. Shareware costs a few dollars—usually around $10 to $15—and is put into circulation in the hope that people who use it and like it will pay for it. You're on the honor system —you mail your payment to the program's creator, who trusts you. Unless otherwise noted, the programs in this section are shareware.

I have not tried all of the programs listed in this appendix, and I do not guarantee any of them. If you obtain and use any of the listed programs, you do so strictly at your own risk. Some freeware and shareware programs have been around a long time, and some even work about as well as most commercially published programs do. But others have problems.

One reason to be cautious is that some freeware and shareware programs—particularly control-panel applications and system extensions —can interfere with the operation of other programs. Even worse, some freeware and shareware can cause your Macintosh to crash without warning—and that means, of course, that if you're working on any files and haven't saved them, they will be lost. So remember: *free*ware, *share*ware, *be*ware! *Caveat emptor,* too.

AIFF Recorder

AIFF Recorder is an Apple Events–aware utility for recording and playing AIFF or AIFF-C sound files of any length, asynchronously—meaning that you can switch Finder layers and work in another program while the sound plays. Features include support for MACE 3:1–ratio compression support,

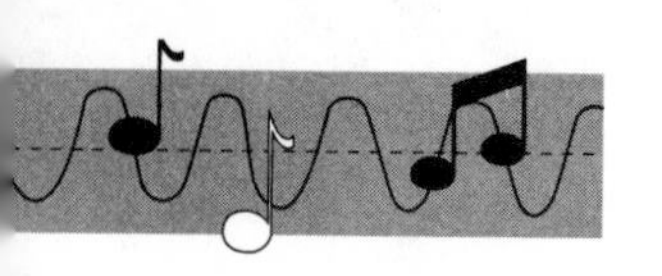

and volume control via arrow keys. It's a small, neat program. You need a recording digitizer, of course, to record sound with AIFF Recorder.

AIFF Recorder records straight to your hard disk in Audio Interchange File Format. There is no memory limitation on a sound's duration. The limit is how much hard disk space you have!

AIFF Recorder is shareware; it costs $20. Contact the author, Kas Thomas, at Box 625, Old Greenwich, CT 06870. AppleLink: THOMAS.KAS. America Online: MIRACLE3.

AIFFStartupSound

AIFFStartupSound is a small system extension that plays an AIFF or AIFF-C file as a startup sound when you start your Macintosh. AIFFStartupSound plays any AIFF sound, compressed or uncompressed, of any size. According to Kas Thomas, the author, AIFFStartupSound doesn't conflict with other system extensions. AIFFStartupSound requires System 6.0.7 or later.

You can download AIFFStartupSound from America Online.

AIFF Toys

Amanda Walker has created two short programs that demonstrate the enhanced Sound Manager's ability to record and play back AIFF files. Files can be played directly from disk, so that sounds no longer have to fit in memory. The programs come with source code, and they're available free from America Online.

AudioData

AudioData, written by Dennis Fleisher, translates MacRecorder or SoundEdit files into numerical data in ASCII format. The converted file can be read by spreadsheets, graphing, and data-analysis programs for audio postprocessing. AudioData may be of use to audio enthusiasts, physicists, engineers, or science teachers. This utility allows you to use the MacRecorder as a general-purpose data-acquisition tool for any transducer that can be connected to the MacRecorder input jack.

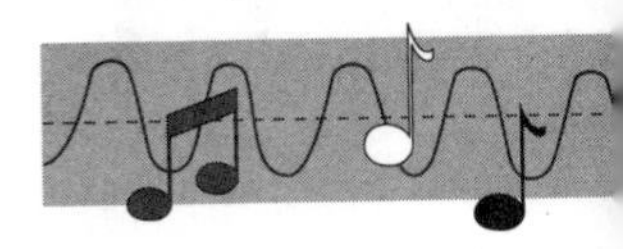

The AudioData package includes the application, instructions, and three sample SoundEdit files for experimentation. You can download it from America Online.

Chime

Chime, by Robert Flickinger, is a popular control panel device that plays sounds in the background on the hour and—if you choose—also on the half hour and on the quarter hour. Chime can also report nautical time by playing ship's bells.

Chime can play up to four user-installed sounds. You can program it to chime like Big Ben, or to toll the hour using any other kind of sounds. It can play its sounds concurrently with other sounds, and it doesn't interfere with other programs that may be running, since it does its work in the background. The current release, version 4.0.2, features support for the PowerBook and Quadra series and a new separate utility that configures the system heap for sounds, simplifying installation.

Chime is free, and you may freely distribute it to your friends; however, the program is copyrighted and you can't sell it or offer it as an incentive for anyone to buy another product. Chime is available from public and commercial bulletin boards, from user groups, or from its author (GEnie: Flick; MCI: RFlickinger; CompuServe: 75156-2563). If all else fails, the author's address is 1957 Laughlin Park Drive, Los Angeles, CA 90027.

Dejal's SndConverter

Dejal's SndConverter, by David Lambert, is an excellent application for converting sounds from one format to another. The program recognizes SoundEdit files and 'snd ' resources, and Sound Mover suitcases. It's System 7-compatible and runs in color on color models of the Macintosh.

Dejal's SndConverter is shareware; it costs $10, and it comes with extensive documentation. You can order the program from Dejal Userware, 12 Scorpio Place, Auckland, New Zealand. You can also download it from CompuServe, America Online, or the Internet (100033.2435@compuserve.com).

Dejal's SndPlayer

Dejal's SndPlayer is a small, System 7-compatible application that allows you to play sounds recorded in many formats. It's a slick shareware application that you can download from CompuServe, the Internet, or America Online. You can also order it from Dejal Userware, 12 Scorpio Place, Auckland, New Zealand.

Echo Chamber

Echo Chamber is an application that algorithmically adds an echo effect to most SoundMaster-type digitized sounds. It lets you select the length and intensity of the echo, so you can simulate any type of echoes. Echoed sounds can be recorded to disk for use with other sound applications. As an extra bonus, you can open the resources in any file, so you can play those mysterious "sound" files that some games use. The program, by Marcio Luis Teixeira, is downloadable from America Online.

ExceptionEdit

Exception Edit is an *exceptions editor*—that is, an application called that lets you create exception files for use with MacinTalk. With an exceptions editor, you can instruct MacinTalk to pronounce specific combinations of letters in specific ways. For example, you can instruct MacinTalk to pronounce the word *HyperCard* correctly each time MacinTalk encounters the word, instead of saying "HipperCard."

Once you place the correct pronunciation of a letter combination in an exceptions file, MacinTalk will pronounce the letter combination in accordance with your instructions, so you don't have to edit the combination manually every time it appears in text. You can also improve MacinTalk's pronunciation by using an exceptions editor. You can download ExceptionEdit from America Online.

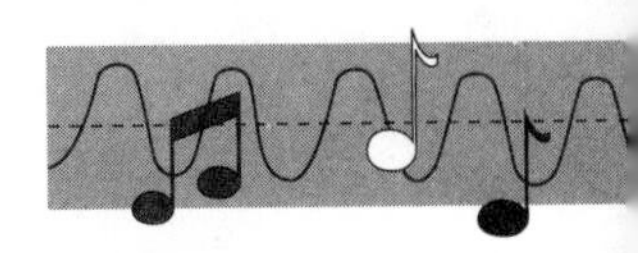

Loudmouth

Loudmouth tells you (literally! it speaks!) the file type of any file that you drag into the Loudmouth icon. Keep an alias of this program on your desktop and drop any file into it, anytime, to hear the type of the file in question. Loudmouth requires System 7.

Loudmouth is available from Kas Thomas, Box 625, Old Greenwich, CT 06870. AppleLink: THOMAS.KAS. America Online: MIRACLE3.

MIDI CD

MIDI CD, written by Jim Nitchals, is an application that plays a 40-minute selection of ten prerecorded songs through any 68020- or 68030-equipped Macintosh, with no extra hardware required. You can download MIDI CD from America Online.

Phil's CD-ROM Audio Player

This no-frills program by Philip Trauring plays audio CDs on a CD-ROM drive. You can play, pause, go to next or previous tracks, and set the track you want to play. This shareware program costs $10 and is available from America Online.

PlayAIFF

PlayAIFF, written by Chris Reed, can play AIFF and AIFF-C files in the background under MultiFinder using some of the new commands in Sound Manager 7.0. Instead of loading a whole sound file into memory, PlayAIFF uses only a small buffer, so huge sounds can be played with no noticeable slowdown of other applications. The program also plays multichannel sounds, and it can open multiple channels of sound at once. As an example AIFF file, HAL saying "I'm sorry Dave, I'm afraid I can't do that" is included.

The PlayAIFF program is available from America Online.

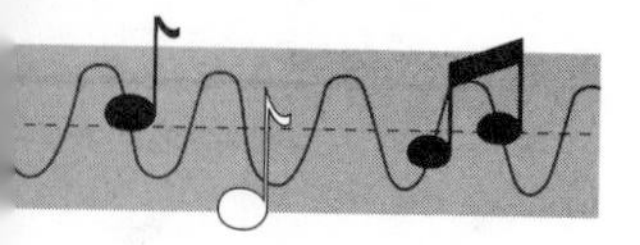

Play All Sounds!

Play All Sounds! is a program that plays all the sounds in all open resource files. Generally, these files include the sounds in your System file, as well as any sound resource files that you have specifically opened with application programs such as SoundWave. Play All Sounds! was written by Adam Stein and can be downloaded from America Online.

Sample Editor

Sample Editor, by Garrick McFarlane, is an update to what many people consider one of the best sound-editing programs available for the Macintosh. With Sample Editor, you can create, play, and edit Audio Interchange (AIFF) files and 'snd ' resources. Figure C–1 shows the Sample Editor screen display.

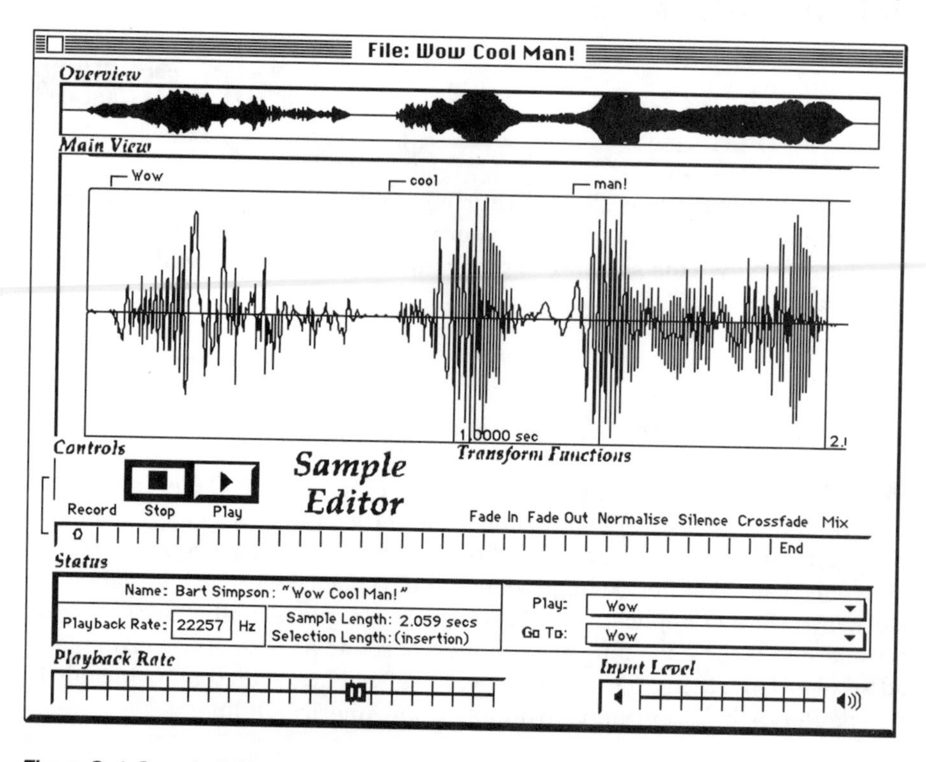

Figure C–1. Sample Editor screen display

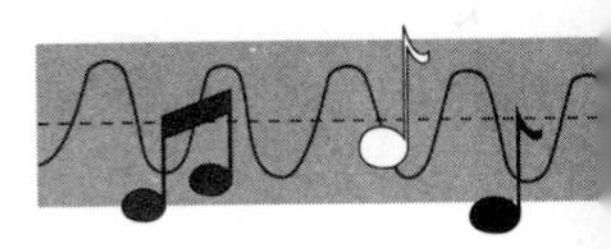

If you have a plug-in microphone or digitizer, you can record your own sounds with Sample Editor. The program displays waveforms of sounds, and you can zoom the display in and out to view waveforms in different levels of detail. You can edit sounds with conventional Macintosh Cut, Copy, Paste, and Clear commands, and you can add special effects such as Fade, Normalise, Crossfade, and Delay.

Sample Editor is freeware; all the author asks is that you send him a note if you like the program. He's at the Department of Computer Science and Applied Mathematics, Aston University, Birmingham, UK. His Internet address is McFarlaneGA@KIRK.ASTON.AC.UK. You can download Sample Editor from the Internet or America Online.

SMP Shareware

SMP Shareware is a compressed file you can find on telecommunications services including CompuServe and America Online. It is a file that contains the Sound Mover application, which is listed under separate headings in this appendix. To obtain Sound Mover, with its instructions, download this package.

SndEditor

SndEditor is a sound-file editor designed for use with ResEdit 2.1.1. To use the editor, you must have a copy of ResEdit and know how to use it. Then you can download the SndEditor file and paste its resources into a copy of ResEdit. Chris Reed wrote SndEditor, and it's available from America Online.

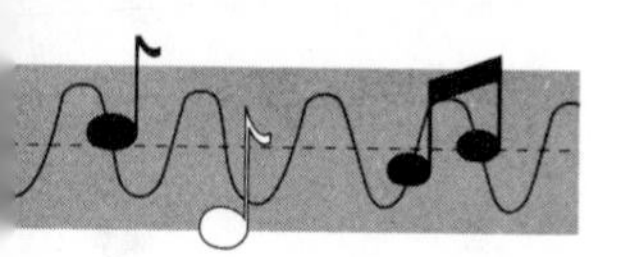

SndPlayer

SndPlayer, according to its author, David Lambert, "lets you quickly and easily listen to sounds stored in several formats." SndPlayer supports SoundEdit, System 7.0 'snd ' files, Sound Mover suitcases, HyperCard stacks, and applications and other files that contain hidden 'snd ' resources.

The program is System 7-compatible, and it has volume control and many other features. It's a $10 shareware application that comes with extensive documentation. The price includes automatic upgrades for five years. SndPlayer is available on America Online.

Sound Converter Utilities

Four programs that can convert sounds to and from various file formats are available from America Online:

- **SCFileConverter:** Converts Sound Cap files to Sound Designer files, and back again.
- **SDFileConverter:** Converts Sound Designer files to Sound Lab files, and back again.
- **SEFileConverter:** Converts SoundEdit files to Sound Designer files, and back again.
- **SSFileConverter:** Converts Studio Session files to Sound Designer files, and back again.

SoundHack

SoundHack, written by Tom Erbe, can translate sound files from one format to another and can manipulate sound files in other ways. Features include a binaural filter, amplitude analysis capability, and a gain change module. SoundHack can read and write sound-file formats including Sound Designer II, AIFF, IRCAM, NeXT, and Sun files. It can also read (but not write), DSP Designer and raw data files. Also, it can now handle 32-bit floating point and (as before) 16-bit linear data encoding.

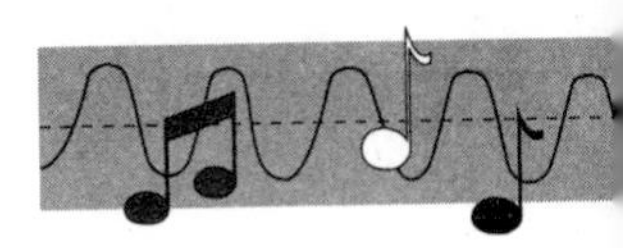

SoundHack requires a Macintosh equipped with an MC68020 processor and a 68881 coprocessor; a 68030 processor and a 68882 coprocessor; or a 68040 processor. At this writing, that means the program requires a Macintosh SE/30; a Macintosh Classic II; a Macintosh II, IIci/cx/ci/fx; or a Macintosh Quadra. SoundHack is available from America Online.

SoundMan

SoundMan, from Tekton Software, is a small application that resembles Sound Mover but has a few different features. SoundMan, like Sound Mover, is patterned after the Apple Font/DA Mover, but it is designed to move sounds. SoundMan is available from America Online.

SoundMaster

SoundMaster, a shareware classic, is a control-panel device written by a well-known Macintosh whiz named Bruce Tomlin. You can program SoundMaster to play any kinds of sounds that you like when your Macintosh performs certain common actions, such as starting up, shutting down, accepting or ejecting a disk, or emptying the trash. Figure C–2 shows the SoundMaster Control Panel.

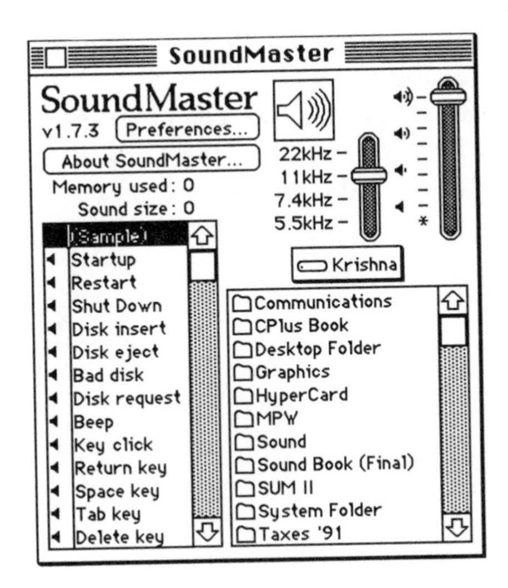

Figure C–2. SoundMaster Control Panel

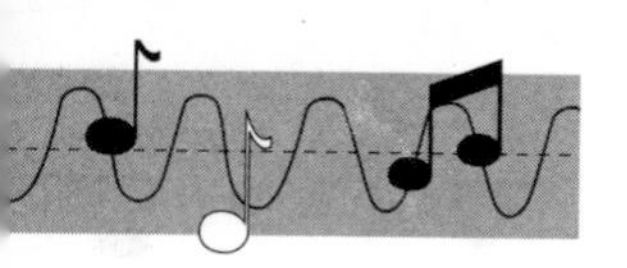

SoundMaster can accompany your computer's actions with sound effects, voice, or music, and the sounds that you select can be as pleasing or as annoying as you like. SoundMaster can even make a sound every time you press a key—and it can make different sounds when you press special keys, such as the Return key, the Space bar, the Delete key, or the Tab key. Also, SoundMaster can toll the passing of the hours by making any kinds of sounds that you choose on the hour and on portions thereof.

SoundMaster is compatible with Sound Cap files, SoundEdit files, and sound resources of type 'sfil' and 'snd '. SoundMaster can also read Sound Mover files that are slightly modified, and modification is easy.

SoundMaster is widely available on public and commercial bulletin boards. You can also download the latest version from the author's personal bulletin board by connecting your Macintosh (with telecommunications software installed, of course) to 512–641–2063. You can also contact the author on America Online: BTomlin.

SoundMaster is a shareware program; if you obtain it, use it, and like it, you are requested to become a registered owner by sending $15 to Bruce Tomlin.

Sound Mover

"Sound Mover is to sounds what Apple's Font/DA Mover is to fonts and desk accessories." Thus spake Riccardo Ettore, the creator of the Sound Mover shareware program. And it's true: Sound Mover is an application with a window that looks and works much like the Apple Font/DA Mover.

With Sound Mover, shown in Figure C–3, you can open any kind of sound that program recognizes, and copy the sound to another file. The program recognizes several resource and sound-file formats, including Format 1 and Format 2 'snd ' resources, and 'FSSD' files and 'DEWF' sound files.

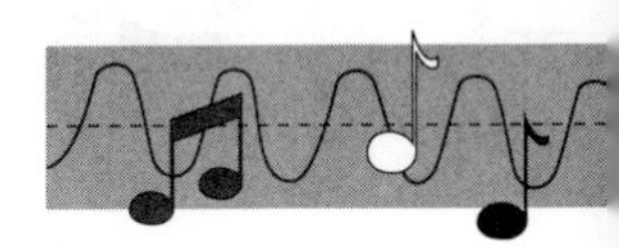

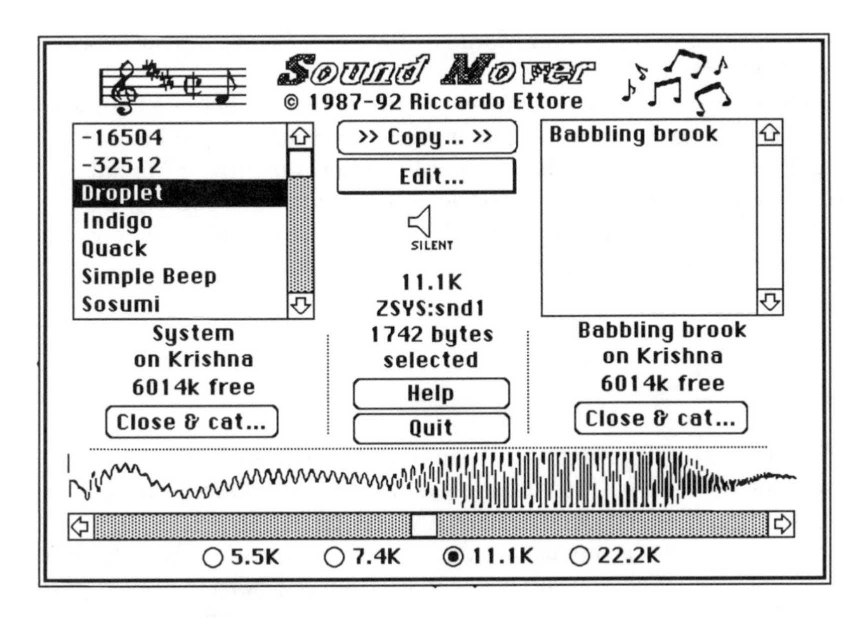

Figure C–3. Sound Mover

When you copy a sound with Sound Mover, the program saves the sound in its new location as a sound *suitcase* file; that is, as a file of type 'SFIL' with a creator ID of 'SMOV'. A sound suitcase is similar to the font and desk accessory suitcases that were used by the Macintosh operating system prior to the introduction of System 7. Sound Mover can place any number of sound resources in a sound suitcase, and it can then place the suitcase in any file. Once a sound has been placed in a suitcase, you can install it as a system sound or copy it to any other destination that recognizes resources, such as a HyperCard stack.

Sound Mover and several other sound-related shareware utilities are bundled together in a collection known as the Sound Manager Package (SMP)—it's only a coincidence that the package has the same name as the Macintosh Toolbox manager called the Sound Manager. Ettore's Sound Manager Package also includes StartupSndInit, which can customize your computer's startup sound; IBeep2, which installs a custom system beep; and SndControl, which can customize the sounds that the Macintosh makes when it performs fifteen common actions.

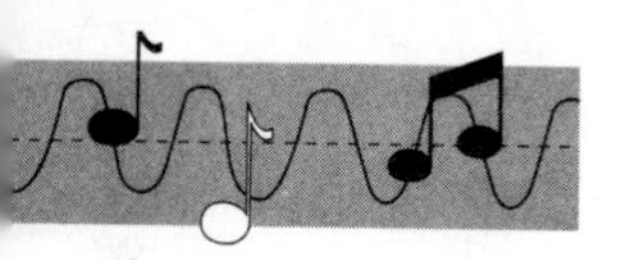

Of the programs in the Sound Manager Package, Sound Mover is far and away the most popular.

The SMP kit costs $25, which you can send to author Richard Ettore in the form of cash, check, money order, or credit-card number and expiration date. You can obtain the kit from public bulletin boards or Macintosh user groups, but you can't get printed documentation until you pay the author. Airmail is recommended, since Ettore's address is 67, rue de la limite, 1970-W Oppem, Belgium.

SpeedBeep

Speed Beep is a utility that lets you keep using your Macintosh while a beep sound (or series of beep sounds) plays. In other words, Speed Beep offers asynchronous sound playing of system beeps.

Also, you can select a group of sounds for your Macintosh to beep from at random (if you wish), and you can cause more than one beep to play at once (if your Macintosh hardware and software support multiple sound playing).

Speed Beep sports an easy-to-use control-panel interface to allow you to change any of the settings.

Speed Beep is shareware; after you use for 15 days, it creates a message asking you to pay $10 for it. When you send the $10, you get a secret code that disables the message. SpeedBeep is downloadable from America Online.

SuperPlay

SuperPlay can play sound files created by SoundCap, and can turn them into resources that you can use in your own programs. The program can also convert resources of type 'ASND' into SoundCap-format files. (An 'ASND' resource has the same format as an uncompressed sound file saved with SoundCap.)

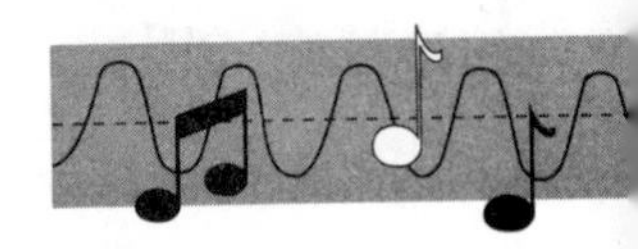

SuperPlay is available on both America Online and CompuServe, or from the author: John Raymonds, 21738 Barbara Street, Torrance, CA 90503.

The Grouch

Place Oscar the Grouch (of "Sesame Street" fame) in your System Folder and reboot. Put something in the trash, and you'll see and hear Oscar gobble up your trash! Great fun!

The Grouch was created by Eric Shapiro of Ann Arbor, Michigan. The program is free, but it is copyrighted and cannot be sold or modified without permission. It is available on public bulletin boards, from Macintosh user groups, or from the author. His address is Rock Ridge Enterprises, 620 Hidden Valley #102, Ann Arbor, MI 48104. His AppleLink address is D1313.

Wallpaper Music

Wallpaper music plays sounds continuously in the background. You can therefore stimulate your ears at given time intervals. "Why is this good?" asks the program's author, Bernhard S. Wieser. "It can break the boredom of your day. You can use it for Macintosh capability demos. Freak out your friends and colleagues. It's up to you."

Specifically, Wallpaper Music lets you play sampled sounds transparently in the background. It consists of two applications. The first is a faceless background task (called the server) that contains a bunch of 'snd ' resources. The second is a simple application (called the client) that can communicate with the background task to configure it.

You can download Wallpaper Music from America Online.

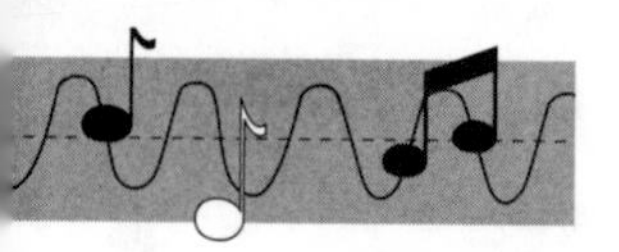

WaveMaker

WaveMaker, by Richard Uhl, is an educational application that lets you create waveforms by combining other waveforms. Specifically, it lets you set the amplitudes of the first seven harmonics to produce a composite waveform. Then you can listen to the results. "In a way," explains the author, "this is additive synthesis with an FM flavor, since you are using sine waves to produce the sound." If you don't know what that means, experiment. You can learn a lot from this program, which you can download from America Online. Figure C–4 shows the Wave Maker screen display.

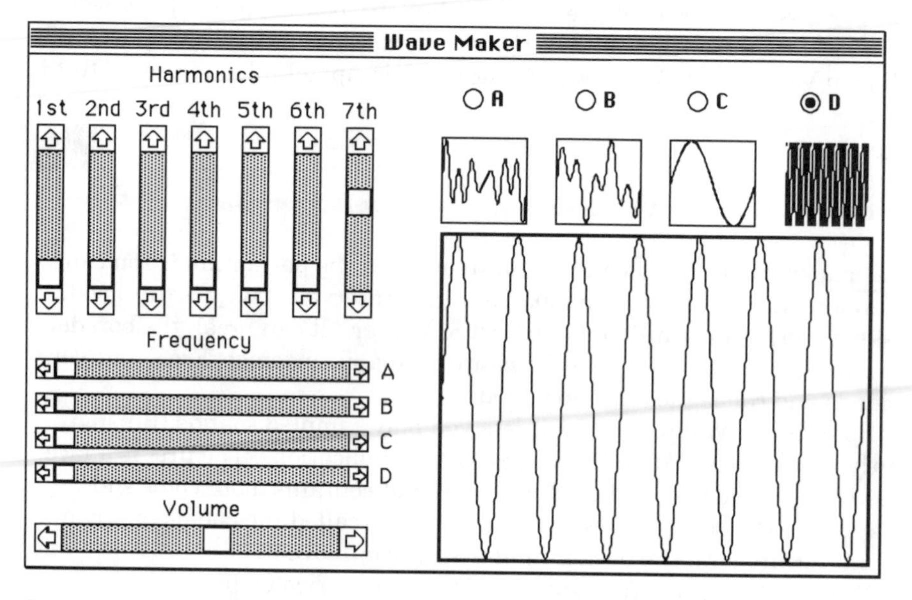

Figure C–4. Wave Maker screen display

Wavicle

Wavicle is a shareware sound editor and recorder that you can download from America Online or from the Internet. It was written by Lee Fyock, whose Internet address is laf@mitre.org.

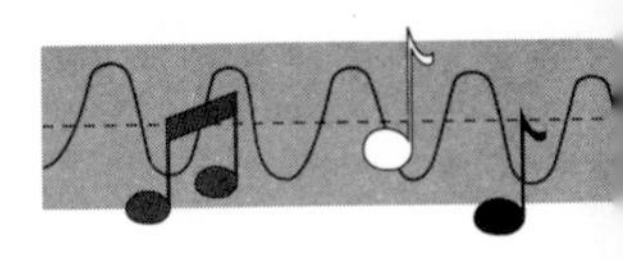

With Wavicle, shown in Figure C–5, you can edit sound files recorded with SoundWave, SoundEdit, SoundEdit Pro, and other applications that can create 'FSSD' format files. Features include reverb, fades, and other special effects. You can cut, copy, and paste sounds using standard Macintosh editing techniques. With Wavicle and a sound digitizer, you can record your own sounds.

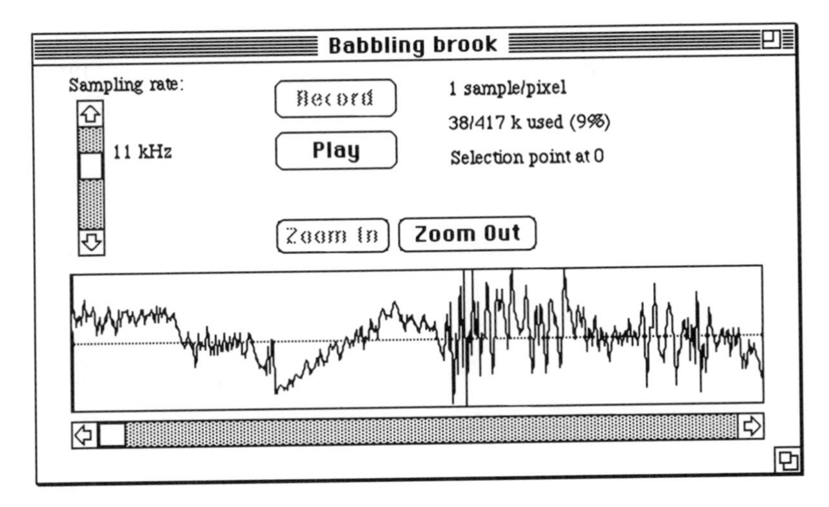

Figure C–5. Wavicle

How Sounds Are Stored in Memory

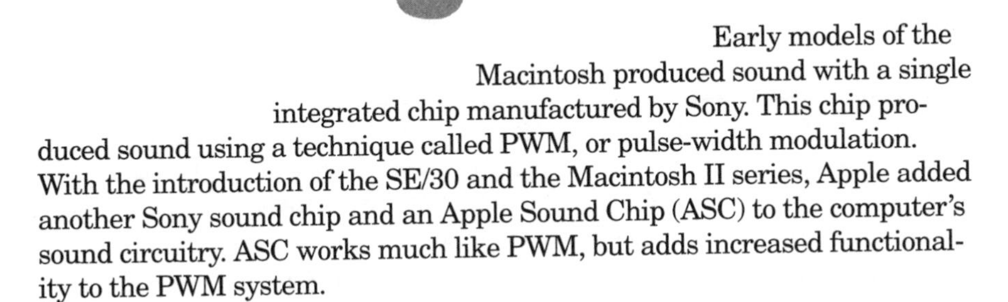

Early models of the Macintosh produced sound with a single integrated chip manufactured by Sony. This chip produced sound using a technique called PWM, or pulse-width modulation. With the introduction of the SE/30 and the Macintosh II series, Apple added another Sony sound chip and an Apple Sound Chip (ASC) to the computer's sound circuitry. ASC works much like PWM, but adds increased functionality to the PWM system.

The PWM Sound System

The PWM sound system uses a technique called pulse-width encoding to create sounds. During each horizontal blanking interval—the period of time when your computer's video screen is not being scanned by an electron beam—the PWM sound circuit reads one 16-bit word in the computer's sound buffer. It uses the high-order byte of the word to generate a pulse of electricity whose duration is proportional to the value in the byte. This pulse is then sent to the Sony sound chip, which produces the waveform needed to generate the sound.

The ASC Sound System

With the premiere of the Macintosh SE/30 and the Macintosh II line, Apple replaced the computer's PWM sound system with the ASC (Apple Sound Chip) system. An ASC circuit is built around three microprocessors: one Apple Sound Chip and two Sony sound chips. The ASC system is compatible with software written for earlier models of the Macintosh, but it also offers stereo sound and other enhancements that are not available in computers that were built during the days of PWM.

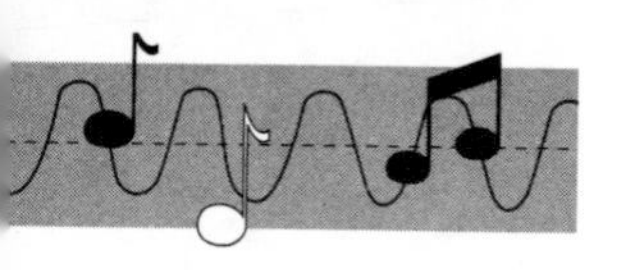

The ASC sound system contains 2K of RAM that can be configured as either two 1K sound buffers or as four 512-byte sound buffers. Because this reserved RAM is available, and because ASC also has special hardware in which sound synthesis can be performed, it requires less processor time than does PWM. Furthermore, ASC—unlike PWM—does not have to be synchronized with the computer's video blanking interval. Thus, it is more efficient in its use of CPU time.

Because of the configuration of its reserved on-board RAM, ASC can operate in any one of four configuration modes, which are summarized in Table D–1.

Table D–1 ASC Configuration Modes

Mode	Configuration
Monophonic single-voice mode	ASC RAM is configured as two 1K buffers. The output of what would otherwise be the left-channel buffer is converted to a PWM signal and is fed to both channels.
Stereophonic single-voice mode	On-board RAM is configured as two 1K buffers. One buffer provides data for a right sound channel, and the other provides data for a left channel. The output of each buffer is converted into a PWM signal. One signal is sent to the left channel of the sound source, and the other signal is sent to the left channel.
Monophonic four-voice synthesis mode	On-board RAM has two 1K buffers. The data stored in these four buffers is synchronized with time periods called sample clock periods. During each sample clock period, a value is read from one buffer. All four values are then summed, and the result is converted to a PWM signal. This signal is then output simultaneously to both channels.
Stereophonic four-voice synthesis mode	As in monophonic four-voice synthesis mode, on-board ASC RAM is configured as four independent 512-byte buffers, and the data in each buffer is synchronized with a sample clock period. During each sample clock period, a value is read from one buffer. These values are then summed in pairs, and the result of each summed pair is converted to a PWM signal. One PWM signal is then output to the right channel, and the other is output to the left channel.

Appendix E

Control Panel Troubleshooting

If your Macintosh displays the wrong kind of Sound Control Panel, or displays an error message when you click on the Add button or try to record a sound, read this appendix before you call for help.

If your computer has a built-in or plug-in recording system, and your Macintosh displays a collapsed Sound Control Panel in a collapsed window rather than an expanded one, these tips may help.

If you have a recording module plugged in, but your Mac displays a collapsed Sound Control Panel instead of an expanded one:

- Check to see if you're running System 6.0.5 or later. If you're running System 7, that's fine.
- Also make sure that a sound driver that's compatible with your sound hardware is installed in your System Folder (or in your Extensions folder, if you're running System 7).
- Check to see that you're using the right kinds of cables, and that they're all plugged in properly.
- If your recording module has a volume control, make sure that the control is not turned all the way off; your recording module may have a volume control that switches off when it is set at its lowest position.

If you have an expanded Sound Control panel, but you get an error message when you click on the Add button or when you attempt to record a sound, try these remedies:

- Make sure that the correct driver icon in the bottom section of your Sound Control Panel is highlighted. If it isn't highlighted, it isn't active.
- Make sure that your System Folder doesn't contain any system extensions, INITs, control panel utilities, or other pieces of software that might interfere with the operation of your sound drivers. Some

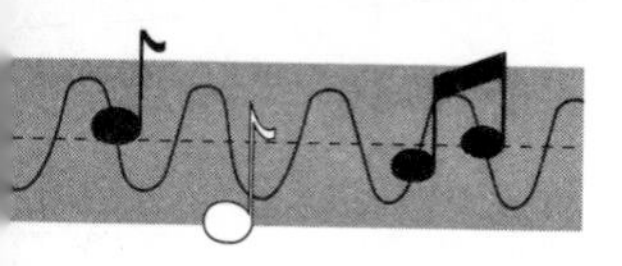

startup utilities, especially freeware or shareware that you get from bulletin boards, can affect the operation of some sound drivers. Virus detectors, in particular, can cause problems. So can some non-Apple CD-ROM drivers.

There are so many kinds of startup utilities that it's difficult to predict which utilities might affect sound drivers. But use only startup utilities that you really need, and always be sure to keep your System Folder as free from potentially dangerous pieces of software as possible.

- If you're using the MacRecorder driver on a Macintosh system equipped with virtual memory, open your Memory Control Panel and turn off virtual memory. Virtual memory interferes with the operation of the MacRecorder driver.

Appendix F

Sound Resources and Sound Files

Since the introduction of the Macintosh in 1984, software developers have created many kinds of sound files. The formats of sound files vary greatly, so software manufacturers and Macintosh fans have created many kinds of sound-conversion programs.

If you do a lot of work with Macintosh sounds—particularly with the libraries of sounds that are available on bulletin boards and from Macintosh user groups—sound-conversion programs can come in handy. Many shareware programs—that is, sound-related programs that are available at little or no cost—are listed in Appendix C. Some of the programs included in Appendix C are sound-conversion programs.

How Sounds Are Stored

When you record a sound on a Macintosh, it is stored in memory as a series of binary numbers. As you learned in Chapters 2 and 3, this series of numbers represents the *waveform* of the sound. When you have recorded the waveform of a sound, you can store it on a disk in a file.

Parts of a Macintosh File

Every Macintosh file is divided into two parts, called *forks*. One of these forks contains only resources and is therefore known as a *resource fork*. The other fork contains data, and is therefore called a *data fork*. You can store sound data in either the resource fork or the data fork of a file. Figure F–1 shows the resource fork and the data fork of a Macintosh file.

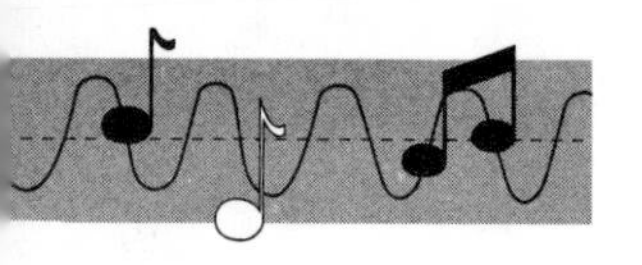

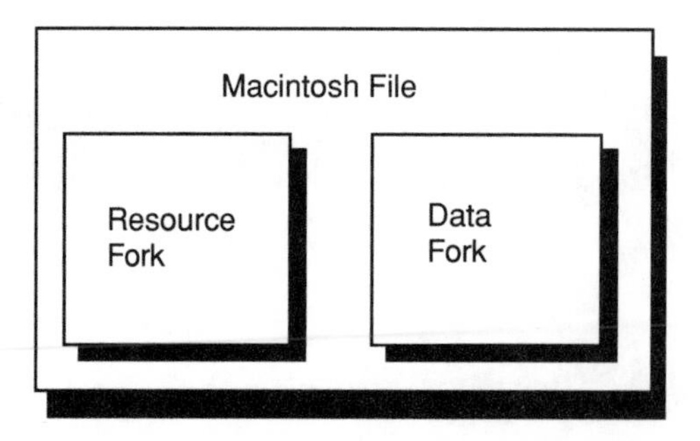

Figure F–1. The two parts of a Macintosh file

Resources, as noted in Chapter 3, are blocks of information that are stored in a special way inside Macintosh files. You could say that a resource is a piece of a file that is important to the Macintosh programmer but is ordinarily invisible to the Macintosh user.

Although the typical Macintosh user knows little, if anything, about resources, almost every Macintosh application contains a large number of resources. For example, most commercial Macintosh programs create their dialog boxes, icons, and text strings from information that is stored in the form of resources. Files that are not applications—for example, files in which sounds are stored—can also contain resources.

A text file—the kind of file that a text editor or word processor creates —often has a data fork that's packed with information, but an empty resource fork. Similarly, a file that contains only a sound might have the information needed to reproduce the sound stored in its data fork, but nothing at all in its resource fork. Alternatively, a file may have sound data stored in its resource fork, but nothing stored in its data fork.

Types of Sounds

If a file has sound information stored in its data fork, the file is called a *sound file.* If a file of any type has sound data stored in its resource fork, the sound that's stored in the resource fork is called a *sound resource.*

It's important to note that a sound resource can be stored in any kind of file—not just in a sound file. For example, a HyperCard stack is a type of file, and sound resources are often stored in HyperCord stacks.

It's also important to remember that a sound file does not always have an empty resource fork. Some sound files have sound data stored in their data forks, but have other kinds of sound-related information stored in their resource forks. For example, when you create a sound file with the SoundWave, the sound's waveform is stored in the file's data fork. However,

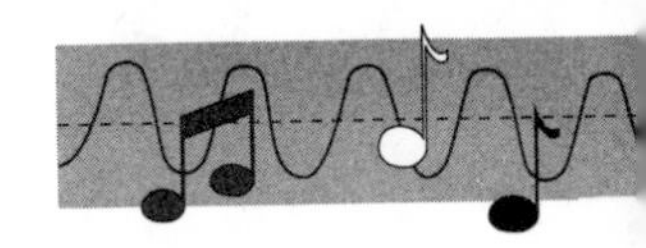

SoundWave also stores essential information about the sound—including the sound's length, the sampling rate at which it was recorded, and any compression data that may be needed to play the sound—in the sound file's resource fork.

Figure F-2 shows how sound data and information about a sound are stored in a data file.

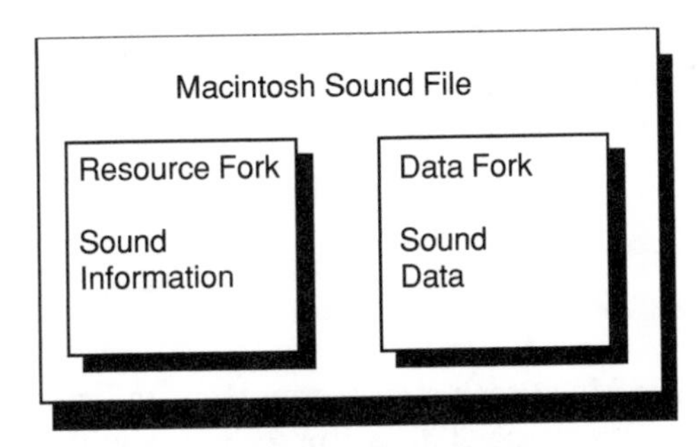

Figure F–2. A Macintosh sound file

(Apple encourages software developers to use resources wherever possible in Macintosh applications because resources can be easily moved from one application to another, and—when they contain text—can be easily translated into different languages.)

The two main sound formats—sound resources and sound files—have their individual advantages and disadvantages. Sound resources use memory efficiently and can be used in HyperCard stacks. Also, *applications* can manipulate sound resources quite easily. But sound files are easier for Macintosh *users* to manipulate, since only one sound is ordinarily stored in a sound file, and the Macintosh operating system treats a sound file like any other kind of file.

Sound files give you more control over sounds than sound resources in other ways, too. For example, if you have a collection of sounds stored as sound files, you can divide your collection into categories that you can then store in separate folders. You could divide a collection of sound files into libraries of musical sounds, libraries of sounds from movies, and so on. That would be difficult to do with a collection of sounds stored as resources. Another advantage of sound files over sound resources is that sound files are generally more suitable than resources for storing very long sounds.

When you record a sound using a HyperCard program—such as the HyperCorder sound-processing program introduced in Chapter 5—the sound winds up stored as a resource in a HyperCard stack. From that point on, if you want to play the sound, you must start up HyperCard and play the sound in the HyperCard environment.

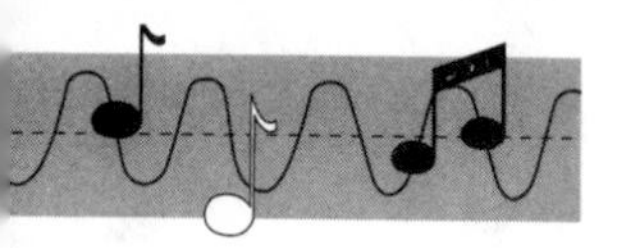

In comparison, most sound-processing programs—such as the SoundWave program introduced in Chapter 4—store sounds as sound files—the data fork contains sound data. When you store a sound on a disk as a sound file, you can play the sound using any sound-processing program that recognizes the kind of file in which the sound is stored. For example, SoundWave can play sounds that were created by the SoundEdit program published by Macromedia. (Fortunately, SoundWave can convert sound resources to sound files, and HyperCorder can convert sound files to sound resources. So the two formats are not completely incompatible. However, SoundWave and HyperCorder can't directly read each other's sound file formats.)

Sound Files

When an application creates a file. the Macintosh stores important information about the file in a *file header.* One piece of data stored in every file header is a four-letter designator called a *file type.* When you open a file, your computer uses the information stored in the file's header to determine several essential facts about the file. For example, the file header tells the Macintosh operating system whether the file is an application, how long the file is, how it should be printed, and how it should be displayed on the screen.

An important piece of information called a *file type designator* is stored in every file header. A file type designator is a series of four characters enclosed in single quotation marks. A file type designator is a very brief description of the contents and format of a file. For example, an application is a file of type 'APPL', a text document is a file of type 'TEXT', and a SoundWave sound file is a file of type 'FSSD'.

When the Macintosh loads a file, the file type designator tells the Macintosh what kind of file has been loaded and what program created the file. The file type designator also tells the Finder what kind of icon to display for the file on the Macintosh desktop.

Creators of Files

Besides a file type designator, every Macintosh file header also contains a *creator ID*—a four-letter designator that tells who created the file. For example, if you examine the header of a SoundWave file, you'll see that the creator is identified as 'JOSH'. I don't know who Josh is, but he has his place in history; he is identified as the creator of every SoundWave file.

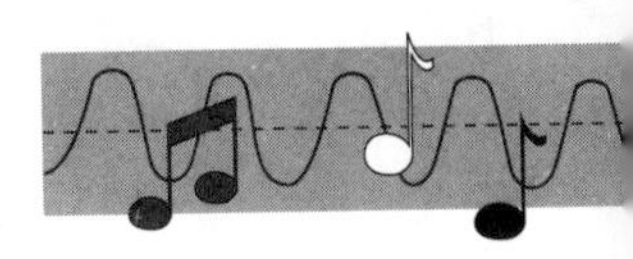

Since every file header contains both a file type designator and a creator ID, some software manufacturers use the creator fields of file headers to specify subtle differences in files of the same type. For example, at least three different kinds of files have the file type 'FSSD', but you can tell those varieties apart by examining their creator IDs. That's because the three varieties of 'FSSD' files have different creator IDs. For example, a SoundWave file is an 'FSSD' file with the creator ID 'JOSH', while a SoundEdit file is an 'FSSD' file with the creator ID 'SFX!'

Accessing File Headers

You can examine the file type designator of any file by opening the file with ResEdit and then choosing the Get Information command from the File menu. You can also read file headers by launching MPW (the Macintosh Programmer's Workshop) and executing the Files command with the –l option. For more information on the Macintosh Programmer's Workshop, see Apple's MPW documentation and *Programmer's Guide to MPW,* Volumes I and II, published by Addison-Wesley.

Apple maintains a registry of file types, and when a software developer creates a new file type, the developer is supposed to register the file type with Apple. That way, Apple can keep track of all existing file types, and software publishers can write programs capable of reading other publishers' files.

Figure F–3 shows the icons of some of the most widely used types of sound files.

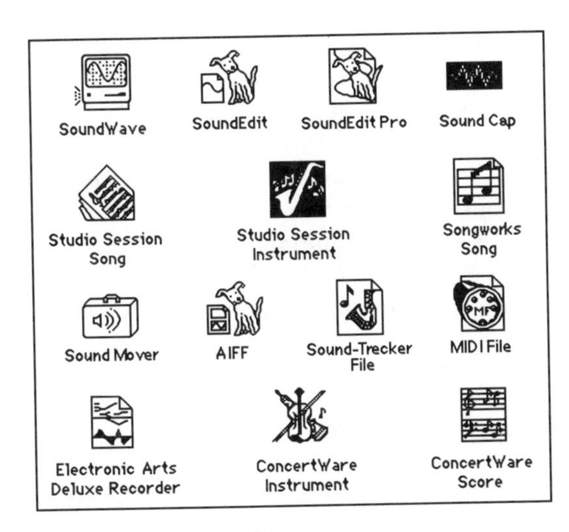

Figure F–3. Types of sound files

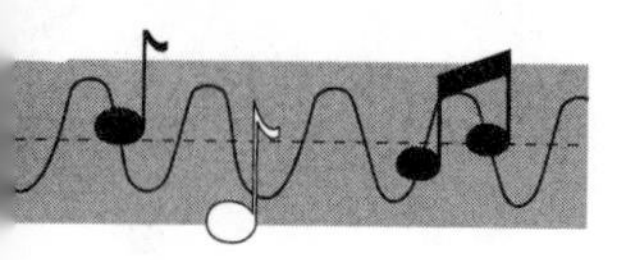

Resource Designators

Just as there are many kinds of Macintosh files, there are many kinds of Macintosh resources. So resources, like files, have designators. Each time a new kind of resource is created, it is assigned a resource type. A resource type is always a four-letter abbreviation (or three letters followed by a space), enclosed in single quotation marks.

To prevent duplications in the file types assigned to resources, Apple maintains a registry of resource types. Each time a software developer creates a new resource type, the developer is requested to register the new resource type with Apple. That way, Apple can keep track of the many kinds of resources that are used in Macintosh applications, and duplications in resource type designators can be avoided.

In a resource type designator, the use of uppercase or lowercase letters is significant. For example, when early versions of the SoundWave program recorded a sound, the program stored information about the sound in a short (8-byte) resource of type 'info'. Later, when SoundWave was upgraded to support the compression of sounds, a longer (64-byte) resource of type 'INFO' was created so that compression information could also be stored in the sound file.

Today, some of the SoundWave files available on bulletin boards and from Macintosh user groups contain 8-byte resources of type 'info', while others contain 64-byte resources of type 'INFO'.

The SoundWave program that is provided on your bonus disk and covered in Chapter 4 can read both kinds of SoundWave files. When SoundWave saves a file, it stores the file in the modern format—the format that includes an 'INFO' resource. If the file originally contained an older 'info' resource, that resource remains part of the file.

To obtain the type designator of a resource, all you have to do is open the sound file containing the resource using ResEdit, a utility that is available from APDA. When you open a file using ResEdit, ResEdit displays a window that contains an icon for each resource in the file. Under each icon, there is a three-letter or four-letter word or abbreviation. Each such word or abbreviation is a resource type designator.

You can also obtain information about resource types by launching MPW (the Macintosh Programmer's Workshop) and executing the DeRez command.

Varieties of Macintosh Sound Files

There are many kinds of Macintosh sound files, but some are used more than others. Some of the varieties of sound files that Macintosh users most often encounter are described under the headings that follow.

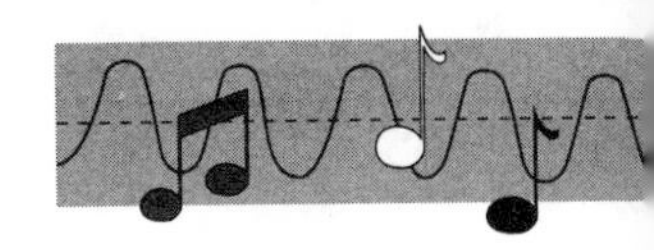

SoundWave Files

A SoundWave file, as mentioned earlier in this section, has a file type designator of 'FSSD' and a creator ID of 'JOSH'. A SoundWave file contains a data fork in which waveform information about a sound is stored. Unlike a Sound Cap file, however, a SoundWave file also contains a resource fork that contains important information about the sound, such as its length and its sampling rate.

SoundEdit Files

The SoundEdit program, now marketed by Macromedia, creates sound files with an 'FSSD' type designator—the same designator used by SoundWave and Sound Cap files. However, SoundEdit files have a unique creator ID: 'SFX!'.

A SoundEdit file, like a modern SoundWave file, has both a data fork and a resource fork. The waveform of a sound is stored in the file's data fork, and important information about the sound is stored in the file's resource fork. There is a difference, however, between the resource fork of a SoundWave file and the resource fork of a SoundEdit file. A SoundEdit file, unlike a SoundWave file, has a resource fork that contains several kinds of resources.

Although a SoundEdit file contains more resource information than a SoundWave file, the SoundWave program that's on your bonus disk can read, edit, and save sound files that are stored in the SoundEdit format, and it can save SoundEdit files in the SoundWave format. You can also play, edit, and store SoundEdit files with the HyperCorder program that's on your bonus disk. That's fortunate, since the SoundEdit format is the most popular format for storing 8-bit Macintosh sounds.

SoundEdit Pro Files

Early in 1992, MacroMind Paracomp (now Macromedia) introduced a new sound-editing software package called SoundEdit Pro and a new sound-file format called the SoundEdit Pro format. The SoundEdit Pro format is an extension of the original SoundEdit format, but it has a different file type designator. A SoundEdit Pro file has the file type designator 'jB1 ' and the creator ID 'jBox'.

The SoundEdit Pro file format supports multitrack recording using either 8-bit or 16-bit sound samples, and sampling rates of up to 48kHz. In a SoundEdit Pro file, waveform information is stored in a data fork. In the file's resource fork, information about the sound in the data fork is stored in resources of eight different resource types: 'CLRS', 'INFO', 'LABS', 'REPT',

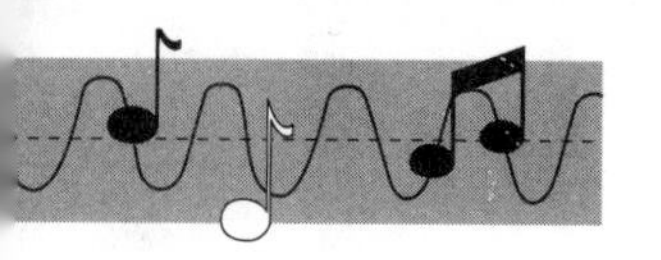

'CUES', 'PReS', 'PRnt', and 'TRKS'. More information about these resource types is provided in the documentation that comes with SoundEdit Pro.

The SoundWave and HyperCorder programs that are on this book's bonus disk can be used to play, edit, and save sounds that are recorded in the SoundEdit Pro format, provided they have a word length of 8 bits and are recorded at sampling rates of 22kHz or less.

Studio Session and Super Studio Session Files

If you've ever searched through the libraries of sounds that are available from computer user groups and bulletin boards, you've probably come across many Studio Session sound files.

There are two kinds of Studio Session files: instrument files and song files. A Studio Session instrument file is a sampled sound of an instrument playing a single note. When you play a Studio Session instrument file, you can play it at any pitch and for any duration you choose.

The file designator of a Studio Session instrument file is 'DEWF'. The creator ID of most Studio Session files is 'FSSC', but you can't depend on that; many Studio Session files have creator IDs that were assigned by different creators.

A Studio Session song file has a file type of 'XSNG', and usually has the creator ID 'XPRT'. However, individual creators also claim the creator fields of many Studio Session song files.

A Studio Session song file is a series of Studio Session instrument files, played at different pitches and strung together to form a musical score, or song. You can create Studio Session files with the Studio Session program published by Bogas Productions—now available in a new and improved version called Super Studio Session.

Super Studio Session creates and plays the same kinds of files as Studio Session. A Studio Session song file is a file of type 'XSNG'. Studio Session instrument files have file type 'DEWF'.

By storing a series of notes in a Studio Session instrument file, and then playing the notes back as a song file, you can produce music in a very memory-efficient manner. And music created with Super Studio Session sounds great, even on the small speaker that's built into the Macintosh.

Many programs, including the SoundWave program introduced in Chapter 4, can play Studio Session instrument sounds at various pitches. Several freeware and shareware programs can also play Studio Session song files. But to create, record, and play back professional-sounding Studio Session songs, you must own the Studio Session or Super Studio Session program.

Super Studio Session has an editor that lets you compose musical scores on your Macintosh screen, and a Jukebox utility that can play

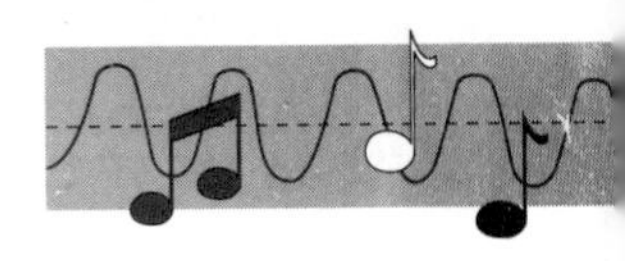

collections of songs in any sequence. With Super Studio Session, you can play hundreds of prerecorded songs and scores, and you can create your own arrangements and your own musical compositions. The Super Studio Session program is examined in more detail in Chapter 7.

Using Studio Session Files A Studio Session file, like a Sound Cap file, stores waveform information in a data fork and has an empty resource fork. Despite this similarity, Studio Session files and Sound Cap files are not compatible; the encoding systems that they use for representing sounds are different.

The SoundWave program on this book's bonus disk can play Studio Session instrument files at various pitches, and it can convert Studio Session instrument files to the SoundWave format. However, SoundWave can't read Studio Session song files, and it doesn't provide any tools for using SoundWave instrument files very effectively. You can cut, edit, and paste Studio Session instrument files using SoundWave, but the work is tedious and the results are not guaranteed.

The HyperCorder program introduced in Chapter 5 is not compatible with Studio Session instrument or song files.

Sound Cap Files

Many collections of sounds that are available on public bulletin boards and from user groups contain sound files known as Sound Cap files. A Sound Cap file is a file of type 'FSSD', with a creator ID of 'FSSC'.

Sound Cap files were originally created by an early sound-processing program called Sound Cap. The Sound Cap program is now out of print, but many sound libraries available on bulletin boards and from Macintosh user groups still contain sounds that were recorded in the Sound Cap format. In Figure F–3, the rightmost icon in the top row is the icon of a Sound Cap file.

Although you can't buy the Sound Cap application any more, newer sound-processing programs—such as the SoundWave program introduced in Chapter 4—can play sounds that were recorded in the Sound Cap format.

Every Sound Cap file has a data fork in which the waveform of a sound is stored. Furthermore, Sound Cap files store waveform information in their data forks in exactly the same format that is used by SoundWave. That's why Sound Cap files and SoundWave files can both use the 'FSSD' file type designator.

However, there is one important difference between a SoundWave file and a Sound Cap file: A SoundWave file has both a data fork and a resource fork. When you record a program with SoundWave, the sound's waveform is stored in the file's data fork, and important characteristics of

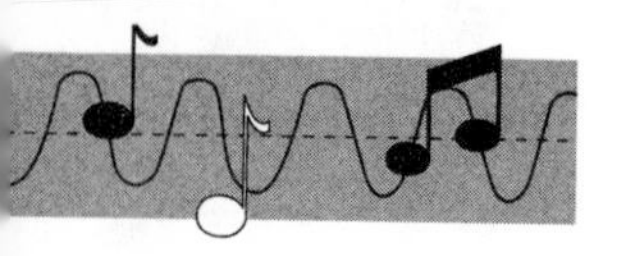

the sound—such as its length and its sampling rate—are stored in the file's resource fork. A Sound Cap file, in contrast, has a data fork but no resource fork (more accurately, a Sound Cap file has an empty resource fork). That means a Sound Cap file has no place to store important information about a sound, such as its length or its sampling rate.

The only way to determine the sampling rate of a Sound Cap sound is by trial and error. Simply listen to the sound using a sound-editing program such as SoundWave, and then adjust the sampling rate until it sounds right. (Usually, the correct sampling rate for a Sound Cap sound is either 11kHz or 22kHz, and that makes the process simpler.) For more information about sampling rates, refer to Chapter 4.

AIFF and AIFF-C Files

The AIFF, or Audio Interchange File Format, is a file type that Apple created so that software publishers could start using universally compatible sound files.

The AIFF-C file type, also created by Apple, is compatible with the AIFF file type but can be used to store compressed sounds. Also, the AIFF-C format can be extended to handle new compression techniques and new application-specific data as needed. For this reason, Apple now encourages software developers to update any applications that currently support only AIFF files so that the applications can also support AIFF-C files. An AIFF file is a file of type 'AIFF'. An AIFF-C file has the type designator 'AIFC'.

Since software publishers are an independent lot and have developed proprietary file formats that they like to stick with, this idea has not yet achieved as much popularity as Apple would like. However, most sound-related programs can now read files that are stored in the AIFF-C format, and multimedia programs that make use of the AIFF-C format are slowly becoming more popular.

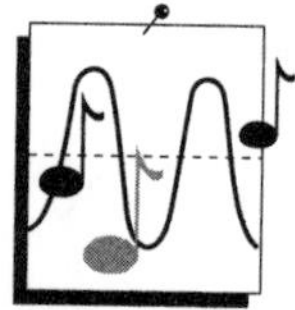

TECH TALK

Playing Sound Files

If a sound is stored as a file of type AIFF or type AIFF-C, the Sound Manager can play it by calling the Sound Manager function SndStartFilePlay. ❍

System 7 Sound Files

Macintosh system alert sounds are normally stored as sound resources. However, the System 7 Finder can copy any system alert sound from the System file into a special kind of sound file called a System 7 sound file. A System 7 sound file contains just one sound. When you have created a System 7 sound file, you can move the file from one folder to another in the same way that you would move any other file. To learn how to copy

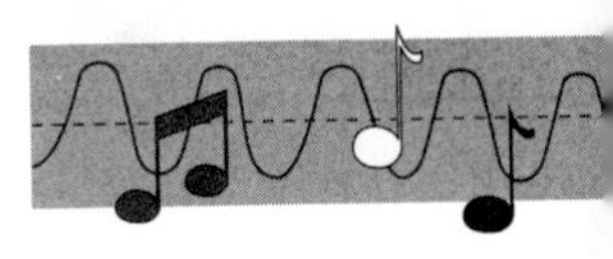

system alert files into sound files, see the section "Moving Sound Resources," later in this appendix.

A System 7 sound file is a file of type 'sfil'. Figure F–4 shows the icons for a sound resource and a System 7 sound file, and the icon for the ResEdit utility.

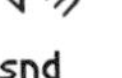

Sound resource icon **System 7 sound file icon** **ResEdit icon**

Figure F–4. Sound resource, System 7 sound file, and ResEdit icons

If you're running System 7, you can copy or move the Quack alert sound from your System file to a System 7 sound file in another folder. Follow these steps:

1. If you want to move the sound out of the System Folder, quit any programs that are running. If you want to make a copy of the sound but leave the original sound in the System Folder, you don't have to quit any applications.
2. Open the System Folder.
3. Double-click on the System file. The Finder then displays the names of the fonts and sounds in the System file.
4. Find the folder that holds the files you have copied from your bonus disk. Open that folder and find another folder labeled Music and Sounds. Open the Music and Sounds folder.
5. Using the mouse, select the icon in the system file that is labeled Quack. Then drag the Quack icon into the Music and Sounds folder while you hold down the Option key. (If you don't hold down the Option key, the Finder removes the sound from the System Folder and moves it to its new location.)
6. When you move a sound from the System Folder to another folder, the sound starts off as a resource but winds up as a file.

When you have moved the Quack sound resource in your System file to a file named Quack in the Sounds and Music folder, double-click on the new Quack file's icon. I won't tell you what kind of sound you will hear, but it should sound something like a duck.

If the destination folder contains an application that can access sounds stored in resource files, then that application can use the sound that you

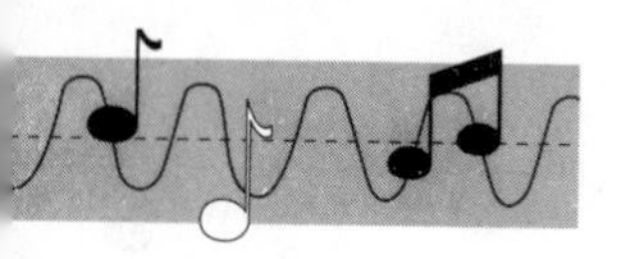

have moved or copied. One application that can play sound resources stored in resource files is SoundApp, which is on your bonus disk and is introduced in Chapter 3.

Other Kinds of Sound Files

Besides the file types described so far in this section, you may run across several other kinds of sound files. Table F–1 lists some of the most often used types of sound files.

Table F–1 Types of Sound Files

Type	Function
'Midi'	Stores MIDI (Musical Instrument Digital Interface) files, created by keyboard synthesizers and other kinds of musical instruments (see Chapter 9)
'CWIF'	Stores sounds created by the ConcertWare and ConcertWare+ music programs
'CWMF'	Stores ConcertWare and ConcertWare+ scores
'MUS '	Stores sounds created by the MusicWorks program
'SFIL'	Stores sound files created by the Sound Designer and Sound Mover programs; 'SFIL' sound files created by Sound Designer have a creator ID of 'XFER', and 'SFIL' sound files created by the Sound Mover program—sometimes referred to as sound file "suitcases"—have a creator ID of 'SMOV' (Sound Mover is a shareware program described in Appendix C)
'WAVE'	Stores sound files created by the Sound Lab program
'SEGM'	Stores sound files created by the Deluxe Recorder program from Electronic Arts

Sound Resources

As noted at the beginning of this appendix, Macintosh sounds can be stored as either sound resources or sound files. Most sound-recording and sound-editing programs store sounds in stand-alone files. But other kinds of sounds—such as the Macintosh system sounds and sounds in HyperCard stacks—are conventionally stored as sound resources.

Sound resources are ordinarily hidden inside other files, but you can create files that contain only sound resources. For example, the two icons in Figure F–5 represent files that contain only sound resources. The file labeled Sound Resources was created with ResEdit. The file labeled Quack was copied from the System Folder using the System 7 Finder. Techniques

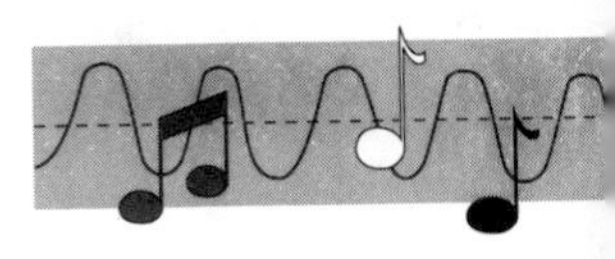

for moving sounds are described later in this appendix, under the heading "Moving Sound Resources."

Figure F–5. Files containing sound resources

Format 1 and Format 2 Sound Resources

There are several kinds of sound resources, but the only resources that are currently in widespread use are resources with the type designator 'snd '. Resources of type 'snd ' are compatible with the current version of the Macintosh Sound Manager, and all other types of sound resources are being phased out.

Resources of the 'snd ' type can be stored in two different formats, known (logically enough) as Format 1 and Format 2.

Format 2 resources were designed to be used with the original version of HyperCard. A Format 2 resource supports only one of the three built-in Macintosh synthesizers: the sampled sound synthesizer. Format 2 resources can contain sounds that are compressed with the MACE compression tool sold by APDA. However, they do not support multichannel sound.

A Format 1 resource is a new kind of resource that can support all three Macintosh synthesizers, and can handle compressed and multichannel sounds.

Because of their built-in limitations, Format 2 sound resources are now obsolete; current versions of HyperCard (version 2 and later) are now compatible with both Format 1 and Format 2 resources, and so are most modern sound-related applications, including the SoundWave and HyperCorder programs that are provided on the bonus disk that comes with this book.

Apple now encourages software developers to use only Format 1 resources when they develop applications, and to forget Format 2 resources.

Sound Resource Headers

In an 'snd ' resource, information about the sound is stored in a structure called a *header*. Usually, waveform information that represents the sound is stored immediately following the resource's header. (There is a technique that program designers can use to store information about a sound in a

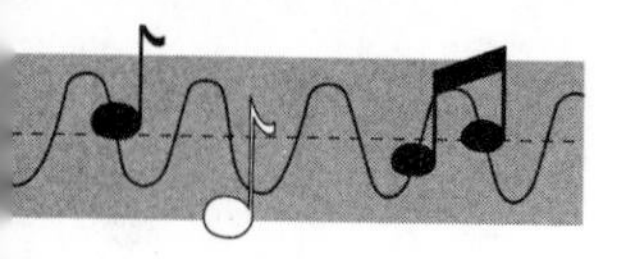

header, and to store the sound itself in a separate file. To date, however, most software developers have not taken advantage of this technique.)

The sound header that appears at the beginning of an 'snd ' resource can contain a large amount of information about the sound, such as the sound's sampling rate (the number of intervals per second used to represent the sound in memory), the length of the sample, and various kinds of information regarding compression. (For more about sampling rates and compression, see Chapter 4.)

An 'snd ' header also contains information telling where the data representing a sound is to be found; that is, whether the data is stored in the resource itself, or whether it is stored in a separate file.

There are three kinds of headers that an 'snd ' resource can use: a *standard sound header* (used for monophonic sounds), an *extended sound header* (used for stereo and 16-bit sounds), and a *compressed sound header* (used for compressed sounds, whether monophonic or stereo).

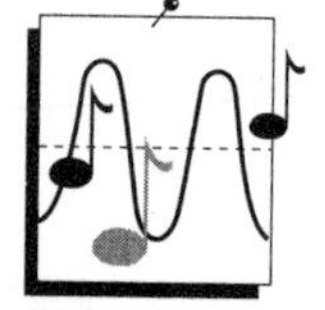

TECH TALK

Playing Sound Resources

If a sound is stored as a resource, an application can play it by passing the handle of a sound resource (a resource of type 'snd ') containing a sound header to the Sound Manager function SndPlay. ❍

Moving Sound Resources

Sometimes it is useful to move a sound resource from one file to another. If you have a sound that an application uses, and you would like to make that sound your alert sound, you can move it into your System file. Then you can open the Sound Control Panel and select the sound that you have moved as your alert sound. You can move sounds from your System file into the trash, or move alert files to other locations so that you can use them with applications or with HyperCard stacks.

There are several ways to move sound resources from file to file. Some applications—such as the SoundWave program and the HyperCorder program on this book's bonus disk—have sound-moving capabilities built in. One shareware program, Sound Mover (described in Appendix C), is specifically designed to move sound files and sound resources.

The ResEdit utility, available from APDA, can move sounds that are stored as resources. You can also do a limited amount of sound moving with the Finder.

One application that is often used to manipulate resources is ResEdit, which you can obtain from APDA. There are also many applications that you can use to record, load, save, and edit sounds that are stored as

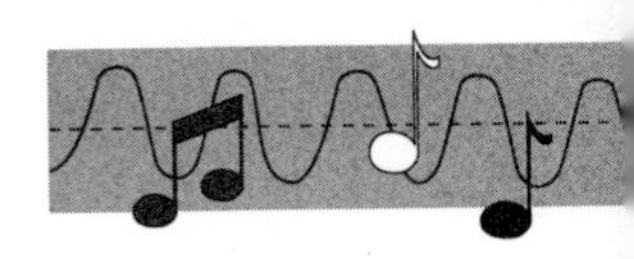

resources. (ResEdit is described in great detail in the Addison-Wesley book *ResEdit Complete,* which is listed in the Bibliography.)

ResEdit is a general-purpose resource-editing program; you can use it to edit all kinds of resources, including sound resources. However, some programs include special-purpose utilities that are specially designed to provide you with some control over sound resources. For example, you can record, load, and save sound resources with the Macintosh Sound Control Panel described in Chapter 1. And with the SoundWave and HyperCorder programs introduced in Chapters 4 and 5, you can record, edit, and save sound resources.

Moving Sounds with ResEdit

To move a sound resource with ResEdit, simply open the file that contains the sound, open the file that you want to copy the sound into, and then copy the sound using standard Macintosh copy and paste techniques.

Moving Sounds with the Finder under System 7

With the System 7 Finder, you can copy any system alert sound from the System to another in the same way that you would move any other file.

Appendix G

The MIDI Message Format

A MIDI message is a series of bytes that can travel in only one direction: from a single source to a single destination. A MIDI message is transmitted through a single MIDI cable.

There are only two kinds of bytes in a MIDI message: a *status byte* and a *data byte.* The status byte serves as a message header: It tells what channel a MIDI message is addressed to, and it tells what kind of MIDI message is being sent.

In every status byte and every data byte, the most significant (leftmost) bit specifies the byte type. If the byte begins with a binary 1, it is a status byte; if the byte begins with a binary 0, it is a data byte.

For example, the following is a three-byte MIDI message—a status byte followed by two data bytes:

```
10010100 01000000 01011001
```

The Status Byte

The first byte in a MIDI message—the status byte—is followed by one or more data bytes. The data bytes in a message contain additional information that the slave device needs to carry out the instruction that is identified in the status byte.

For example, the status byte in the preceding message alerts the receiving device that a Note On message is about to be transmitted on MIDI Channel 4.

When the device receiving the message receives the status byte, it makes preparations to receive a Note On message on MIDI Channel 4.

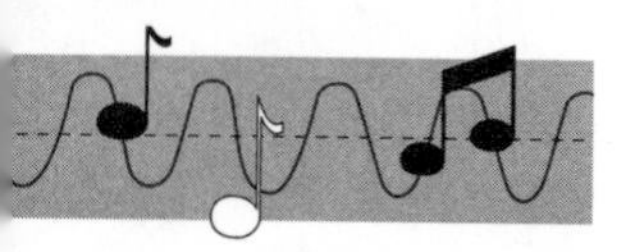

Data Bytes

When the transmitting device finishes sending the status byte, it starts sending data bytes. The data bytes contain any additional data that the receiving device may require in order to carry out the instructions in the message being sent.

For example, if the MIDI message being transmitted is a Note On message, the data byte tells the receiving device what the note is, what the note's attack velocity is, and so on. When the receiving device has received the status byte and all the data bytes that follow, the receiving device has all the information it needs to carry out the instructions contained in the message.

The MIDI language contains some codes—such as Note On and Note Off—that every MIDI device understands. However, there are other MIDI codes that different devices interpret in different ways. For example, synthesizers can receive *system-exclusive* messages that different kinds of synthesizers are free to respond to in different ways. To find out what kinds of system-exclusive messages a given synthesizer can understand, you must refer to documentation that deals with that specific instrument.

The meanings of the bytes in MIDI messages are defined in a table called the *MIDI Implementation Chart.* Every MIDI device has a MIDI Implementation Chart that tells how it interprets MIDI messages. Therefore, to find out how a specific device responds to MIDI messages, you must consult its MIDI Implementation Chart.

A Note On Message

Here's another look at the same Note On message that you have been examining:

```
10010100 01000000 01011001
```

The first byte in the message begins with a 1, so it's a status byte. The next two bytes begin with 0s, so they're data bytes.

The second through eighth bits in the status byte alert the receiving device that a Note On message is about to be sent on MIDI Channel No. 4.

The second and third bytes in the message begin with binary 0s, so they are data bytes. The first data byte tells the receiving device that the note to be played is MIDI Note No. 64. The second data byte tells the receiving device that the attack velocity, or volume level, of the note is 89.

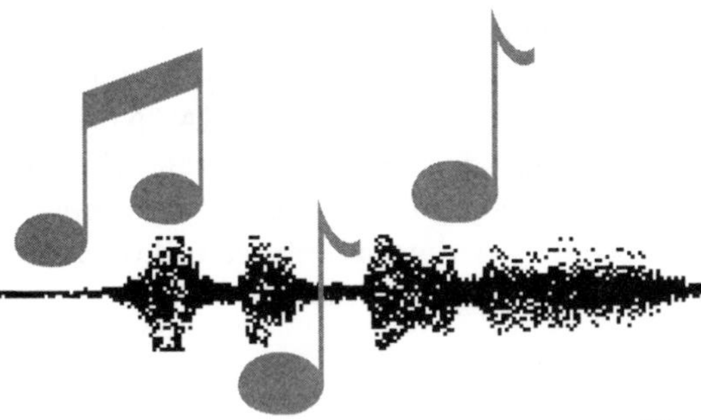

It's the Law

This section is provided to meet legal requirements for publishing the software that is included with this book. On the bonus disk that comes with this book, there are eight programs. Each numbered heading in this section contains information about the free software program that goes with the heading.

In addition, the following two paragraphs apply to HyperCorder, HyperLab, the IIfx Serial Switch, MacinTalk, the Audio Palette, and all programs listed in the appendices:

ADDISON-WESLEY, PARVATI PRODUCTIONS, AND MARK ANDREWS MAKE NO WARRANTIES, EXPRESS OR IMPLIED, INCLUDING WITHOUT LIMITATION THE IMPLIED WARRANTIES OF MERCHANTABILITY AND FITNESS FOR A PARTICULAR PURPOSE, REGARDING THE SOFTWARE. ADDISON-WESLEY, PARVATI PRODUCTIONS, AND MARK ANDREWS DO NOT WARRANT, GUARANTEE OR MAKE ANY REPRESENTATIONS REGARDING THE USE OR THE RESULTS OF THE USE OF THE SOFTWARE IN TERMS OF ITS CORRECTNESS, ACCURACY, RELIABILITY, CURRENTNESS, OR OTHERWISE. THE ENTIRE RISK AS TO THE RESULTS AND PERFORMANCE OF THE SOFTWARE IS ASSUMED BY YOU. THE EXCLUSION OF IMPLIED WARRANTIES IS NOT PERMITTED BY SOME JURISDICTIONS. THE ABOVE EXCLUSION MAY NOT APPLY TO YOU.

IN NO EVENT WILL ADDISON-WESLEY, PARVATI PRODUCTIONS, AND MARK ANDREWS, THEIR LICENSORS, AND THEIR DIRECTORS, OFFICERS, EMPLOYEES, OR AGENTS (COLLECTIVELY LICENSOR OF ADDISON-WESLEY, PARVATI PRODUCTIONS, AND MARK ANDREWS) BE LIABLE TO YOU FOR ANY CONSEQUENTIAL, INCIDENTAL, OR INDIRECT DAMAGES (INCLUDING DAMAGES FOR LOSS OF BUSINESS PROFITS, BUSINESS INTERRUPTION, LOSS OF BUSINESS INFORMATION, AND THE LIKE) ARISING OUT OF THE USE OR INABILITY TO USE THE SOFTWARE EVEN IF THE LICENSOR OF

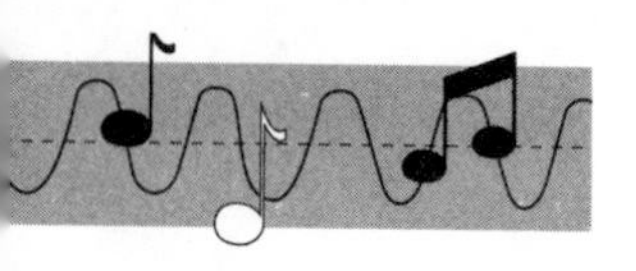

1. Macintosh Sound

2. The Science of Sound

3. Sampled Sound

4. Sound Processing

5. HyperCard Sound

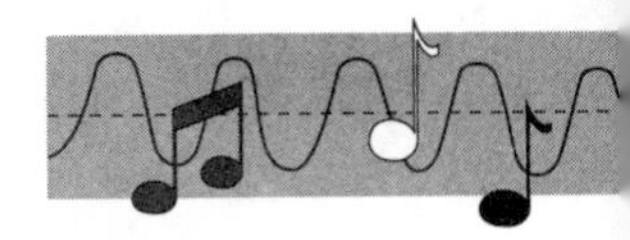

6. Speech Synthesis

7. Macintosh Music

8. Melody and Harmony

9. MIDI and the Mac

Chapter 9, "MIDI and the Mac," is illustrated with pictures from The Book of MIDI, a HyperCard stack published by Opcode Systems. The pictures are used with permission from Opcode Systems.

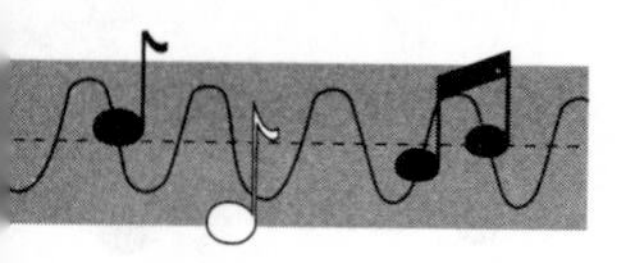

Software and fonts in machine-readable form for backup purposes only. You must reproduce on such copy the Apple copyright notice and any other proprietary legends that were on the original copy of the Apple Software and fonts. You may also transfer all your license rights in the Apple Software and fonts, the backup copy of the Apple Software and fonts, the related documentation and a copy of this License to another party, provided the other party reads and agrees to accept the terms and conditions of this License.

2. Restrictions. The Apple Software contains copyrighted material, trade secrets, and other proprietary material and in order to protect them you may not decompile, reverse engineer, disassemble, or otherwise reduce the Apple Software to a human-perceivable form. You may not modify, network, rent, lease, loan, distribute, or create derivative works based upon the Apple Software in whole or in part. You may not electronically transmit the Apple Software from one computer to another or over a network.
3. Termination. This License is effective until terminated. You may terminate this License at any time by destroying the Apple Software, related documentation and fonts, and all copies thereof. This License will terminate immediately without notice from Apple if you fail to comply with any provision of this License. Upon termination you must destroy the Apple Software, related documentation and fonts, and all copies thereof.
4. Export Law Assurances. You agree and certify that neither the Apple Software nor any other technical data received from Apple, nor the direct product thereof, will be exported outside the United States except as authorized and as permitted by the laws and regulations of the United States. If the Apple Software has been rightfully obtained by you outside of the United States, you agree that you will not re-export the Apple Software nor any other technical data received from Apple, nor the direct product thereof, except as permitted by the laws and regulations of the United States and the laws and regulations of the jurisdiction in which you obtained the Apple Software.
5. Government End Users. If you are acquiring the Apple Software and fonts on behalf of any unit or agency of the United States Government, the following provisions apply. The Government agrees: (i) if the Apple Software and fonts are supplied to the Department of Defense(DoD), the Apple Software and fonts are classified as "Commercial Computer Software" and the Government is acquiring only "restricted rights" in the Apple Software, its documentation and fonts as that term is defined in Clause 252.227–7013(c) (1) of the DFARS; and (ii) if the Apple Software and fonts are supplied to any unit or agency of the

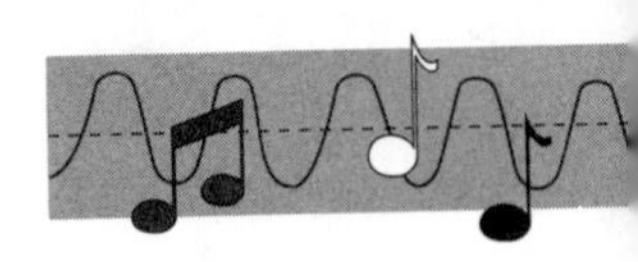

United States Government other than DoD, the Government's rights in the Apple Software, its documentation and fonts will be as defined in Clause 52.227–19(c) (2) of the FAR or, in the case of NASA, in Clause 18–52.227–86(d)of the NASA Supplement to the FAR.

6. Disclaimer of Warranty on Apple Software. You expressly acknowledge and agree that use of the Apple Software and fonts is at your sole risk. The Apple Software, related documentation and fonts are provided "AS IS" and without warranty of any kind and Apple and Apple's Licensor(s) (for the purposes of provisions 6 and 7, Apple and Apple's Licensor(s) shall be to as "Apple") EXPRESSLY DISCLAIM ALL WARRANTIES, EXPRESS OR IMPLIED, INCLUDING, BUT NOT LIMITED TO, THE IMPLIED WARRANTIES OF MERCHANTABILITY AND FITNESS FOR A PARTICULAR PURPOSE. APPLE DOES NOT WARRANT THAT THE FUNCTIONS CONTAINED IN THE APPLE SOFTWARE WILL MEET YOUR REQUIREMENTS, OR THAT THE OPERATION OF THE APPLE SOFTWARE WILL BE UNINTERRUPTED OR ERROR-FREE, OR THAT DEFECTS IN THE APPLE SOFTWARE AND THE FONTS WILL BE CORRECTED. FURTHERMORE, APPLE DOES NOT WARRANT OR MAKE ANY REPRESENTATIONS REGARDING THE USE OR THE RESULTS OF THE USE OF THE APPLE SOFTWARE AND FONTS OR RELATED DOCUMENTATION IN TERMS OF THEIR CORRECTNESS, ACCURACY, RELIABILITY, OR OTHERWISE. NO ORAL OR WRITTEN INFORMATION OR ADVICE GIVEN BY APPLE OR AN APPLE AUTHORIZED REPRESENTATIVE SHALL CREATE A WARRANTY OR IN ANY WAY INCREASE THE SCOPE OF THIS WARRANTY. SHOULD THE APPLE SOFTWARE PROVE DEFECTIVE, YOU (AND NOT APPLE OR AN APPLE AUTHORIZED REPRESENTATIVE) ASSUME THE ENTIRE COST OF ALL NECESSARY SERVICING, REPAIR, OR CORRECTION. SOME JURISDICTIONS DO NOT ALLOW THE EXCLUSION OF IMPLIED WARRANTIES, SO THE ABOVE EXCLUSION MAY NOT APPLY TO YOU.

7. Limitation of Liability. UNDER NO CIRCUMSTANCES INCLUDING NEGLIGENCE, SHALL APPLE BE LIABLE FOR ANY INCIDENTAL, SPECIAL, OR CONSEQUENTIAL DAMAGES THAT RESULT FROM THE USE OR INABILITY TO USE THE APPLE SOFTWARE OR RELATED DOCUMENTATION, EVEN IF APPLE OR AN APPLE AUTHORIZED REPRESENTATIVE HAS BEEN ADVISED OF THE POSSIBILITY OF SUCH DAMAGES. SOME JURISDICTIONS DO NOT ALLOW THE LIMITATION OR EXCLUSION OF LIABILITY FOR INCIDENTAL OR CONSE-

QUENTIAL DAMAGES, SO THE ABOVE LIMITATION OR EXCLUSION MAY NOT APPLY TO YOU. In no event shall Apple's total liability to you for all damages, losses, and causes of action (whether in contract, tort (including negligence), or otherwise) exceed the amount paid by you for the Apple Software and fonts.

8. Controlling Law and Severability. This License shall be governed by and construed in accordance with the laws of the United States and the State of California, as applied to agreements entered into and to be performed entirely within California between California residents. If for any reason a court of competent jurisdiction finds any provision of this License, or portion thereof, to be unenforceable, that provision of the License shall be enforced to the maximum extent permissible so as to effect the intent of the parties, and the remainder of this License shall continue in full force and effect.
9. Complete Agreement. This License constitutes the entire agreement between the parties with respect to the use of the Apple Software, related documentation and fonts, and supersedes all prior or contemporaneous understandings or agreements, written or oral, regarding such subject matter. No amendment to or modification of this License will be binding unless in writing and signed by a duly authorized representative of Apple.

Bibliography

Papers

Audio Palette Developer Note. Cupertino, CA: Developer Technical Publications, Apple Computer, Inc., 1990.

Books

Alchemy Owner's Manual, Third Edition. Half Moon Bay, CA: Passport Designs, Inc., 1989.

Alley, Peter, and Strange, Carolyn. *ResEdit Complete.* Reading, MA: Addison-Wesley, 1991.

Apel, Willi. *Harvard Dictionary of Music,* 2nd Edition, revised and enlarged. Cambridge, MA: Belknap Press of Harvard University Press, 1972.

DeFuria, Steve, and Scacciaferro, Joe. *Synthesis with Style!* Pompton Lakes, NJ: Third Earth Publishing, Inc., 1989.

Evans, Jeffrey. *Windows on Music,* second edition. Kirkland, WA: Ars Nova Software, 1989.

Fryer, Terry. *Digital Sampling.* Milwaukee, WI: Hal Leonard Publishing Corporation, 1989.

Goldberg, Michael. *The Ultimate Home Studio.* Menlo Park, CA: Digidesign, Inc., 1991.

Hindemith, Paul. *Elementary Training for Musicians.* London: Schott and Company, Ltd., 1946.

Hindemith, Paul. *Traditional Harmony.* London: Schott and Company, Ltd., 1968.

Huber, David Miles. *The MIDI Manual.* Carmel, IN: Sams (a division of Macmillan Publishing), 1990.

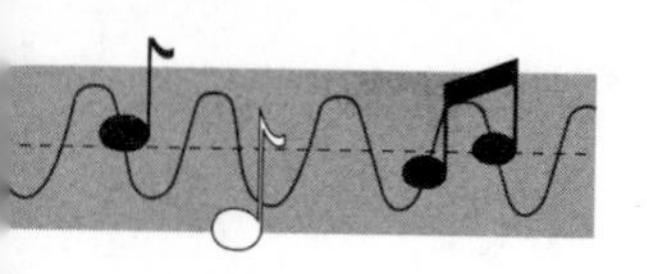

Huber, David Miles. *Random Access Audio: An Introduction.* Menlo Park, CA: Digidesign, Inc., 1990.

HyperCard: Getting Started. Cupertino, CA: Apple Computer, Inc., 1989–1990.

HyperCard New Features Guide. Cupertino, CA: Apple Computer, Inc., 1989–1990.

HyperCard Reference. Cupertino, CA: Apple Computer, Inc., 1989–1990.

HyperCard Script Language Guide. Cupertino, CA: Apple Computer, Inc., 1989–1990.

HyperCard Script Language Guide: The HyperTalk Language. Reading, MA: Addison-Wesley, 1989.

HyperTalk: Beginner's Guide to Scripting. Cupertino, CA: Apple Computer, Inc., 1989–1990.

Inside Macintosh, Volumes I – VI: Reading, MA: Addison-Wesley, 1985–1990.

MacRecorder User's Guide. Emeryville, CA: Farallon Computing, Inc., 1987, 1990.

Mash, David. *Computers and the Music Educator: A Curriculum and Resource Guide.* Menlo Park, CA: Digidesign, Inc., 1991.

May, John C., and Whittle, Judy B. *Extending the Macintosh Toolbox.* Reading, MA: Addison-Wesley, 1991.

Meadow, Anthony. *System 7 Revealed.* Reading, MA: Addison-Wesley, 1991.

Multimedia: Authorware Professional for Macintosh. Minneapolis: Authorware, Inc., 1987–1990.

Penfold, R.A. *Synthesizers for Musicians.* Kent, Great Britain: PC Publishing, 1989.

Persichetti, Vincent. *Twentieth Century Harmony: Creative Aspects and Practice.* New York: W.W. Norton & Co., 1961.

Randel, Don Michael. *Harvard Concise Dictionary of Music.* Cambridge, MA: Belknap Press, 1978.

Reference: Authorware Professional for the Macintosh. Minneapolis: Authorware, Inc., 1987–1990.

Schoenberg, Arnold. *Structural Foundations of Harmony,* revised edition with corrections, (Leonard Stein, editor). New York: W.W. Norton & Co., 1969.

Shafer, Dan: *The Complete Book of HyperTalk 2.* Reading, MA: Addison-Wesley, 1991.

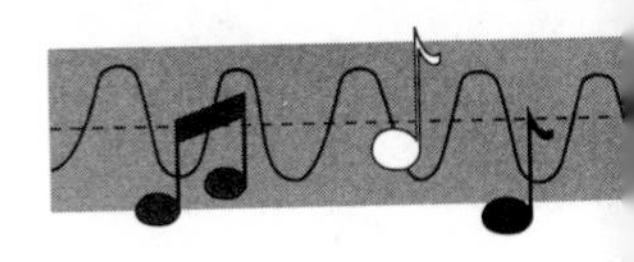

Tutorial: Authorware Professional for the Macintosh. Minneapolis: Authorware, Inc., 1987–1990.

Voice Recorder User Manual. Woburn, MA: Articulate Systems, Inc., 1991.

Wheddon, C., and Linggard, R., editors. *Speech and Language Processing.* London: Chapman and Hall, 1990.

Index

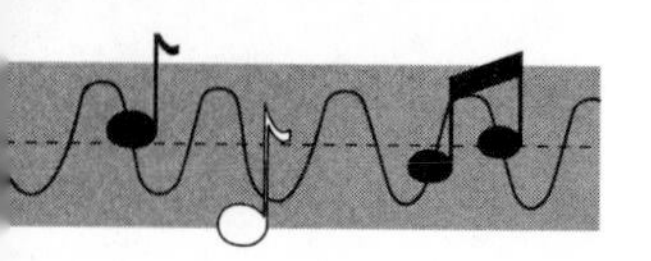

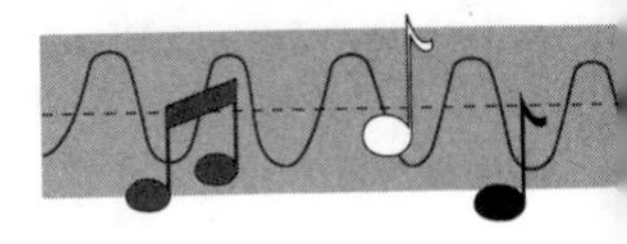

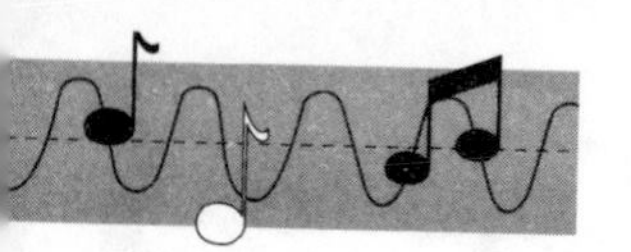

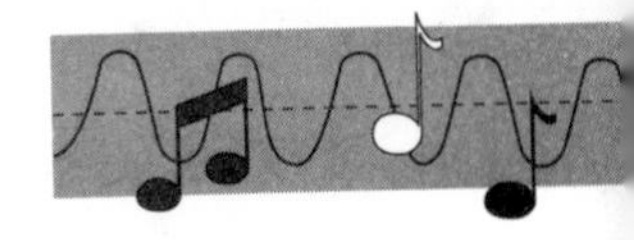

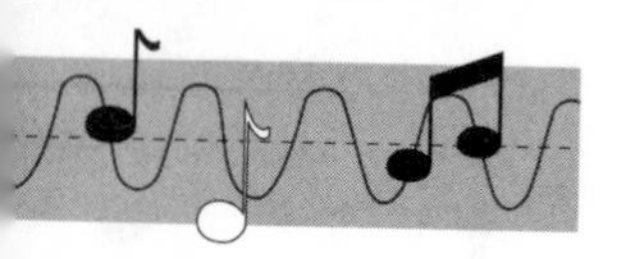

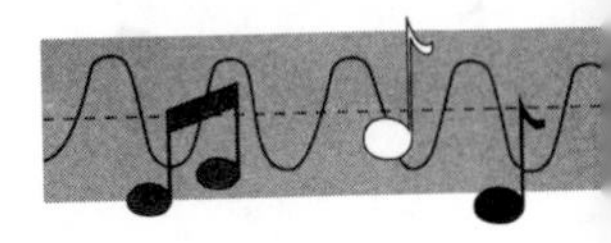

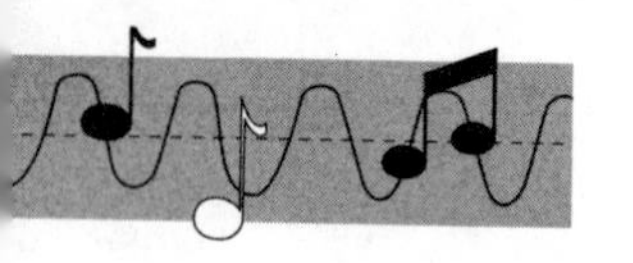

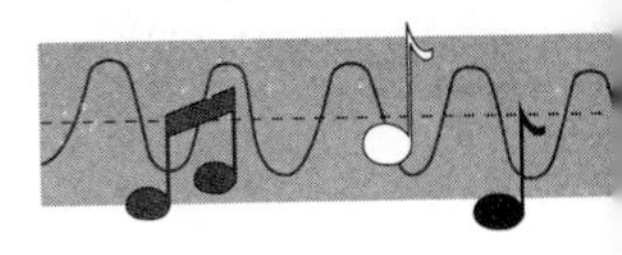

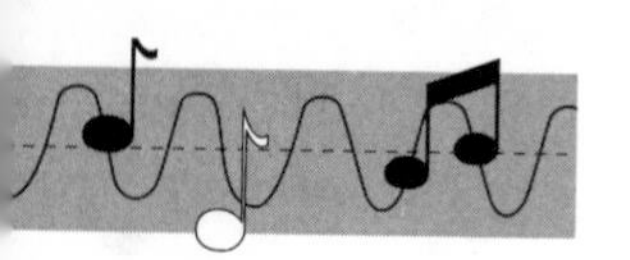

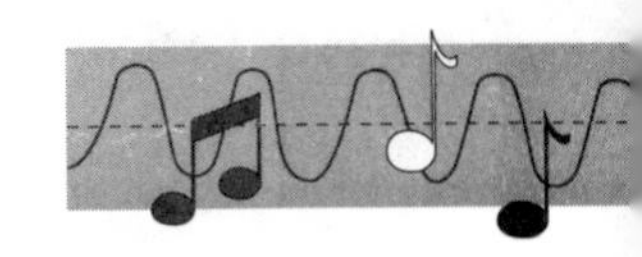

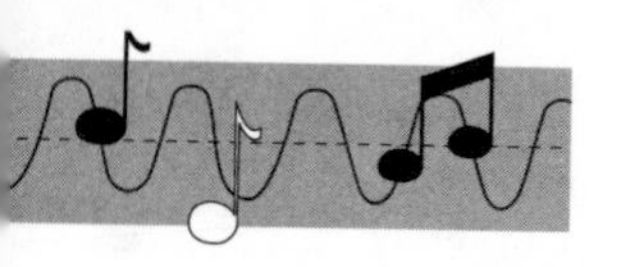

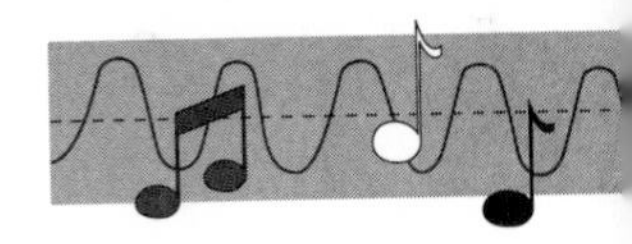

Addison-Wesley warrants the enclosed disk to be free of defects in materials and faulty workmanship under normal use for a period of ninety days after purchase. If a defect is discovered in the disk during this warranty period, a replacement disk can be obtained at no charge by sending the defective disk, postage prepaid, with proof of purchase to:

Addison-Wesley Publishing Company
Editorial Department
Trade Computer Books Division
One Jacob Way
Reading, MA 01867

After the 90-day period, a replacement will be sent upon receipt of the defective disk and a check or money order for $10.00, payable to Addison-Wesley Publishing Company.

Addison-Wesley makes no warranty or representation, either express or implied, with respect to this software, its quality, performance, merchantability, or fitness for a particular purpose. In no event will Addison-Wesley, its distributors, or dealers be liable for direct, indirect, special, incidental, or consequential damages arising out of the use or inability to use the software. The exclusion of implied warranties is not permitted in some states. Therefore, the above exclusion may not apply to you. This warranty provides you with specific legal rights. There may be other rights that you may have that vary from state to state.

Unpacking Your Bonus Disk

Before you can use the programs on the bonus disk, you must unpack, or decompress, the files in which the programs are stored. The files are compressed with Compact Pro, a data compression and expansion program written by Bill Goodman and licensed for use with this volume.

It's easy to decompress the programs on your bonus disk and transfer them to another disk in their original form. You don't need a copy of Compact Pro to do that, because the compressed files are self-extracting.

If you're extracting your bonus disk archives onto a hard disk, or onto a blank 1.4Mb floppy disk, you can copy both of the archives that are on your bonus disk into the same folder. If you're copying the files onto 800K floppies, you need two blank disks. Extract the Incredible Sound 1 file onto one disk, and extract the Incredible Sound 2 icon onto the other.

To expand and copy the programs on your bonus disk, just follow these steps:

1. Open your bonus disk. You'll see two icons that represent archives of compressed files.
2. Double-click the icon labeled Incredible Sound 1.
3. Compact Pro displays a dialog box with instructions. Click the OK button, then do what the message says: select the volume and folder where you want your decompressed software to go, and then click the button labeled Extract. That decompresses the files in the archive, and copies them to your chosen destination. When you've finished extracting the files in Incredible Sound 1, do the same thing with Incredible Sound 2.

When you've finished copying the files, be sure to store your original bonus disk somewhere for safekeeping.

When you've decompressed the Incredible Sound on your bonus disk, you can start running the Incredible Sound programs that the disk contains. Each program on the disk is thoroughly documented in the text.

The Incredible Sound Machine Bonus Disk

Powerful Applications, Utilities, and Drivers

SoundWave™ —A complete working version of the state-of-the-art sound recording and editing program specially licensed for this book from Macromedia, Inc. SoundWave is the sound editor for Authorware Professional for Macintosh®, 1990 Eddy Award Winner.

HyperCorder—A new HyperCard® program created for this book that lets you add sounds to stacks. You can convert sound files into HyperCard sounds and save HyperCard sounds as standalone sounds.

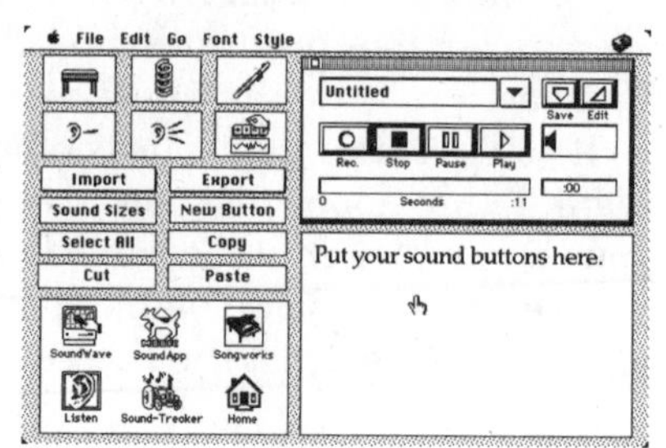

Built into HyperCorder, ***Audio Palette*** is a HyperCard recording and sound utility that is supplied only with microphone-equipped models of the Macintosh. Now, all Macintosh users can use the Audio Palette licensed from Claris® with their HyperCard stacks.

MacRecorder® Driver—A system extension utility that can interface your Macintosh with a sound recording module enabling you to record your own sounds.

SoundApp—An entertaining and instructional program from Apple designed to demonstrate the three sound synthesizers built into every Macintosh.

HyperLab—Just type text into this application and have your computer read it back to you in a variety of ways with Apple's voice synthesizer. HyperLab is a HyperCard-based application exclusively written for the book that demonstrates MacinTalk™, Apple's voice synthesizer. MacinTalk is also included on the disk.

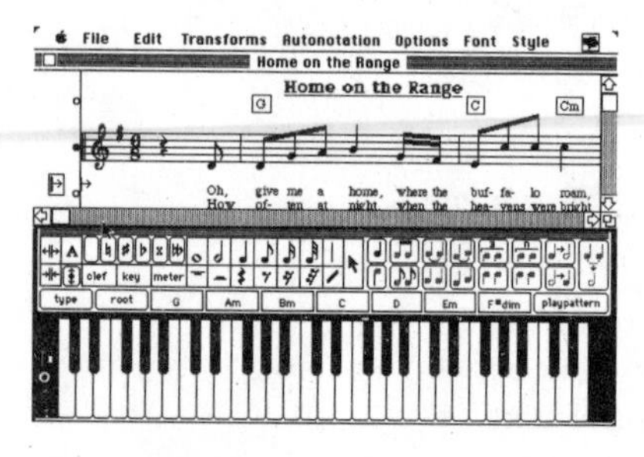

Songworks Demo—This special demonstration version from Ars Nova Software enables you to compose musical scores on your Macintosh. After writing your composition, you can play, edit, add a chord accompaniament, or transpose the score into a different key.

Listen™ ***Demo from Imaja Software***—A musical training demonstration program, Listen puts both a piano keyboard and a guitar fretboard on your screen and lets you play either instrument. Exercises teach you about notes, chords, and other topics musicians and hobbyists need to understand.

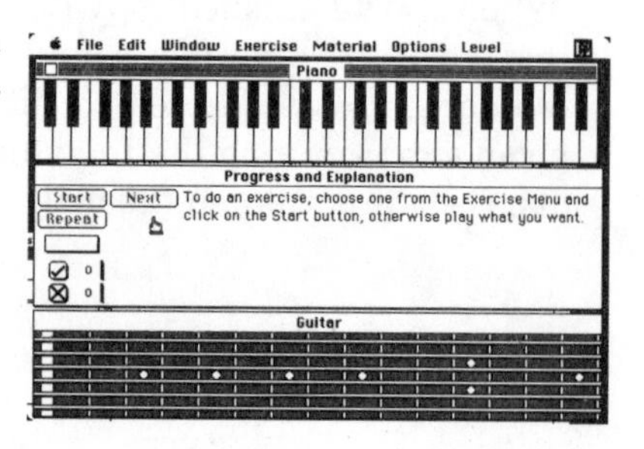

Sound-Trecker—A shareware program that allows you to play multi-channel sound in stereo, while displaying waveforms in real time on an oscilloscope-like screen.

See "Unpacking Your Bonus Disk" on the previous page for instructions on how to decompress the files on the disk.